Civil Peace and the Quest for Truth

Civil Peace and the Quest for Truth

The First Amendment Freedoms in Political Philosophy and American Constitutionalism

Murray Dry

LEXINGTON BOOKS
Lanham • Boulder • New York • Toronto • Oxford

LEXINGTON BOOKS

Published in the United States of America
by Lexington Books
An imprint of The Rowman & Littlefield Publishing Group, Inc.
4501 Forbes Boulevard, Suite 200, Lanham, Maryland 20706

PO Box 317
Oxford
OX2 9RU, UK

British Library Cataloguing in Publication Information Available

Library of Congress Cataloging-in-Publication Data

Dry, Murray.
   Civil peace and the quest for truth : the First Amendment freedoms in political
philosophy and American constitutionalism / Murray Dry.
      p. cm.
   Includes bibliographical references and index.
   ISBN 0-7391-0746-1 (cloth : alk. paper) — ISBN 0-7391-0931-6 (pbk. : alk. paper)
   1. Freedom of religion—United States. 2. Freedom of speech—United States.
3. Civil rights—United States—Philosophy. I. Title.
   KF4783.D79 2004
   342.7308'52—dc22
                                                                    2004009947

Printed in the United States of America

⊚™ The paper used in this publication meets the minimum requirements of
American National Standard for Information Sciences—Permanence of Paper for
Printed Library Materials, ANSI/NISO Z39.48-1992.

To my wife, Cecelia,
To my daughters, Rachel and Judith,
To my brother, Paul, and sister, Bonnie,
To my mother, Shirley Dry,
And to the memory of my father, Sidney Dry

Contents

Acknowledgments

I began writing this book in 1996 and 1997 in Palo Alto on sabbatical leave from Middlebury College. Thanks to the late Gerald Gunther, I was a visiting scholar at Stanford Law School. I am grateful to Kathleen Sullivan for allowing me to audit and fully participate in her wonderful First Amendment course in the fall of 1996. Thanks to the generosity of Peter Minowitz, who was then chair of Santa Clara University's political science department, I was able to teach a course on the subject of this book during the winter of 1997. As a result of my experience teaching that course, I decided to enlarge the scope of the book to include a discussion of religious freedom as well as freedom of speech.

My interest in connecting American constitutional law to the American founding, and both to political philosophy, ancient and modern, originates in my graduate school study at the University of Chicago under Herbert Storing, Leo Strauss, and Joseph Cropsey. Without claiming that my teachers would agree with my argument in every particular, I believe it reflects and is consistent with their approach to political philosophy and American constitutionalism.

I am also indebted to three other people who have been teachers, in all but the formal sense. In his numerous essays on American constitutionalism and his book *Taming the Prince*, Harvey C. Mansfield Jr. helped me to think about the essence of American constitutionalism and its evolution. In her essay on Madison's *Memorial and Remonstrance*, Eva Brann taught me about the importance of toleration and the new meaning that John Locke gave to that term. Gerald Gunther's comprehensive *Constitutional Law* casebook—now edited by Kathleen Sullivan—as well as his important law review article about the Hand-Holmes exchange on freedom of speech has been indispensable to my continuing study of First Amendment freedoms.

Thanks to funds made available by Middlebury College, I received research assistance from the following students: Damjan deKrnjevich Miskovich, Irakly Areshidze, Sam Dettmann, Peter Nestor, Giorgi Areshidze, Uzair Kayani, and Kiernan McAlpine.

Peter Minowitz and James Stoner read and commented on the entire manuscript. Peter provided important specific questions and detailed editing. Jim's presentation and defense of my argument was especially generous, since I give less weight to the common law understanding of the First Amendment freedoms than does he in his books *Common Law and Liberal Theory: Coke, Hobbes, and the Origins of American Constitutionalism* and *Common Law Liberty.*

Barry Sullivan and Winnifred Fallers Sullivan also read and commented on the entire manuscript, thus providing me with the perspective of trained lawyers and scholars. Michael Zuckert also read and commented on chapter six.

I received encouragement and constructive criticism from several colleagues: Paul Nelson, Russ Leng, and Kateri Carmola in my own department and Eve Adler and Marc Witkin in the classics department. And Hans Raum, Middlebury College's associate librarian, helped me with government documents and other bibliographic matters.

Paul Dry assisted me in three ways: he was a constant source of prodding and encouragement to me to get on with the business of writing; he carefully went over the introduction; and he put me in touch with his partner at Paul Dry Books, John Corenswet. John rigorously edited the manuscript, querying me with numerous detailed questions for every chapter of the book. Whether or not readers agree with my argument, thanks to John they should be able to follow it.

Parts of the book are revisions of previously published articles or public lectures given at Middlebury College and St. John's College in Annapolis and for the Supreme Court Historical Society (for citations to the articles see the bibliography). More than anything else, the book reflects my teaching at Middlebury since I arrived here in 1968. This has been a wonderful place to teach and to write, and I have thought of my students, past and present, as my readers. Since so many have asked me over the years when I was going to write a book, I am pleased to be able to say that I have finally done it. I look forward to their responses.

Introduction

First Things First

Congress shall make no law respecting an establishment of religion, or prohibiting the free exercise thereof; or abridging the freedom of speech, or of the
press, or the right of the people peaceably to assemble, and to petition the
Government for redress of grievances.

Though apparently straightforward, the First Amendment's language has
produced an increasing amount of constitutional debate among scholars and
Justices in recent years. In large part, the debate concerns the prominent
concept of neutrality in judicial interpretations of the First Amendment freedoms. As applied to speech, neutrality means that government regulation
may not restrict or in any way punish speech on the basis of its viewpoint or
even its content. As applied to religion, neutrality means that government
may not use religion as a category of action, either to provide a benefit or exact a punishment. Most studies of the First Amendment ignore or pay scant
attention to the American founding and to classic texts in the history of political philosophy. This is a mistake, because the Enlightenment philosophers
of the seventeenth and eighteenth centuries intended to change, and did
change, the way good government is understood. The thought of those
philosophers shaped the American founders' understanding of republican
government and continues to influence the Supreme Court's interpretations
of the First Amendment freedoms.

Not until the twentieth century did freedom of speech and religious freedom become prominent parts of American constitutional law, when the
Supreme Court applied First Amendment doctrines, via the Fourteenth
Amendment, to the states.[1] However, the framers' understanding of republican government had already provided the foundation for such a development. And philosophic arguments from Enlightenment thinkers provided
the fundamental bases of that understanding.

American constitutional doctrines concerning free speech and religious
freedom follow the philosophic principles that Locke, Spinoza, Montesquieu,
and, to a lesser extent, Bacon, Hobbes, and Milton advocated.[2] These
thinkers tried to liberate philosophy from the restraints imposed by revealed
religion. To do this, they had to liberate government from any responsibility
for the salvation of the souls of its citizens. Each philosopher, in his own fashion, advocated "limited government." Government should limit itself to securing rights and thus establishing civil peace. Government should not use
its coercive power to try to save souls or to inculcate moral virtue.

Most books on the First Amendment cover either speech or religion but
not both.[3] There are two reasons why we should study the two freedoms together. First, both freedom of speech and freedom of religion, understood as
individual rights, arise out of limited government. The Enlightenment
philosophers, especially Spinoza and Locke, sought to replace any form of religious politics with limited government. Montesquieu followed Spinoza and
Locke when he first identified political liberty as the object of government
and then defined that liberty as security. He categorized offenses against religion as non-criminal law. Alexis de Tocqueville, who praised religion for
maintaining the mores ("moeurs") necessary for free government, also supported the separation of religion from government. Indeed, Tocqueville criticized the Puritans for turning to the Old Testament for their criminal laws.
Montesquieu and Tocqueville both advocated freedom of speech (and of the
press) as a necessary part of political liberty. Since the two freedoms both presuppose limited government, we should study them together in relation to
limited government. In addition, it is often difficult to separate the claim of
one freedom from the claim of the other. Here, then, is my second reason for
studying the freedoms together: We can't clearly separate them and study
them apart.

When the American founders wrote new state constitutions from 1776
to 1790 and the new U.S. Constitution in 1787, they adopted the ideas of
the Enlightenment thinkers on limited government[4] and the separation of
religion from government. These new constitutions differed from the old
colonial charters in two important ways: The new constitutions redefined

the purpose of government, and they liberalized suffrage and office-holding requirements. In Virginia, James Madison and Thomas Jefferson thought that limited government required a complete separation of government from religion; George Washington and Patrick Henry thought that for the sake of morality government could, and should, support religion in a non-preferential manner.[5]

Notwithstanding legal limits, Americans of the founding period enjoyed a great deal of freedom of speech (and of the press), and the Constitution protected federal lawmakers against any liability for what they said in the legislative chambers. The legal limits took the form of the English common law's "no prior restraint" rule.[6] While administrative approval could not be required before publication, subsequent punishment for libel, including seditious libel, could follow. Seditious libel meant criticism of any government official "in order to provoke him to wrath, or expose him to public hatred, contempt, and ridicule."[7] In response to the passage of the Sedition Act by the Federalist-controlled Congress in 1798, Madison and other Republicans, who previously had expressed no opposition to the English common law rule on freedom of the press, reconsidered their views. As an advocate of popular government, Madison opposed seditious libel laws.

The Supreme Court confronted First Amendment controversies for the first time in the twentieth century.[8] In free speech cases, the Court drew on the argument that truth wins out in a contest with falsehood. Milton first claimed this power on behalf of truth; after him, Locke did the same, in a limited context, and Mill expanded the claim and its application.[9] The Court also propounded pragmatic arguments similar to those that Spinoza and Montesquieu had made. The most prominent Supreme Court justifications for the importance of freedom of speech were: (1) it facilitates the search for truth; (2) it is an essential part of self-government; and (3) it allows for individual self-realization.[10] Each of these justifications echoes the philosophic arguments of Milton, Locke, and Mill on the one hand, and Spinoza and Montesquieu on the other.

For its understanding of religious freedom, the Court, starting in the 1940s, turned to Madison and Jefferson, both of whom followed Locke. The reigning judicial interpretation of the religion clauses (Establishment and Free Exercise) emphasizes neutrality.[11] This is the "strict separationist" position. Government should be neutral as between religion and non-religion; religion should not be an activity that confers a benefit or exacts a punishment. Another interpretation of the Establishment Clause, which follows Washington and Henry, and which Chief Justice Rehnquist advocates,[12] maintains that government should be able to express general non-discriminatory support for religion, say in the form of school prayer or religious symbols, as long as no coercion is involved. Advocates of this position are referred to as "non-preferentialists." On matters affecting the Free Exercise Clause, the strict separation position would uphold a law that has a constitutional purpose and neutral application, even if it incidentally burdens practitioners of religion. Those favoring more accommodation to religious freedom advocate a stricter standard of review whenever such a law significantly burdens a religious practice.[13]

Free speech and religious freedom ensure a general right of conscience—a right to be left alone—absent a legitimate government purpose. At the same time, the Establishment Clause suggests that religious activity is distinctive, and hence that free speech and religious freedom are not identical. On the basis of the Free Exercise Clause, individuals sometimes claim special exemptions from otherwise valid laws. And on the basis of the Establishment Clause, government is forbidden to support religious expression. The Supreme Court's handling of a controversy that involved both free exercise and free speech claims illustrates the overlapping relationship between the two First Amendment freedoms. The controversy also illustrates the Supreme Court's reliance on neutrality in its interpretation of both freedoms.

In 1940, the Supreme Court handed down its opinion in the first "flag salute" case: *Minersville School District v Gobitis*.[14] Lillian and William Gobitis,[15] brother and sister aged twelve and ten, were expelled from the public schools of Minersville, Pennsylvania, for refusing to salute the flag and to say the following: "I pledge allegiance to my flag, and the Republic for which it stands; one nation indivisible, with liberty and justice for all." The Gobitis family, affiliates of the Jehovah's Witnesses, were raised to believe that such a gesture of respect for the flag amounted to bowing down to a graven image and was forbidden by Exodus 20:4. They claimed that the requirement violated the Free Exercise Clause as applied to them. After the lower courts decided in favor of the Gobitis family, the Supreme Court reversed, eight-to-one. Justice Frankfurter, who wrote the Court opinion, explained the principle embodied in the religion clauses: "Conscientious scruples have not, in the course of the long struggle for religious toleration, relieved the individual from obedience to a general law not aimed at the promotion or restriction of religious beliefs."[16] Since free exercise claimants could raise no special claim against the government, Justice Frankfurter only had to find a legitimate government end and a reasonable connection to it.[17] In his dissent Justice Stone argued that both freedoms of speech and religion should have protected these religious convictions.[18] While Justice Stone was less willing to defer to the school board in such matters of conscience, he did not make clear whether this free exercise case was any different from a free speech case. Would he have voted the same way if the objection to the required flag salute had no basis in religious belief?

The Court answered that question when it decided the second flag salute case, *West Virginia State Board of Education v Barnette*.[19] The plaintiffs, Walter Barnette and his children, maintained that the West Virginia school board's flag salute requirement for all public school pupils violated their free exercise of religion.[20] They offered periodically and publicly to pledge their support to the flag and "their allegiance and obedience to all the laws of the United States that are consistent with God's law as set forth in the Bible." [21] The lower court, notwithstanding the *Gobitis* precedent, decided in favor of the Barnettes.[22] Justice Jackson, newly appointed, wrote the Supreme Court opinion affirming the lower court's decision. He began by redefining the issue in terms of speech, or forced utterance. "To sustain the compulsory flag salute we are required to say that a Bill of Rights which guards the individual's right to speak his own mind, left it open to public authorities to compel him to utter what is not in his mind."[23] For Justice Jackson and the Court, viewing a compulsory flag salute in terms of freedom of speech led to its rejection as unconstitutional. He held that the First Amendment not only protects many kinds of speech, but also in this case prohibits government from compelling it.

> If there is any fixed star in our constitutional constellation, it is that no official, high or petty, can prescribe what shall be orthodox in politics, nationalism, religion, or other matters of opinion or force citizens to confess by word or act their faith therein.[24]

In other words, the First Amendment freedom of unorthodox speech implies a freedom from an enforced orthodoxy.

The flag salute controversy reveals three important features of the Supreme Court's interpretation of our First Amendment freedoms. First, cases involving freedom of conscience tend to blur the distinction between freedom of speech and free exercise of religion. Second, framing the issue in terms of coerced speech frees the Court from having to determine what is and what is not a legitimate religious belief. If the Court had decided for the Barnettes on free exercise grounds, as the five other Justices in the majority were willing to do, the required flag salute ceremony would have been constitutional for all children except those who objected on religious grounds. Third, the *Barnette* Court's "fixed star" regarding orthodoxy becomes the basis for what is later called "content neutrality" in free speech cases, and it also resembles the neutrality approach that the Court takes in religion cases.[25]

The Court's "no orthodoxy" principle in *Barnette* provides a different emphasis to American constitutionalism from the famous statement in the Declaration of Independence on the purpose of government:

> We hold these truths to be self-evident, that all men are created equal, that they are endowed by the creator with certain unalienable rights, among which are life, liberty and the pursuit of happiness. To secure these rights, governments are instituted among men, deriving their just powers from the consent of the governed.

The American founders affirmed natural equality as America's political orthodoxy.[26] The Declaration asserts not only that government is founded on truths, but also that those truths require a kind of liberty that allows all human beings to pursue happiness freely. The truths do not direct human beings toward a particular activity or way of life.

One can imagine the need to preserve free government by restraining expressions of support for tyranny. In that spirit, a school board might decide to inculcate a love of country and a love of freedom in the nation's youth by requiring students to salute the flag in public schools. Justice Jackson's opinion in *Barnette* placed a more hardy emphasis on individual freedom without departing from the Declaration's "self-evident truth." First, he would have required a greater threat to national unity than was shown before allowing the compulsion to express a belief. In addition, Justice Jackson did not actually deny the statement of the Declaration. While he wrote that "no official . . . can prescribe what shall be orthodox . . . or force citizens to confess by word or act their faith therein," he made it clear that required civics courses in school were a constitutional means of inculcating patriotism.[27] A voluntary pledge ceremony was also permissible.[28]

In another important (and later) free speech case, Justice Powell wrote the following for the Court: "We begin with the common ground. Under the First Amendment there is no such thing as a false idea."[29] This sentiment resembles Justice Jackson's in his *Barnette* opinion, and it is what Justice Holmes meant when he wrote, in a dissent that has since been adopted in spirit by the Court, that "the best test of truth is the power of the thought to get itself accepted in the competition of the market, and that truth is the only ground upon which their wishes safely can be carried out."[30]

The Court's understanding of the First Amendment freedoms reveals the importance of two themes: civil peace and the quest for truth. Civil peace is the object of a government dedicated to the securing of rights and limited by the consent of the governed. It is true that civil peace can also be understood as the prevention of strife regardless of the regime. But the political philosophers who emphasized civil peace, including Hobbes, as well as Spinoza, Locke, and Montesquieu, appealed to what Tocqueville calls "self interest well understood."[31] People understand that it is in their interest to respect the rights of others. As a result, civil peace with stability is attained when individual rights are secured from other individuals as well as from government. The quest for truth describes both philosophic activity—which transcends but may threaten, or appear to threaten, the foundations of government— and political activity, especially such activity as is associated with democracy. We shall see that Spinoza, in order to secure freedom for philosophy, deliberately blurred the distinction between a philosophic and a political quest for the truth. The acceptance of this view of the quest for truth has secured substantial freedom of expression and led to increased skepticism about the ascertainment of truth, for philosophy or politics.

The teachings of classical political philosophy—Plato, Aristotle, and Thucydides[32]—illustrate the distinctive project of the Enlightenment philosophers. Each regards freedom of speech as essential to democracy. Each, however, accepts religion as an important part of political life. For example, when Socrates defends himself, in Plato's *Apology of Socrates*, against the charge of not believing in the gods of the city, he does not argue: "Athens is a free city. No official, no judge . . . may tell me what I shall, or shall not, teach or think."[33] Since the ancients do not regard democracy as the best regime, they present the strengths and weaknesses of unlimited freedom of speech. These philosophers expect good government to provide its citizens with more than civil peace. As a result, they do not advocate an unlimited freedom of inquiry.

The Enlightenment philosophers refused to accept the political limitations on freedom of thought and speech that the ancients did. These philosophers wanted to philosophize, to study, and to publish *in peace*. Religious strife threatened that peace. They fashioned their arguments for religious freedom in terms of toleration. Nevertheless, they grounded toleration in right, or legitimate, government. In his *Theological-Political Treatise*, Spinoza first argued for philosophic freedom against claims on behalf of revealed religion; then he argued for political freedom.[34] Milton and Locke expressed confidence in the truth's winning out in a free exchange with falsehoods, but they wrote rhetorically. They argued against theologically based restrictions on philosophy. They meant that philosophic freedom, the quest for truth, would not harm the body politic. Each philosopher limited freedom of speech or religion so that neither threatened civil peace. As *the* condition for peace, Hobbes advocated absolute sovereignty, whereby the sovereign must control freedom of speech and of religion. Hobbes also supported the emancipation of the peaceful passions—acquisition via commerce, not war—which leads to the development of these freedoms. Spinoza, who advocated religious freedom, was the first philosopher to argue that democracy best allowed each person to develop his rational faculties; therefore he supported freedom of speech. But Spinoza knew the difference between philosophic reason and non-philosophic, or democratic, reason. The philosopher attempts "to know things through their primary causes"; the democratic citizen relies on society "to live in security and good health."[35] Spinoza's argument for democratic freedom, and hence for freedom of speech, can be viewed as philosophically self-interested as well as humanitarian. Because he feared the rule of the priests in an aristocracy, Spinoza thought that democracy was the best regime for the philosophers.

Montesquieu's definition of political liberty as the tranquility of spirit that comes from an individual's opinion of security led him to argue that speech should be punishable only when it prepares or accompanies a criminal act. Mill then extended the arguments of Milton, Locke, Spinoza, and Montesquieu by arguing that full freedom for political as well as religious opinions will lead to truth's eventual victory. Milton is the first writer to introduce the metaphor of Truth winning out in a battle with falsehood. Mill never explained what he meant by truth, but he was most interested in providing for individual self-development. He was confident that freedom of speech would not lead to any harm. Mill allowed restrictions on speech only when it incited a crowd to unlawful action.

> An opinion that corn-dealers are starvers of the poor, or that private property is robbery, ought to go unmolested when simply circulated through the press, but may justly incur punishment when delivered orally to an excited mob assembled before the house of a corn-dealer, or when handed about among the same mob in the form of a placard.[36]

Justice Oliver Wendell Holmes turned this into the famous "clear and present danger" test for punishable speech, and then offered his own confident assertion that truth will win out.

> Persecution for the expression of opinions seems to me perfectly logical. If you have no doubt of your premises or your power and want a certain result with all your heart, you naturally express your wishes in law and sweep away all opposition. To allow opposition by speech seems to indicate that you think the speech impotent, as when a man says that he has squared the circle, or that you do not care wholeheartedly for the result, or that you doubt either your power or your premises. But when men have realized that time has upset many fight-

ing faiths, they may come to believe even more than they believe the very foundations of their own conduct that the ultimate good desired is better reached by free trade in ideas—that the best test of truth is the power of the thought to get itself accepted in the competition of the market, and that truth is the only ground upon which their wishes safely can be carried out. That at any rate is the theory of our Constitution.[37]

By adopting Mill's metaphor of truth winning out in a marketplace of ideas, Holmes made the notion a staple of American constitutional law, one applicable to speech cases and some religion cases as well.[38] When the Court adopts a "content neutrality" approach to regulation of speech, the Justices reveal their confidence in the beneficent outcome of contending views. Some critics challenge this approach when it leads to protection for nude dancing, cross burning, flag burning, or pornography on the Internet.[39] Indeed, the Court's compromising approach to campaign finance—"money is speech," but contributions may be limited while independent expenditures may not be—has drawn criticism from both sides; some say it restricts core political speech, and others say it restricts government's ability to assure fair elections.[40]

In the name of required government neutrality in religion, the Court prohibits government-encouraged prayer in public schools or at public school graduation ceremonies. The Court also struck down required "creation science" courses where public schools teach evolution.[41] On the other hand, the Court now allows most forms of government assistance to parochial schools, including tuition vouchers,[42] and some forms of governmental display of religious symbols.[43] As for the Free Exercise Clause, the Court now holds that laws neutral in their purpose toward religion do not have to pass a "compelling state interest" test to be upheld.[44] But, the Court protects religious activity on the part of student groups at public universities, as speech contributing to the marketplace of ideas.[45]

Do these decisions amount to a coherent view, one that we citizens can readily understand and support? They surely seem to be far removed from the founders' constitution. In the first part of this book, I show how the American constitutional founding, from 1776 to 1790, established limited government. In the middle section, I turn to some political philosophers, from Plato to Mill, to gain a full appreciation of what limited government really means. By studying the philosophic origins of both our understanding of government as a whole and the First Amendment freedoms, we can better understand the strengths and weaknesses of our own form of government and way of life. Both "civil peace" and "the quest for truth" are central to my discussion because they point to the prominence of security and prosperity on the one hand, and freedom of inquiry and self-development on the other. We must not take the marketplace of ideas metaphor too seriously, however. The philosophers who made that argument knew the difference between philosophic freedom and political freedom. The former involves disinterested inquiry into causes; the latter involves interested action.

With these philosophic foundations in place, I conclude with a study of the constitutional doctrines that the Supreme Court has developed in its interpretation of freedom of speech and religious freedom. I explain why I think the judicial emphasis on neutrality, for free speech and for religious freedom, provides the best support for the freedom that limited government secures. Limited government supports wide-ranging philosophic and scientific inquiry and extensive forms of political and individual expression. The two constitutional doctrines of neutrality (one applied to religion and the other to content- and viewpoint-based expression) implement the objectives of civil peace and freedom of inquiry. We probably have to accept vulgarity in expression and dilution of religious convictions as the price of tolerance and individual freedom.

To preserve that freedom, at a time when any claim to a transcendent truth is suspect, we need to appreciate the importance of moderation. Moderation—a classical virtue—protects and preserves political freedom *and* intellectual inquiry. It is worth noting at the conclusion of this introduction that the virtue of moderation, which limited government requires, is something limited government cannot legislate into existence. It is my hope that a careful study of our First Amendment freedoms may encourage us in our practice of moderation.

Notes

1. Originally, the first ten amendments applied only to the federal government, not to the states. When the Supreme Court interpreted the Freedom of Speech, Free Exercise, and Establishment Clauses to apply to the states under the Fourteenth Amendment's Due Process clause, it also started to give the First Amendment freedoms increased protection. I discuss this in Part Three.

2. Following Leo Strauss and Harvey Mansfield, I acknowledge Machiavelli as the founder of modern political philosophy. The philosophers of the seventeenth century, including Bacon, Hobbes, Spinoza, and Locke, began the process of "taming the prince," as Mansfield has put it, *Taming the Prince: The Ambivalence of Executive Power*, (New York: The Free Press, 1989) or channeling Machiavellianism into peaceful pursuits, as Strauss put it, *Natural Right and History* (Chicago: University of Chicago, 1953) and *What is Political Philosophy?* (Chicago: University of Chicago Press, 1959).

3. There are some exceptions. See Daniel A. Farber, *The First Amendment* (New York: Foundation Press, 1998); Walter Berns, *The First Amendment and the Future of American Democracy* (New York: Basic Books, 1976); and David Lowenthal, *No Liberty For License: The Forgotten Logic of the First Amendment* (Dallas: Spence Publishing Company, 1997) slightly revised as *Present Dangers: Rediscovering the First Amendment* (Dallas: Spence Publishing Company, 2002).

4. In America, there was no hereditary nobility; limited government would also be republican government.

5. See Thomas Curry, *The First Freedoms: Church and State in America to the Passage of the First Amendment* (New York: Oxford University Press, 1986), 140–3.

6. The best book on the subject is Leonard W. Levy, *Emergence of a Free Press* (New York; Oxford University Press, 1985)

7. William Blackstone, *Commentaries on the Laws of England*, facsimile of the First Edition of 1765–1769 (Chicago: University of Chicago Press, 1979), vol. 4, 150.

8. This book does not examine the development of the First Amendment freedoms in state court decisions in the nineteenth century. For free speech, see David M. Rabban, *Free Speech in its Forgotten Years* (Cambridge: Cambridge University Press, 1997); for religion, see Mark DeWolfe Howe, *The Garden and the Wilderness: Religion and Government in American Constitutional History* (Chicago: University of Chicago Press, 1965).

9. John Milton, "Areopagitica," in *Areopagitica and Education*, George H. Sabine, ed. (Arlington Heights, Illinois: Harlan Davidson, Inc., 1951); John Locke, *A Letter Concerning Toleration*, James H. Tully, ed. (Indianapolis: Hackett Publishing Company; 1973); John Stuart Mill, *On Liberty and Other Writings*, Stefan Collini, ed. (Cambridge: Cambridge University Press, 1989).

10. See Thomas I. Emerson, *The System of Freedom of Expression* (New York: Vintage, 1971) 6-7; Daniel A. Farber, *The First Amendment* (New York; Foundation Press, 1998), 3-6; Kathleen Sullivan and Gerald Gunther, *Constitutional Law*, 14th ed. (New York: Foundation Press, 2001), 959-962.

11. This position was first stated in *Everson v Board of Education*, 330 U.S. 1 (1947).

12. *Wallace v Jaffree*, 472 U.S. 38 (1985).

13. See *Sherbert v Verner*, 374 U.S. 398 (1963). The application of this rule was severely limited in *Employment Div Dept of Human Resources of Oregon v Smith* 494 U.S. 872 (1990).

14. 319 U.S. 586 (1940).

15. The family name actually was Gobitas. A letter that Billy Gobitas wrote to "Our School Directors" dated November 5, 1935, in the Library of Congress JPG picture files.

16. 310 U.S. 586, 594.

17. "National unity is the basis of national security. To deny the legislature the right to select appropriate means for its attainment presents a totally different order of problem from that of the propriety of subordinating the possible ugliness of littered streets to the free expression of opinion through the distribution of handbills." Id. at 595.

18. "I cannot conceive that in prescribing, as limitations upon the power of government, the freedom of the mind and spirit secured by the explicit guaranties of freedom of speech and religion, they intended or rightly could have left any latitude for a legislative judgment that the compulsory expression of belief which violates religious convictions would better serve the public interest than their protection." Id. 605.

19. 319 U.S. 624 (1943).

20. They also cited Exodus 20:4, as the Gobitis family did.

21. 319 U.S. 624, 629.

22. The three-judge district court cited *Jones v Opelika*, 316 US 584 (1942) as support for a change in position by the Supreme Court.

23. Id. 634.

24. Id. 642.

25. The difference between free speech neutrality and establishment clause neutrality is that a voluntary flag salute school exercise is constitutional, whereas voluntary prayer in public schools is not. On July 26, 2002, the ninth circuit, voting 2–1, decided that the 1954 amendment to the Pledge of Allegiance (adding "under God") violated the Establishment Clause (*Newdow v Congress*, 292 F. 3rd 597). On February 28, 2003, a divided circuit court, sitting en banc, refused to entertain a rehearing of the case (328 F. 3d 466 CA92003). On June 14, 2004, the Supreme Court reversed, holding that Newdow, who was not the custodial parent of his daughter, did not have standing to challenge the school district's policy (see *Elk Grove Unified School District v Michael A. Newdow*, 2004 U.S. Lexis 4478 Justice Stevens's opinion of the court at note 8). Chief Justice Rehnquist and Justices O'Connor and Thomas each wrote separate opinions indicating that they would have reached the merits and decided the case against Newdow. Justice Scalia did not participate in the decision. No justice expressed support for the ninth circuit's position on the pledge.

26. The framers knew that slavery conflicted with the Declaration. See John Rutledge's speech in the Federal Convention, where he rejects the application of the Declaration to matters of government. ("Religion and humanity had nothing to do with the question—Interest alone is the governing principle with Nations.") 21 August 1787, in Max Farrand ed., *Records of the Federal Convention* (New Haven: Yale University Press, 1937), vol. 2, 364.

27. See Id. 631, where Justice Jackson quotes with approval the remark in Chief Justice Stone's *Gobitis* dissent on the appropriateness of required civics courses. If a civics course is regarded as inculcating love of country, Justice Jackson should have used the conjunction "and," not "or," in his famous sentence.

28. See Id. at 630, 638, 641.

29. *Gertz v Welch*, 418 U.S. 323, 339 (1974).

30. *Abrams v United States*, 250 U.S. 616, 630 (1919).

31. Alexis de Tocqueville, *Democracy in America*, translated by Harvey C. Mansfield and Delba Winthrop (Chicago: University of Chicago Press, 2000) vol. 1 part two, chapter eight, 500-503 (hereinafter cited as *Democracy in America*).

32. I include Thucydides for reasons Leo Strauss gave for including him, along with Aristotle and Plato, in his book *The City and Man* (Chicago: Rand McNally,

1964). By covering cities at war, he provides "a supplement [to the philosopher's speech on the best city] which the philosopher cannot give" (140); in addition, his work "lets us see the universal in the particular event which he narrates . . ." (143).

33. Alexander Meiklejohn offers that interpretation of Socrates' defense speech in *Political Freedom: The Constitutional Powers of the People* (Oxford: New York, 1965), 22.

34. *Theological-Political Treatise*, translated by Samuel Shirley (Indianapolis: Hackett Publishing Company, 1998).

35. Id. chap. 3, 38

36. *On Liberty*, supra n. 5, 56.

37. *Abrams v United States* 250 U.S. 616, 630 (1919).

38. *Rosenberger v Rector University of Virginia*, 515 U.S. 819 (1995) involves both religion clauses and the Free Exercise Clause. Justice Kennedy uses the phrase in his Court opinion upholding the right of a student organization to receive funds to publish a religious newspaper. See p. 831.

39. Robert Bork has been a strident critic of the Court's interpretation of the First Amendment. See his essay in *First Things*, Nov 1996, no. 67, p. 23; reprinted in *The End of Democracy? Judicial Usurpation of Politics*. 15; *The Tempting of America: The Political Seduction of the Law* (New York: Free Press, 1990), 126-28, 246-47, 333-36; *Slouching toward Gomorrah: Modern Liberalism and American Decline* (New York: Regan Books, 1996), 98–102. Other scholars who have criticized the Court's interpretation of the First Amendment from a conservative perspective include Walter Berns, *The First Amendment and the Future of American Democracy* (New York: Basic Books, 1976), and David Lowenthal, *No Liberty For License: The Forgotten Logic of the First Amendment* (Dallas: Spence Publishing, 1997). The five-to-four flag burning decisions of 1989 and 1990 led to an attempt to pass a constitutional amendment to permit the protection of the flag. Recent decisions regarding pornography on the Internet have also been controversial. These will be discussed in Part Three.

40. Vincent Blasi supports spending limits in "Free Speech and the Widening Gyre of Fund-Raising: Why Campaign Spending Limits May Not Violate the First Amendment After All," 95 *Columbia Law Rev* 1281 (1994), and Cass Sunstein has proposed "A New Deal for Speech," in *The Partial Constitution* (Cambridge: Harvard University Press, 1993), chapter 7. Kathleen Sullivan took the other side in "Against Campaign Finance Reform," 1998 *Utah Law Review* 311.

41. *Edwards v Aguillard*, 482 U.S. 578 (1987).

42. *Zelman v Simmons-Harris*, 536 U.S. 639 (2002).

43. *Lynch v Donnellly*, 465 U.S. 668 (1984).

44. As applied to Free Exercise cases, the "compelling state interest test puts the burden on the government to justify the application of a neutral law to anyone who objects on the basis of religious belief or practice." The Court first applied the test to Free Exercise cases in 1963 and it reconsidered and rejected that approach in 1990. See *Sherbert v Verner*, 374 U.S. 398 (1963) and *Employment Division, Department of Human Resources v Smith*, 494 U.S. 872 (1990). These cases are discussed below in chapter 13.

45. In addition to *Rosenberger*, cited above, the most recent case is *Good News Club v Milford Central School*, 533 U.S. 98 (2001).

PART ONE

RELIGIOUS FREEDOM AND FREEDOM OF SPEECH IN THE AMERICAN FOUNDING

The American constitutional founding starts with the Declaration of Independence, includes the subsequent state constitutions and the Articles of Confederation, and culminates in the work of the Federal Convention of 1787, whose members wrote the American Constitution, and the state ratification conventions of 1787–1788, which established the Constitution as the supreme law of the land. For our purposes, we will need to view the American founding in a more extended sense: looking at the early views on religious freedom and freedom of speech, from the Puritan beginnings, and looking at the debate on the meaning of freedom of speech that arose out of the controversy over the Sedition Act of 1798. The most instructive and well-known writing on the Sedition Act is Madison's Virginia Report, which is an elaboration of his Virginia Resolutions.

Following in the footsteps of Herbert Storing's study of the Anti-Federalists[1], I am looking for the fundamental principles in documents and expressions of opinion. Such materials are important because political thought affects American government significantly, as Joseph Cropsey has pointed out. Taking the regime to refer to what Americans stand for—freedom, equality, and rights— he asks:

Why is our political essence obscure to us if it is embodied in words that can be studied and comprehended? Experience shows that the words are subject to construction, and that the unchanging text of the First Amendment, for example, means different things to different judges. Apparently something, call it for the moment thought, mixes itself with the documents that embody the regime—in fact then mixes itself with the regime—and in so doing clarifies but also perplexes our understanding of the regime, and hence of ourselves—what we stand for and what our goals are.[2]

Thought has such a large and potentially unnerving or destabilizing effect on our regime, on who we are as a people, due to what Cropsey describes as our own regime's "self limitation in the name of freedom. It is obvious that regulation of religion, of art, of thought, and the expression of it, of science, and of many aspects of private life is intentionally ruled out by the regime."[3] That self-limitation, which the term "liberal democracy" describes, was not a part of Puritan democracy. The philosophic thought about politics that is identified with the Enlightenment accounted for significant changes in the way Americans understood the purpose of government. Our current understanding of religious freedom and freedom of speech derives from the view that government's purposes are limited to securing individual, natural rights, as is stated in the Declaration of Independence and in state bills of rights.[4] That limited view of government was not the view of the first immigrants, especially the Puritans. A comparison of colonial charters and constitutions reveals a comprehensive view of government that does not delineate the political from the theological. The state constitutions that were enacted during the Revolutionary period have more to say about religion than about speech, but the provisions concerning religion are consistent with the Enlightenment view that government's purposes were related to security and well being in this world. Viewed in a political sense, religion served government by inculcating proper morals. Viewed in terms of salvation of the soul, religion was a private matter, separate from government.

My first task is to use documents and commentaries to illustrate the significance of the difference between a theological approach to politics and a philosophic approach rooted in the principle of the rights of man. I will start by comparing the Declaration's of Independence with John Winthrop's "A Model of Christian Charity," a sermon delivered on board the *Arbella* in 1630.

Notes

1. Herbert Storing, *What the Anti-Federalists Were For!* (Chicago: University of Chicago Press, 1981), 6.

2. "The United States as a Regime," in Joseph Cropsey, *Political Philosophy and the Issues of Politics* (Chicago, University of Chicago Press, 1977) p. 2.

3. Id. 2.

4. Eight of the original thirteen states had bills of rights attached to their constitutions: Virginia, Pennsylvania, Delaware, Maryland, North Carolina, Connecticut, Massachusetts, and New Hampshire. See The Roots of the Bill of Rights: An Illustrated Source Book of American Freedom, ed. by Bernard Schwartz (New York, N.Y.: Chelsea House Publishers; 1980).

CHAPTER ONE

The American Founding and the Puritan Origins

Students of the American Founding tend to start with the Declaration of Independence as the document that set forth a philosophic account of legitimate government as well as a detailed brief against the English government, cataloging its acts of tyranny. The Resolution of Independence, passed in June 1776, a month earlier than the Declaration, called on the several states to adopt new constitutions and to form a confederation; this led to eleven new state constitutions and the framing and eventual ratification of the Articles of Confederation. Yet Americans already had a century and a half of experience in government. Why not start with the earliest social compacts? Alexis de Tocqueville, the most famous foreign observer and commentator on America, did just that. In the second chapter of his *Democracy in America*, titled "Concerning Their Point of Departure and Its Importance for the Future of the Anglo-Americans," Tocqueville emphasized beginnings, for peoples as well as for individual human beings. "Peoples always feel [the effects of] their origins. The circumstances that accompanied their birth and served to develop them influence the entire course of the rest of their lives."[1] Convinced that in America "we can watch the natural quiet growth of society," Tocqueville asserted that this chapter, which describes the Puritan immigrants, provides "the seed of what is to follow and the key to almost the whole work."[2] If Tocqueville is right, the differences between Winthrop's understanding of government and that of the signers of the Declaration of Independence are minimal. Let us consider the differences and then return to Tocqueville.

The Declaration of Independence begins with Jefferson's version of the language of section one of the Virginia Bill of Rights.

When in the Course of human Events, it becomes necessary for one People to dissolve the Political Bands which have connected them with another, and to assume among the Powers of the Earth, the separate and equal Station to which the Laws of Nature and Nature's God entitle them, a decent respect for the Opinions of Mankind requires that they should declare the causes which impel them to the Separation.

We hold these truths to be self-evident, that all Men are created equal, that they are endowed by their creator with certain unalienable Rights, that among these are Life, Liberty, and the Pursuit of Happiness—That to secure these Rights, Governments are instituted among men, deriving their just powers from the Consent of the Governed, that whenever any Form of Government becomes destructive of these ends, it is the Right of the People to alter or abolish it, and to institute new Government, laying its foundation on such Principles, and organizing its Powers in such Form, as to them shall seem most likely to effect their safety and Happiness. Prudence, indeed, will dictate that Governments long established should not be changed for light and transient Causes; and accordingly all Experience hath shewn, that Mankind are more disposed to suffer, while evils are sufferable, than to right themselves by abolishing the Forms to which they are accustomed. But when a long Train of Abuses and Usurpations, pursuing invariably the same Object, evinces a design to reduce them under absolute Despotism, it is their Right, it is their duty, to throw off such Government, and to provide new guards for their future security.[3]

Paraphrasing the argument of John Locke's *Second Treatise of Government*, the Declaration presents the American revolutionary position that the principles of government come from natural law, starting with individual rights of life, liberty, and the pursuit of happiness. After presenting the extensive bill of particulars against the king, the Declaration concludes as follows:

We therefore, the Representatives of the United States of America, in General Congress, Assembled, appealing to the Supreme Judge of the World for the Rectitude of our Intentions, do, in the Name, and by the Authority of the good people of these Colonies, solemnly Publish and Declare, That these United Colonies are, and of Right ought to be, FREE AND INDEPENDENT STATES; that they have full power to levy War, conclude Peace, contract Alliances, establish Commerce, and to do all other Acts and Things which INDEPENDENT STATES may of right do. And for the support of this Declaration, with a firm Reliance on the Protection of divine Providence, we mutually pledge to each other our Lives, our Fortunes, and our sacred Honor.

Jefferson's draft of the Declaration referred to "nature's god," in the first paragraph, but it was not capitalized. His draft of the final paragraph did not include mention of "the Supreme Judge" or "divine Providence."[4] Do these additions mean that while Jefferson can be associated with Enlightenment philosophy, the framers of the Declaration, and hence the document itself, cannot? To understand the significance of these terms, let us turn to a comparable kind of document for some of the first Puritan settlers of the New World.

John Winthrop's sermon, delivered on aboard the *Arbella* (1630) in a voyage from Great Britain to New England,[5] resembles the Declaration of Independence in three respects. First, it is a statement to a group of individuals who, by having chosen to remove themselves to the New World, have established themselves as a distinct people. Second, it is a statement of that people's principles or aspirations. Third, it describes the people's work as a covenant, or contract. In the first part of the sermon, Winthrop refers to both the law of nature, also called the moral law, and to the law of grace, also called the law of the gospel. The fundamental difference between the Puritan body politic, illustrated by this sermon, and the later American body politic, illustrated by the Declaration of Independence, concerns the understanding of natural law.

For Winthrop, the law of nature is consistent with inequality. That is because "God almighty" is "delighted to show forth the glory of his wisdom in the variety and difference of the creatures." No man is made "more honorable than another or more wealthy, etc. out of any particular and singular respect to himself, but for the glory of his creator and the common good of the creature, man."[6] Furthermore, while justice and mercy are the "two rules whereby we are to walk one toward another," Winthrop ranks mercy above justice. Citing the Gospel of Matthew, Winthrop identifies all precepts of the moral law with man's duty to "love his neighbor as himself."

As the law of nature applies to man "in the estate of innocency," the law of grace, or the gospel, applies "in the estate of regeneracy." (This key distinction is not present in the Declaration.) While both laws apply, the law of nature "propounds one man to another," whereas the law of grace pertains to "a brother in Christ . . . and so teacheth us to put a difference between Christians and others." While this is a special concern for Christians, it also commands "love to an enemy" in a way that the law of nature cannot. Christians must at times "give beyond their ability," as well as "do good to them that hate you."[7]

Winthrop's "mercy" seems to span both laws. Each law is an aspect of God's law. Summarizing his discussion of giving, lending, and forgiving,

Winthrop quotes Matthew again: "Whatsoever ye would that men should do to you, do ye the same to them also."[8] The law of nature from the Declaration, in contrast, is best understood as dictating action from the negative: as Hobbes put it, do not do that to others what you do not want done to you.[9] The security of rights replaces the primacy of duty to others, let alone a duty to act with mercy.

Winthrop next discusses love as "the affection from which the exercise of mercy must arise." Love, and not any form of dialogue or argument, is the preferred way "to draw men to works of mercy," and its source is said to be Scripture. Adam's fall accounts for selfish love, which continues until "Christ comes and takes possession of the soul and infuseth another principle, love to God and our brother."[10] Winthrop continues: "And the party loving reaps love again . . . which the soul covets more than all the wealth in the world. [Moreover], nothing yields more pleasure and content to the soul than when it finds that which it may love fervently, for to love and live beloved is the soul's paradise, both here and in heaven."[11]

In his concluding part of the sermon, known as the Application,[12] Winthrop moves from these divine principles of human life to the task confronting his fellow settlers upon their imminent landing. First, "we are a company professing ourselves fellow members of Christ." Second, "[i]t is by a mutual consent, through a special overvaluing providence and a more than ordinary approbation of the churches of Christ, to seek out a place of cohabitation and consortship under a due form of government both civil and ecclesiastical." Third, "the end is to improve our lives to do more service to the Lord; the comfort and encrease of the body of Christ whereof we are members; that ourselves and posterity may be the better preserved from the common corruptions of this evil world, to serve the Lord and work out our salvation under the power and purity of his holy ordinances." Fourth, the means must be more extraordinary than those practiced in England, since these Puritans in the New World regard themselves as specially chosen by God, as the ancient Israelites were. Winthrop then summarizes their condition:

Thus stands the cause between God and us. We are entered into covenant with him for this work. We have taken out a commission, the Lord hath given us leave to draw our own articles. We have professed to enterprise these actions, upon these and those ends, we have hereupon besought him of favor and blessing. Now if the Lord shall please to hear us, and bring us in peace to the place we desire, then hath he ratified this covenant and sealed our commission, [and] will expect a strict performance of the articles contained in it. But if we shall neglect the observation of these articles which are the ends we have propounded and, dissembling with our God, shall fall to embrace this present world and prosecute our carnal intentions, seeking great things for ourselves and our posterity, the Lord will surely break out in wrath against us, be revenged of such a perjured people, and make us know the price of the breach of such a covenant.[13]

To avoid such an end, Winthrop quotes the counsel of Micah—to do justly, love mercy, and walk humbly with our God—as well as the exhortation of Moses concerning the choice of life and good over death and evil. He also paraphrases Matthew to the effect that they "shall be as a city upon a hill."[14]

Winthrop assumes that government is responsible for cultivating a complete human being, one who follows the commands and precepts of the Old and the New Testaments. The covenant is, accordingly, between the different men and God, not simply among men. Colonial government in America reflected this view, as we can see by looking at charters and constitutions. For example, the Mayflower Compact (1620) contains the following statement of purpose:

Having undertaken for the Glory of God and advancement of the Christian Faith, and the Honor of our King and Country, a Voyage to plant the first Colony in the northern Parts of *Virginia*; Do by these Presents, solemnly and mutually, in the Presence of God and one another, covenant and combine ourselves together into a civil Body Politic, for our better Ordering and Preservation, and Furtherance of the Ends aforesaid: And by Virtue hereof do enact, constitute, and frame, such just and equal Laws, Ordinances, Acts, Constitutions, and Officers, from time to time, as shall be thought most meet and convenient for the general Good of the Colony; unto which we promise all due Submission and Obedience.[15]

The Fundamental Orders of Connecticut, dated January 14, 1639, provided for the following oath for magistrates: "I . . . doe sweare by the great and dreadful name of the everliving god to promote the publike good and peace of the same, according to the best of my skill, . . . and will further the execution of Justice for the tyme aforesaid according to the righteous rule of Gods word; so help me God, etc."[16]

Another example comes from William Penn's Charter of Liberties and Frame of Government of the Province of Pennsylvania in America, dated May 5, 1682. After referring in his preface to the "divine right of government . . . to terrify evil doers . . . [and] to cherish those that do well," Penn writes that "government seems to me a part of religion itself, a thing sacred in its institution and end. For if it does not directly remove the cause, it crushes the effects of evil, and is as such . . . an emanation of the same Divine Power, that is both author and object of pure religion . . . ."[17] All magistrates "shall be such as possess faith in Jesus Christ," and all persons "who confess and acknowledge the one Almighty and eternal God, to be the Creator, Upholder, and Ruler of the world" and who "live peaceable and justly in civil society, shall, in no ways be molested or prejudiced for their religious persuasion, or practice in matters of faith and worship, nor shall they be compelled . . . to frequent or maintain any religious worship, place or ministry whatever."[18]

Another article describes criminal offenses this way:

> That as a careless and corrupt administration of justice draws the wrath of God upon magistrates, so the wildness and looseness of the people provoke the indignation of God against a country: therefore, that all such offences against God, as swearing, cursing, lying, prophane talking, drunkenness, drinking of healths, obscene words, incest, sodomy, rapes, whoredom, fornication, and other uncleanness (not to be repeated) all treasons, murders, duels, felonies, seditions, maims, forcible entries, and other violences to the persons and estates of the inhabitants within this province; all prizes, stage-plays, cards, dice, May-games, gamesters, masques, revels, bull-baiting, cock-fighting, bear baitings, and the like, which excite the people to rudeness, cruelty, looseness, and irreligion, shall be respectively discouraged, and severely punished, according to the appointment of the Governor and freemen in provincial Council and General Assembly."[19]

The Massachusetts Body of Liberties, dated December 1641, includes a provision for religious liberty in the form of conscientious objection. The provision allowed a statement and recording of dissent, but this did not release the dissenter from the obligation of the order or law (75).[20] Another section makes the following capital crimes: worshipping "any other god but the lord god;" being "a witch;" blaspheming "the name of God;" homosexuality, adultery, and theft (94). In addition, persons were allowed to join a church "Provided they do it in a Christian way, with due observance of the rules of Christ revealed in his word" (95, 1). The churches had the liberty of self-government. Another article referred to all "rites, freedoms, Immunities, Authorities and Priviledges, both Ecclesiastical and Civil," as laws and thereby urged all magistrates "not to fail to inflict condign and proportionable punishments upon every man impartiallie, that shall infringe or violate any of them" (96).

Finally, in the Pennsylvania Charter of Liberties of 1701, William Penn extended full religious liberty to everyone "who shall confess and acknowledge *One* [italics in original] almighty God, the Creator, Upholder, and Ruler of the world." To be able to serve in government, it was also necessary to "profess to believe in Jesus Christ, the savior of the World."[21]

In contrast to the early charters and constitutions, the post Revolutionary state constitutions no longer contained statements concerning the theological purpose of government. The Massachusetts Constitution of 1780, for example, stated in its preamble that "the end . . . of government is to secure the existence of the body politic, and to protect it, and to furnish the individuals who compose it with the power of enjoying in safety and tranquillity their natural rights, and the blessings of life." The importance of equality and natural rights was reaffirmed in Article I.

Article III stated that the happiness of the people and the preservation of good government depend on "piety, religion, and morality," which depend on "the public worship of God." This is an argument for a "civil religion"; the people have the right to invest their legislature "with power to authorize and require" through towns, parishes, and precincts, support for "public Protestant teachers of piety, religion, and morality." Moreover, the people also had the right to invest their legislature with the authority to require attendance. In addition, all magistrates were required to take an oath declaring their belief in the Christian religion.[22] New Hampshire's Constitution of 1784 copied the Massachusetts Constitution up to the point of authorizing public support for teachers of the Christian religion, but it did not authorize requiring attendance.[23] Massachusetts did not amend those parts of its Constitution that authorized public support and required attendance until 1833.[24]

The changing view about religion and its relation to government from the colonial charters to the state constitutions prompts a question about Tocqueville's account of the importance of the Puritans and religion in general for America. What does Tocqueville have in mind by emphasizing the continuity from the Puritan beginnings to the later American constitutional founding? He describes the Puritans as republican in their politics as well as deeply religious. Their religion is praised in some respects and criticized in others. For example, Tocqueville quotes Connecticut's 1650 code of laws to show how religion was used to support education:

> It being one chief project of that old deluder, Satan, to keep men from the knowledge of scriptures, as in former times, keeping them from an unknown tongue, so that in these latter times by persuading them from the use of tongues. . . . And that learning may not be buried in the grave of our forefathers, in church and commonwealth, the Lord assisting our endeavors.

After noting that the law obliges parents to send their children to school or risk losing their guardianship rights to society, Tocqueville concludes that "in America it is religion that leads to enlightenment; it is the observance of divine laws that guides man to freedom."[25]

Religion sets the limits to the Puritans' political independence, and in Tocqueville's opinion that is very good. As he puts it, "in the moral world," which is informed by religion, "everything is classified, coordinated, foreseen, decided in advance. In the political world, everything is agitated, contested, uncertain. In the one, there is passive though voluntary obedience; in the other, there are independence, contempt for experience, and jealousy of every authority." Religion thus buttresses political freedom:

> Religion sees in civil freedom a noble exercise of the faculties of man; in the political world, a field left by the Creator to the efforts of intelligence. Free and powerful within its sphere, satisfied with the place that is reserved for it, it knows that its empire is all the better established when it reigns by its own strength alone and dominates over hearts without support.
>
> Freedom sees in religion the companion of its struggles and its triumphs, the cradle of its infancy, and the divine source of its rights. It considers religion as the safeguard of mores, and mores as the guarantee of laws and the pledge of its own duration.[26]

Tocqueville praises the Puritans by attributing to them the position on religion that developed in New England after the Revolution: the position of separation, with religion still influential, since it sets the mores of the people. Tocqueville's criticism of Puritanism pertains to its criminal laws. Connecticut's code apparently followed Massachusetts's of nine years earlier, discussed above. After noting that idolatry, adultery, blasphemy, sorcery, rape, and homosexuality are capital crimes, Tocqueville writes: "In this way they carried the legislation of a rude and half-civilized people into the heart of a society whose spirit was enlightened and mores mild; so one never saw the death penalty laid down more profusely in the laws, or applied to fewer of the guilty."[27] He then reminds his reader that "these ridiculous and tyrannical laws" were self-imposed.

What should we make of this remarkable account of the Puritans? Tocqueville seems to contradict himself by saying that all is foretold in these beginnings and then by celebrating a separation between religion and politics and a liberalized criminal law—Enlightenment developments that the Puritans resisted. Tocqueville may have played down the break from a religious polity to a liberal one in order to make a stronger case in his own country for the constructive use of religion in the democratic society of post Revolutionary France.

While Tocqueville seems to have assumed that the Puritans' adoption of criminal law from the Old Testament would not last and that religion would become separate from politics, he did not mention Roger Williams, the one American religious figure who espoused such a position. Perhaps that is because Williams's thought was theological and Tocqueville was interested in "civil religion."[28] Williams not only insisted on separation, but also coined the metaphor "wall of separation," which Jefferson later used in a letter to the Baptists from Danbury, Connecticut. Mark DeWolf Howe, in his book *The Garden and the Wilderness*, points this out and argues that "the faith of Roger Williams played a more important part than the doubts of Jefferson" in establishing the Constitutional barrier between church and state.[29] For Howe, a proper historical understanding of Williams's influence on the religion clauses of the First Amendment would have prevented the Supreme Court from adopting "a secularist's view of separation." Furthermore, "the rule of separation was no less a postulate of faith than it is an axiom of doubt."[30] Howe argues that if the Supreme Court came to appreciate Williams's influence, it would then be able to acknowledge "what may fairly be described as a *de facto* establishment of religion."[31] Howe seems to agree with Tocqueville, who wrote: "Religion, which among Americans never mixes directly in the government of society, should therefore be considered as the first of their political institutions."[32] But Williams's fundamentally theological position cannot become the basis for principles of religious freedom that are part and parcel of limited government, of a regime of rights and consent. Let us consider Howe's argument and the two versions of the "wall of separation."

Jefferson wrote the following to A Committee of the Danbury Baptist Association in Connecticut, dated January 1, 1802.

> Believing with you that religion is a matter which lies solely between man and his God, that he owes account to none other for his faith or his worship, that the legislative powers of government reach actions only, and not opinions, I contemplate with sovereign reverence that act of the whole American people which declared that their legislature should 'make no law respecting an establishment of religion, or prohibiting the free exercise thereof,' thus building a wall of separation between Church and State. Adhering to this expression of the supreme will of the nation in behalf of the rights of conscience, I shall see with sincere satisfaction the progress of those sentiments which tend to restore to man all his natural rights, convinced he has no natural right in opposition to his social duties.[33]

Williams's version appeared in 1644, in his response to John Cotton's letter, published in 1643, which told Williams why he was banished from Massachusetts. Williams summarizes the issues between them by quoting the following from Cotton's letter:

"Mr. Williams, saith he, "holds forth these four particulars:

"First, that we have not our land by patent from the King, but that the natives are the true owners of it, and that we ought to repent of such a receiving it by patent.

"Secondly, that it is not lawful to call a wicked person to swear, to pray, as being actions of God's worship.

"Thirdly, that it is not lawful to hear any of the ministers of the parish assemblies in England.

"Fourthly, that the civil magistrate's power extends only to the bodies and goods and outward state of men.[34]

Williams's response to Cotton included the following:

First, the faithful labors of many witnesses of Jesus Christ, extant to the world, abundantly proving that the church of the Jews under the Old Testament in the type and the church of the Christians under the New Testament in the antitype were both separate from the world; and that when they have opened a gap in the hedge or wall of separation between the garden of the church and the wilderness of the world, God hath ever broke down the wall itself, removed the candlestick, and made His garden a wilderness of the world, as at this day. And that therefore if He will ever please to restore His garden and paradise again, it must of necessity be walled in peculiarly unto Himself from the world; and that all that shall be saved out of the world are to be transplanted out of the wilderness of this world, and added unto His church or garden.[35]

Williams's "typology," as Perry Miller explains, is the key to his separationist version of Puritanism. According to a typological interpretation of Scriptures, everything in the Old Testament has an allegorical correspondence to the New Testament. The relationship is one in which the sense of the Old Testament can only be discerned from the teachings of the New Testament. Most Puritans who came to New England, such as John Winthrop, tried to organize themselves as a church after the model of God's covenant with Abraham. In Williams's version of typology, with the coming of Christ and the New Testament, the Old Testament ceases to have any significance for the Christian. Separatism began by referring to independence from the established church in England. Williams's version of separatism went to the limit of its logic. As Miller writes:

[Williams's] immense distinction is that, involved with the Massachusetts oligarchy over the question of whether they should or should not declare themselves Separationists, he was forced to go farther than he had intended, and so to maintain the utter impossibility of New England magistrates, or of any other rulers or sachems in the world, being antitypes of Israel's sovereigns. The more earnestly they imitated Jewish governors, the more he was obliged to accuse them of becoming traitors to the Christian dispensation.[36]

This accounts for how Williams got to his separationist position from a theological perspective. What does it mean for politics? Surely Williams supports toleration in so far as he opposes persecution in the name of conscience. "[I]f thou huntest any for cause of conscience, how canst thou say thou followest the Lamb of God who so abhorred that practice?"[37]

Williams argues that government should not use its coercive authority in matters of conscience, but liberty and happiness in this world do not have the same rank for him as they do for advocates of liberal constitutionalism.[38]

Howe celebrates Williams' contribution to the First Amendment's religion clauses by playing down the difference between skeptic and believer, and emphasizing their agreement to "safeguard . . . the spiritual realm from the encroachments of government."[39] But for Williams, "spirit" means the truth of the New Testament; for an adherent of the rights of man, it means the liberty to develop one's faculties. The pursuit of happiness is not the same as following the love of God by living a Christian life in self-denial of bodily pleasures.

Howe thinks the First Amendment is "more the expression of Roger Williams' philosophy than that of Jefferson's" because "by and large, American opinion in 1790 accepted the view that religious truth was identifiable and beneficent. It was, in large part, because that was the prevailing view that it seemed peculiarly appropriate to safeguard that truth from the rough and corrupting hand of government."[40]

But Enlightenment philosophy affected the American founders' understanding of religious truth. After all, the Declaration of Independence, which Jefferson said reflected the "harmonizing sentiments of the day,"[41] referred to the law of nature and Nature's God, not to the Biblical God, and certainly not to Jesus Christ. That is consistent with the replacement of any Biblical account of the good life with a relegation of the entire question to the individual, in the language of "life, liberty, and the pursuit of happiness." It may be true that many Americans thought of themselves as Christians, but what they understood by that was undergoing a transformation, as we can see in the authoritative documents of the Founding period.

Notes

1. Tocqueville, Alexis de, *Democracy in America*, edited by Harvey C. Mansfield and Delba Winthrop (Chicago: University of Chicago press 2000) vol. 1, pt. 1, chap. 2, 28

2. Id. at 29.

3. Boyd, Julian P. ed. *Papers of Thomas Jefferson*, vol. 1 (Princeton: Princeton University Press, 1950), 429–30. For section 1 of the Virginia bill of rights, see Francis Newton Thorpe, ed., *The Federal and State Constitutions, Colonial Charters and Other Organic Laws of the States Territories and Colonies Now or Heretofore Forming The United States of America* (Washington, D.C.: GPO, 1909) vol. 3, 1841.

4. Id. 423, 427.

5. Winthrop had previously been chosen governor of the "Governor and Company of the Massachusetts Bay in New England [sic]." He and his associates "sailed in March 1630, reaching Salem (Mass.) on the 12th of June, accompanied by a large party of Puritan immigrants." See *The Encyclopedia Britannica*, eleventh edition (New York: Encyclopedia Britannica, 1910–1911), vol. 28, 736.

6. John Winthrop, "A Model of Christian Charity," in Heimert, Allen and Andrew Delbanco, eds., *The Puritans in America: A Narrative Anthology* (Cambridge: Harvard University Press, 1985), 83.

7. See Matthew 5: 44.

8. 7:22, in Winthrop, "A Model of Christian Charity," 85.

9. *Leviathan*, ed. by Richard Tuck (Cambridge: Cambridge University Press, 1991) chap. 14, 92, and chap. 15, 109. The first reference is in Latin, the second in English.

10. In Winthrop, "A Model of Christian Charity," 87.

11. Id. at 88.

12. I am grateful to my colleague Professor John McWilliams for this term.

13. In Winthrop, "A Model of Christian Charity," at 90–91.

14. Id. 91.

15. In Thorpe, vol. 3, 1841. The text comes from William Bradford's *Plimouth Plantations*. Italics in text.

16. From Thorpe, vol. 1, 519–23 .

17. Id. vol. 5, 3053.

18. Id. vol. 5, p. 3063; articles XXXIV and XXXV of the laws agreed to.

19. Id. vol. 5, p. 3063, article XXXVII.

20. The Massachusetts Body of Liberties is published in *Colonial Origins of the American Constitution*, Donald S. Lutz, ed. (Indianapolis: Liberty Fund, 1997), 70–87. The numbers cited in parentheses identify the sections that have been paraphrased or quoted.

21. Thorpe, vol. 5, 3077.

22. Id., vol. 3, 1889–90.

23. Thorpe, vol. 4, 2454 (resolution 6).

24. See Thorpe vol. 3, 1914, article XI of the amendment articles, and 1922, for the ratification date.

25. Tocqueville, *Democracy in America*, 41–42. The Connecticut code is in *Colonial Origins*, 241–249; the part Tocqueville quotes is at 247–48. Massachusetts' Laws and Liberties, 1647, contained a similar provision; see *Colonial Origins*, 129.

26. Id., 43–44.

27. Id., 38

28. Rousseau used this term in his *Social Contract*; it is the title of book IV, chap. 8.

29. Mark DeWolf Howe, *The Garden and the Wilderness* (Chicago: University of Chicago Press, 1965), 7.

30. Id., 10.

31. Id., 11.

32. Tocqueville, *Democracy in America*, 280.

33. *The Portable Thomas Jefferson*, ed. by Merrill D. Peterson (New York, Penguin Books, 1975), 303–4

34. Miller, Perry, *Roger Williams: His Contribution to the American Tradition* (New York: Atheneum; 1962), 93.

35. Id., 98.

36. Id., 38.

37. Roger Williams, "The Bloody Tenent, of Persecution, for cause of Conscience, discussed, in A Conference betweene Truth and Peace," quoted in Miller, *Roger Williams*, 109.

38. For a view of Williams that emphasizes his tolerance and "civility," see James Calvin Davis, "A Return to Civility: Roger Williams and Public Discourse in America," *Journal of Church and State*, vol. 43 autumn, 2001, (no. 4), 689–706. Even Davis, however, acknowledges that "[r]eligion, not politics, was, of course, Williams' truly ultimate concern" (699, n. 33).

39. Howe, *Garden*, 18.

40. Id., 19.

41. Letter to Henry Lee, May 8, 1825, in *Thomas Jefferson: Selected Writings*, ed. By Harvey C. Mansfield, Jr. (Arlington Heights, Il: AHM Publishing Corp. 1979), 12.

CHAPTER TWO

Religious Freedom and Freedom of Speech in the State Constitutions of the Confederation Period

Thus far, the discussion has focused on religion because the shift from a religious polity to religious freedom is fundamental. Religious freedom and freedom of speech both presuppose a regime that is dedicated to securing individual rights. From 1776 to 1784, eleven of the original thirteen states drafted new constitutions; Connecticut and Rhode Island continued to be governed under Crown colony charters, dating from the 1660s. By 1798, several states had revised their constitutions, and Vermont and Kentucky, both of which entered the Union in the 1790s, also framed new constitutions. Following is a chronological chart of these constitutions, including the two seventeenth-century charters.

I am looking at these constitutions for two reasons: (1) to confirm the shift from religious polities, which are reflected in Colonial charters and speeches, to liberal polities—with their emphasis on individual freedoms—which are reflected in these constitutions; and (2) to understand the range of views on religious freedom and freedom of speech that emerged during the American Founding. Our interest, therefore, is in general constitutional statements about the purpose of government, as well as specific provisions regarding religious freedom and freedom of speech. Since the culminating act of the American Founding is the framing and ratifying of the Constitution of 1787, along with the addition of the Bill of Rights, let us note the relevant provisions in the Constitution itself, as well as the language of the First Amendment.[1]

Table 2.1. Chronology of State Constitutions

	Date	State[1]	Bill or Declaration of Rights?
	1662	Connecticut	no
	1663	Rhode Island	no
	1776	New Hampshire	no
	1776	Virginia	yes
	1776	Pennsylvania	yes
D of I ———>			
	1776	Delaware	no
	1776	Maryland	yes
	1776	North Carolina	yes
	1776	South Carolina	no
	1777	Georgia	no
	1777	New York	no
	1777	Vermont	no
	1778	South Carolina	no
	1780	Massachusetts	yes
	1784	New Hampshire	yes
	1786	Vermont	no
	1789	Georgia	no
	1790	Pennsylvania	no
	1792	Kentucky	no
	1793	Vermont	no
	1798	Georgia	no

[1] The states that appear more than once had more than one constitution during the period surveyed. The constitutions are all in Francis Newton Thorpe, ed., *The Federal and State Constitutions, Colonial Charters and Other Organic Laws of the States, Territories, and Colonies Now or Heretofore Forming The United States of America* (Washington, D.C.: GPO, 1909) seven volumes.

The Constitution contains a preamble that makes no reference to religion:

We the People of the United States, in Order to form a more perfect Union, establish Justice, insure domestic Tranquility, provide for the common defence, promote the general welfare and secure the Blessings of Liberty to ourselves and our Posterity, do ordain and establish this Constitution for the United States of America.

In the body of the Constitution, one clause in Article I Section 6 secures freedom of speech for members of Congress:

The Senators and Representatives . . . shall, in all cases except Treason, Felony, and Breach of the Peace, be privileged from Arrest during their Attendance at the Session of their respective Houses, and in going to and coming from the same; and for any Speech or Debate in either House, they shall not be questioned in any other place.

This clause reflects British "parliamentary privilege"; it addresses the political speech of lawmakers. Another clause, in Article VI, prohibits the use of any religious test for office holding ("no religious Test shall ever be required as a Qualification to any Office or public Trust under the United States").

The First Amendment reads as follows: "Congress shall make no law respecting an establishment of religion or abridging the free exercise thereof; or abridging the freedom of speech, or of the press, or the right of the people peaceably to assemble, and to petition the Government for a redress of grievances."

The First Amendment's Free Speech Clause may be viewed as a "republicanized" version of the Speech and Debate Clause. Of course, the clause may be interpreted to reach beyond political speech to a general right to say what one wants, short of some clear showing of direct injury.[2]

These constitutional provisions may be categorized as follows: (1) general statements of the purpose of government, (2) religious affiliation and oaths, and (3) freedom of speech and freedom of the press. The Constitution's framers clearly drew on the state constitutions for these provisions. The state constitutional provisions, especially those that are part of a declaration of rights, reveal a fuller account of the purpose of government and a more complex and varied account of the key elements of religious freedom. I will use the schema presented above as a means of describing the relevant provisions in the state constitutions.

General Statements of the Purpose of Government

The two seventeenth century charters still in operation during the Confederation period, in Connecticut (1662) and Rhode Island (1663), both start this way: "Charles the Second, by the Grace of God, King of England, Scotland, France and Ireland, Defender of the Faith." This language reflects the religious character of the American colonial polities, as well as English monarchy.

The six new state constitutions that contained separate bills of rights were:

Virginia: framed (i.e., drafted) May 6, adopted June 12, 1776
Pennsylvania: framed July 15, completed September 28, 1776
Maryland: framed August 14, completed November 11, 1776

North Carolina: framed November 12, completed December 18, 1776
Massachusetts 1780: drafted in convention from September 1779 to
    March 1780; ratified by the people, by a two-thirds vote, by June 1780
New Hampshire 1784: approved by the people June 4, 1784[3]

We look to these state bills of rights for a general declaration of the purpose of government. Here are the first three provisions of Virginia's Declaration of Rights.

> Section 1: That all men are by nature equally free and independent and have
> certain inherent rights, of which, when they enter into a state of society,
> they cannot, by any compact, deprive or divest their posterity; namely, the
> enjoyment of life and liberty, with the means of acquiring and possessing
> property, and pursuing and obtaining happiness and safety.
> Sec. 2 [sic]: That all power is vested in, and consequently derived from, the
> people; that magistrates are their trustees and servants, and at all times
> amenable to them.
> Sec. 3: That government is, and ought to be, instituted for the common bene-
> fit, protection, and security of the people, nation, or community; of all the
> various modes and forms of government, that is best which is capable of
> producing the greatest degree of happiness and safety, and is most effectu-
> ally secured against the anger of maladministration; and that, when any
> government shall be found inadequate or contrary to these purposes, a ma-
> jority of the community hath an indubitable, inalienable, and indefeasible
> right to reform, alter, or abolish it, in such manner as shall be judged most
> conducive to the public weal.[4]

All the other state bills of rights contain language similar to Section 1 of
Virginia's bill of rights. Even Massachusetts's bill of rights, which treats religion differently from Virginia's, begins with similar provisions on the purpose
of government.[5]

Religious Freedom
Among the new state constitutions, Virginia's was the first. Its religious freedom provision reads as follows:

> That religion, or the duty we owe to our Creator, and the manner of discharg-
> ing it, can be directed only by reason and conviction, not by force or violence;
> and therefore, all men are equally entitled to the free exercise of religion, ac-
> cording to the dictates of conscience; and that it is the mutual duty of all to
> practice Christian forbearance, love, and charity towards each other.[6]

Table 2.2. Religious Freedom in the State Constitutions

No Compelled Support	General Statement of Freedom	Some Form of Aid to Religion	Establishment of Protestantism, But No Compelled Support
Pennsylvania	Virginia	Massachusetts	South Carolina
New Jersey	North Carolina	New Hampshire	
New York	Delaware	Maryland	
Georgia			
Vermont			
Kentucky			

Notwithstanding this language, Virginia's legislature proposed to support teachers of the Christian religion in 1784. Leaving that aside, we can describe the following general positions on religious freedom in table 2.2.[7]

The provisions of the Massachusetts Constitution of 1780, which resembled the Provision in the Maryland Constitution of 1776, and which New Hampshire's Constitution of 1784 followed closely, provide a good contrast to most of the other constitutions. The second article reads:

It is the right as well as the duty of all men in society, publicly, and at stated seasons, to worship the SUPREME BEING, the great Creator and Preserver of the universe. And no subject shall be hurt, molested, or restrained, in his person, liberty, or estate, for worshipping GOD in the manner and season most agreeable to the dictates of his own conscience; or for his religious profession of sentiments; provided he doth not disturb the public peace, or obstruct others in their religious worship.[8]

The third article moves from the generally accepted view that government depends upon piety, religion, and morality, or a well-formed citizenry, to the controversial view that government may require both attendance at religious worship and financial support, for both construction and instruction.[9] The authors of this article saw no contradiction between it and the previous article's guarantee of religious liberty, as long as the attendance was at the church of one's choice and the support went to that church or the local parish or precinct in which the money was raised. While these provisions were understood to serve the governmental purpose of securing rights, not salvation of souls, they were omitted from the New Hampshire Constitution in 1792, the Massachusetts Constitution in 1833, and the Maryland Constitution of 1851.

Religious Affiliation and Oaths

Most of the state constitutions contain provisions indicating a preference for Protestants or Christians. In some cases, an acknowledgment of the existence of God was necessary either to hold office or to vote. Several constitutions affirmed that no Protestant or no one who believed in God and in future rewards and punishments would be denied any civil rights. The constitutions did not specify what, if any, civil rights were denied to non-Protestants or nonbelievers. In addition, six of the state constitutions contained provisions prohibiting clergymen from holding civil offices. Table 2.3 identifies these provisions.

These state constitutional provisions dealing with religion reflect the predominance of Protestantism in America as well as the tendency to move away from any constitutional, and hence any governmental, recognition of that fact. The best way to illustrate this development is to focus on Virginia. The discussion started with the framing of the Constitution of 1776, and continued with a debate over general assessment for the support of religious instruction. This debate first provoked Jefferson's Bill for Establishing Religious Freedom, in 1777, and then Madison's "Memorial and Remonstrance against Assessment," in 1785. Madison succeeded in defeating the Assessment Bill of 1784 and then in getting the legislature to adopt Jefferson's bill

Table 2.3. Religious Preferences in State Constitutions

State	Office-Holding Provisions	Civil Rights
Virginia 1776		
Pennsylvania 1776	belief in God/R&P	acknowledge God (1)[1]
New Jersey 1776		Protestant
Delaware 1776	Christian (2)/no clergy	
Maryland 1776	Christian	Christian (rel. liberty)
North Carolina 1776	Protestant/no clergy	
New York 1777	no clergy	
Georgia 1777	Protestant (4)/no clergy	
Vermont 1777	belief in God	acknowledge God oath to vote
South Carolina 1778	Protestant (3)/no clergy	acknowledge God R&P
Massachusetts 1780	Christian (5)	
New Hampshire 1784	Protestant	Christian
Kentucky 1792/1799	no clergy (1799)	

[1] (1) Pennsylvania's 1790 constitution omitted any reference to the Old and New Testaments and to rewards and punishments.
(2) Delaware's 1792 constitution changed the oath of office to require simple adherence to the constitution.
(3) South Carolina's constitution of 1790 eliminated its reference to Protestantism as the established religion. Also, the five-part credo, and the religious requirement (Protestant) for offices were eliminated.
(4) In Georgia's constitution of 1789, the requirement that representatives be Protestant was eliminated.
(5) The Massachusetts constitution's requirement that the Governor be a Christian was eliminated in 1821.

in 1786. I will focus on the contributions of Jefferson and Madison, as they led the movement away from assessments and any other form of governmental support for religion.

Madison's contribution began with what became section 16 of the Virginia bill of rights.

> That religion, or the duty we owe to our Creator, and the manner of discharging it, can be directed only by reason and conviction, not by force or violence; and therefore, all men are equally entitled to the free exercise of religion, according to the dictates of conscience; and that it is the mutual duty of all to practice Christian forbearance, love, and charity towards each other.[10]

George Mason's proposal and the legislative committee's first draft read "that all men should enjoy the fullest toleration." Madison objected to "toleration" since it implied the granting of a privilege rather than the recognition of a right.[11] He proposed this language:

> That religion, or the duty which we owe to our Creator, and the manner of discharging it, being under the direction of reason and conviction only, not of violence or compulsion, all men are equally entitled to the full and free exercise of it according to the dictates of Conscience; and therefore that no man or class of men ought, on account of religion to be invested with peculiar emoluments or privileges; nor subjected to any penalties or disabilities unless under color of religion the preservation of equal liberty and the existence of the state be manifestly endangered.[12]

The reference to no "emoluments or privileges" was apparently too much of a threat to the Anglican establishment in Virginia to be accepted. When Patrick Henry, whom Madison enlisted to introduce his resolution, explained that he did not intend it to disestablish the Anglican Church in Virginia, the Convention rejected the amendment.[13] Then Madison proposed an alternate version, which is very close to the language ultimately adopted.[14]

> That religion, or the duty which we owe to our Creator, and the manner of discharging it, can be directed only by reason and conviction, not by force or violence; and therefore, that all men are equally entitled to enjoy the free exercise of religion, according to the dictates of conscience, unpunished and unrestrained by the magistrate, Unless the preservation of equal liberty and the existence of the State are manifestly endangered; And that it is the mutual duty of all to practice Christian forbearance, love, and charity towards each other.[15]

The omission of the prohibition on "peculiar emoluments and privileges" meant that the Virginia Constitution embraced both freedom of conscience and some form of establishment. For example, by having references to the King replaced by references to the Virginia magistrates, the men of the Virginia Convention "continued to regard themselves as the legislative body for the church."[16] The legislature that met in 1776 continued to assert control over the established church while it repealed British acts that conflicted with freedom of religion and kept open the question of a general assessment for different religious societies.[17]

In the next decade, two efforts were made to pass a General Assessment bill in support of religious instruction. The first effort was made in 1779, partly in response to Jefferson's bill for establishing religious freedom. The second effort was made in 1784, and this aroused Madison to write his "Memorial and Remonstrance against Assessment." As a result of Madison's efforts, along with the support of the Baptists and (eventually) the Presbyterians, the Assessment bill was defeated and Jefferson's bill was passed in 1786.

Jefferson's bill, which was drafted in 1777, and first considered in the legislature in 1779, began as follows:

> Well aware that the opinions and belief of men depend not on their own will, but follow involuntarily the evidence proposed to their minds; that Almighty God hath created the mind free, and manifested his supreme will that free it shall remain by making it altogether insusceptible of restraint; that all attempts to influence it by temporal punishments, or burthens, or by civil incapacitations, tend only to beget habits of hypocrisy and meanness, and are a departure from the plan of the holy author of our religion, who being lord both of body and mind, yet chose not to propagate it by coercions on either, as was in his Almighty power to do, but to extend it by its influence on reason alone.[18]

By emphasizing the influence of reason alone, Jefferson disavowed any Biblical support for the separation of religion from politics. After attacking compelled contributions for religion, even for those teachers one would favor, Jefferson continued:

> that our civil rights have no dependance [sic] on our religious opinions, any more than our opinions in physics or geometry; that therefore the proscribing any citizen as unworthy the public confidence by laying upon him an incapacity of being called to offices of trust and emolument, unless he profess or renounce this or that religious opinion, is depriving him injuriously of those privileges and advantages to which, in common with his fellow citizens, he has a natural right; . . . that to suffer the civil magistrate to intrude his powers into

the field of opinion and to restrain the profession or propagation of principles on supposition of their ill tendency is a dangerous falacy [sic], which at once destroys all religious liberty, because he being of course judge of that tendency will make his opinions the rule of judgment, and approve or condemn the sentiments of others only as they shall square with or differ from his own; that it is time enough for the rightful purposes of civil government for its officers to interfere when principles break out into overt acts against peace and good order; and finally, that truth is great and will prevail if left to herself; that she is the proper and sufficient antagonist to error, and has nothing to fear from the conflict unless by human interposition disarmed of her natural weapons, free argument and debate; errors ceasing to be dangerous when it is permitted freely to contradict them.[19]

By denying that civil rights have any dependence on religious opinion, Jefferson went beyond the argument for separation, for one might maintain that religious opinions voluntarily held are the basis for political opinions that support civil rights.

Jefferson's remark that truth is great and will prevail if left to herself drew on Milton and Locke, as we shall see below,[20] and referred to religious opinions. He did not think it applied to political opinions, since the political truths were known. Moreover, in his First Inaugural, Jefferson referred to a republican creed that needed to be taught in the schools, and, in his Second Inaugural, he recommended that the state governments prosecute libelous speech. Furthermore, the bill resolved that "no man shall be compelled to frequent or support any religious worship, place or ministry," or in any way "suffer on account of his religious opinions or belief."[21]

When Jefferson was elected governor, in 1779, sentiment shifted away from his position and toward Assessment. The legislature took up the following bill.

For the encouragement of religion and virtue, and for removing all restraints on the mind in its inquiries after truth, Be it enacted by the General Assembly, that all persons and Religious Societies who acknowledge that there is one God and a future state of rewards and punishments, and that God ought to be publickly worshiped, shall be freely tolerated.

The Christian Religion shall in all times coming be deemed, and held to be the established Religion of this Commonwealth; and all Denominations of Christians demeaning themselves peaceably and faithfully, shall enjoy equal privileges, civil and Religious.[22]

The bill described the incorporation of religious societies that must subscribe to five precepts: "there is one Eternal God and a future state of Rewards and Punishments"; "God is publickly to be Worshiped;" "that the Christian religion is the true religion"; " the Holy Scriptures . . . are of divine inspiration, and are the only rule of Faith"; and "It is the duty of every Man . . . to bear Witness to truth."[23] All societies following this creed and selecting their pastors or teachers accordingly would be taxed for the support of those teachers.[24] This bill was shelved and never allowed to come to a vote after its introduction.[25]

The next attempt at an Assessment bill came in 1783 and 1784, after the conclusion of the Revolutionary War. This bill did not mention the establishment of Christianity and it had no required precepts. Its preamble stated:

> Whereas the general diffusion of Christian knowledge hath a natural tendency to correct the morals of men, restrain their vices, and preserve the peace of society, which cannot be effected without a competent provision for learned teachers, who may be thereby enabled to devote their time and attention to the duty of instructing such citizens as from their circumstances and want of education cannot otherwise attain such knowledge; and it is judged that such provision be made by the Legislature, without counteracting the liberal principle heretofore adopted and intended to be preserved by abolishing all distinctions or preeminence amongst the different societies or communities of Christians.[26]

Madison led the opposition to the bill in the House of Delegates and Patrick Henry led the supporters until his election as governor in 1784. Madison assisted in getting Henry elected Governor, and that reduced support for the Assessment bill in the House.[27] Madison then got final action on the bill postponed until after the next election. This gave him the time and opportunity to write out his objections to the bill and send them to his political friends, who circulated them among the people, urging them to deliver to the legislature resolutions opposing the bill.

While the thirteen circulated copies of Madison's Memorial collected 1,552 signatures, another—anonymous—petition, which argued against the bill from a strictly Christian perspective, garnered three times as many signatures.[28] Thus Madison's arguments cannot be credited with single-handedly defeating the Assessment Bill. But because we are interested in the position that both affirms the natural rights foundation of good government and then insists on the separation of religion from politics, and because Madison drafted the federal Bill of Rights four years later, his argument merits our attention.

Madison's "Memorial and Remonstrance" takes the form of a petition from the people addressed to the legislature and consists of fifteen points. Madison's first point reveals his distinctive understanding of religion and his judicious treatment of the subject.[29]

Because we hold it for a fundamental and undeniable truth, "that Religion or the duty we owe to our Creator and the Manner of discharging it, can be directed only by reason and conviction, not by force and violence." The religion then of every man must be left to the conviction and conscience of every man; and it is the right of every man to exercise it as these may dictate. This right is in its nature an unalienable right. It is unalienable because the opinions of men, depending only on the evidence contemplated by their own minds, cannot follow the dictates of other men: It is unalienable also, because what is here a right towards men, is a duty towards the Creator. It is the duty of every man to render to the Creator such homage, and such only, as he believes to be acceptable to him.[30]

Madison offers two reasons for regarding religion as apart from society as well as government: opinions depend on evidence and cannot follow the dictates of men, and what is a right toward men is a duty toward the Creator. Like Jefferson, Madison refers to the opinions of men without distinguishing religious opinions. Perhaps he subsumes religious and philosophic opinions under the category of speculative opinions. (One might ask whether most men in fact form their opinions without reference to the opinions, if not the dictates, of other men.) Either religious opinions are distinctive or they are not. If they are distinctive, how are they defined? Are they encompassed by the duty we owe to our Creator? What about opinions that deny creation as the basis of human and non-human things? If religious opinions are like other opinions, either government may control all opinions or none at all, until they harm others directly. Both Madison's and Jefferson's discussions of religious opinions remind us of the possible connection between religious freedom and freedom of speech.

Madison's second argument links natural rights with a divine Creator; as a result, what would otherwise be viewed as starting from individual claims is said to have its source in a duty that precedes any natural right or any social duty.[31] How does such a formulation of man's relation to his Creator relate to Christianity? Brann makes two comments about this point. First: "Religion as defined in the passage from the Declaration of Rights which Madison quotes is a conflation of the Roman notion of obligatory performance and the biblical idea of obedience to the Creator, while the Christian salvational sense, to be introduced in the middle paragraphs, is here missing."[32] Since the divine duty is a right in relation to other men, it must be "*individually* discharged."[33] Second, Brann points out how Madison's account of the separation of the realms of religion and government differs from Roger Williams's account of the "garden of the church and the *wilderness* of the world:"

In contrast, the precedence of the religious realm set out in the Memorial is not seen from the perspective of the world beyond, but from the position of a practicing citizen of *this* world, albeit with prior obligations. This is precisely why the functionaries of civil society may not invade the realm of religion—because that realm is here conceived as belonging to the active life of the world, not to civil society but certainly to society. The suspicion and contempt of the world, on the other hand, against whose intrusions the soul and the church must be guarded, belongs to *Christian* liberty, *a theological condition* and not a *civil right* [Brann's emphasis].[34]

Brann says that Madison is proposing a "civil theology in which the political arena is circumscribed by religion." She also notes that unlike Jefferson's bill establishing religious freedom, which referred to the extension of "our religion" by "its influence on reason alone," "Madison's civil theology," because it encompassed all religions, "is a far more genuine grounding for religious pluralism."[35] At the same time, the prominence that Madison gives to "the active life of the world" agrees with Jefferson's position on religion and politics, in contrast to Roger Williams's preference for the "garden of the church" over the "wilderness of the world."[36] This tells against Howe's argument that Williams's influence on the First Amendment was greater than Jefferson's.[37]

Madison denies that "the civil magistrate is a competent judge of religious truth, or that he may employ religion as an engine of civil policy,"[38] without suggesting that the truth will win out. The closest he comes to that thought is to say that Christianity "existed and flourished, not only without the support of human laws but in spite of every opposition to them."[39] He goes on to say that governmental support for religion both harms religion, by instilling pride in the clergy, and does not help government, because rulers can use religion to subvert public liberty. Madison's position toward religion resembles the account Tocqueville gave of Americans some fifty years later, when he wrote that they succeeded in "combining marvelously" "the spirit of religion and the spirit of freedom."[40]

There does seem to be at least one difference between Madison and Tocqueville on religion and its relation to politics. This concerns the relationship between man's duty to pursue the truth about God—if one can describe religion's ultimate aim in that manner—and man's exercise of his intellectual faculties in the world of politics and society. Tocqueville appears to acknowledge that religion provides an important framework for human action in this world, even if it remains beyond political control.[41] This may simply be a richer version of "civil theology" than Madison provides. Or it may elaborate the meaning of Madison's conjoining the natural rights teaching with a person's duty to "render to the Creator such homage, and such only, as he believes to be acceptable to him."[42] Still, for Madison and for Tocqueville, that homage, no matter how individual, is consistent with the rights of man. Such civil theology is fundamentally different from a view of religion that understands it as providing the truth about the whole, and hence about how man should live in this world in preparation for the next.

Freedom of Speech and Freedom of the Press

We can trace in table 2.4 three distinct provisions concerning freedom of speech and of the press from the state constitutions of the Confederation period to the Constitution of 1787 and the First Amendment.

The constitutions of Virginia and Pennsylvania contain typical clauses: "That the freedom of the press is one of the great bulwarks of liberty, and can never be restrained." [43] Or:

"That the people have a right to freedom of speech, and of writing, and publishing their sentiments; therefore the freedom of the press ought not to be restrained."[44] But what does freedom of the press mean? Here is a more detailed clause from the Delaware constitution:

> The press shall be free to every citizen who undertakes to examine the official conduct of men acting in a public capacity; and any citizen may print on any subject, being responsible for the abuse of that liberty. In prosecutions for publications investigating the proceedings of officers, or where the matter published is proper for public information, the truth thereof may be given in evi-

Table 2.4. Freedom of Speech in State Constitutions

Lawmakers' Speech and Debate Protection	People's Right to Freedom of Speech; Prohibition on Abridging the Press	People's Right to Assemble, Petition Government, etc.
Maryland	Virginia	Pennsylvania
Massachusetts	Pennsylvania	Delaware
New Hampshire	Delaware	Maryland
	Maryland	North Carolina
	North Carolina	Vermont
	Georgia	Massachusetts
	Vermont	New Hampshire
	Massachusetts	Kentucky
	New Hampshire	
	Kentucky	

dence; and in all indictments for libels, the jury may determine the acts and the law, as in other cases.[45]

This reflects a liberal version of the English common law view of freedom of the press, which allowed no prior restraint but permitted subsequent punishment for libel. Here a jury is allowed to determine the law as well as the facts, and truth may be given in evidence as a defense against libel.[46]

The Americans of the founding generation followed the English common law; William Blackstone's *Commentaries of the Laws of England* was their authority. Blackstone described liberty of the press at the end of his chapter "Of Offences against the Public Peace," in particular after his discussion of libel, especially seditious libel. One might say that the common law starts with an interest in punishing offenses against the public peace, including those in writing and speech; liberty of the press, and free speech generally, is not abridged as long as the punishment of such offenses takes place after their publication or utterance. In an earlier volume, Blackstone discussed wrongs respecting the rights of persons, and remedies. He distinguished between libel as a public offense, which "has a tendency to break the peace, or provoke others to break it," and other libels (we would call them civil or private), for which the remedy "is to repair the party in damages for the injury done him." In that case only, the defendant may "justify the truth of the facts, and shew that the plaintiff has received no injury at all."[47] Libels as public offenses are

> malicious defamations of any person, and especially a magistrate, made public by either printing, writing, signs, or pictures, in order to provoke him to wrath, or expose him to public hatred, contempt, and ridicule. The direct tendency of libel is the breach of the public peace, by stirring up the objects of them to revenge, and perhaps to bloodshed.[48]

Hence, "it is immaterial with respect to the essence of a libel [as a public offense], whether the matter be true or false, since the provocation, and not the falsity, is the thing to be punished criminally."[49] Blackstone notes that in a civil action, normally against a private individual, "a libel must appear to be false as well as scandalous; for, if the charge be true, the plaintiff has received no private injury, and has no ground to demand a compensation for himself, whatever offence it may be against the public peace . . . ." In a criminal prosecution, on the other hand, "the tendency which all libels have to create animosities, and to disturb the public peace, is the sole consideration of the law. . . . [T]he only facts to be considered are . . . the making or publishing of the book or writing; and . . . whether the matter be criminal."[50]

At this point Blackstone says that "the *liberty of the press*, properly understood, is by no means infringed or violated."

> The liberty of the press is indeed essential to the nature of a free state: but this consists in laying no *previous* restraints upon publications, and not in freedom from censure for criminal matter when published. Every freeman has an undoubted right to lay what sentiments he pleases before the public: to forbid this, is to destroy the freedom of the press: but if he publishes what is improper, mischievous, or illegal, he must take the consequence of his own temerity. To subject the press to the restrictive power of a licenser, as was formerly done, both before and since the revolution, is to subject all freedom of sentiment to the prejudices of one man, and make him the arbitrary and infallible judge of all controverted points in learning, religion, and government. But to punish (as the law does at present) any dangerous or offensive writings, which, when published, shall on a fair and impartial trial be adjudged of a pernicious tendency, is necessary for the preservation of peace and good order, of government and religion, the only solid foundation of civil liberty.[51] [Emphasis original]

Thus, in so far as government needs religion to shape and maintain character, that dependence justifies a restriction on freedom of the press.[52]

But, as Leonard Levy pointed out, it is not clear whether Blackstone would allow the jury to decide the question of criminality or whether the judge would do that, leaving only the question whether or not the statement was actually printed or published to the jury.[53] If the judge decides on criminality, and if criminality includes even truthful statements as long as they expose a public official to "hatred, contempt, or ridicule," then liberty of the press does no more than substitute the judgment of a judge after the fact for a licenser before the fact of publication. Of course, if there is a jury trial, even if the jury is only entrusted with determining the fact and matter of publication, the defendant's lawyer might be able to persuade the jury to ignore the judge's instructions and find the defendant "not guilty." [54]

This occurred in the famous American libel case involving John Peter Zenger in 1735. A dispute between William Cosby, the newly appointed Governor of New York, and Rip Van Dam, the acting Governor, led Cosby to sue Van Dam in the Supreme Court of New York. Cosby convened the Supreme Court, whose members the Governor controlled through appointment and removal, to act as a court of equity, thus dispensing with the jury. He did this to avoid a jury, which he feared would be sympathetic to Van Dam. When Chief Justice Lewis Morris published a dissent, Governor Cosby retaliated by removing him from the Court. That led to an intense political battle in which Morris joined Van Dam and launched the *New York Weekly*

Journal as a vehicle for carrying on their opposition to Governor Cosby. John Peter Zenger was the printer, but James Alexander, the lawyer who represented Morris and later represented Zenger, was the "guiding genius and effective editor."[55] The attack on Cosby took the form of pseudonymous letters to the editor and sham advertisements.[56]

Alexander's contentions that calumnies and lies will not destroy an innocent man and that the truth will prevail over falsehood probably came from "Cato's Letters," which were popular in America. The Letter on "Freedom of Speech" was twice published in the *New York Journal*.[57] In this context, both Cato and Alexander acknowledged the need for libel laws, but, contrary to the common law as Blackstone later presented it, they contended that truthful statements about government and government officials could not be regarded as criminal.[58]

The Zenger trial took place on August 4, 1735.[59] His attorney, Andrew Hamilton,[60] made the same argument in court that Alexander had made in print. Since Zenger was charged with "printing and publishing *a certain false, malicious, seditious, and scandalous libel*," Hamilton required the prosecuting attorney to prove "the words *false* in order to make us guilty."[61] Shortly after, Hamilton cited the authority of Justice John Powell to the effect that "*to make it a libel it must be false and malicious and tend to sedition.*"[62] Hamilton then acknowledged that "the opinions of the three other judges were against him," but he claimed that Powell's judgment had won approbation.[63] Later, in an exchange with the Chief Justice on the matter of a special verdict, in which the jury only decides on publication, Hamilton wrote that "leaving it to the judgment of the Court *whether the words are libelous or not* in effect renders juries useless (to say no worse) in many cases" [emphasis original].[64] The argument for the jury's right to hand down a general verdict and take truth into account was:

> [W]hen a ruler of a people brings his personal failings, but much more his vices, into his administration, and the people find themselves affected by them, either in their liberties or properties, that will alter the case mightily, and all the high things that are said in favor of rulers, and of dignities, and upon the side of power, will not be able to stop people's mouths when they feel themselves oppressed, I mean in a free government.[65]

After chastising Mr. Hamilton for suggesting that the jury disregard the judge's instructions, the Chief Justice said that since the fact of publication was admitted "[t]he only thing that can come in question before you is whether the words as set forth in the information make a libel. And that is a matter of law, no doubt, and which you may leave to the Court."[66] Zenger concluded his narrative by noting that, after withdrawing for a short time, however, the jury nevertheless returned with a verdict of "Not Guilty, upon which there were three huzzas in the hall which was crowded with people and the next day I was discharged from my imprisonment."[67]

The Zenger case thus revealed a tension between the common law rule and the effect of jury participation in a case with a popular defendant who was charged with libeling the government. The constitutions of Delaware, Pennsylvania (1790), and Kentucky included language reflecting the liberalized "Zenger" position on juries and truth as a defense, while the seven other state constitutions (out of fifteen) that included a freedom of speech provision did not address the subject.

Notes

1. The first federal constitution, the Articles of Confederation, did not address individual rights, as that was assumed to be the task of the state constitutions and governments.

2. Likening the Bill of Rights to "an echo" of the state declarations of natural rights, Herbert Storing wrote: "This is especially true of the First Amendment, which might be described as a statement in matter-of-fact legal form of the great end of free government, to secure the private sphere, and the great means for preserving such a government, to foster an alert and enlightened citizenry." See "The Constitution and the Bill of Rights," in *Writings of Herbert J. Storing: Toward a More Perfect Union*, ed. by Joseph M. Bessette (Washington D.C. AEI, 1995) p. 128.

3. The first four constitutions were not submitted to the people for ratification. This information comes from Thorpe, *The Federal and State Constitutions*. Vermont's Constitution of 1777 also contained a separate bill of rights. Vermont's special status was due to its originally having been claimed by Massachusetts, New Hampshire, and New York. All claims were not settled until 1790, when Vermont entered the Union as the fourteenth state. For each of these six states, general statements about the purpose of government are found at the beginning of the bill or declaration of rights part of the constitution. The other state constitutions, with the exception of Delaware, begin with a preamble that recounts the reasons for their declaration of independence from Great Britain and the subsequent right to establish a government.

4. Thorpe, supra, p. 3813.

5. See the Massachusetts' Preamble, in Thorpe, vol. 3 p. 1889.

6. Bill of Rights, sec. 16, from Thorpe, supra, p. 3814. Pennsylvania's bill of rights contained a similar provision, but it also contained some explicit prohibitions. See Thorpe, 3082, Res II.

7. This excludes the two charter states—Connecticut and Rhode Island—and includes Vermont and Kentucky.

8. Thorpe, vol. 3, p. 1889.

9. Thorpe, 1889–1890.

10. Bill of Rights, sec. 16, from Thorpe, supra, p. 3814.

11. See Brann, Eva, "Madison's Memorial and Remonstrance," in *The Past-Present: Selected Writings of Eva Brann*, (Annapolis, MD, St. John's College Press, 1997), p. 225.

12. Quoted in Gaillard Hunt, "James Madison and Religious Liberty," *Annual Report of the American Historical Association*, 1901, vol. 1, pp. 166–67. I was led to this work by Eva Brann's essay, cited in the previous footnote.

13. See Curry, *The First Freedoms; Church and State in America to the Passage of the First Amendment*, (New York, Oxford University Press, 1986) p, 135; see also Thomas E. Buckley, *Church and State in Revolutionary Virginia* 1776–1787 (University Press of Virginia 1977), pp. 18–19.

14. See above, text at note 10.

15. *The Papers of James Madison* (Chicago: University of Chicago Press, 1962), vol. 1, pp. 174–75 (hereinafter cited as *Papers of James Madison*).

16. Buckley, supra, p. 21.

17. Id. at pp. 33–37.

18. Peterson, Merrill, ed., *The Portable Jefferson*, New York: Penguin Books, 1977, p. 251.

19. Id. at pp. 252–53.

20. Part two, chapter 6

21. *The Portable Jefferson*, supra note 21, at p. 253.

22. Buckley, supra, p. 185.

23. Id. p. 186.

24. Id. at pp. 186–87.

25. Id. at p. 60.

26. Id. at 188; see also Brann, supra note 11, p. 211.

27. Id. pp. 100–101. In addition, Richard Henry Lee, who also supported the bill, was then serving as president of the Confederation Congress. Lee argued that "the experience of all times shews Religion to be the guardian of morals—And he must be a very inattentive observer in our country, who does not see that avarice is accomplishing the destruction of religion, for want of a legal obligation to contribute something to it." This is from James Curtis Ballagh, ed., *The Letters of Richard Henry Lee*, (rept., New York, 1970) 2:304–5, as quoted in Buckley, *Church and State in Revolutionary Virginia*, p. 102

28. Brann, supra, p. 212.

29. My interpretation of Madison's Memorial has benefited greatly from Eva Brann's essay.

30. Hunt, Gaillard, *The Writings of James Madison*, ed., 9 vols. (New York: Putnam, 1900–1910), vol. 2, p. 184; *Papers of James Madison* vol. 8, p. 299. Madison's internal quote is from the Virginia Bill of Rights (XVI).

31. Consistent with this formulation of duty, Madison proposed an amendment to the Federal Constitution recognizing conscientious objection to rendering military

service. See Veit, Helen E, ed., *Creating the Bill of Rights* (Baltimore, Johns Hopkins University Press, 1991) p. 12.

32. Brann, supra, note 14, p. 216.

33. Id. p. 217, emphasis original.

34. Id. p. 217.

35. Id. pp. 217–18, quoting from Jefferson's "Bill for Establishing Religious Freedom," in Peterson, supra, note 21, p. 251.

36. See chapter 1, text at note 36 and note for citation.

37. Mark DeWolf Howe, supra, p. 19. Howe contrasted the Enlightenment philosopher to "American opinion in 1790 [which] accepted the view that religious truth is identifiable and beneficent" (p. 19). But Madison's argument here, which may be said to have nearly harmonized the sentiments of the day on religion, affirms natural rights philosophy and the importance of this world, without disparaging religious truth. Howe would be right only if he could show that most Americans in 1790 regarded this world as a wilderness, in contrast to the otherworldly garden of the church. See also chapter 1 above.

38. Memorial, fifth paragraph.

39. Memorial, sixth paragraph.

40. Tocqueville, *Democracy in America*, translated by Harvey Mansfield and Delba Winthrop (Chicago: University of Chicago, 2000), p. 43; (italics in original).

41. See vol. II, part I, chapter 5, p. 418.

42. Memorial paragraph 1.

43. Virginia, section 12, in Thorpe, vol. 7, p. 3814.

44. Pennsylvania section 12, in Thorpe, vol. 5, p. 3083.

45. Thorpe, vol. 1, p. 569. This is article I, section 5 of the state constitution of 1792. The article, which describes rights of individuals, was not in the state constitution of 1776.

46. The constitutions of Pennsylvania (1790) and Kentucky (1792) included similar provisions.

47. William Blackstone, *Commentaries of the Laws of England*, facsimile of first edition of 1765–1769 (Chicago and London, University of Chicago Press, 1979) vol. III, chapter 8, pp. 125–26.

48. Id. at IV, ch. 2, p150.

49. Id.

50. Id. at p. 151.

51. Id. at pp. 151–52.

52. "Blackstone's century protected liberty by punishing licentiousness; that is, the preservation of liberty lay in curbing its excesses. As a pragmatic, working constitutional doctrine, the concept of liberty taught not what the individual was free to do, but what the rule of law permitted." John Phillip Reid, *The Concept of Liberty in the Age of the American Revolution* (Chicago: University of Chicago Press, 1988), p. 118

53. Levy, Leonard, *Emergence of a Free Press* (New York: Oxford University Press, 1985), p. 13, note 23.

54. This is called "jury nullification."

55. Alexander, James, *A Brief Narrative of the Case and Trial of John Peter Zenger* [*hereinafter Zenger*] (Cambridge, MA: Belknap Press of Harvard University, 1963). The material quoted comes from Stanley Katz's Introduction, p. 8.

56. See number 2, Monday November 12, 1735, in Id. pp. 113–14.

57. One passage from Cato's Letter on libel must have come from Milton's *Areopagitica*: "Truth has so many Advantages above Error, that she wants only to be shewn, to gain Admiration and Esteem." Discourse on Libels," in *Cato's Letters*, (sixth edition, London, 1765) vol. III, no. 100, October 27, 1722, pp. 298–99.

58. Katz points out that Alexander was not always consistent, that in one number he claims that "any speech which endangers the state or society ought to be punished," Zenger p. 15.

59. For a detailed account of the events leading up to the trial, see Katz' Introduction, pp. 17ff.

60. James Alexander, his previous attorney, was disbarred when he tired to turn the defense into an impeachment of the Cosby Administration. See Katz' introduction, p. 20.

61. Id. pp. 68, 69. The emphasis, here and in the following passages, are in the original.

62. Id. p. 72.

63. Id.

64. Id. at p. 78.

65. Id. at p. 78.

66. Id. at p. 100.

67. Id. at p. 101.

CHAPTER THREE

The Federal Constitution and the Bill of Rights

The Federal Convention

The framers of the federal Constitution, who met from May until December 1787 at the Federal Convention in Philadelphia, hardly mentioned the subjects of freedom of speech or religion. When Charles Pinckney proposed a series of bill of rights provisions on August 20, they included these two: "The liberty of the press shall be inviolably preserved; No religious test or qualification shall ever be annexed to any oath of office under the authority of the U.S."[1] They were submitted to the Committee on Detail. When the latter was presented to the Convention, on August 30, it was unanimously approved, with only Roger Sherman thinking it "unnecessary, the prevailing liberality being a sufficient security against such tests."[2] The prohibition on religious tests or oaths became Article VI, section 3 of the Constitution. This decision may have reflected the emerging view that religion could best prosper without government support; or it may have reflected the view that such matters were for the state governments to decide.[3] At any rate, we saw that several state constitutions that provided for oaths including a religious test were amended to eliminate them.[4]

The Committee on Detail did not offer a provision for liberty of the press. When George Mason proposed that the plan of government be prefaced with a declaration of rights, Sherman argued that such a declaration was not necessary since the state declarations "are not repealed by this Constitution," the cases requiring jury trial could not be determined, and "the Legislatures may be safely trusted."[5] That was the dominant view. Eldridge

Gerry's motion for a committee to prepare a bill of rights, which Mason seconded, was defeated 0–10–1. Later, on September 14, Pinckney and Gerry moved to insert "that the liberty of the Press should be inviolably observed." Sherman repeated his earlier remark that the provision was not necessary as "the power of Congress did not extend to the press," and the Convention defeated the motion 4–7.[6]

The Ratification Debate and Madison's Reconsideration of a Bill of Rights

From today's perspective, the absence of a bill of rights from the crowning achievement of the American Founding is difficult to understand. Moreover, the cries for a bill of rights which arose during the ratification debate reflected the fundamental issue of federalism: the Anti-Federalist critics either proposed a convention to consider amendments such as a bill of rights, knowing that a second convention would allow them to reconsider the structure and powers of the new government; or they proposed amendments which cut back on the powers, especially the powers to tax and to raise an army, or which restricted the powers of the Senate.[7]

The Anti-Federalists had a good argument for adding a bill of rights to the Constitution, as Madison came to see, precisely because the new form of federalism that they created with the Federal Constitution no longer relied on the state governments for their authority or their effective power. As a result, the case for a federal bill of rights was the same as the case for a state bill of rights; to the extent that a statement of rights in a written constitution served any good purpose, such as reminding the people of important principles, it applied to the federal government as well. As the Anti-Federalists tended to emphasize the importance of limitations of government authority, Federal Farmer viewed a written statement of rights as an educational device for the people:

> We do not by declarations change the nature of things, or create new truths, but we give existence, or at least establish in the minds of the people truths and principles which they might never otherwise have thought of, or soon forgot. If a nation means its systems, religious or political, shall have duration, it ought to recognize the leading principles of them in the front page of every family book.[8]

The Anti-Federalist arguments in support of a bill of rights were persuasive enough that the Constitution would not have been ratified without the promise, first made in the Massachusetts Ratification Convention, that Congress would consider proposed amendments immediately following ratification of the Constitution.[9]

Madison was reconsidering his own views on a bill of rights—partly, no doubt, as a result of his constituents' interest in it, but also as a result of Jefferson's arguments. Jefferson's first reaction to the proposed Constitution was largely supportive, but he did lament the absence of a bill of rights.[10] Madison's reply indicated that "a constitutional declaration of the most essential rights" probably "will be added," but he remained skeptical. Claiming he was always in favor of a bill of rights, as long as it did not "imply powers not meant to be in the enumeration," he "never thought the omission a material defect," and his inclination to support a bill of rights was "that it is anxiously desired by others."[11] Nevertheless, Madison acknowledged, following Federal Farmer, that "political truths declared in that solemn manner [may] acquire by degrees the character of fundamental maxims of free Government, and . . . counteract the impulses of interest and passion." Madison also noted that abuse of power might come from the government, not from a popular majority, in which case "a bill of rights will be a good ground for an appeal to the sense of the community."[12]

In reply, Jefferson started with Madison's account of the case for a bill of rights. "In the arguments in favor of a declaration of rights, you omit one which has great weight with me, the legal check it puts into the hands of the judiciary. This is a body, which if rendered independent, and kept strictly to their own department merits great confidence for their learning and integrity."[13] Madison repeated this in his speech in support of a bill of rights in the First Congress.[14]

In the course of the ratification debate little was said about the meaning of freedom of the press or freedom of speech,[15] though remarks were made about religion. For example, Federal Farmer objected to the Constitutional provision against a religious oath: "It can be no objection to the elected, that they are Christians, Pagans, Mahometans, or Jews."[16] Storing summarized the Anti-Federalist position this way:

> Many Anti-Federalists supported and would even have strengthened the mild religious establishments that existed in some states. . . . More generally, the Anti-Federal position was not so much that government ought to foster religion as that the consolidating Constitution threatened the healthy religious situation as it then existed. The religious diversity of the whole United States seemed so great as to strain to breaking point any publicly useful religious foundation for the nation as a whole.[17]

This is why the framers of the Bill of Rights were not able to make perfectly clear what they intended with respect to religion. They might have been able to agree on a prohibition on Congress, but they would not have agreed on a uniform rule for the states. Storing contrasts the Federalists' and the Anti-Federalists' views on religion in this manner:

> The Constitution and its defenders deliberately turned away from religion as the foundation of civil institutions. Among the Anti-Federalists, on the other hand, there was a great deal of sympathy with views like those of Charles Turner: "without the prevalence of Christian piety and morals, the best republican Constitution can never save us from slavery and ruin." He expressed a central Anti-Federal thought when he urged that the new rulers should turn their attention to the task, which surpasses the framing of constitutions, of fostering religion and morals, thereby making government less necessary by rendering "the people more capable of being *a Law to themselves*."[18]

The Framing of the First Amendment: The First Congress

That free speech and religious freedom are part of the First Amendment is accidental. James Madison, the father of the Bill of Rights as well as the Constitution, proposed placing the amendments within the existing Constitution; the religious freedom and free speech clauses would have been added to Article I, section 9. Many advocates of a bill of rights assumed they would come at the head of the Constitution, as they did in those state constitutions that had bills of rights. But Roger Sherman prevailed in having the amendments placed at the end. As a result, the original document, which thirty-nine framers signed, remained unchanged. While the House version separated the religion clauses from the speech and press clauses, the Senate version put them together, and the Joint Committee chose to keep them together.[19] When it was finalized by Congress and sent to the states for ratification, what became the First Amendment was the third article of the proposed Bill of Rights. Only when the first two articles failed to gain ratification did the free speech and religious freedom provisions become the First Amendment.[20]

On June 8, 1789, Madison introduced his proposed amendments to the Constitution with a major speech. Noting that many opponents of the Constitution supported federalism but questioned the supporters' devotion to liberty and republican government, Madison wanted to "conform to their wishes, and expressly declare the great rights of mankind secured under this constitution."[21] Madison reminded his fellow lawmakers that two states had yet to ratify the Constitution (North Carolina and Rhode Island), and he thought that prompt passage of amendments aimed at guarding against an abuse of power would change public sentiment in those states. Madison made clear, however, that he had no intention of reopening any question concerning the structure or powers of the new government, "because I doubt, if such a door was opened, if we should be very likely to stop at that point which would be safe to the government itself: But I do wish to see a door opened to consider, so far as to incorporate those provisions for the security of rights, against which I believe no serious objection has been made by any class of our constituents."[22]

Madison introduced his amendments in nine numerically separate resolutions.[23] His first proposed amendment was a threefold statement of the purpose of government, similar to the first sections of the Virginia Declaration of Rights.

> That all power is originally vested in, and consequently derived from the people.
>
> That government is instituted, and ought to be exercised for the benefit of the people; which consists in the enjoyment of life and liberty, with the right of acquiring and using property, and generally of pursuing and obtaining happiness and safety.
>
> That the people have an indubitable, unalienable, and indefeasible right to reform or change their government, whenever it be found adverse or inadequate to the purposes of its institution.[24]

His fourth proposed amendment included ten separate additions to Article I, section 9. Most of these provisions, which describe individual rights secured against Congress, became part of the first ten amendments. When he discussed his proposed amendments, Madison said, "The first of these amendments, [comma in original] relates to what may be called a bill of rights."[25] I believe that Madison meant to include both his threefold perambulatory statement and his proposed restrictions on Congress. This interpretation is confirmed by observing that Madison skips over the fourth resolution when he takes up all the other resolutions to his proposal, and in order.

Just as there was division over the necessity of a written bill of rights, there was a division over form: many of the state constitutional provisions were imprecatory—they were couched in the language of "ought" or "should."[26] Those of Madison's proposals that were adopted were couched in the mandatory language of binding law. This was consistent with Madison's reminder, taken from Jefferson, that "If [these provisions] are incorporated into the constitution independent tribunals of justice will consider themselves in a peculiar manner the guardians of those rights; they will be an impenetrable bulwark against every assumption of power in the legislative or executive."[27] Madison had also managed to solve the problem of an incomplete enumeration of rights; he proposed a statement, which later became the ninth amendment, that "exceptions . . . made in favor of particular rights, shall not be so construed as to diminish the just importance of other rights retained by the people."[28]

We turn now to Madison's version of the provisions for religious liberty and freedom of speech as they were to be applied to Congress. This is part of what he proposed to be inserted in Article I, section 9:

> The civil rights of none shall be abridged on account of religious belief or worship, nor shall any national religion be established, nor shall the full and equal rights of conscience be in any manner, or on any pretext infringed.
>
> The people shall not be deprived or abridged of their right to speak, to write, or to publish their sentiments; and the freedom of the press, as one of the great bulwarks of liberty, shall be inviolable.[29]

This statement on religious freedom covers more than rights of conscience, and hence might be taken to prohibit general assessment as well as restrictions on belief or worship. The statement of freedom of speech and freedom of the press is full, but it makes no reference to seditious libel or to the role of the jury in such cases.

Madison's amendments, along with others proposed by the states, were committed to a Select Committee of the House on July 22, and that Committee issued its report on July 28. On August 15, the full House took up Madison's religion proposal, which now read: "no religion shall be established by law, nor shall the equal rights of conscience be infringed." Mr. Sylvester feared the language might "have a tendency to abolish religion altogether." Mr. Gerry suggested "no religious doctrine shall be established by law." Mr. Sherman thought the amendment unnecessary, which was Madison's original position on all the proposed bill of rights amendments. Mr. Carroll thought the amendment would conciliate the minds of the people. Madison explained "that congress should not establish a religion, and enforce the legal observation of it by law, nor compel men to worship God in any manner contrary to their conscience."[30] He observed that some critics had expressed the concern that Congress might pass laws under the necessary and proper clause—especially taxes—that would infringe on the rights of conscience or establish a national religion. Mr. Benjamin Huntington asked what effect the amendment might have on religious establishments in the states. While he understood the amendment to mean what Madison said, he nonetheless thought that it could be interpreted to threaten those New England states that had established religions. In particular, he feared that federal courts would not be able to uphold obligations against individuals for support of ministers or the building of places of worship. In reply, Madison was willing to reinsert the word "national," which had been in his original proposal but had brought an objection from Mr. Gerry—on the grounds that the government was federal not national. This discussion had already occurred in the Federal Convention. Mr. Livermore proposed an amendment to read "congress shall make no laws touching religion, or infringing the rights of conscience," and after Madison withdrew his motion, the House passed Livermore's, 31–20. Then on August 20, the House accepted Mr. Ames's motion to change the resolution to read "Congress shall make no law establishing religion, or to prevent the free exercise thereof, or to infringe the rights of conscience." The final House version substituted "prohibiting" for "to prevent."[31]

On September 3, the Senate agreed to replace "religion" with "any particular denomination of religion in preference to another," and to strike the reference to the rights of conscience. Then on September 9, it agreed to incorporate the religion and the speech clauses into one amendment:

> Congress shall make no law establishing articles of faith or a mode of worship, or prohibiting the free exercise of religion or abridging the freedom of speech, or the press, or the right of the people peaceably to assemble, and petition to the Government for the redress of grievances.[32]

Finally, in a joint conference committee, both Houses agreed to the final language:

> Congress shall make no law respecting an establishment of Religion, or prohibiting the free exercise thereof; or abridging the freedom of Speech, or of the Press; or the right of the people peaceably to assemble and petition the Government for a redress of grievances.[33]

This examination of the history of the framing of religion clauses of the first amendment does not yield definitive answers to the kind of constitutional questions that have come before the United States Supreme Court. Those favoring a broad view of the Establishment Clause point out that the rejected versions of the clause more pointedly addressed the problem in terms of "non-preferentialism" than the final language.[34] The accepted language, they insist, is perfectly consistent with the interpretation the Supreme Court gave to the clause in its 1947 *Everson* decision, when it held that government must be neutral not just with regard to different religions, but also between religion and nonreligion.[35] On the other hand, those favoring a limited view of the Establishment Clause point to the state establishments and the indefinite article "an."[36] Even compared to the other language that was considered in the House and the Senate, one can argue that nonestablishment should be understood only to require neutrality among different religions, but that certain forms of support for religion, if noncoercive and nondiscriminatory, would be permissible.

But that is not clearly the case, since the framers did not agree on what was consistent with religious freedom and what was not. In particular, as Thomas Curry has pointed out, a majority from Virginia thought that a general assessment violated the rights of conscience but a majority from Massachusetts did not.[37] And Huntington, who feared federal interference with state laws supporting religion, considered a system of support for local ministers, as in New Hampshire and Massachusetts, a violation of the Establishment Clause.

After voting on the religion clauses on August 15, the House considered this proposal for freedom of speech: "The freedom of speech and of the press, and the right of the people peaceably to assemble and consult for their common good, and to apply to the government for redress of grievances shall not be infringed."[38] The only reply, from Mr. Sedgwick, was to suggest that since freedom of speech implied the right of assembly the latter need not be mentioned, and he moved that it be dropped. This prompted Mr. Tucker to speak in support of the provision and to suggest that the people's right to instruct their representatives should be added. Right after Mr. Sedgwick's motion was defeated, Mr. Tucker moved to add the people's right "to instruct their representatives"; this provoked a full discussion—much longer than the two separate discussions on religion put together—on democracy, representation, and popular sovereignty. When it was over, Madison, who spoke cogently against the people's right of instruction and who was ably assisted by Mr. Hartley, prevailed on the House to defeat the motion by a vote of 10 to 41.[39] The major argument for the right to instruct representatives derived from the notion of popular sovereignty. Some supporters of instructions maintained that they would not be binding. Since Hartley emphasized the importance of relying on representatives for gaining full information and deliberating well, Madison pointed out that the people already had the right, by means of freedom of speech and of the press, to communicate their sentiments and wishes to their representatives. On the matter of popular sovereignty, Madison said: "My idea of the sovereignty of the people is, that the people can change the

constitution if they please, but while the constitution exists, they must conform themselves to its dictates."[40]

Since the original Constitution contains a Speech and Debate Clause,
which protects members of Congress against legal liability when they carry
out their legislative duties,[41] freedom of speech for lawmakers was guaranteed
before a comparable freedom of speech was recognized for individual citizens.

Two days later, the House considered Madison's proposal to restrain the
states. He wanted the following provision added to Article I, section 10, between clauses one and two: "No state shall violate the equal rights of conscience, or the freedom of the press, or the trial by jury in criminal cases."[42]
When this proposal came up for discussion in the House, Tucker moved to
strike it out, claiming that it was best "to leave the state governments to
themselves."[43] When Madison replied that he thought "it was the most valuable amendment on the whole list," the House kept it in, changing the form
from negative to positive: "the equal rights of conscience, the freedom of
speech, or of the press, and the right of trial by jury in criminal cases shall
not be infringed by any state."[44] For some reason the original negative word-
ing was retained in the House Resolution and Articles of Amendment, dated
August 24, 1789. On September 7, however, the Senate opposed that
amendment, and it was deleted.[45]

On August 17, the House engaged in a full discussion of Madison's proposed amendment concerning militias.

> A well-regulated militia, composed of the body of the people, being the best
> security of a free state; the right of the people to keep and bear arms shall
> not be infringed, but no person, religiously scrupulous, shall be compelled to
> bear arms.[46]

Mr. Gerry feared that this could be used to prevent certain people from
bearing arms by declaring them "religiously scrupulous."[47] He seemed to
think that Congress could use this provision to justify providing a standing
army.[48] Most of the comments turned on the question whether this privilege
should be constitutionally compelled or left to legislative discretion. Some
who favored it as a constitutional right would have attached the requirement that an equivalent payment be made. Mr. Sherman pointed out that
those with conscientious objections would likewise object to making such a
payment. Sherman thought this could be left to the states' discretion, since
they would be responsible for raising the militia. Mr. Benson moved to strike
the clause and "leave it to the benevolence of the legislature. . . . No man
can claim this indulgence of right. It may be a religious persuasion, but it is

not a natural right." The motion to strike the clause was defeated by a close vote of 22–24.[49] Further discussion took place on August 20, and the language was changed to "No person religiously scrupulous shall be compelled to bear arms in person."[50] As reported by the House on August 24, the militia amendment concluded with the language "but no one religiously scrupulous of bearing arms, shall be compelled to render military service in person."[51] But on September 4, the Senate amended that article to read: "A well regulated militia, being the best security of a free state, the right of a people to keep and bear arms shall not be infringed."[52] This left to legislative discretion the granting of exemptions from military service for those with religious objections.

Deliberations in the First Congress thus shed some light on the meaning of the two religion clauses but did not settle matters. Practical political considerations, including varying opinions and laws among the states, prohibited the First Congress from providing a uniform solution but not from placing limits on Congress. As Thomas Curry put it: "Granted not all the states would have concurred on a single definition of religious liberty; but since they were denying power to Congress rather than giving it, differences among them on that score did not bring them into contention."[53] Consider the Establishment Clause. Does the prohibition on passing any law respecting an establishment of religion require only neutrality between religions, which is known as "non-preferentialism"? Or does it require strict neutrality between religion and irreligion, as the Supreme Court held in 1947? The ambiguities derive partly from the language and partly from the varied practices in the several states. We can conclude from the discussion that the framers intended to leave state practices alone. That is why Madison's separate proposal to prohibit the states from violating the rights of conscience failed. Additionally, when Madison was arguing in the Virginia Ratification Convention against the need for a bill of rights, he asserted that Congress had no right to "intermeddle with religion." He surely did not change his mind on this matter. Curry, citing Madison, argues against "non-preferentialism." He also notes that Americans did not make a distinction between permissible and impermissible forms of establishment. "American history offers abundant examples of writers using the concept of preference, when, in fact, they were referring to a ban on all government assistance to religion."[54] Adams's characterization of Massachusetts's mild establishment referred to its qualifications for office, not assessment. The disputes over assessment, in New England and Virginia, Curry claims, were not over establishment but over the meaning of "freedom of religion."[55] And on that point, the position of Jefferson and Madison prevailed.

Perhaps Curry is right, but I think the evidence is inconclusive. Here is another illustration of the dual character of the American founding. The only point that needed to be clear was that the religion clauses would leave the states unaffected; anything beyond that risked serious disagreement. This illustrates why a constitutional founding is never complete. The language may be majestic but as cases arise in courts, judges will be required to ascend from the particular details of history to a principled understanding of the meaning of freedom of religion.

Notes

1. *The Records of the Federal Convention of 1787*, Max Farrand, ed., vol. II, p. 341–42.

2. Id. at II, p. 468.

3. In post-Convention writings on this clause, Madison and Randolph both deny that it implies any federal authority over religion. See Farrand, op. cit.. vol. III, pp. 297, 310. see also Storing's remark at text at note 17 below.

4. See above, chapter 2, table 2.3.

5. Id. at II, p. 588.

6. Id. at II, p. 617–18.

7. See the chart in Murray Dry, "The Debate Over Ratification of the Constitution," in *The Encyclopedia of the American Constitution*, p. 480 and also the chart on p. 482; see also Storing, Herbert, *What the Anti Federalists Were For !* (Chicago: University of Chicago Press, 1981).

8. Federal Farmer XVI, in Storing, *The Complete Anti-Federalist* (Chicago, University of Chicago Press, 1981) 2.8.196.

9. See Dry, Murray, "The Debate Over Ratification of the Constitution," in *Encyclopedia of the American Revolution*, ed. by Jack P. Greene and J. R. Pole (Cambridge Ma. Blackwell, 1991) p. 482 and Rutland, Robert, *The Birth of the Bill of Rights: 1776–1791.* (Boston, Northeastern University Press, 1991).

10. See his letter to Madison dated 20 December 1787, in *The Portable Jefferson*, pp. 428–32. Jefferson was America's Minister to France from 1785 to 1789.

11. Letter to Jefferson of 17 October 1788, in *Madison Papers*, vol. XI, pp. 295–300.

12. *Madison Papers*, vol. XI, pp. 298–99.

13. Jefferson to Madison, March 15, 1789, in Peterson, supra, p. 438.

14. see Madison's June 8 speech, in Veit et. al. *Creating the Bill of Rights*, pp. 83–84.

15. Centinel II, 2.7.30, in Storing, *The Complete Anti-Federalist.*

16. Federal Farmer, in Storing, 2.8.150 in Id.

17. *What the Anti-Federalists Were For!*, supra, p. 23. See also text at note 3 above.

18. Id. at p. 23, quoting from Turner, at 4.18.12, emphasis original.

19. See *Creating the Bill of Rights: The Documentary Record From the First Federal Congress*, ed. by Helen E. Veit, Kenneth R Bowling, and Charlene Bangs Bickford,

(Baltimore and London: Johns Hopkins University Press, 1991), pp. 37–41, 47–50.

20. The original first two amendments covered apportionment and compensation for members of Congress. The latter was ratified as the twenty-seventh amendment in 1992.

21. Veit, supra, p. 78.

22. Id. at p. 79.

23. Id. at pp. 11–14.

24. Id. at pp. 11–12.

25. Id. p. 80 (June 8 speech)

26. See Storing, Herbert J., "The Constitution and the Bill of Rights," in *Writings*, p. 123.

27. Veit et. al. *Creating the Bill of Rights*, pp. 83–84.

28. Id. at pp. 13, 83.

29. Id. at p. 12.

30. Id. p. 157.

31. Id. at p. 30.

32. Id. at p. 38, note 8.

33. Id. at pp. 50–51.

34. Leonard Levy, *The Establishment Clause: Religion and the First Amendment*, (New York, MacMillan, 1986) chapter 4, especially pp. 81–84.

35. *Everson v Board of Education* 330 U.S. 1 (1947).

36. See Michael Malbin, *Religion and Politics: The Intention of the Authors of the First Amendment* (Washington D.C.: American Enterprise Institute, 1978).

37. See Curry, *The First Freedoms*, p. 202 and see above discussion of Madison's campaign against Virginia's general assessment.

38. *Creating the Bill of Rights*, p. 159.

39. Id. p. 177.

40. Id. at p. 167.

41. "They [members of Congress] shall in all cases, except treason, felony, and breach of the peace, be privileged from arrest during their attendance at the session of their respective Houses, and in going to and returning from the same; and for any speech or debate in either House, they shall not be questioned in any other place." Article I, section 6.

42. Veit et. al., *Creating the Bill of Rights*, p. 13.

43. Id. at p. 188.

44. Id at p. 189; see also p. 31, note 23.

45. Id. at p. 41, note 19.

46. Id. at p. 183.

47. Id. at p. 182.

48. The attempt to limit Congress's power to provide for standing armies, by requiring a super majority of 2/3rds in both houses, failed to pass in the House or the Senate

49. Id. at p. 184.

50. Id. at pp. 198–99.

51. Id., p. 38.

52. Id., p. 39. This became the Second Amendment.

53. Curry, Thomas, *The First Freedoms: Church and State in America to the Passage of the First Amendment* (New York, Oxford University Press), 1986, p. 194.

54. Id. at p. 211. Curry quotes Madison's Virginia ratification convention remark at p. 208. It comes from John Elliot, ed., *The Debates in the State Conventions on the Adoption of the Federal Constitution*, 5 vols., 2nd ed., (Philadelphia: J.B. Lippincott Company, 1981) vol. 3, p. 330, (June 12). Hereinafter Elliot.

55. Id. at pp. 211, 213.

CHAPTER FOUR

The Postfounding Debate on Freedom of Speech: The Sedition Act, the Kentucky and Virginia Resolutions, and the Virginia Report

The first controversy over interpreting the Free Speech clause of the Constitution arose in 1798. In response to the Federalist passage of the Alien and Sedition Acts, the Republicans passed the Virginia and Kentucky Resolutions.[1] Madison wrote the Virginia Resolutions and the more extensive Virginia Report of 1800; Jefferson wrote the Kentucky Resolutions. John Marshall wrote the Minority Report of the Virginia Legislature. The debate was more about federalism than it was about speech, since the major argument of the Republicans was that Congress had no authority to pass a sedition act. In his fullest statement on the matter, however, Madison confronted the question: Is the English common law rule of "no prior restraint" sufficient for republican government? In his Virginia Report, Madison suggested that sedition laws were themselves incompatible with republican government. Marshall argued in support of the constitutionality of the Sedition Act.

The Sedition Act had four sections. Section 1 punished sedition, including speech or writing that advocated such sedition. Section 2 proscribed seditious libel:

That if any person shall write, print, utter, or publish, or shall cause or procure to be written, printed, uttered or published, or shall knowingly and willingly assist or aid in writing, printing, uttering or publishing any false, scandalous and malicious writing or writings against the government of the United States, or either house of the said Congress or the said President, or to bring them, or either of them, into contempt or disrepute; or to excite against them, or either of any of them, the hatred of the good people of the United States or to stir up sedition within the United States, or to excite any unlawful combinations therein, for opposing or resisting any law of the United States, or any act of the President of the United States, done in pursuance of any such law, or of the powers in him vested by the constitution of the United States or to resist, oppose, or defeat any such law or act, or to aid, encourage or abet any hostile designs of any foreign nation against the United States, their people or government, then such person, being thereof convicted before any court of the United States having jurisdiction thereof, shall be punished by a fine not exceeding two thousand dollars and by imprisonment not exceeding two years.[2]

Section 3 incorporated the Zengerian principles.

That if any person shall be prosecuted under this act, for the writing or publishing of any libel aforesaid, it shall be lawful for the defendant, upon the trial of the cause, to give in evidence in his defence, the truth of the matter contained in the publication charged as a libel. And the jury who shall try the cause, shall have a right to determine the law and the fact under the direction of the court, as in other cases.

Section 4 provided that the law would remain in force until March 3, 1801, the last day of the current Administration.[3]

Republican Albert Gallatin opposed the bill in the House. He argued for a strict construction of the enumerated powers and against a federal common law of crimes. Then he interpreted the First Amendment to forbid Congress to exercise any power over speech or press. He made the point that a "no prior restraint" rule would not fit speech, which could only be punished subsequently, and therefore the First Amendment could not be so limited.[4] Leonard Levy comments that "in rejecting subsequent restraints, Gallatin should have also rejected the concept of seditious libel, but he did not."[5] Levy points out that the Federalist position was that "one might say what he pleased subject to his responsibility under the law for malice, falsehood, seditiousness, and the like."[6] Gallatin also argued that making truth a defense did not adequately protect speech, since "writings containing animadversions on public measures almost always contained not only facts but opinions. And how could the truth of opinions be proven by evidence?"[7] John Nicholas had made the same point in a speech earlier that day: "If this bill be passed into law, the people will be deprived of that information on public measures, which they have a right to receive, and which is the life and support of a free Government." Printers would "not only refrain from publishing anything of the least questionable nature, but they would be afraid of publishing the truth, as though true, it might not always be in their power to establish the truth to the satisfaction of a court of justice."[8] For Levy, this meant that the Republicans were beginning to develop a broader view of freedom of speech, but they had yet to repudiate the concept of seditious libel.[9]

The Virginia and Kentucky Resolutions intended to organize Republican opposition to the sedition act and the other three Federalists statutes.[10] These famous Resolutions anchored their opposition to the Sedition Act on the position that Congress had no power whatsoever over freedom of speech or freedom of the press.[11]

Jefferson's draft of the Kentucky Resolutions asserted that when a power was assumed that was not specifically delegated, "a nullification of the act is the rightful remedy: that every state has the natural right in cases not within the compact ...to nullify of their own authority all assumptions of powers by others within their limits."[12]

Madison never made a "states' rights" argument in that form. For Madison the addressees were the people in the states. As a result, while the Virginia Resolutions declared "that the acts aforesaid are unconstitutional," they limited themselves to asserting "that the necessary and proper measures will be taken by each [of the other states] for co-operating with this state, in maintaining unimpaired the authorities, rights, and liberties reserved to the states respectively, or to the people."[13]

Madison's Resolutions also discuss freedom of speech:

> The other of which acts [sedition] exercises, in like manner, a power not delegated by the Constitution, but, on the contrary, expressly and positively forbidden by one of the amendments thereto—a power which, more than any other, ought to produce universal alarm, because it is leveled against the right of freely examining public characters and measures, and of free communication among the people thereon, which has ever been justly deemed the only effectual guardian of every other right.[14]

Madison went on to quote from the Virginia Ratification Convention's affirmation that "the liberty of conscience and the press cannot be cancelled, abridged, restrained or modified, by any authority of the United States."[15] He did so in order to argue that the Virginia ratifiers of the Constitution took freedom of speech seriously. But by referring to "any authority of the United States," Madison conflated two distinct arguments. One, identified with federalism, focuses on the combination of the enumeration of the powers of Congress and the First Amendment. The other addresses the question, "What is the freedom of speech in America?" Madison did not address that question in detail until the Virginia Report. Hence, in effect Madison, like Jefferson, did present a "states' rights" argument.

John Marshall's argument, from the Minority Report of the Virginia Legislature, accepted the common law understanding of freedom of speech and the press and drew on the Constitution's "Necessary and Proper" clause to uphold the Sedition Act. Following the common law position on seditious libel, Marshall moved from the power to punish resistance to government to the implied power to punish "those acts, which are criminal in themselves, and which obviously lead to and prepare resistance."[16] The argument assumed that calumnies against the government, by themselves, were likely to lead to resistance to government. Marshall's argument on the merits also elides the case for civil libel with criminal libel. He claims that writing or printing calumnies against an individual, with intent to defame him, "constitute[s] an offense against the government" justifying indictment. This is distinct from publishing "malicious calumnies against government itself," which is "an injury to all those who have an interest in government."[17] Marshall may not have been convinced of the merits of his own argument here, however; in his campaign for Congress in 1798, he declared himself "not an advocate of the Alien and Sedition Bills" at the same time that he expressed his opposition to the states' rights arguments made against the laws.[18]

We have noted that Republican Congressmen Nicholas and Gallatin took issue with the common law rule of no prior restraint without repudiating seditious libel altogether. In February 1799, when the House considered repealing the Sedition Act but ended up reaffirming it, Nicholas stated the minority Republican position at length. Levy identifies this as the first statement of "the new libertarianism," by which he means an opposition to seditious libel laws. In this speech, Nicholas denied that the law of libels remained part of the state codes:

> At the Revolution, the State laws were either the law of England, or were built on it, and, of course, they would contain the monarchical doctrine respecting libels. When the State Constitutions were formed, the old law was continued in force indiscriminately, and only a general exception made of what should be found inconsistent with the State Constitutions. Now to prove that the States have considered the law of libels consistent with the freedom of the press, gentlemen should show that this law has been practiced on since the Revolution, and that the attention of the States had been called to it by its execution, and that it still remains in force. I believe this cannot be done. So far as I know, it has been a dead letter. I mean the law of libels against magistrates; and, if so, the argument is reversed and is wholly on my side.[19]

Levy thinks that Nicholas was wrong on the facts,[20] but he is interested in what appears, from the entire argument, to constitute a repudiation of seditious libel as inconsistent with freedom under republican government. Other Republicans who adopted this new libertarian position included George Hay, Tunis Wortman, and Madison.

Given Madison's prominence in the framing of the Constitution and the Bill of Rights, we will focus on his arguments. Levy notes that Madison's Virginia Report "carries an uncommon authority not on the original meaning of the First Amendment but on the meaning that it ought to have."[21]

While Madison repeated his federalism, or states' rights, arguments against the Alien and Sedition Acts in the Virginia Report, we are interested in his remarks about freedom of speech, which includes freedom of the press. Supporters of the Sedition Act claimed that the understanding of freedom of the press came from the common law, which prohibited prior restraints, and that therefore the First Amendment, which prohibited abridgments to that freedom, allowed regulations that either reflect, or in this case reflect and liberalize, the common law understanding. This argument assumes a liberal construction of the enumerated power to provide against insurrections.

Madison replied that the common law understanding of freedom of the press did not exhaust the meaning of the freedom in republican America.

> In the British government, the danger of encroachments on the rights of the people, is understood to be confined to the executive magistrate. . . .
>
> In the United States, the case is altogether different. The people, not the government, possess the absolute sovereignty. The legislature, no less than the executive, is under limitations of power. Encroachments are regarded as possible from the one, as well as from the other. Hence in the United States the great and essential rights of the people are secured against legislative, as well as against executive ambition. They are secured, not by laws paramount to prerogative but by constitutions paramount to laws. The security of the freedom of the press, requires that it should be exempt, not only from previous restraint by the executive, as in Great Britain; but from legislative restraint also; and this exemption, to be effectual, must be an exemption, not only from the previous inspection of licenses, but from the subsequent penalty of laws.[22]

Madison then addressed the contention that, notwithstanding these differences, "the actual legal freedom of the press must determine the degree of freedom which is meant by the terms and which is constitutionally secured."[23]

> The nature of governments elective, limited, and responsible, in all their branches, may well be supposed to require a greater freedom of animadversion,

than might be tolerated by the genius of such a government as that of Great Britain. In the latter, it is a maxim, that the king, an hereditary, not a responsible magistrate, can do no wrong; and that the legislature, which in two thirds of its composition, is also hereditary, not responsible, can do what it pleases. In the United States, the executive magistrates are not held to be infallible, nor the legislatures to be omnipotent; and both being elective, are both responsible. Is it not natural and necessary, under such circumstances, that a different degree of freedom, in the use of the press, should be contemplated?[24]

Moreover, Madison maintained that the freedom enjoyed in England was more extensive than the law prescribed and "the practice in America must be entitled to much more respect."[25]

Madison then argued that the First Amendment "was meant as a positive denial to Congress, of any power whatever on the subject [of freedom of speech]," thus leaving full responsibility over the subject to the states.

The peculiar magnitude of some of the powers necessarily committed to the federal government; the peculiar distance of the seat of its proceedings from the great body of its constituents; and the peculiar difficulty of circulating an adequate knowledge of them through any other channel; will not these considerations, some or other of which produced other exceptions from the powers of ordinary governments, all together, account for the policy of binding the hand of the federal government, from touching the channel which alone can give efficacy to its responsibility to its constituents; and of leaving those who administer it, to a remedy for injured reputations, under the same laws, and in the same tribunals, which protect their lives, their liberties and their properties.[26]

Madison's confidence in state governments accords more with the Anti-Federalist argument against the Constitution than with Madison's argument for the extended sphere in the *Federalist Papers*. In addition, since Madison included a provision that became the Tenth Amendment, and since he disclaimed, in his speech introducing the amendments, any intention to change the structure or powers of the proposed government, the reasonable interpretation of the First Amendment is that it was intended to affirm the same limitation on Congress that state bills of rights affirmed on state legislatures.[27]

Finally, since Madison suggested leaving it to state governments to deal with the matter of injured reputations and did not refer to a lack of confidence in government, which could cause disturbances of the peace, he seems to have had in mind civil libel laws only, not criminal (including seditious) libel laws.[28] This position would apply to the states as well as to the federal government. While Congress should be viewed as having no power over speech and press, the state governments are tacitly limited to providing protection for government officials against civil libel; criminal, or seditious libel, seems to be ruled out, by default.[29]

The strongest part of Madison's argument seems to be the one against laws punishing seditious libel, not the one against Congress possessing the power to do so. He quotes from the Virginia Resolutions to the effect that the power "is leveled against that right of freely examining public characters and measures, and of free communication among the people thereon, which has ever been justly deemed the only effectual guardian of every other right."[30] If that is the case, it must apply to state governments as well, even if one has more confidence in them than in the federal government. And, as Madison well knew and hinted at, the most deeply fought partisan controversies had produced a contest between federal and state authorities, with the result that under this federal sedition law Republicans were prosecuted, just as under a Virginia sedition law Federalists would be prosecuted.[31]

At this point, Madison addressed the claim that since truth is a defense, the Sedition Act does not threaten freedom. His response was very persuasive, and again this applies to state seditious libel laws as well as federal law. First, Madison noted that even if the matter concerned facts alone, it could be difficult to provide "the full and formal proof, necessary in a court of law."[32] Second, "opinions and inferences, and conjectural observations, are not only in many cases inseparable from the facts, but may often be more the objects of the prosecution than the facts themselves."[33] Nor did the "intent to defame" requirement provide adequate security:

For omitting the inquiry, how far the malice of the intent is an inference of the law from the mere publication; it is manifestly impossible to punish the intent to bring those who administer the government into disrepute or contempt, without striking at the right of freely discussing public characters and measures: because those who engage in such discussions, must expect and intend to excite these unfavorable sentiments so far as they may be thought to be deserved. To prohibit therefore the intent to excite those unfavorable sentiments against those who administer the government, is equivalent to a prohibition of the actual excitement of them; and to prohibit the actual excitement of them, is equivalent to a prohibition of discussions having that tendency and effect; which again, is equivalent to a protection of those who administer the government, if they should at any time deserve the contempt or hatred of the people, against being exposed to it, by free animadversions on their characters and conduct. Nor can there be a doubt, if those in public trust be shielded by penal laws from such strictures of the press, as may expose them to contempt or disrepute, or hatred, where they may deserve it, that in exact proportion as

they may deserve to be exposed, will be the certainty and criminality of the intent to expose them, and the vigilance of prosecuting and punishing it; nor a
doubt, that a government thus entrenched in penal statutes, against the just
and natural effects of a culpable administration, will easily evade the responsibility, which is essential to a faithful discharge of its duty.[34]

Madison concluded by asserting that "the right of electing the members of
the government constitutes . . . the essence of a free and responsible government."[35] He has thus laid out the case against sedition laws in free government: in the name of protecting against breaches of the peace, such laws protect the government and its officials from the very criticism that consent of
the governed requires.

Madison made another argument intending to demonstrate that the words
of the First Amendment deny to the federal government any authority over
freedom of the press. If Congress had any power to regulate one right, he
pointed out, it must have a comparable power to regulate others, in particular, religion:

> For if Congress may regulate the freedom of the press, provided they do not
> abridge it; because it is said only "they shall not abridge it"; and is not said,
> "they shall make no law respecting it": the analogy of reasoning is conclusive,
> that Congress may regulate and even abridge the free exercise of religion; pro-
> vided they do not prohibit it; because it is said only "they shall not prohibit it";
> and is not said, " they shall make no law respecting or no law abridging it."[36]

But Madison already likened the federal protection to a state's protection of
freedom of speech. In general, one must know what "the freedom of speech"
is before one can determine whether a regulation abridges it.

The American founders did not have the occasion to think deeply about
the proper understanding of freedom of speech in 1787 and 1788, because the
freedom was enjoyed in practice and ensuring its security was not the reason
for calling the Federal Convention to frame a new constitution. The controversy over the new country's proper relationship to Revolutionary France and
to monarchical England gave rise to a law that outlawed seditious libel, and
the circumstances provided an occasion for the Federalists to stifle Republican opposition. This caused the thoughtful Madison, among others, to reconsider the meaning of freedom of speech for republican America.

What do we make of the meaning of the First Amendment's freedom of
speech and press clauses in light of America's liberal practice and in light of
Madison's argument?[37] Walter Berns, in a law review article and later in a
book chapter, contends that the Republicans argued from states' rights, not

from freedom of speech.[38] More important, he claims that republican government may require the use of a sedition act and that as long as such an act allows a general jury verdict and makes truth and good motive a defense, such an act is compatible with freedom. Berns concludes his chapter "Free Speech and the Founding Principle" with a discussion of a state libel case. Harry Croswell was sued for libel in New York when he printed an article accusing "Jefferson of paying James Callender for 'calling Washington a traitor, a robber, and a perjurer [and] for calling Adams a hoary-headed incendiary.'"[39] At his trial (which had, Berns points out, "a Republican judge presiding,"), Croswell was not allowed to prove the truth of his accusations and hence, with the jury left only to decide whether he published the words, he was convicted. On appeal to the state supreme court, Alexander Hamilton, serving as his lawyer, attempted to persuade the court that the trial judge erred in not allowing Croswell to prove the truth of his accusations. The legal question was whether Fox's Libel Act of 1792, which liberalized the jury's role, was the new common law for New York.

The state court, with Judge James Kent dissenting, held that the Fox Libel Act did not apply to America, as it was a revision and not a declaration of the common law.[40] Berns points out that the later Libel Act of 1843 in England clearly made truth a defense when the publication was for a public benefit. This is meant to show how the Federal Sedition Act liberalized the English common law. But Berns's main point is that this was Hamilton's and Kent's position in the Croswell case and that this is the sound position on libel in republican government, "both because it permitted truth as a defense in a trial of public libels (when the allegations were published with good motives and for justifiable ends) and because it enlarged the role of the jury in the determination of the intent and tendency of the publication."[41] For Berns, this standard is consistent with the Declaration of Independence's statement of the political truth about politics:

> Thus, the natural law dictated the form of the Constitution, and, through the vehicle of the common law, the manner in which government was to be administered under it: "all men were to be free to publish opinions on public men and measures—the provisions respecting freedom of the press guaranteed this—but their publications were not to be maliciously false. The truth was to be the standard of political life.[42]

Berns thinks that seditious libel laws that incorporate truth as a defense reflect the political truth of the Declaration of Independence, whereas Madison and Levy doubt that such a position suffices when people are prosecuted for the expression of political opinions. That is because facts and opinions get mixed together, and the jury defense will work only if the defendant's criticism of government has popular support.

Berns relates freedom of speech and religion in a manner that provides a good transition to the next part of this study. He quotes from a letter Madison wrote to Jefferson to make the point that political opinions are different from religious opinions.[43] Berns notes that "the United States is not founded on a religious truth," but that it is "founded on a 'political creed,' the self evident truths of the Declaration of Independence."[44] Berns returns to this point when he takes issue with Levy's argument that all opinions had to be regarded as relative, with respect to truth or falsity, before freedom of speech could be recognized as a civil liberty. For Berns, the American founders "were fully convinced that the Constitution derived from a self-evident truth respecting man's nature and the government appropriate to it. In fact, toleration of different religious opinions rests, and can only rest, on this political truth."[45] This becomes the basis of Berns' disagreement with the free speech doctrines of the modern Supreme Court.[46]

But if Madison was right, as I think he was, that the character of modern republican government is incompatible with seditious libel, then the line between protected and unprotected speech needs to be drawn closer to prohibited conduct. Furthermore, it turns out that there is support for such a position in modern political philosophy.

Berns's remarks have nicely touched on both First Amendment freedoms as I have considered them in this examination of the American founding. His distinction between a religious truth and a political truth reflects the differences we have noted between Puritan political ideas and early American charters, which incorporated religion into a political life that looked up to salvation, and the treatment of religious freedom and freedom of speech in the Revolutionary state constitutions. Controversy over the meaning of freedom of speech depends on a shift from a religious polity to a liberal constitutional polity that could still make use of religion to secure its basis. With that shift, more emphasis is given to individual rights, and as a result, freedom of speech becomes more important. Acknowledging the significance of that shift, Berns still argues for retention of seditious libel as a necessary means of preserving liberty without having it collapse into dangerous license. I disagree with his argument at that point, for reasons Madison gave and the Supreme Court gives in some of its free speech decisions. I have presented Berns's position in detail, however, because it is an excellent example of the contemporary conservative critique of the Supreme Court's approach to free speech, which I will discuss in part three.

Notes

1. As the Federalists controlled Congress during John Adams's presidency, the newly emerging Republican Party controlled the state legislatures in Virginia and Kentucky.

2. U.S. Statutes at Large Vol. 1, pp. 596–97.

3. Id.

4. *The Debates and Proceedings in the Congress of the United States, (Annals of Congress)*, (Washington, D.C.: Gales and Seaton, 1851). 5th Congress, 2nd Session, pp. 2,155–56, 2,160–61.

5. Leonard Levy, *Emergence of a Free Press* (New York, Oxford University Press, 1985) p. 303.

6. Id. p. 304.

7. *Annals*, supra, p. 2162.

8. Id. at pp. 2041.

9. See Levy, supra, note 5, chapter 9.

10. The other acts were the Naturalization Act, the Alien Friends Act, and the Alien Enemies Act; see U.S. Statutes at Large, Vol. I, pp. 566ff.

11. The authors of these Resolutions, Madison, and Jefferson had both made "strict construction" arguments in 1790, against the constitutionality of the national bank. For Madison's speeches on the national bank in the First Congress, see *Annals of Congress*, vol. II, pp. 1,894–1,902 (February 2, 1791) and pp. 1,956–60 (February 8). For Jefferson's opinion on the national bank, addressed to President Washington, see Merrill Peterson, ed., *The Portable Jefferson* (New York; Penguin Books, 1977) pp. 261–67.

12. Peterson, supra, note 11, p. 287. The Kentucky legislature omitted nullification, claiming that "the co-States, recurring to their natural right in cases not made Federal, will concur in declaring these acts void and of no force, and will each unite with this Commonwealth in requesting their repeal at the next session." Henry Steele Commager, *Documents of American History*, 7th ed., vol. 1 (New York: Appleton-Century-Crofts, 1963), pp. 181–82.

13. Id. at p. 183.

14. Id. at p. 182.

15. Id. p. 182, from Elliot vol. III, p. 529.

16. John Marshall, Report of the Minority on the Virginia Resolutions, J. House of Delegates (Va.) 6:93–95 (1798–99), as found in *The Founders' Constitution*, edited by Phillip Kurland and Ralph Lerner (Chicago, University of Chicago Press, 1987), vol. 5, no. 20, p. 137.

17. Id. p. 137.

18. Albert J. Beveridge, *The Life of John Marshall*, in four volumes (Boston and New York, Houghton Mifflin Company 1919), vol. 2, pp. 388–89. The quotation comes from the *Times and Virginia Advertiser*, Alexandria, Virginia, October 11, 1798.

19. *Annals*, 5th Congress, third session, p. 3009; see also Levy, *Emergence of a Free Press*, at pp. 310–11.

20. ("He inaccurately claimed that the states did not retain the law of libels in their criminal codes."), Levy, supra, note 5, p. 311.

21. Id. p. 315.

22. *Papers of James Madison*, ed. by David B. Mattern et. al. (Charlottesville; University of Virginia Press), vol. XVII, pp. 336–7.

23. Id. at p. 337.

24. Id. p. 337.

25. Id. p. 338.

26. Id. at p. 341.

27. Levy seems to agree with this position; see *Emergence of a Free Press*, p. 323.

28. On Blackstone's formulation, a criminal libel law is justified as a means of preventing breaches of the peace. If the libel that threatens the peace is directed against the government or a government official, it is seditious libel; if not, the threatening speech is still a criminal libel.

29. Both Berns and Levy assumed that Madison wrote "An Address of the General Assembly to the People of the Commonwealth of Virginia," to accompany the Virginia Resolutions. This is because Gaillard Hunt, who edited Madison's Writings, included it in his volumes. That address includes the following statement:

"Calumny injures individuals, usurpation, States. Calumny may be redressed by the common judicatures; usurpation can only be controlled by the act of society. Ought usurpation, which is most mischievous, to be rendered less hateful by calumny, which, though injurious, is in a degree less pernicious? But the laws for the correction of calumny were not defective. Every libelous writing or expression might receive its punishment in the State courts, from juries summoned by an officer, who does not receive his appointment from the President, and is under no influence to court the pleasure of Government, whether it injured public officers or private citizens." *Writings of Madison*, VI, 334.

As Levy points out, it is not clear whether the punishing of libels in state courts refers to civil libels only or seditious libels as well. If it includes criminal punishment as well, and if the author of this Address was Madison, as Levy and Berns assumed, then Madison did change his mind the following year. The editors of the Madison Papers do not believe that Madison composed either the Address or a Note on the Virginia Resolutions. See *Papers of Madison*, vol. XVII, pp. 199–206.

30. Papers of James Madison, vol. xvii, p. 341, from Virginia Resolutions, in Commager, p. 182.

31. "And it will not be a breach, either of truth or of candour, to say, that no persons or presses are in the habit of more unrestrained animadversions on the proceedings and functionaries of the state governments, than the persons and presses most zealous, in vindicating the act of Congress for punishing similar animadversions on the government of the United States." Id. p. 338.

32. Id., p. 343.

33. Id. p. 343.

34. Id. at p. 344.

35. Id. at p. 344.

36. Id. at p. 347.

37. The discrepancy between legal theory and practice caused Leonard Levy to moderate his argument and change the title of his book when he revised it. See preface in Levy, Leonard, *Freedom of Speech and Press in Early American History: Legacy of Suppression* (New York: Harper and Row, 1960); compare to his preface in his revision, called *Emergence of a Free Press* (New York, Oxford University Press, 1985).

38. "Freedom of the Press and the Alien and Sedition Acts: A Reappraisal," in *The Supreme Court Review, 1970* (Chicago, University of Chicago, 1970), pp. 107–59; a revised version appears in *The First Amendment and the Future of American Democracy* (New York, Basic Books, 1976) chapter 3 ("Free Speech and the Founding Principle," pp. 80–146).

39. Berns, *The First Amendment and the Future of Democracy*, p. 128.

40. Id. at p. 131.

41. Id. at p. 138.

42. Id. at p. 140.

43. Id at pp. 82–3; from Hunt, *Writings of Madison*, IX, 220.

44. Id. at p. 83.

45. Id. p. 146.

46. See Berns, chapter 4. David Lowenthal, in his book, *No Liberty For License: The Forgotten Logic of the First Amendment* (Dallas, Spence Publishing Company, 1997), slightly revised in *Present Danger: Rediscovering the First Amendment* (Dallas, Spence Publishing Company, 2002), makes a similar argument; see chapters 2–3.

PART TWO

THE FIRST AMENDMENT FREEDOMS IN POLITICAL PHILOSOPHY

The philosophic writings to which I now turn shed light on the struggle to draw the boundaries between religion and politics and the development of the important and related freedoms of religion and speech. These philosophic arguments were made against an older philosophic tradition, as well as prevailing religious traditions. To illustrate what that means for freedom of speech and religious freedom, I will contrast modern, or Enlightenment, philosophy with classical philosophy. The modern philosophers who advanced the Enlightenment arguments and who addressed religion and/or speech in detail include Milton, Hobbes, Spinoza, Locke, Montesquieu, Rousseau, and Mill. The classical philosophers whom they opposed were Plato and Aristotle. The modern philosophers provide the foundation for the American founders' thinking about politics and its relation to truth. My intention is not to point out a pattern of influence, but to pursue the question: How are freedom of religion and freedom of speech related to each other, and what do they mean?

The modern philosophers' aim, I believe, was to provide for civil peace and to protect the human desire for knowledge and the quest for the truth. The classical philosophers emphasized "the best regime" rather than civil peace. In addition, while they wanted to maintain a place for philosophy, that is, the quest for truth, they did not confront religion in the direct manner of the modern philosophers.

Contemporary justifications for freedom of speech draw on political philosophy. Constitutional law scholars and academic philosophers typically identify the following justifications for protecting freedom of speech: (1) to promote individual self-expression and self-realization, (2) to promote "representative democracy and self-government," and (3) to promote "the search for knowledge and 'truth' in the marketplace of ideas."[1]

Another reason that is frequently offered reflects general distrust or fear of governmental authority. One scholar refers to it as an argument from governmental incompetence.[2] In this case, the government is held unable to make the proper distinctions "in determinations of truth and falsity"; likewise, it is based on "an appreciation of the fallibility of political leaders, and a somewhat deeper distrust of governmental power in a more general sense."[3] Another calls it "the checking function." In this case, the argument is that while limited government may punish civil disobedience, it "must . . . preserve a climate in which citizens can seriously consider the option to engage in civil disobedience as a means of combating abuses of official power."[4] Or, less provocatively, freedom of speech is "a method of achieving a more adaptable and hence a more stable community, of maintaining the precarious balance between healthy cleavage and necessary consensus."[5] This version suggests that skepticism toward governmental authority in general supports private expression as well as public speech. Each of these justifications can be traced to one or more of the philosophers whose works I examine in this part.

Notes

1. Kathleen Sullivan and Gerald Gunther, *Constitutional Law*, 14th ed., (Westbury, N.Y., Foundation Press, 2001), pp. 959–63; the casebook editors draw on two works of Thomas Emerson: *The System of Freedom of Expression*, (New York, Random House, 1970), and *Toward a General Theory of the First Amendment*, (New York, Random House, 1964).

2. Frederick Schauer, *Free Speech: A Philosophical Enquiry*, (New York, Cambridge University Press, 1982), p. 86.

3. Id.

4. Vincent Blasi, "The Checking Value in First Amendment Theory," in *American Bar Association Research Journal*, 1977, no. 3, pp. 648.

5. Emerson, *System of Freedom of Expression*, supra, note 1, p. 7.

CHAPTER FIVE

Ancient Political Philosophy: Plato, Aristotle, and Thucydides

Plato and Aristotle offer versions of the justifications of freedom of speech I just discussed. Their presentations differ from John Stuart Mill, whom I discuss below and who is usually identified with them, because Plato and Aristotle highlight virtue, or human excellence, not individual freedom. We can learn about the strengths and weaknesses of democracy and free speech in Plato, Aristotle, and Thucydides. I include Thucydides, because his account of key speeches and deeds, especially of the Athenians, provides a concrete illustration of democracy and freedom of speech. In addition, the classical philosophers accept religion as having a legitimate place in political life. I will start with the general accounts of Aristotle and Plato and then turn to Thucydides's account of democratic Athens. I begin with Aristotle, whose *Politics* contains, as Leo Strauss has written, "the original form of political science: that form in which political science is nothing other than the fully conscious form of the common sense understanding of political things."[1]

In the *Politics*, Aristotle identifies the democratic conception of justice with equality, meaning that each person has an equal claim to govern.[2] The best argument in support of democracy is the superiority of collective wisdom: "The many, of whom none is individually an excellent man, nevertheless can when joined together be better—not as individuals but all together—than those [who are best], just as dinners contributed [by many] can be better than those equipped from a single expenditure."[3] In addition to offering an equal right to deliberate and decide on law and policy, democratic freedom also means "to live as one wants. For this is, [the democrats] assert, the work of freedom since not living as one wants is characteristic of a slave."[4]

While Aristotle does not expressly mention freedom of speech, it is clear that collective deliberation requires freedom of speech, just as "living as one wants" does. Put differently, the "self-government" and "truth" justifications for free speech are joined in Aristotle's account of democracy, since the case for political equality is based, at least in part, on the superior wisdom of collective deliberation. In addition, the freedom to be left alone to do what one wants must also—for the sake of self-development—include the freedom of expression.

Aristotle's assessment of democracy is complicated. As democracy emphasizes the equality of free birth, so oligarchy emphasizes wealth. Because he acknowledges the contributions of both wealth and free birth—as well as prudence—Aristotle favors the mixed regime over either democracy or oligarchy, and his best regime is an aristocracy, or the rule of the best.[5] Yet, he supports democracy with reference to the collective wisdom of the many. His explanation reveals an argument similar to the "distrust of government" justification for free speech.

> For having them [free persons or the multitude] share in the greatest offices is not safe: [one might argue that] through injustice and imprudence they would act unjustly in some respects and err in others. On the other hand, to give them no part and for them not to share [in the offices] is a matter for alarm, for when there exist many who are deprived of prerogatives and poor, that city is necessarily filled with enemies. What is left, then, is for them to share in deliberating and judging. Hence Solon and certain other legislators arrange to have them both choose officials and audit them, but do not allow them to rule alone.[6]

The case for democratic freedom is rooted more in political expediency, related to security. The city needs the active support of those who will be able and willing to defend it against its enemies, foreign and domestic; therefore, an extensive enfranchisement is sound. On the other hand, certain tasks of government require special skills. These include law and treaty making, as well as executing the offices of treasurer or general. It is best that the many be allowed to choose these special, or discontinuous, offices rather than to have them held by all, either at the same time or by lot. We are reminded of the significance of representation for modern republican, or liberal democratic, government. Aristotle's understanding of democracy was both less and more democratic than American democracy.[7] In addition, when Aristotle's

advocacy of democracy as the regime that provides superior collective deliberation is considered in light of his subsequent reminder of the expediency of
having citizens participate in political life to some extent, we must conclude
that Aristotle does not think that truth, even political truth, necessarily wins
out in "the marketplace of ideas."

Aristotle does not say much about religion, but what he does say conveys
his view that political authorities supervise worship of the gods and that the
regime's focus is on living well in this life.[8]

Plato expressly links freedom of speech with democracy in the *Republic*.
Plato's Socrates identifies democracy with the rule of the poor, since offices
are filled by lot and most men are poor. He then describes the democratic citizen: "In the first place, then, aren't they free? And isn't the city full of freedom and free speech? And isn't there license in it to do whatever one
wants?"[9] Socrates then says that "just like a many-colored cloak decorated in
all hues, this regime, decorated with all dispositions, would also look fairest,
and many . . . would judge it to be the fairest regime." In addition, "it's a convenient place to look for a regime."[10] When this last remark is put together
with the realization that the best regime cannot be actualized, and that
Socrates and his interlocutors are actually carrying on their conversation
outside of democratic Athens, democracy begins to look better—from the
perspective of individual self development—than its low ranking—from the
perspective of political virtue—implies.

When he turns to describe the democratic man, also called the "private
man," Socrates notes a lack of training and moderation. These young men
"naming shame simplicity . . . push it out with dishonor, a fugitive; calling
moderation cowardliness and spattering it with mud, they banish it; persuaded that measure and orderly expenditure are rustic and illiberal, they join
with many useless desires in driving them over the frontier."[11] Thus the
regime of freedom and freedom of speech, which started out as charming in
its many colors, moves beyond any reasonable measure:

> Then I suppose that afterward such a man lives spending no more money, ef-
> fort, and time on the necessary than on the unnecessary pleasures. However,
> if he has good luck and his frenzy does not go beyond bounds—and if, also as
> a result of getting somewhat older and the great disturbances having passed
> by, . . . then he lives his life in accord with a certain equality of pleasures he
> has established.[12]

Plato's *Apology of Socrates*, in its dramatic depiction of the trial, conviction, and sentencing to death of the philosopher Socrates, reveals another

side of Athenian democracy. The democratic regime may be the most open of all regimes, and yet in its nonliberal version it does not separate religion, or opinions about the gods, from political life. The political claims are all encompassing.

In Plato's version of the trial, Meletus, Anytus, and Lycon make the following charge: "Socrates does injustice by corrupting the young, and by not believing in the gods in whom the city believes, but in other diamonia [daimonic, or godlike, things or beings] that are novel."[13] After Socrates is found guilty, by a vote of approximately 280 to 220, the accusers, on behalf of the city, propose the death penalty. The jury—after hearing Socrates first playfully propose what befits heroes, "meals in the Prytaneum," the equivalent of "tenure for life" as his "penalty," and then propose a fine—settles on death.[14]

The *Apology* is the only Platonic dialogue in which Socrates is presented in a conversation with the entire city of Athens, that is, with the randomly selected five hundred jurors. In all the other dialogues in which Socrates appears, he speaks with a select few. Socrates insists that his interlocutor and he must be the judges, not some external jury, and that question and answer, rather than long speeches, be employed. Likewise, in the *Phaedrus*, Socrates criticized writing as frozen speech, which says the same thing to everyone, and he praised speaking for allowing the speaker to tailor his remarks to the specific audience.[15]

Socrates has a large, hostile audience in the *Apology*. Such an audience will affect his ability to instruct his listeners, and hence it will affect what he says. At the beginning of his speech, he claims that unlike his accusers, who are clever speakers but liars, he will tell the simple, unadorned truth; it is, he claims, the only way he knows, since at age seventy this is his first time in a law court as a defendant. Socrates implies that all that is necessary for justice is truth telling. But at the end of the dialogue, he contradicts his first statement by indicating that he could have spoken differently. Now it appears that if he had wanted to save his life at any cost, he could have spoken shamelessly, saying what needed to be said to please his listeners.[16] The latter statement is consistent with Socrates' remark about the flexibility of speaking, whereas the first statement about simply telling the truth is not. Socrates' two accounts of his manner of speaking give some indication of the meaning of Socratic irony and suggest the need to approach the critical arguments on the charges carefully.

Socrates begins by explaining that the current charges arose out of a slander initiated by earlier unnamed accusers (who, he suggests, got the idea from Aristophanes). These old unnamed accusers said: "[T]here is a certain

Socrates, a wise man, a thinker on the things aloft, who has investigated all things under the earth, and who makes the weaker speech the stronger." Since people think the student of nature does not believe in gods, this is a serious accusation. Socrates then turns this into a formal indictment by paraphrasing it thus: "Socrates does injustice and is meddlesome, by investigating the things under the earth and the heavenly things, and by making the weaker speech the stronger, and by teaching others the same thing."[17] Socrates refers to Aristophanes' description of him in *The Clouds* as the source for this account, which he calls "drivel." He replies by asserting that he does not teach for pay and then by disclaiming any knowledge of the virtue of human being and citizen. No one, he asserts, would come to him for guidance.[18]

The next part of his argument anticipates the question, "What got you into trouble, Socrates, if you are so innocent?" The answer that Socrates provides suggests that, notwithstanding his professed ignorance, Socrates does offer a teaching on how one should live, and while he does not accept pay for it, his sometimes public presentations upset many important people. Socrates tells the story of his deceased friend Chaerephon's going to the oracle at Delphi to inquire whether there was anyone wiser than Socrates and having the priestess reply that no one was wiser. Socrates, convinced of his own ignorance, set out to disprove the oracle's reply, which he treated as a divination, by seeking out and conversing with others whom he took to be superior to himself in wisdom. After talking with politicians, poets, and craftsmen, Socrates reported that the politicians seemed to be wise but were not, the poets were capable of inspired utterances but "do not make what they make by wisdom," and the craftsmen, who knew their particular crafts, erred in thinking that they were "wisest also in all other things, the greatest things."[19] Thus, what started as a denial of the gods' wisdom turned into a confirmation: Socrates is the wisest human being because he "has become cognizant that in truth he is worth nothing with respect to wisdom."[20]

Socrates gets himself into trouble in the course of examining others because the young men of Athens who have leisure enjoy following him and watching him confound those with pretensions to knowledge. These people do not like being shown up, especially in the company of the young, including perhaps their own sons. They fall back on common charges against philosophers: that they conduct their own studies of nature without believing in the gods and that they make the weaker speech appear the stronger.[21] "Therefore," Socrates says, "it would be a wonder to me if I should be able in this short time to take away from you this slander which has become so great."[22]

What starts out as an act of defiance against the gods becomes a divine justification for Socrates' pursuit of his way of life, which, as we shall see, involves questioning others and trying to get them to change their ways. Socrates concludes this part of his defense by claiming that the hatred he incurs by his deeds "is also a proof that I speak the truth."[23] That might not hold up as a general proposition, but if it turns out to be true in Socrates' case and some others, we are confronted with a tension between democratic freedom and the freedom of speech of the philosopher. As we shall see, this tension becomes greater with the development of Christianity.

Let us turn now to the formal accusation of Meletus, Anytus, and Lycophon. Socrates begins with the corruption charge. He asks, Who makes the youth better? After first saying that the laws do, in response to Socrates' prodding, Meletus gives the democratic answer that the citizen judges—the jurors ("all of them")—are able to educate the young. Socrates notes that in the training of horses it is the few, rather than the many, who know how to make them better.[24] Socrates thus suggests two possible bases for rearing the young: knowledge of human excellence and knowledge of what a given political association, or body politic, looks up to.

The second charge against Socrates is that he teaches the youth "not to believe in the gods in whom the city believes, but in other daimonia that are novel." After getting Meletus to expand on the charge by asserting that he is an atheist,[25] Socrates can point out that Meletus has contradicted his own indictment, according to which Socrates believes in, or introduces, daimonia that are novel.[26] As Leo Strauss has pointed out, "this refutation is so beautiful because it leaves entirely open whether Socrates believes in the gods of the city."[27]

Perhaps Socrates does not believe in the gods of the city, and the city may rightfully be concerned about that. Plato's Socrates does not expect, or even hope, that a philosopher can live in full harmony with a city—that is, a political community. The complex relationship between philosophy, or the life of the mind, and politics involves more than the city's having a claim on its citizens, however, because Socrates has a claim on the city. Socrates presents a second account of his way of life by constructing a hypothetical proposal on behalf of the jurors: that they will acquit him on condition that he "no longer spend time in this investigation or philosophize; and if you are caught doing this you will die." To this Socrates would respond:

> I, men of Athens, salute you and love you, but I will obey the god rather than you; as long as I breathe and am able to, I will certainly not stop philosophizing, and I will exhort you and explain this to whomever of you I happen to

meet, and I will speak just the sorts of things I am accustomed to: "Best of men, you are an Athenian, from the city that is greatest and best reputed for wisdom and strength: are you not ashamed that you care for having as much money as possible, and reputation, and honor, but that you neither care for nor give thought to prudence, and truth and how your soul will be the best possible?"[28]

In this popular presentation of philosophy, the emphasis is on exhortation rather than inquiry, the care of the soul is moral rather than intellectual, and the activity, like law-abidingness, can be expected of everyone. On this formulation, philosophy does not threaten democratic politics. If Plato's Socrates was serious about this account, then an overzealous democratic city made a tragic mistake because it was unable to recognize the moral and intellectual contribution that Socrates was making to the city.[29] But there is abundant evidence in the *Apology*, which is confirmed by the *Republic*, that Socrates' popular presentation of his philosophic way of life should not be taken literally. First, we noted how the simple unadorned truth does not necessarily get itself accepted by a democratic jury, precisely because, as Meletus's remarks revealed, a democratic people is suspicious of any claim that any one person or any few persons possess political wisdom. Second, Socrates' refusal to address the relationship between the city's gods and his way of life—apart from his unverifiable story about the oracle of Delphi—suggests that there is not a simple harmony between the requirements of politics and the life of the mind. Socrates acknowledges this shortly after by likening himself to "some gadfly" who awakens a "great and well-born horse who is rather sluggish" and then by saying that he has had to avoid political life to survive. "For know well, men of Athens, if I had long ago attempted to be politically active, I would long ago have perished. . . . Rather, if someone who really fights for the just is going to preserve himself even for a short time, it is necessary for him to lead a private rather than a public life."[30]

In the second part of the dialogue, after Socrates is found guilty, he explains again why he cannot keep silent: "If I say that this even happens to be a great good for a human being—to make speeches every day about virtue and the other things about which you hear me conversing and examining both myself and others—and that the unexamined life is not worth living for a human being, you will be persuaded by me even less when I say these things."[31]

Socrates does not equate philosophy with exhortation, as he did before, and he does not imply that the activity is accessible to all. The *Republic* gives a fuller account of why the philosophic life is necessarily in conflict with the demands of politics. The desires of most human beings are for goods that are connected to the particularity of body and hence cannot be truly shared. On the other hand, if political life is to reflect true human dignity, it needs to respect and support the universal human capacity for thought and reflection on the nature of things. That activity transcends politics but also ultimately dignifies it.[32] In that sense, Socrates was not simply speaking foolishly when he described himself as a gadfly or when he proposed what amounted to "lifetime tenure" as his "punishment."

Both Plato and Aristotle describe philosophy as the best human life because it involves the fullest form of human activity, inquiry into the nature of things. Since the philosophic way of life is characterized by the fullest freedom of thought and inquiry, in that sense it can be identified with the life devoted to the fullest freedom of speech—that is, reasoned speech about how things are. And yet when these philosophers reflect on freedom generally and freedom of speech in political terms, they remind us of the need for two kinds of limits. One applies to the many nonphilosophers, and that is moderation in the pursuit of pleasures and pains related to the body. The other applies to the philosophic few, who must show respect for those regimes that tolerate their activity even though the regimes, guided as they are by subphilosophic thought and opinions, cannot truly appreciate and honor philosophy.

I have discussed Plato and Aristotle to show that freedom of speech is most prominent in democracy although it is not fully recognized in classical or preliberal democracy, and freedom of religion is not recognized at all. Thucydides' account of Athenian democracy confirms this. In his *History of the Peloponnesian War* we see actual cities involved in war; in addition to the deeds, Thucydides presents speeches that approximate what he thinks would have been said under the circumstances. Justice Brandeis, author of one of the most famous judicial defenses of freedom of speech—against laws punishing subversive advocacy[33]—apparently drew on the Athenians, and especially Pericles's Funeral Oration, for his inspiration.[34]

The Funeral Oration is surely one of the great political speeches. With it, and what he says right after it, Thucydides conveys his measured assessment of Athenian democracy. In the speech, Pericles praises Athens, and thus himself, in these terms, among others: "we cultivate refinement without extravagance and knowledge without effeminacy"; "instead of looking on discussion as a stumbling-block in the way of action, we think it an indispensable preliminary to any wise action at all"; "as a city, we are the school of Hellas"; and "Athens alone of her contemporaries is found when tested to be greater than her reputation, and alone gives no occasion to her assailants to blush at the antagonist by whom they have been worsted, or to her subjects to question her title to rule by merit."[35] Pericles ends that section of his speech with the statement "we have forced every sea and land to be the high-way of our daring, and everywhere, whether for evil or good, have left imperishable monuments behind us."[36]

This statement contrasts with Thucydides' account, in his own name, of why he wrote his history: "The absence of romance in my history will, I fear, detract somewhat from its interest; but if it be judged useful by those inquirers who desire an exact knowledge of the past as an aid to the understanding of the future, which in the course of human things must resemble if it does not reflect it, I shall be content."[37] The Thucydidean contribution concerns thought and understanding about cities and men at war. Pericles' contribution, as Thucydides presents it, lies in the field of practical action, not thought, and even in its most positive and boastful form, it reveals itself as a mixture of good and ill deeds.

Pericles' boastfulness concealed some truths, as Thucydides reveals immediately. Shortly after the speech, a plague swept through Athens, causing much pain and suffering, especially since Pericles had everyone stay within the walled city. To contain the incipient revolt, Pericles had to tell the people what he did not say in the Funeral Oration: that their greatness did not cause other cities to accept Athenian dominance, that in fact they were regarded as a tyrant city by the rest of Greece and they would be subject to reprisals unless they kept their wits about themselves and kept to his war policy.

Many Athenians interpreted the plague as a divine punishment, although Pericles' speech revealed a total absence of piety in his boastful claims to be able to control political life. Whether or not Thucydides agreed with Pericles about the cause of the plague, the author conveys to the reader the need for a ruler in democratic Athens to take account of the piety or superstitions of the people.[38]

Thucydides presents his judgment of Pericles in a eulogy: "For as long as he was at the head of the state during the peace, he pursued a moderate and conservative policy; and in his time its greatness was at its height." Furthermore, Pericles' "foresight concerning the war became better known after his death," when the people did not follow Pericles' advice and suffered as a result. Pericles alone, "by his rank, ability, and known integrity," was able to control the Athenian people. "In short," Thucydides writes, "what was nominally a democracy was becoming in his hands government by the first citizen."[39]

As confirmation of this statement about the remarkable character of Athenian democracy under Pericles, Thucydides presents a debate between

Cleon, a crude man of the people, and Diodotus, perhaps a fictitious character, over what should be done to the Mytilenians. The Athenians had already executed the actual participants in the revolt after they put it down.
The question concerned the remaining population of men, women, and
children.

Their initial decision was to kill all the Mytilenian men and to make
slaves of the women and children, on the grounds that this was a city that
had revolted even though it had been allowed to remain free, albeit in a
subordinate relationship to Athens. Having sent a galley to deliver the
news to their forces at Mytilene, they had second thoughts and went into
a conference to reconsider the decision. On the merits, Cleon argues from
justice that the Mytilenians deserve their punishment because of their in-
gratitude, and he argues from expediency that any sign of softness will encourage more revolts. Diodotus makes no explicit argument from justice,
let alone compassion. Rather, he argues from expediency that if the Athenians extract the fullest measure of revenge against a people who revolted
and then surrendered, in subsequent revolts—and subjected cities *will* try
to revolt—the cities will fight to the last man, knowing that surrendering
will gain them nothing. Diodotus's argument carries the day, and the
Athenian rowers manage to get to Mytilene just in time to prevent the
harsher punishment.

In addition to debating the punishment issue on the merits, Cleon, who
spoke first, attacked the very act of deliberating; that is to say, this man of the
people—the crude version of Pericles—spoke against speeches as he taunted
the people with the charge that their government was a tyranny and they
had to be tough and stand firm or they would lose their preeminence. Cleon
likens a proposal to change a resolution with a proposal to change a law, and
hence he attributes to those advocating change a desire to show off, to appear wiser than the laws.[40] Then Cleon goes on to question the good faith of
those who demanded the reconsideration. "Such a man must plainly either
have such confidence in his rhetoric as to attempt to prove that what has
been once for all decided is still undetermined, or be bribed to try to delude
us by elaborate sophistic arguments."[41] Finally, the "three failings most fatal
to empire" are "pity, sentiment, and indulgence."[42]

Diodotus, for his part, begins by defending freedom of deliberation and
turns the tables on Cleon on the matter of bad faith:

> As for the argument that speech ought not to be the exponent of action, the
> man who uses it must be either senseless or personally interested: senseless if
> he believes it possible to deal with the uncertain future through any other

medium; interested if wishing to carry a disgraceful measure and doubting his ability to speak well in a bad cause, he thinks to frighten opponents and hearers by well-aimed calumny. What is still more intolerable is to accuse a speaker of making a display in order to be paid for it. . . . The city is no gainer by such a system, since fear deprives it of its advisers; . . . The good citizen ought to triumph not by frightening his opponents but by beating them fairly in argument; and a wise city, without overdistinguishing its best advisers, will nevertheless not deprive them of their due, and far from punishing an unlucky counselor will not even regard him as disgraced.[43]

This noble defense of freedom of speech succeeds in this case, although protection against speakers who slander speakers might require that public speakers or officials be protected. In addition, Diodotus may not have relied on a straightforward argument on the merits in order to gain the decision. His explicit argument was made solely in terms of expediency, and yet it appears that the full argument for Diodotus's leniency must include some consideration of compassion, or decency. His failure to make that argument reveals another fact about freedom of speech in democracy: the most persuasive argument is not necessarily the most truthful one.

For each of these political thinkers, democracy is an important regime—although not the best—and freedom of speech is an important part of democracy. While Aristotle makes an argument for the collective wisdom of the many, and Thucydides has Pericles celebrate Athenian democracy in terms that might have provided the model for Justice Brandeis, neither Thucydides, Aristotle, nor Plato thinks that freedom of speech is likely to yield the truth. Perhaps the reason why they did not have to make such a claim is that the religion of the Greek cities bolstered their regimes but did not pose a special threat to philosophic inquiry. Philosophy was possible in democratic Athens, even though the city eventually put Socrates to death in the name of piety.

Two millennia later, philosophers began to make a case for freedom of speech that blurred the distinction between the philosophers' speech and the speech of the nonphilosophers. This case was made after philosophers argued, on behalf of philosophy as well as peace, that religion had to be separated from and subordinated to a politics limited to security. The theological-political question—which inquires into the relationship between religion and philosophy as well as between religion and politics—precedes the political question regarding free speech. Only when the former is settled, on grounds that take religion out of politics, can the free speech argument be made fully.

Notes

1. Leo Strauss, *The City and Man* (Chicago: Rand McNally & Company, 1964), p. 12.

2. Aristotle, *The Politics*, tr. by Carnes Lord (Chicago, University of Chicago Press), 1984, III: 9.

3. Id. III: 11, p. 101.

4. Id. VI: 2, pp. 183–84.

5. Aristotle continually returns to the case for the absolute rule of the one wise man in the latter half of book three, but the absolute rule of one is not a political regime in the strict sense, since there is only one citizen, i.e., a person who participates, or even has the right to participate, in office. For that definition of citizenship, see book III, chapter 1.

6. See *The Politics*, book three, chapter 11, p. 101.

7. There were slaves, public and private, in Greece, and there were selected magistrates. But in democratic Athens the deliberative function, which is broader in scope than the legislative power, was vested in a large popular counsel, consisting of all the citizens, at least in important respects. We call this direct democracy, and we take it for granted that it is not feasible; moreover, most of the founders, especially the Federalists, preferred the refining effect of even popular elections. See *Federalist* 10 and 63.

8. In the *Nicomachean Ethics*, Aristotle discusses the virtues, moral and intellectual, without devoting special attention to piety. Also, in his *Politics*, Aristotle makes no reference to piety or the priests when he discusses the different claims to rule in the central discussion of the work. And when Aristotle does mention the priests, in his account of the best regime in book seven, his treatment suggests polite deference.

9. *The Republic of Plato*, tr. by Allan Bloom, Book VIII, 557b, p. 235.

10. Id., 557c.

11. Id. 560d.

12. Id. 561a–561b.

13. *Plato and Aristophanes: Four Texts on Socrates*, translated with notes by Thomas G. West and Grace Starry West (Ithaca, New York: Cornell University Press, 1984), p. 73 (24b–c).

14. Id. pp. 90 (36d), 92 (38b).

15. See *Phaedrus*, 275c–2777d.

16. *Four Texts on Socrates*, supra. note 13, p. 93 (38d).

17. Id., p. 66 (19b).

18. Id., p. 66 (19c) ff.

19. Id., pp. 70–71 (21d–22d).

20. Id., p. 72 (23b).

21. Id., p. 72 (23d).

22. Id., p. 72 (23e).

23. Id., p. 73 (24a).

24. Id. at 25a–b.

25. [S] "Or do you assert that I myself do not believe in gods at all and that I teach this to others?" [M] "This is what I say, that you do not believe in gods at all." *Id.* p. 76 (26c).

26. Id. pp. 76–78 (26b–27d). Perhaps the daimon is Plato's Socrates' ironic way of describing some of his actions, such as a decision to stay out of political life; he refers to it later in the dialogue as not having opposed his form of defense.

27. "Plato's Apology of Socrates and Crito," in Leo Strauss, *Studies in Platonic Political Philosophy* (University of Chicago 1983), p. 44. This is especially noteworthy because as Thomas and Grace West have pointed out, the Greek word that is translated "believe in" ("nomizein") can also mean "acknowledge" or "respect," and in Xenophon's version of Socrates' defense, he has Socrates deny the charge by asserting that "not only others, who were with me, have seen me sacrificing at the common festivals, and on the public altars, but Meletus himself might have seen me if he had desired to do so." See *Four Texts on Socrates,* supra, note 13, p. 76 note 44.

28. *Four Texts on Socrates,* supra, note 13, p. 81 (29d–e).

29. Alexander Meiklejohn interpreted the dialog this way. See his *Political Freedom: The Constitutional Powers of the People* (New York: Oxford UP, 1960) pp. 22–23.

30. *Four Texts on Socrates,* p. 83 (31D-E). See Joseph Cropsey, *Plato's World: Man's Place in the Cosmos,* (Chicago: University of Chicago Press, 1995), p. 157.

31. *Four Texts on Socrates,* supra, note 13, p. 92 (38a).

32. See Leo Strauss, "Liberal Education and Responsibility," in *Liberalism: Ancient and Modern* (New York, Basic Books, 1968), pp. 14–15.

33. *Whitney v California* 274 U.S. 357 (1927). See part three.

34. Brandeis did not draw our attention to his Greek source, but his biographer Philippa Strum asserts that Brandeis was comparing the American founders to the Athenians in his *Whitney* opinion. Moreover, she claims, on the authority of Paul Freund, late law professor, first clerk and lifelong friend of Brandeis, that the phrase "[t]hey believed liberty to be the secret of happiness and courage to be the secret of liberty" came from Pericles' Funeral Oration. (See Vincent Blasi, "The First Amendment and the Ideal of Civic Courage: The Brandeis Opinion in *Whitney v California,*" 29 *Wm and Mary L. Rev* 653, 691, quoting from Philippa Sturm's biography of Brandeis.)

35. *The Landmark Thucydides: A Comprehensive Guide to The Peloponnesian War,* ed. by Robert B. Strassler, tr. by Richard Crawley (New York; The Free Press, 1996), book II, sections 40–41.

36. Id. at II, 41.

37. Id. at I, 22.

38. That the people's religion plays an important part in Athenian politics is revealed later in the book, when Alcibiades, chief advocate and coleader of the expedition to Sicily, whose leadership is essential for Athenian success, is charged with acts of impiety and called to return for trial. Since he knows his political enemies were behind the charges and that he will be found guilty, he flees first to Persia and

then to Sparta, and seeks refuge with the Spartans whom he helps. And later, when retreat from Syracuse is required, Nicias, the remaining general in charge, calls everything to a halt when he sees an eclipse of the moon, thus sealing the fate of the Athenian invaders.

39. Id. II, 65.

40. "The [more gifted fellows] are always wanting to appear wiser than the laws, and to overrule every proposition brought forward, thinking that they cannot show their wit in more important matters, and by such behavior too often ruin their country, while those who mistrust their own cleverness are content to be less learned than the laws, and less able to pick holes in the speech of a good speaker; and being fair judges rather than rival athletes, generally conduct affairs successfully." III, 37.

41. Id. III, 38.

42. Id. III, 40.

43. Id. III, 42.

CHAPTER SIX

Seventeenth-Century Political Philosophy: Bacon, Hobbes, Milton, Locke, and Spinoza

Today, the First Amendment supports religious freedom by separating religion from government, and it upholds freedom of speech and press on the conviction that the truth wins out in the free exchange of ideas. A deliberate project initiated by philosophers in the seventeenth century called for these results, or something similar. That project intended to establish civil peace in order to ensure the conditions for the quest for truth—that is, for the pursuit of philosophy or science. In making that argument, the philosophers made rhetorical use of the notion that the truth wins out in a free exchange of opinions. Francis Bacon was the first philosopher to espouse civil peace as the aim of government and to hold religious controversy responsible for unnecessary strife. Thomas Hobbes then made a full argument for government limited to securing rights. Notwithstanding his arguments for absolute sovereignty, and for censorship as a means of securing civil peace, Hobbes's account of natural right and the precepts of reason prepared the way for the doctrines, developed later, of religious freedom and freedom of speech. John Milton, in his *Areopagitica* presents the first explicit argument in favor of freedom of the press, and he also makes an argument for toleration. Then John Locke and Benedict Spinoza combined arguments for freedom of speech and religious freedom with arguments for limited government. Spinoza in particular argued that democracy was the best form of government, and he made the fullest argument for freedom of speech.

Francis Bacon

Francis Bacon expressed his views about religion and science candidly in a letter he wrote in 1609: "Myself am like the miller of Huntingdon, that was wont to pray for peace among the willows; for while the winds blew, the wind-mills wrought, and the water mill was less customed. So I see that controversies of religion must hinder the advancement of sciences."[1]

In his *Advancement of Learning* (1605), Bacon reveals his procedure for resolving religious controversies. He first distinguishes natural theology, or divine philosophy, from revealed theology. His rejection of Aristotle's final cause and his reinterpretation of Aristotle's formal cause into an efficient cause make divine philosophy no different from natural philosophy, with the latter limited to material and efficient causes. Bacon says that there is no way "to induce any verity or persuasion concerning the points of faith" "out of the contemplation of nature." At the end of the *Advancement* he returns to revealed theology:

> The prerogative of God extendeth as well to the reason as to the will of man; so that as we are to believe His word, though we find a reluctation in our reason. For if we believe only that which is agreeable to our sense, we give consent to the matter and not to the author; which is no more than we would do toward a suspected and discredited witness.[2]

Bacon goes on to adopt the Biblical perspective by arguing "more worthy it is to believe than to know as we know now." That Bacon writes rhetorically here can be confirmed by checking his more straightforward work, *The New Organon,*

> The human understanding is of its own nature prone to abstractions and gives a substance and reality to things which are fleeting. But to resolve nature into abstractions is less to our purpose than to dissect her into parts; . . . Matter rather than forms should be the object of our attention, its configurations and changes of configuration, and simple action, or motion; for forms are figments of the human mind, unless you will call those laws of action forms.[3]

Putting the two passages together, does not the "author of matter," as Bacon puts it, turn out to be a figment of the human mind? Put differently, when Bacon writes in the *Advancement* that the "farthest end of knowledge" is "the glory of God and the relief of man's estate," the first half of that statement is rhetorical, while the second half directs theory, or science, toward practice, or relief of suffering and prolongation of life. Civil peace is the condition for the quest for useful truths.

Hobbes

In his *Leviathan* (1651), Hobbes, like Bacon, tries to tame religion. While his argument for absolute sovereignty sounds foreign to American constitutionalism, Hobbes's account of natural right and the subsequent natural laws, which turn out to be precepts of reason whereby we can attain peace, is not that far removed from instituting a government to secure individual rights. By using the term "natural law" and then expressly disowning it, Hobbes indicates his rejection of a divine lawgiver.[4] And his title, *Leviathan*, suggests that man can imitate God—who used nature to create the world—by using art to create the Leviathan. But Hobbes reminds his readers of the Biblical story of Leviathan, the sea monster whom God referred to when he replied to Job's entreaties by saying, in effect, until you can create Leviathan do not ask me for an accounting.[5]

Hobbes discusses freedom of speech briefly, and in connection with the question of the truth. One of the sovereign's rights is to be judge of what doctrines are to be taught: "And though in matters of doctrine, nothing ought to be regarded but the truth; yet this is not repugnant to regulating the same by Peace. For Doctrine repugnant to Peace, can no more be true, than Peace and Concord can be against the Law of Nature."[6] In other words, the political truth is that peace requires absolute sovereignty.

Hobbes presents another account of truth at the end of his book. He claims that he wrote nothing "contrary either to the Word of God, or to good Manners or tending to the disturbance of the public peace." He plans to "return to my interrupted Speculation of Bodies Naturall; wherein, (if God give me health to finish it,) I hope the Novelty will as much please as in the Doctrine of the Artificial Body it useth to offend. For such Truth, as opposeth no mans profit, nor pleasure, is to all men welcome."[7]

Both Bacon and Hobbes pay lip service to religion while their common aim is to make sure that religion does not undermine civil peace, which is the condition for the peaceful pursuit of natural philosophy or science.

Milton's *Areopagitica*

John Milton's *Areopagitica* (1644) is the first work to contain an explicit defense of freedom of speech, in the form of freedom of the press. Writing in defense of learning, and hence the liberty to publish without prior approval from government, Milton urges Parliament to rescind its recently enacted licensing law. Milton's argument is famous for its contention that "though all the winds of doctrine were let loose to play upon the earth, so

Truth be in the field, we do injuriously by licensing and prohibiting to mis-
doubt her strength."[8] In addition, Milton's argument for freedom of speech
eventually includes an argument for toleration, and hence for religious
freedom. Of course, each argument is limited: toleration is not extended to
"popery," and "mischievous and libellous" publications are subject to subsequent punishment. If Milton truly believed that truth would win out in
the field of contention with falsehood, his limits on toleration are puzzling.
In addition, Milton does not necessarily have limited government, or modern constitutionalism, in mind. If that is correct, then the first thinker to
argue for the related freedoms of speech and religion did not understand
them in terms of a government whose purposes were limited to security. At
the same time, Milton's defense of freedom, especially his advocacy of
virtue tested by vice, differs from both the Biblical and the Aristotelian accounts of virtue.

Likening himself to Socrates, who addressed the Athenian assembly about
the Areopagitican magistrates, Milton addresses the Parliament of England
with a plea that it reconsider and "call in" a published order "to regulate
printing: that no book, pamphlet, or paper shall be henceforth printed, unless the same be first approved and licensed by such or at least one of such as
shall be thereto appointed."[9] Milton offers a fourfold argument:

> first the inventors of [licensing] to be those to whom ye will be loath to own;
> next, what is to be thought in general of reading, whatever sort the books be;
> and [third] that this Order avails nothing to the suppressing of scandalous,
> seditious, and libellous books, which were mainly intended to be suppressed.
> Last, that it will be primely to the discouragement of all learning, and the stop
> of truth, not only by disexercising and blunting our abilities in what we know
> already, but by hindering and cropping the discovery that might be yet further
> made, both in religious and civil wisdom.[10]

While he claims that licensing "crept out of the Inquisition," Milton does acknowledge that "blasphemous, and atheistical, or libellous" materials were
censored in ancient Greece, and the case was similar in Rome.[11] In this section, Milton argues that "revolutions of ages do not oft recover the loss of a
rejected truth, for the want of which whole nations fare the worse."[12]

Milton's defense of reading includes the argument that knowledge of good
is interwoven with knowledge of evil:

> As therefore the state of man now is, what wisdom can there be to choose,
> what continence to forbear, without the knowledge of evil? He that can ap-
> prehend and consider vice with all her baits and seeming pleasures, and yet ab-

stain, and yet distinguish, and yet prefer that which is truly better, he is the true warfaring Christian.[13]

Since therefore the knowledge and survey of vice is in this world so necessary to the constituting of human virtue, and the scanning of error to the confirmation of truth, how can we more safely and with less danger scout into the regions of sin and falsity than by reading all manner of tractates, and hearing all manner of reason? And this is the benefit which may be had of books promiscuously read.[14]

Milton's third point is that licensing "conduces nothing to the end for which it was framed." He suggests that Plato's censorship "seems to tolerate no kind of learning" and applied only to his imagined republic. In addition, Plato himself, Milton points out, would have been expelled under his own laws, on the basis of his own writings and his reading of Sophron, Mimus, and Aristophanes. Milton argues that unwritten laws, or manners and morals, will have to serve as "sustainers of every written statute," since he expects "all licensing will be easily eluded." "Impunity and remissness, for certain, are the bane of a commonwealth; but here the great art lies, to discern in what the law is to bid restraint and punishment, and in what things persuasion only is to work."[15] While it is hard to know how far Milton intends to take this argument, the position becomes the basis of Locke's argument for toleration. In general, modern limited government, which later becomes liberal democracy, is characterized by an emphasis of rights over duties and by an expansion of the sphere of persuasion and a contraction of the sphere of coercion.

Milton connects his argument to religion in this manner: "For God sure esteems the growth and completing of one virtuous person more than the restraint of ten vicious."[16] He provides no Scriptural source for this however. Milton follows this up with the argument that the job of censor, to be done right, must be filled by a learned man and that such a person is not likely to seek out the position.[17]

Finally, Milton argues that licensing laws will both threaten what is already known and impede the quest for more complete knowledge:

Well knows he that uses to consider, that our faith and knowledge thrives by exercise, as well as our limbs and complexion. Truth is compared in Scripture to a streaming fountain; if her waters flow not in a perpetual progression, they sicken into a muddy pool of conformity and tradition. A man may be a heretic in the truth; and if he believe things only because his pastor says so, or the Assembly so determines, without knowing other reason, though his belief be true, yet the very truth he holds becomes his heresy.[18]

By "heretic in truth," Milton likens someone who does not have knowledge of the truth to someone who does not truly believe. Milton does not go into a comparison of Scriptural truths with philosophic investigations into nature. The argument on its face resembles one that Mill makes in *On Liberty*, written two hundred years later.

As for new knowledge, Milton introduces a classical image with the Christian end:

> Truth indeed came once into the world with her divine Master, and was a perfect shape most glorious to look on: but when He ascended, and His apostles after Him were laid asleep, then straight arose a wicked race of deceivers, who, as that story goes of the Egyptian Typhon with his conspirators, how they dealth with the good Osiris, took the virgin Truth, hewed her lovely form into a thousand pieces, and scattered them to the four winds. From that time ever since, the sad friends of Truth, such as durst appear, imitating the careful search that Isis made for the mangled body of Osiris, went up and down gathering up limb by limb still as they could find them. We have not yet found them all, Lords and Commons, nor ever shall do, till her Master's second coming; He shall bring together every joint and member, and shall mould them into an immortal feature of loveliness and perfection. Suffer not these licensing prohibitions to stand at every place of opportunity forbidding and disturbing them that continue seeking, that continue to do our obsequies to the torn body of our martyred saint.[19]

In his commentary on *Areopagitica*, Paul Dowling points out that only in Milton's story of Osirus, not in Plutarch's, "does the search last so long as to counsel long-term patience with doctrinal differences."[20]

After issuing a warning about not looking directly at the sun, Milton continues: "To be still searching what we know not by what we know, still closing up truth to truth as we find it (for all her body is homogeneal and proportional), this is the golden rule in theology as well as in arithmetic, and makes up the best harmony in a church. . . . "[21] But are the truths the same? Dowling contrasts the theological truth of the golden rule with the arithmetic truth that, given three terms, a fourth can be derived. The searching process appears to fit only the arithmetic golden rule. Dowling suggests that Milton joins them because "only when Protestants allow each other freedom will the English nation be allowed to pursue philosophic and scientific freedom."[22] The difference between the two kinds of rules suggests the difference between philosophic freedom and a freedom to act in a variety of intemperate ways, which might have been provoked by books. Milton's rejoinder I presume would be that laws may provide for subsequent punishment. Toward the end of his argument about the ill effects of licensing, Milton defends his country-men against charges of schism as he pleads for tolerance with this image:

> Yet these are the men cried out against for schismatics and sectaries; as if, while the temple of the Lord was building, some cutting, some squaring the marble, others hewing the cedars, there should be a sort of irrational men who could not consider there must be many schisms and many dissections made in the quarry and in the timber, ere the house of God can be built. And when every stone is laid artfully together, it cannot be united into a continuity, it can but be contiguous in this world; neither can every piece of the building be of one form; nay, rather the perfection consists in this, that out of many moderate varieties and brotherly dissimilitudes that are not vastly dispropor-tional arises the goodly and the graceful symmetry that commends the whole pile and structure.[23]

Milton urges Parliament not to heed the advice of those who counsel sup-pression: "If it be desired to know the immediate cause of all this free writing and free speaking, there cannot be assigned a truer than your own mild, and free, and humane government."[24] Even assuming Milton writes ironically here—since, among other things, the country is involved in civil war and Parliament did in fact pass a licensing statute—he does advocate free and hu-mane government, and he identifies it with freedom of speech and press: "Give me the liberty to know, to utter, and to argue freely according to con-science, above all liberties."[25] Still, while Milton's free government is as-suredly republican, it does not invoke individual rights, as Hobbes's govern-ment does.

In his conclusion, Milton presents two striking images of truth winning over error, followed by an argument for tolerance that emphasizes the pres-ence of "indifferent things." Then he describes the limits of toleration and how laws should deal with inappropriate writing or speaking. After referring to a fallen Parliamentary hero, Lord Brooke, whose final words opposed epis-copacy and supported unlimited freedom, Milton writes his most famous pas-sages in support of freedom and truth:

> And though all the winds of doctrine were let loose to play upon the earth, so Truth be in the field, we do injuriously by licensing and prohibiting to mis-doubt her strength. Let her and Falsehood grapple; who ever knew Truth put to the worse in a free and open encounter?[26]
> For who knows not that Truth is strong next to the Almighty? She needs no policies, nor stratagems, nor licensing to make her victorious; those are the shifts and the defences that error uses against her power: give her but room,

and do not bind her when she sleeps, for then she speaks not true, as the old Proteus did, who spake oracles only when he was caught and bound, but then rather she turns herself into all shapes except her own, and perhaps tunes her voice according to the time, as Micaiah did before Ahab, until she be adjured into her own likeness.[27]

If the first part of the case for tolerance is not to fear for truth is strong and will prevail, the second part is that not all differences are fundamental, or that truth "may have more shapes than one."[28]

Milton then offers his moderate position on toleration:

Yet if all cannot be of one mind—as who looks they should be?—this doubt-less is more wholesome, more prudent, and more Christian: that man be toler-ated rather than all compelled. I mean not tolerated popery and open super-stition, which as it extirpates all religions and civil supremacies, so itself should be extirpate, provided first that all charitable and compassionate means be used to win and regain the weak and the misled: that also which is impious or evil absolutely, either against faith or manners, no law can possibly permit that intends not to unlaw itself: but those neighboring differences, or rather indif-ferences, are what I speak of, whether in some point of doctrine or of disci-pline, which though they may be many, yet need not interrupt the unity of spirit, if we could but find among us the bond of peace.[29]

Milton concludes his argument for liberty of the press and for limited tol-eration this way:

And as for regulating the press, let no man think to have the honor of advis-ing ye better than yourselves have done in that order published next before this, "that no book be printed unless the printer's and the author's name, or at least the printer's, be registered." Those which otherwise come forth, if they be found mischievous and libellous, the fire and the executioner will be the timeliest and the most effectual remedy that man's prevention can use.[30]

I assume that "those which otherwise come forth" refers both to those who have and those who have not registered their names. Mischievous and li-belous books are still subject to punishment, although it means that the bur-den is on the government to prove its case, rather than the burden being on the printer or author to satisfy the licenser.

Why, however, if Milton believed that the truth was strong and would pre-vail over falsehood, did he place limits on toleration? Dowling thinks that Milton never held to the truth "wins out" position, but that he only pre-sented it for rhetorical purposes, since other partisans of toleration who were well respected in Parliament espoused that view of truth.[31] Dowling may be right, but that view seems to require that we discount all of Milton's affirmations of belief in the truth of Christianity, and that is not easy to do. Surluck offers a political and a theological explanation. The political explanation, which Dowling shares, is that Catholicism threatened the independence of England by making a universal claim on the allegiance of all Christians, regardless of their citizenship. As Milton wrote in "Of True Religion" (1673), "The Pope . . . pretends right to Kingdoms and States, and especially to this of *England*, Thrones and Unthrones Kings, and absolves the people from their obedience to them."[32] For the theological argument, Surluck draws on the same work: "True Religion is the true Worship and Service of God, learnt and believed from the Word of God only. . . . He hath Reveal'd and taught it us in the holy Scriptures . . . with strictest command to reject all other traditions or additions whatsoever."[33] Surluck then connects that to Milton's statement about searching "what we know not by what we know, still closing up truth to truth as we find it." and comments: "[B]ut the fundamental thing 'we know' is, for Milton, precisely what Roman Catholicism denies. Hence it cannot claim the protection of the toleration argument, and self-defense requires its proscription."[34] If Milton is fundamentally a Puritan, he can take the position that people will come to the truth about God only if they are permitted to interpret Scripture on their own, not as interpreted by ecclesiastical authority. If he is fundamentally a philosopher, he can take the position that philosophers should be permitted to publish freely, and since security of government justifies libel laws, they should be prudent enough to write so as not to run afoul of such laws. In either case, Milton has made an argument for freedom of speech and tolerance, or religious liberty, that celebrates learning and the quest for the truth, but he has deliberately overstated the capacity of truth to triumph in the field of controversy against falsehood. For that argument we must look elsewhere.

Locke's *Letter Concerning Toleration*

In his *Letter Concerning Toleration*[35] (1689), John Locke argues for the complete separation of religion, whose jurisdiction is concern about the soul, from government, whose jurisdiction is the body. The magistrate, Locke argues, should manifest no concern for speculative doctrines, since they do not pertain to the civil interests of "life, liberty, health and indolency of body; and the possession of outward things, such as money, lands, houses, furniture and the like."[36] In addition, "the care of the souls cannot belong to the civil magistrate, because his power consists only in outward force; but true and saving religion consists in the inward persuasion of the mind, without which nothing can be acceptable to God."[37] Furthermore, even if laws with penalties could change men's minds, they could not help "in the salvation of their souls." Locke then defines a church as a "voluntary society of men, joining themselves together of their own accord, in order to the publick [sic] worshipping of God."[38] Since the church is a private association, it is not bound by the duty of toleration to retain anyone who "offend(s) against the laws of the society." Its power is limited to excommunication.[39]

As for the magistrate, he may teach or admonish but he may not prescribe by laws or compel by punishment in the matter of an individual's soul. Locke makes this point first with respect to forms and rites of worship and then with respect to doctrines. Forms of worship must be voluntary to be pleasing to God. Locke then considers whether that means "that I deny unto the magistrate all manner of power about indifferent things, which if it be not granted, the whole subject matter of law-making is taken away."[40] Locke replies: "No, I readily grant that indifferent things, and perhaps none but such, are subjected to the legislative power. But it does not therefore follow, that the magistrate may ordain whatever he pleases concerning anything that is indifferent."[41] The test for government is the "public good," which is "the rule and measure of all law-making."[42]

J. W. Gough traces "indifferent things" to the Stoics, for whom the term "adiaphoros" referred to "actions neither good nor bad." In Christian theology "the word was applied to acts neither commanded nor forbidden by God, and in religious worship it came to mean external elements whose observance was not necessary for salvation."[43] Locke uses the concept to support his argument for toleration in two ways: first, he explains what government can and cannot regulate in matters concerning outward worship; second, he suggests that specific religious practices were originally indifferent and derive their authority from the divine positive law.[44] As we shall see, that will turn out to be the free choices of individuals composing a church.

To elaborate on the first point, Locke maintains that each individual and each church is free to worship as he or it pleases, so long as the magistrate does not have a legitimate reason to interfere. "The only business of the Church is the Salvation of Souls: and it no ways concerns the Commonwealth or any Member of it, that this, or the other Ceremony be there made use of."[45] Locke uses the washing of an infant with water as his example of "an indifferent thing."[46] If the magistrate thought it was necessary to prevent disease, a law could require washing, but not baptism. Government may not require baptism or interfere with baptism. Likewise, the religious use of bread and wine is not a concern of government: "both [are] in their own nature and in the ordinary occasions of life, altogether indifferent."[47]

Locke explains the sprinkling of water and the use of bread and wine in the religious celebration of Communion this way: "Will any man therefore say that these things could have been introduced into Religion, and made a part of Divine Worship. If not by Divine Institution?"[48] But what does it mean for Locke that an indifferent thing, which includes the sacramental use of bread and wine as well as the sacrifice of a dog or a goat, becomes a part of religious ritual? What is the difference between divine institution (divine positive law) and human institution? Locke considers this next when he asks, "If nothing belonging to Divine Worship be left to human discretion, how is it then that Churches themselves have the power of ordering any thing about the Time and Place of Worship, and the like?" He answers his own question by distinguishing the circumstances of worship ("the Time and Place of Worship, the Habit and Posture of him that worships")[49] from the fact of worship itself; the latter only seems to be appointed by God, whereas the former are particular instances of "things indifferent." While "amongst the Jews," "the time, place, and manner of worship" and the habits of worship were "a part of the worship itself," these things, "to Christians under the liberty of the Gospel, are meer circumstances of worship."[50]

Locke's argument for toleration is two-pronged: he limits the legitimate sphere of government to matters of life, liberty, and estate, and he interprets the different forms of religious ritual as matters of individual choice regarding intrinsically indifferent things.

Lest he be misunderstood about the limits of religious freedom in the matter of rituals, Locke makes clear that government may prohibit human sacrifices.[51] "These things are not lawful in the ordinary course of life, nor in any private house; and therefore neither are they so in the worship of God, or in any religious meeting."[52] The standard for the limit on religious practices is the law of nature; it, and not religion, provides the basis for what government may and may not do. The line that Locke draws can be identified with neutrality, since it prescribes the same limitations on religious as on nonreligious associations. "Whatsoever is lawful in the Commonwealth, cannot be prohibited by the Magistrate in the Church. Whatsoever is permitted unto any of his subjects for their ordinary use, neither can nor ought to be forbidden by him to any Sect of People for their religious uses."[53] To the query, "What if a Church be idolatrous," Locke replies: "What power can be given to the Magistrate for the suppression of an idolatrous church, which may not, in time and place, be made use of to the ruine of an Orthodox one? For it must be remembered that the civil power is the same every where and the religion of every Prince is Orthodox to himself."[54]

When Locke turns to articles of faith, he distinguishes the speculative from the practical: since the former articles "terminate simply in the understanding" they are "required only to be believed." His elaboration draws on Milton's argument concerning the truth:

> The magistrate ought not to forbid the preaching or professing of any speculative opinions in any church, because they have no manner of relation to the civil rights of the subjects. If a Roman Catholick [sic] believe that to be really the Body of Christ, which another man calls bread, he does no injury thereby to his neighbor. . . . The power of the magistrate, and the estates of the people, may be equally secure whether any man believes these things or no. I readily grant that these opinions are false and absurd. But the business of laws is not to provide for the truth of opinions, but for the safety and security of the commonwealth, and of every particular mans goods and person. And so it ought to be. For truth certainly would do well enough, if she were once left to shift for herself. She seldom has received, and I fear never will receive much assistance from the power of great men, to whom she is but rarely known, and more rarely welcome. She is not taught by laws, nor has she any need of force to procure her entrance into the minds of men. . . . Thus much for speculative opinions. Let us now proceed to practical ones.[55]

Locke's apparent confidence in truth's supremacy can also be understood as his indifference. Whatever the results of such speculation, which he has equated with faith, they cannot be imposed upon anyone else. Also, since Locke holds that each person is orthodox to himself,[56] we must wonder whether he thinks that speculation concerning the soul, and hence the divine, can lead to knowledge. In other words, Locke, following Milton, wants to make sure that doctrinal division does not upset civil peace by becoming a part of governmental strife. Moreover Locke's true position on the soul reduces it to a self that pursues interests connected to the desires of the body.[57]

In support of this contention, consider how Locke discusses the sphere of practical opinions, which "influence the will and manners." First, he acknowledges that "moral actions belong . . . to the jurisdiction both of the outward and the inward court . . . both of the magistrate and conscience."[58] But Locke proceeds to limit concerns of the soul to salvation. First, "the care of each man's salvation belongs only to himself."[59] Then Locke considers government: "But besides their souls, which are immortal, men have also their temporal lives here upon earth."[60] Since men are apt to prey upon the fruits of other men's labors, this requires the establishment of civil society.

Notwithstanding this limitation on the power of government, Locke addresses the question, *"What if the magistrate should enjoin any thing by his Authority that appears unlawful to the Conscience of a private Person?"*[61] Locke's first reply is that "if the government be faithfully administered, and the counsels of the magistrate be indeed directed to the public good, this will seldom happen."[62] If it does happen, Locke continues, and we should note that an individual may think it is the case when it is not, or when others would not so see it, then

> such a private person is to abstain from the action that he judges unlawful; and he is to undergo the punishment, which it is not unlawful for him to bear. For the private judgment of any person concerning a law enacted in political matters, for the public good, does not take away the obligation of that law, nor deserve a dispensation.[63]

Locke concludes by indicating that a government dedicated to securing toleration need not extend toleration to the following opinions or persons: (1) opinions contrary to the fundamental conditions of civil society; (2) persons who claim a right to act on their own in disregard of the civil rights of the community; (3) any church whose source of authority is another government; and (4) any person who denies the being of a god.[64] The principle informing the first three limitations is that the maintenance of tolerance may require intolerance, or nonacceptance, of intolerant persons or associations. Lack of trust accounts for Locke's fourth limitation: "promises, covenants, and oaths, which are the bonds of humane society, can have no hold upon an Atheist."[65]

Locke's argument gave a new meaning to the term "tolerance." Eva Brann has pointed out that Locke,

> by a typical cunning twist, shifts the meaning of the term: not *granted* to dissenting Christians, by the ecclesiastical establishment and its state sponsors, toleration is *required* of the magistrate toward all churches—Mohammetan, Pagan, idolaters (though *not*—and here Madison differed—to atheists); the magistrate has no right to interfere with either the internal or the external aspects of religion. This "tolerance" was no longer the notion Tom Paine excoriated in the *Age of Reason* as "not the *opposite* of Intolerance, but . . . the *counterfeit* of it," but a demand for a right under cover of a less aggressive term.[66]

As for Madison's extending tolerance to atheists as well, I interpret that as a broader application of the same principle, made possible perhaps by the success of the more limited application of the principle.[67] In addition, today we may have less confidence in the ability of oaths to ensure truth telling by anybody, religious or not.

Locke's *Letter Concerning Toleration* completes the argument of his *Second Treatise*, which describes how every individual's natural right to act to preserve himself leads to a government, based on consent, whose purpose is the protection of property, understood as life, liberty, and estate.

As further illustration of Locke's true understanding of the soul, and hence his ironic treatment of truth winning out in the field of speculative religious doctrines, in his chapter on property Locke quotes from St. Paul's Letter to Timothy that "God has given us all things richly," and then demonstrates that in fact nature compels human beings to labor to produce or they perish.[68] Whereas Paul states that the love of money is the root of all evil, Locke's natural law restriction on acquisition is limited to a prohibition on spoilage, and the introduction of money eliminates that as an effective restriction.[69] Locke also writes that the "increase of lands and the right employing of them is the great art of government."[70] Locke thus emancipates the desire for wealth in the course of claiming to demonstrate in a manner consistent with reason and revelation how men come to have a title to property. We are decidedly outside a Christian teaching on the soul.[71]

Readers of Locke's *The Reasonableness of Christianity* may think otherwise. In that work, Locke argues that "faith and repentance, i.e., believing Jesus to be the Messiah and a good life, are the indispensable conditions of the new covenant, to be performed by all those who would obtain eternal life."[72] But later on, Locke indicates that Christianity's "reasonableness" consists in its offering the people something they can understand and believe ("The greatest part cannot know and therefore they must believe"[73]), and it will restrain the pursuit of "the enjoyments of this life."[74] "The view of heaven and hell will cast a slight upon the short pleasures and pains of this present state, and give attractions and encouragements to virtue, which reason and interest, and the care of ourselves, cannot but allow and prefer."[75] Locke's account of the New Testament aims at unifying Christians in a manner that supports toleration; he refers to general beliefs that support morality, he refers to no specific rituals, and government has nothing to do with it. Locke advocates, in short, a civil religion for the sake of peace and moderation.[76]

Locke's own speculative quest for the truth is presented in his *Essay on Human Understanding*, in which he denies the existence of innate ideas. To the extent to which his work can be read and understood by other thoughtful and interested human beings, the quest for truth is surely advanced, at least among those who are able to understand the argument. This all depends upon the work's being available. The civil peace that Locke has in mind benefits the philosophic few as well as the nonphilosophic many; the former may more freely pursue the life of the mind as the latter more freely pursue the life of acquisition. To make this possible, Locke, drawing on Milton's metaphor, wrote in support of speculative doctrines on the grounds that the truth would win out.

Spinoza's Theological-Political Treatise

I have saved Spinoza's *Theological-Political Treatise* for last, even though it was published in 1670, about twenty years before Locke's *Letter Concerning Toleration*, because Spinoza argues both for democracy and for free speech. He does this after having established his major point, which concerns the separation of philosophy from theology. Spinoza summarizes that argument in chapter 14:

> For we have shown that faith demands piety rather than truth; faith is pious, and saving only by reason of the obedience it inspires, and consequently nobody is faithful except by reason of his obedience. . . .
> It now remains for me finally to show that between faith and theology on the one side and philosophy on the other there is no relation and no affinity, a point which must now be apparent to everyone who knows the aims and bases of these two faculties, which are as far apart as can be. The aim of philosophy is, quite simply, truth, while the aim of faith, as we have abundantly shown, is nothing other than obedience and piety.[77]

Spinoza arrives at that conclusion by means of a special interpretation of prophets and prophecy, the Jews as the chosen people, divine law and ceremonial law, miracles, the status of the books of the Bible, and the true nature of religion and divine law. Spinoza identifies prophecy with the imagination of the prophets and the gullibility of the people.[78] He says that any people that prospers is a "chosen people."[79] He explains miracles in terms of an incomplete understanding of nature. That is, since "nothing happens in Nature that does not follow from her laws," "her laws cover everything that is conceived even by the divine intellect," and "Nature observes a fixed and immutable order," "the word miracle can be understood only with respect to men's beliefs and means an event whose natural cause we—or at any rate the writer or narrator of the miracle—cannot explain by comparison with any other normal event."[80] To show that theology and philosophy occupy separate spheres, Spinoza writes from two perspectives: one is his true philosophic position, and the other assumes the Biblical perspective.[81] For example, Spinoza offers two definitions of the divine law: the first is the true knowledge and love of God;[82] the second is "to love God above all things and one's neighbor as oneself."[83] The effect of the first argument, which is Spinoza's philosophic position, is to deny the cognitive status of anything in the Bible. Spinoza contrasts the Bible to Euclid: the latter has an intelligible order that must be discerned; the former has no inherent order, so the order must be imposed on it.[84] In the course of making this argument, Spinoza criticizes Maimonides's claim that the Bible contains a rational teaching. Spinoza quotes from a passage in Maimonides's *Guide of the Perplexed* to show that Maimonides can only claim that the Bible contains a rational teaching by interpreting everything in it metaphorically.[85] But Maimonides goes on, in the passage Spinoza quotes from, to assert that the creation of the world cannot be understood metaphorically, since that would "destroy the foundations of the Law."[86] He then adds that since Aristotle did not succeed in proving the eternity of the world, it is possible to affirm the truth of the Law. Spinoza ignores this. I will shortly offer a suggestion as to why Spinoza treated Maimonides' argument unfairly.

Having established his separation of philosophy from theology, Spinoza next turns to the task of political philosophy proper. The argument proceeds as follows: Whether on the basis of hope of security to enjoy life or fear of violence, each individual will agree to form a compact to preserve a commonwealth, which is identified as the highest good.[87] Some will come to this realization by themselves, on the basis of hope, while others will need to be "persuaded" by fear. Spinoza's argument combines, and thereby blurs the distinction between, formal legality and political expediency. He argues, for example, that there is no danger in forming a body politic with absolute authority, since rational self-interest will restrain the government. This is especially true in a democracy where "it is practically impossible for a majority of a single assembly, if it is of some size, to agree on the same piece of folly. Then again, . . . it is the fundamental purpose of democracy to avoid the follies of appetite and to keep men within the bounds of reason, as far as possible, so that they may live in peace and harmony."[88]

Earlier in his *Treatise*, Spinoza identified three objects of desire: "to know things through their primary causes; to subjugate the passions; i.e. to acquire the habit of virtue; and to live in security and good health."[89] He then said that the first two lie within the bounds of human nature, meaning an individual philosopher could attain them, but the third required government. Spinoza breaks with Aristotle and Plato in identifying democracy as the best and most rational regime because, as far as government is concerned, he has limited reason's task to individual calculation concerning the requirements of security.

Spinoza's discussion of the Hebrew nation brings into relief his concern about religion. "[I]n this state civil law and religion . . . were one and the same thing; the tenets of religion were not just teachings but laws and commands; piety was looked upon as justice, impiety as crime and injustice."[90] This produced a bitter hatred between the Jews and other peoples and the strictest obedience among Jews: "No one ventured to pass judgment in matters of religion; they had to obey all that was commanded them on the authority of God's answer received in the temple, or of the Law established by God, without any resort to reason."[91] The remedy for this, Spinoza says, "is to define piety and religious observance as consisting only in works, that is, simply in the exercise of charity and just dealing, and to allow individual free judgment in all other matters."[92]

So that religion can make no claim on the sovereign, however, Spinoza makes clear that the sovereign defines justice and charity.

At this point, the argument from the biblical perspective gives way to the philosophic argument. Here is how Spinoza puts it, with devastating clarity;

> The divine teachings, whether revealed by the natural light or prophecy do not acquire the force of command from God directly; they must acquire it from those, or through the medium of those who have the right to command and issue decrees, and consequently it is that we can conceive of God as reigning over men and directing human affairs according to justice and equity. This conclusion is supported by experience, for indications of divine justice are to be found only where just men reign; elsewhere . . . we see the same fate befalling the just and the unjust, the pure and the impure.[93]

Spinoza and Hobbes both propose to subordinate religion to absolute sovereignty, whereas Locke proposes the separation of spheres. Each philosopher intends to bring about the same result, civil peace, or security. But only Spinoza favors democracy, and as a result, he makes a full argument for freedom of speech in his final chapter.

The chapter heading is "It is shown that in a free commonwealth every man may think as he pleases, and say what he thinks." Spinoza does not argue that truth wins out in the marketplace of ideas. Rather, he appeals from the sovereign's rights to his interests. First he provides the high-toned justification for free speech that complements his support for democracy:

> It is not, I repeat, the purpose of the state to transform men from rational beings into beasts or puppets, but rather to enable them to develop their mental and physical faculties in safety, to use their reason without restraint and to refrain from the strife and the vicious mutual abuse that are

prompted by hatred, anger, or deceit. Thus the purpose of the state is, in reality, freedom.[94]

Spinoza can identify democracy with rationality on the basis of his previous limitation of rationality to instrumental calculations concerning one's hopes and fears. Spinoza's argument deliberately blurs the distinction between fully rational activity, which means philosophy, and the sub—or instrumental—rational activity of calculating hopes and fears. Why would Spinoza blur the distinction between the philosophic few and the nonphilosophic many, especially since he emphasizes the difference between philosophers and nonphilosophers in other contexts? My suggested answer also applies to my earlier question, why did Spinoza treat Maimonides' argument about Biblical interpretation unfairly? Spinoza feared that under the circumstances any aristocracy would have been of the priestly class and therefore would have threatened philosophy.[95] This also accounts for his vehement rejection of the ancient Jewish republic—philosophy cannot thrive there. [96] He may have thought that the only way to prevent the rule of priests, which threatens the activity of philosophers as well as the subrational freedom of all, was to make an argument against any form of governmental hierarchy. Such an argument is essential for the establishment of liberal democracy.

Spinoza's argument for freedom of speech reflects the special character of democratic rationality. He starts with a statement in support of moderate restraints on the expression of opinions, similar to those expressed by Milton and by Locke. Men should not deny the supremacy of government. They should acknowledge that promises should be kept, because of the harmful deeds that might follow from those opinions. But Spinoza goes on to support a more extensive freedom, in the name of what works:

> He who seeks to regulate everything by law will aggravate vices rather than correct them. What cannot be prohibited must necessarily be allowed, even if harm often ensues. . . . Furthermore, . . . this freedom is of the first importance in fostering the sciences and the arts, for it is only those whose judgment is free and unbiased who can attain success in these fields.
>
> But let it be supposed that this freedom can be suppressed and that men can be kept under such control that they dare not whisper anything that is not commanded by the sovereign. . . . It would thus inevitably follow that in their daily lives men would be thinking one thing and saying another, with the result that good faith, of first importance in the state, would be undermined and the disgusting arts of sycophancy and treachery would be encouraged. This is the source of false dealing and the corruption of all honest ac-

complishments. But it is far beyond the bounds of possibility that all men can be made to speak to order. On the contrary, the greater the effort to deprive them of freedom of speech, the more obstinately do they resist: not indeed the greedy, the flatterers and other poor-spirited souls who find their greatest happiness in gloating over their money-bags and cramming their bellies, but those to whom a good upbringing, integrity and a virtuous disposition have given a more liberal outlook. Men in general are so constituted that their resentment is most aroused when beliefs which they think to be true are treated as criminal, and when that which motivates their pious conduct to God and man is accounted as wickedness. In consequence they are emboldened to denounce the laws and go to all lengths to oppose the magistrate, considering it not a disgrace but honorable to stir up sedition and to resort to any outrageous action in this cause.[97]

Free speech may foster the sciences and the arts, but the example of the former Soviet Union shows that the sciences can also develop without free speech. Spinoza's main argument is that any attempt to restrain the expression of the form or content of opinion is likely to be met with such a spirited opposition, and from the respectable members of society not just the low-lifes, that as a practical matter it is better to limit the restraints of law to overt acts. This low but solid argument in support of free speech in democracy supports the Supreme Court's protection of a substantial range of expression.[98]

I conclude from these seventeenth century philosophers that lowering the objectives of government served the interest of philosophy at the same time that it made peace and prosperity more easily attainable. The project required the reining in of religion, or, differently stated, the elimination of a religious polity. The philosophers reinterpreted Biblical religion to harmonize it with the principle of toleration. Milton and Locke also employed the notion that truth will win out to support toleration.

Two models of religious freedom were offered: the secular sovereignty could either control religion by reducing it to an expression of dogmas consistent with government's limited objectives, or it could insist on a separation of religion from politics and umpire the division. Spinoza proposed the former, starting with "God, that is, a Supreme Being, exists, supremely just and merciful, the exemplar of true life."[99] American constitutionalism followed Locke's separation argument. While some favor non-preferential support for religion, very few people are interested in a return to an ecclesiastical polity.

Regarding freedom of speech, Spinoza's argument deliberately blurs the distinction between philosophy and politics by equating the rational life with the life of material well-being. His free speech argument has nothing to do with truth winning out in the marketplace but rather with a consideration of the kinds of restraint that most people will accept.

Locke treats freedom of speech in his *Second Treatise* when he discusses the people's right of freedom of speech in connection with their consent-giving power to dissolve government. The prince alters the form of government when he "hinders the Legislative from assembling in its due time, or from acting freely. . . .

> for 'tis not a certain number of men, no, nor their meeting, unless they have also freedom of debating, and leisure of perfecting what is for the good of society wherein the legislative consists. . . . For it is not names that constitute governments, but the use and exercise of those powers that were intended to accompany them; so that he who takes away the freedom or hinders the acting of the legislative in its due seasons, in effect takes away the legislative and puts an end to government.[100]

A bit later, Locke explains what he means by saying that the executive acts contrary to his trust when he corrupts the representatives or threatens fair elections in any way:

> For the people having reserved to themselves the choice of their representatives, as the fence to their properties, could do it for no other end, but that they might always be freely chosen, and so chosen, freely act and advise, as the necessity of the Commonwealth and the public good should, upon examination, and mature debate, be judged to require. This, those who give their votes before they hear the debate, and have weighed the reasons on all sides, are not capable of doing. To prepare such an assembly as this, and endeavor to set up the declared abettors of his own will, for the true Representatives of the People, and the law-makers of the society, is certainly as great a breach of trust, and as perfect a Declaration of a design to subvert the Government, as is possible to be met with.[101]

Locke's argument complements Spinoza's without saying anything about truth winning out in a free exchange of opinions. Rather, freedom of speech is seen as a necessary corollary to the consent the people give to government by means of elected representatives. In addition to the right of election, they must have the right to communicate their views to those representatives. While Spinoza's argument makes the case for a substantial freedom of speech immune from government regulation, Locke makes the case for communication with one's elected representatives.

Notes

1. "A Letter to Mr. Matthew, upon sending to him Part of 'Instauratio Magna,'" in *Francis Bacon: A Selection of His Works*, ed. by Sidney Warhoft (The Odyssey Press, 1981) pp. 468–69.

2. *The Advancement of Learning*, ed. G. W. Kitchin, intro by Jerry Weinberger (Philadelphia: Paul Dry Books, 2001), XXV, 1.

3. *The New Organon*, ed. Fulton H. Anderson (Indianapolis: Bobbs-Merrill Educaional Publishing, 1960). Aphorism LI, p. 53.

4. Hobbes, *Leviathan*, Tuck ed. (Cambridge: Cambridge University Press, 1991); compare chapter 14, pp. 91–92 with chapter 15 end, p. 111. Hobbes shifts, in part three (chapter XXXII), to the Christian Commonwealth, and examines the "prophetical," as opposed to the "natural word of God." And he writes: "For though there be many things in God's Word above Reason; that is to say which cannot by naturall reason be either demonstrated, or confuted; yet there is nothing contrary to it," p. 256. Later in that chapter he writes: "Seeing therefore that Miracles now cease, we have no sign left, whereby to acknowledge the pretended Revelations, or Inspirations of any private man; nor obligation to give ear to any Doctrine, farther than it is conformable to the Holy Scriptures...." (p. 259). Hobbes's interpretation of the Scriptures is consistent with his earlier account of nature and natural law.

5. Id. author's introduction, p. 9 and chapter 28, pp. 220–21.

6. Id. chapter 18, pp. 124–25.

7. Id. A Review and Conclusion, p. 491.

8. Milton, *Areopagitica* and *Of Education*, ed. by George H. Sabine (Arlington Heights, Ill.: Harlan Davidson, Inc. 1951), p. 50.

9. Id. p. 5.

10. Id.

11. Id. pp. 6–7.

12. Id. p. 6.

13. Id. at p. 18.

14. Id. at pp. 18–19.

15. Id. at p. 25.

16. Id. at p. 26.

17. Id. at p. 28.

18. Id. at p. 37.

19. Id. at pp. 41–2.

20. Paul M. Dowling, *Polite Wisdom: Heathen Rhetoric in Milton's Arepagitica* (Lanham, Md.: Rowman and Littlefield, 1995), p. 75.

21. *Areopagitica*, p. 43.

22. Dowling, p. 77.

23. *Areopagitica*, pp. 45–46.

24. Id. p. 48.

25. Id. p. 49.

26. Id. at p. 50.

27. Id. at p. 51.

28. Id., p. 51.

29. Id. at p. 52. Milton scholar Ernest Surluck notes that whereas, in earlier writings, on divorce, Milton argued for the separation of religion from politics, he did not make that argument in *Areopagitica*, when it would have supported tolerance. Rather, according to Surluck, Milton chose to develop the argument about indifferent matters and not to make the separation argument, in order to gain the support of the Erastians, who might have been able to persuade the lay Presbytereans in Parliament to oppose licensing. The Erastians would not have supported a complete separation of church and state, however. According to this interpretation, Milton had to make the Erastians think that the Parliamentary majority was intent on introducing a theocracy. Surluck, Ernest, in *The Complete Prose Works of John Milton* (New Haven: Yale University Press, 1959), pp. 168–69, 175–77.

30. *Areopagitica*, supra, p. 55.

31. Dowling, pp. 97ff.

32. Surluck quotes from *Of True Religion* in *Milton's Works*, vol. II, p. 179.

33. Surluck, supra, 181.

34. Id. p. 181. Surluck is quoting again from Milton's *Of True Religion*.

35. Translated by William Popple, ed. by James Tulley (Indianapolis: Hackett Publishing 1983), hereinafter cited as Tulley.

36. Id. p. 26.

37. Id. p. 27.

38. Id. p. 28.

39. Id. p. 30.

40. Id. p. 39.

41. Id.

42. Id.

43. John Locke, *Epistola de Tolerantia: A Letter on Toleration*, bilingual edition edited by Raymond Klibansky, translated with intro and notes by J. W. Gough (Oxford: Clarendon Press, 1968), note 35, pp. 157–58.

44. Tully ed. p. 40.

45. Id. p. 39.

46. Id. p. 40.

47. Id. p. 40.

48. Id. p. 40.

49. Id. p. 41.

50. Id. p. 41.

51. Id. pp. 41–42.

52. Id. p. 42.

53. Id.

54. Id. See also p. 32.

55. Id. p. 46. Compare this to Jefferson's bill for establishing religious freedom, in chapter 3 above.

56. Id. p. 23.

57. "Society is the realm of the soul, or what passes for the soul, the self." And, "in societies attempting to maintain a distinction between state and society, in time one hears less of soul and more of self, then less of self-control and more of self-expression." Harvey C. Mansfield Jr., "The Religious Issue and the Origin of Modern Constitutionalism," in *America's Constitutional Soul* (Baltimore and London: John's Hopkins University Press, 1991), p. 103.

58. Locke, Letter, p. 46.

59. Id. p. 47.

60. Id.

61. Id., p. 48. (Italics in original.)

62. Id.

63. Id. Locke's account thus differs from civil disobedience, as Martin Luther King explained it. King seems to assume that there will be a consensus on when the law or government practice is unjust; Locke assumes that there will be conscientious objections to just laws.

64. Id. at pp. 50–51.

65. Id., p. 51.

66. Eva Brann, "Madison's Memorial and Remonstrance: A Model of American Eloquence," in *The Past-Present: Selected Writings of Eva Brann* (Annapolis: St. John's College Press), p. 225 (emphasis original). Brann makes this point while explaining why Madison, who followed Locke, still took exception to George Mason's proposed "fullest tolerance in the exercise of religion," for Virginia's Bill of Rights. See the discussion of this above in part 1.

67. See Harvey C. Mansfield Jr., "Party Government and the Settlement of 1688," *American Political Science Review*, 933–46 ("The sound principle of the Toleration Act was the widest practicable toleration. . . . It is possible that a general toleration is of necessity inspired by intolerance of the intolerant," p. 941).

68. John Locke, *Two Treatises of Government*, ed. Peter Laslett, *Second Treatise* (Cambridge: Cambridge University Press, 1960), chapter 5, section 31ff. Hereinafter cited as *Second Treatise*.

69. For the natural law prohibition on spoilage, see V, 37, lines 35 to 41. As a possible additional limit on acquisition, Locke does say, at the end of 27, that labor gives right to property, "at least where there is enough, and as good left in common for others." Since labor accounts for 99.9 percent of the wealth (43, line 7), Locke suggests that as long as the "industrious and rational" do not spoil natural wealth, by converting natural wealth to money before it spoils, everyone is better off. Locke's argument supports regulation of property, but not the imposition of upper limits.

70. Locke, *Second Treatise*, chapter 5, section 42, pp. 292–98.

71. My understanding of Locke on religion follows Leo Strauss, *Natural Right and History* (Chicago: University of Chicago, 1953), chapter 5b and "Locke's Doctrine of Natural Law," in *What is Political Philosophy? And Other Studies* (Glencoe, Illinois: The Free Press, 1959), chapter 7, as well as Harvey Mansfield," The Religious Issue and the Origin of Modern Constitutionalism," in supra note 57, and Michael P. Zuckert, in

Natural Rights and the New Republicanism (Princeton: Princeton University Press, 1994), chapter 9, and *Launching Liberalism: On Lockean Political Philosophy* (Lawrence, Kansas: University Press of Kansas, 2002), especially chapter 6. Two scholars who interpret Locke as a Christian thinker are: John Dunn, *The Political Thought of John Locke: An Historical Account of the 'Two Treatises of Government'"* (Cambridge: Cambridge University Press, 1969), and "What is Living and What is Dead in John Locke," in *Interpreting Political Responsibility: Essays 1981–1989* (Princeton, Princeton: University Press, 1990) chapter 2; and Jeremy Waldron, *God, Locke and Equality: Christian Foundations of John Locke's Political Thought* (Cambridge: Cambridge University Press, 2002). Without attempting to present a definitive account of this scholarly disagreement, I note that Dunn believes that "unlimited capitalist appropriation and intensive agricultural labor were equally apt vessels" for "the [Christian] duty of endless aspiration," *Political Thought of John Locke*, p. 217. And Waldron understands Locke to argue that "religious argumentation about equality. . . . is indispensable," p. 237. Waldron cites Locke's Reasonableness of Christianity for this position, p. 241. I discuss this text shortly.

72. John Locke, *The Reasonableness of Christianity, with a Discourse of Miracles and part of a Third Letter Concerning Toleration*, ed. by I. T. Ramsey (Stanford: Stanford University Press, 1958), section 172, pp. 44–45.

73. Id. section 243, p. 66.

74. Id. section 245, p. 69.

75. Id. section 245, p. 70. I am grateful to Michael P. Zuckert for directing me to these passages in Locke's *Reasonableness of Christianity*. See his *Launching Liberalism: On Lockean Political Philosophy* (Lawrence: University of Kansas Press, 2002), chapter 6, "Locke and the Problem of Civil Religion: Locke on Christianity," pp. 147–68.

76. Michael Zuchert, in the work cited in the previous note, thinks Locke went too far in this direction; see *Launching Liberalism*, pp. 162–66.

77. Benedict Spinoza, *Theological-Political Treatise*, Samuel Shirley translation (Indianapolis: Hackett Publishing Company, 1998), chapter 14, pp. 168–69. Hereinafter cited as Spinoza.

78. Id. chapters 1–2.

79. Id. chapter 3, p. 39.

80. Id. chapter 6, pp. 74–75.

81. Leo Strauss made this point when he discussed the Preface and chapter 1 of the *Theological-Political Treatise* in his course at the University of Chicago in 1959. In his essay, "How to Study Spinoza's Theological-Political Treatise," in his book, *Persecution and the Art of Writing* (Glencoe, Illinois: The Free Press, 1952), Strauss refers to Spinoza's contradicting himself on the "central subject of his book," whether "certain knowledge of truths which surpass the capacity of human reason is possible," p. 169. Spinoza's true position was the philosophic one, Strauss argued, but he wrote as he did because he was trying to persuade Christians who were potential philosophers to turn to philosophy and he knew that others would be reading his book as well. See p. 184.

82. Id. chapter 4, p. 50.
83. Id. chapter 12, p. 155.
84. Id. chapter 7, p. 101.
85. Id. chapter 7, pp. 103–4.
86. *The Guide of the Perplexed*, translated by Sholomo Pines (Chicago: University of Chicago Press, 1963) 2 volumes, vol. 2 chapter 25, p. 329.
87. Spinoza, chapter 16, p. 182.
88. Id. chapter 16, p. 184.
89. Id. chapter 3, p. 38.
90. Id. chapter 17, p. 196.
91. Id. pp. 205, 206.
92. Id. chapter 18, p. 216.
93. Id. chapter 19, p. 222.
94. Id. chapter 20, p. 232.
95. Leo Strauss made this point in the course on Spinoza that he taught at the University of Chicago in 1959.
96. About the ancient Hebrew state, Spinoza wrote: "No one [in it] ventured to pass judgment in matters of religion; they had to obey all that was commanded them on the authority of god's answer received in the temple, or of the Law established by God, without any resort to reason." Spinoza, chapter 17, p. 206.
97. Id., chapter 20, p. 234.
98. See below, part three, chapters 9–10.
99. Id. chapter 14, p. 167. Spinoza offers six more dogmas. They are, in brief, "God is one alone," "God is omnipresent," "God has supreme right and dominion over all things," "Worship of God and obedience to him consists solely in justice and charity, or love towards one's neighbor," "All who obey God by following this way of life, and only these, are saved," and "God forgives repentant sinners."
100. *Second Treatise*, chapter XIX, section 215.
101. Id. section 222.

CHAPTER SEVEN

Montesquieu's Constitution of Liberty: *The Spirit of the Laws*

Montesquieu's *Spirit of the Laws* (1748) was the most widely quoted book in the debate over the ratification of the American Constitution.[1] Moreover, the Federalists and the Anti-Federalists both claimed that Montesquieu supported their positions on federalism and the separation of powers. In light of his account of republics, monarchies, and England, whose constitution secures political liberty, we see that Montesquieu celebrated a new form of republican government, which did not have virtue as its "spring," or source of motion, was not restricted in size, and contained the monarchical principle, a strong executive.[2] In addition, this new form of republican government had limited criminal laws and in that way, among others, secured religious liberty and freedom of speech.

Montesquieu defines political virtue as love of equality and love of the homeland.[3] Using this definition, Montesquieu identifies republics with ancient government.[4] He notes that, whereas the education of ancient peoples was consistent, that is no longer the case:

> Today we receive three different or opposing educations: that of our fathers, that of our school masters, and that of the world. What we are told by the last upsets all the ideas of the first two. This comes partly from the opposition there is for us between the ties of religion and those of the world, a thing unknown among the ancients.[5]

Much of what Montesquieu says about religion, and especially Christianity, addresses this problem for the moderns. By making the education that moderns receive internally consistent, Montesquieu prepares the way for a republican form that does not rely on political virtue as self-denial. Montesquieu indicates his disapproval of republican virtue when he gives two modern equivalents of the legendary Spartan founder Lycurgus—the American Quaker William Penn and the Jesuits—and then likens the citizens' dedication to their body politic with the monks' dedication to their monastic community.[6]

A monarchy, in contrast to a republic, has intermediate bodies, and its spring, or principal passion, is honor: "the prejudice of each person and each condition takes the place of the political virtue of which I have spoken and represents it everywhere." Consequently, "each person works for the common good, believing he works for his individual interests."[7]

Montesquieu calls republics and monarchies moderate governments and despotisms immoderate governments, and he clearly favors moderate governments. It seems as if England, Montesquieu's preferred constitution, is closer to monarchy than republicanism. Yet Montesquieu describes England as a republic hiding in the form of a monarchy.[8] What does that mean and why does Montesquieu prefer it?

After he describes the separation of powers in England,[9] Montesquieu says that contemporary monarchies "do not have liberty as their direct purpose as the one we have just mentioned; they aim only for the glory of the citizens, the state, and the prince."[10] While glory can produce "a spirit of liberty that can . . . produce equally great things and can perhaps contribute as much to happiness as liberty itself," the separation of powers is not perfected there and hence political liberty can only be approximated. In his next chapter, Montesquieu ascribes the perfection of English government to the transformation of the government of the medieval Germanic nations.[11] Montesquieu's preferred constitution of liberty has the structure of a mixed government. To find out why he refers to it as a republic in the form of monarchy and why it nonetheless differs fundamentally from his original account of the principle of republics, we should turn to his account of political liberty in book XI.

Montesquieu begins this account by distinguishing political liberty in relation to the constitution from political liberty in relation to the citizen: the former requires the separation of powers, properly understood; the latter requires a proper knowledge of the limits of criminal law. Montesquieu defines liberty in two ways: as "having the power to do what one should want to do and in no way being constrained to do what one should not want to do;" and as "the right to do everything the laws permit."[12]

The first definition focuses on duty, the second on right. Montesquieu may have begun with a definition based on duty to indicate the difference between ancient republics and the modern republic he is about to describe. He proceeds to emphasize the need for power to check power: "A constitution can be such that no one will be constrained to do the things the law does not oblige him to do or be kept from doing the things the law permits him to do."[13] This emphasis on checks suggests that the definition starting from rights is the correct one.

Concerning the institutional arrangements, the powers may be legislative, executive, and judicial, but the institutional balance is due to a bicameral legislature and a single executive, with a veto over the laws. Montesquieu identifies the judging power with popular juries. In addition, the people have the right to elect representatives for one branch of the legislature, but they do not have the power to direct government. Speaking about this constitution in a later place, Montesquieu identifies the two visible powers as the legislative and the executive. He also says that most people do not appreciate the importance of each; "the multitude is ordinarily not fair or sensible enough to have equal affection for both of them." Then he describes the passions of the people in England:

> As all the passions are free there, hatred, envy, jealousy, and the ardor for enriching and distinguishing oneself would appear to their full extent, and if this were otherwise, the state would be like a man who, laid low by disease, has no passions because he has no strength.
> The hatred between the two parties would endure because it would always be powerless.[14]

This explains why Montesquieu describes England as a republic hiding as a monarchy. It differs markedly from the austere republic Montesquieu identified with ancient governments.

In the first book on commerce, Montesquieu describes England as follows:

> Other nations have made commercial interests give way to political interests: England has always made its political interests give way to the interests of its commerce.
> This is the people in the world who have best known how to take advantage of each of these three great things at the same time: religion, commerce, and liberty.[15]

Montesquieu seems to have in mind the replacement of the warlike passions by the peaceful passions, as a means of shifting from virtue as selfless patriotism to political liberty as security.[16] To effect this change, he will have to discuss religion and its relation to civil society. Montesquieu discusses religion in book I, on laws in general, in book XII, in relation to the citizen, and in books XXIV and XXV, which are expressly on religion.

Book I's three chapters are titled: "On laws in relation to the various beings," "On the laws of nature," and "On positive laws." The first chapter begins with a definition of laws as "the necessary relations deriving from the nature of things."[17] Montesquieu discusses laws relating to: the divinity, the material world, the intelligences superior to man, the beasts, and man. On the first point, Montesquieu rejects atheism out of hand: "There is, then, a primitive reason; and laws are both the relations that exist between it and the different beings, and the relations of these various beings to each other."[18] Montesquieu then equates primitive reason with God, as "creator and preserver" of the universe. Since the material world, now just called the world, "formed by the motion of matter and devoid of intelligence, still continues to exist, its motions must have invariable laws."[19] Particular intelligent beings, previously called intelligences superior to man, have laws that they made and others that they did not make. As an example of the latter, "before laws were made there were possible relations of justice. To say that there is nothing just or unjust but what positive laws ordain or prohibit is to say that before a circle was drawn, all the radii were not equal."[20] This suggests a natural justice similar to geometry. This intelligent world, Montesquieu says, is not as well governed as the material, since intelligent beings are subject to error. Apparently they do not have to follow their laws, either their primitive laws or the ones they give themselves. As for beasts, "[t]hey have natural laws because they are united by feeling; they have no positive laws because they are not united by knowledge."[21] Montesquieu's equation of natural laws with feeling, in contrast to knowledge, conflicts with his account of primitive laws and primitive reason. Finally, man is described as a dual being: governed as a physical being by natural laws like other bodies, and as an intelligent being "he constantly violates the laws god has established and changes those he himself establishes." As a finite being, he is subject to ignorance and error:

> As a feeling creature, he falls subject to a thousand passions. Such a being could at any moment forget his creator; god has called him back to him by the laws of religion. Such a being could at any moment forget himself; philosophers have reminded him of himself by the laws of morality. Made for living in society, he could forget his fellows; legislators have returned him to his duties by political and civil laws.[22]

Given the variety of laws affecting man, we wonder how they relate to the divinity and to particular intelligent beings and their possible relations of justice. Montesquieu's reply, presented in the next chapter, is to introduce the laws of nature, meaning human nature, as "prior to all these laws," presumably referring to those in the previous chapter. Montesquieu begins with "the idea of a creator" as "the first of the *natural laws* in importance, though not first in the order of these laws."[23]

Montesquieu, who has rejected "blind fate" as an inadequate account of the origins of life, now describes primitive man as thinking of preservation before speculating on origins. "Such a man would at first feel only his weakness. . . . Such men would not seek to attack one another and peace would be their first natural law."[24] Human beings have to come together and lose their feelings of weakness before the state of war, which necessitates civil society, develops. The second law of nature is that man seeks nourishment. Then comes pleasure from sexual intercourse, and, finally, when human beings gain knowledge, sharing it provides another reason for uniting in society. The third chapter discusses the formation of civil society, which is based on political and civil right, and relations among civil societies, which is based on the right of nations. The spirit of the laws refers to the diverse relations of the laws to every other relevant consideration for civil society.[25] In the best case, the laws are used to establish political liberty both with respect to the constitution and to the citizen.

Montesquieu's enigmatic account of the divine laws in book I, as well as his later treatment of religion, reflects his cautious presentation of a bold project. His intention, I believe, is to eliminate "the opposition there is for us between the ties of religion and those of the world, a thing unknown among the ancients."[26] Montesquieu reveals an important part of this opposition in book XII, where he discusses political liberty from the perspective of the citizen.

Unless the criminal law is properly limited, the separation of powers may be able to secure a collective political liberty but individual citizens will not have the liberty of security. Montesquieu refers to the right to be heard when one is confronted with charges,[27] and the requirement that no man can be condemned to death without the testimony of two witnesses.[28] Then, in a chapter entitled "That liberty is favored by the nature of penalties and by their proportion," Montesquieu identifies four sorts of crimes: those that run counter (1) to religion, (2) to mores, (3) to tranquility, and (4) to the security of citizens. He contends that only the fourth sort of crime should be subject to punishment, or criminal law in the strict sense.[29] For the crime of sacrilege, the penalty should be ostracism. In those matters that wound the divinity but do not disturb the tranquility or security of the state, where there is no public action, there is no criminal matter; it is all between the man and god who knows the measure and the time of his vengeance. For if the magistrate, confusing things, even searches out hidden sacrifice, he brings an inquisition to a kind of action where it is not necessary; he destroys the liberty of citizens by arming against them the zeal of both timid and brash consciences.[30]

Crimes against mores involve "the violation of public or individual continence, that is, of the police concerning how one should enjoy the pleasures associated with the use of one's senses and with corporal union."[31] By "police," Montesquieu means noncriminal rules of society. The remedies here include fines, shame, and at most "expulsion from the town and from society."[32] Likewise, "the crimes that run counter to the citizen's tranquility, and the penalties for them should be drawn from the nature of the thing and relate to that tranquility, such as deprivation, exile, corrections, and other penalties that restore men's troubled spirits and return them to the established order."[33] Only the penalties for the last crimes are "punishments. They are a kind of retaliation, which causes the society to refuse to give security to a citizen who has deprived or has wanted to deprive another of it."[34] The death penalty should be limited to such cases; crimes against property should be punished with loss of property.

Montesquieu's next examples come from religion. He pairs heresy with magic, and then mentions "the crime against nature." All three were punished by burning. Montesquieu indicates his view by saying that magic does not exist, heresy is "susceptible in infinite distinctions, interpretations and limitations," and homosexuality is often hidden.[35] As for the latter, he is satisfied that as long as it is not encouraged, the natural pleasure of producing offspring will suffice to limit homosexual practices.[36]

Montesquieu next argues that the crime of treason should be viewed strictly. He cites as a "violent abuse" of the name of high treason "a law of the emperors [which] pursued as sacrilegious those who called the prince's judgment into question and doubted the merit of those he had chosen for certain employments."[37] He also criticizes the law that made an attempt on the prince's ministers an act of treason, as if it were an act against the prince.[38]

Montesquieu seems to oppose seditious libel laws as well. A short chapter "On thoughts," which concludes with the statement that "laws are charged with punishing only external actions," leads to a chapter "On indiscreet speech." In this chapter, Montesquieu presents the "speech-action" distinction that has become so important in American constitutional law.

He examines the subject from a practical perspective, reminiscent of Spinoza: "Discourse is so subject to interpretation, there is so much difference between indiscretion and malice and so little in the expressions they use, that the law can scarcely subject speech to a capital penalty, unless it declare explicitly which speech is subject to it."[39] Montesquieu goes on to propose the following approach to speech:

> The words that are joined to an act take on the nature of that action. Thus a man who goes into the public square to exhort the subjects to revolt becomes guilty of high treason, because the speech is joined to the act and participates in it. It is not speech that is punished but an act committed in which speech is used. Speech becomes criminal only when it prepares, when it accompanies, or when it follows a criminal act. Everything is turned upside down if speech is made a capital crime instead of being regarded as the sign of a capital crime.[40]

While allowing that written words "contain something more permanent than speech," Montesquieu nonetheless argues "when they do not prepare the way for high treason, they are not material to the crime of high treason."[41]

In book XIX, chapter 27, Montesquieu describes England as a place where the laws contribute to the forming of the mores, manners, and character of a nation, and as a place where "all the passions are free." Furthermore, "[t]his nation, made comfortable by peace and liberty, freed from destructive prejudices, would be inclined to become commercial."[42] And religion in England reflects the importance of peace and liberty. Some people would be indifferent, others would embrace the dominant religion, but all would resist any attempt to impose a religion on them.[43]

Montesquieu describes the individuals as "confederates more than citizens," which indicates the distinctively individualist character of liberty in this new republic. He also connects liberty with reason this way: "In a free nation it often does not matter whether individuals reason well or badly; it suffices that they reason; from that comes the liberty that protects them from the effects of these same reasonings."[44] Montesquieu, like Spinoza, identifies free speech with modern republican government because it follows from an emancipation of the peaceful passions. This preoccupation with self-interest as the root of liberty in the form of security applies to thought, and especially to religious thought, as well as to external goods.

Montesquieu's two books on commerce come immediately after this summary discussion of laws, manners, and mores and their effect on the spirit of a nation. Commerce cures destructive prejudices and goes together with gentle mores; its natural effect is "to lead to peace."[45] The ancient republics were largely military; the modern republic is commercial. In addition, its commerce is more extensive and varied as improvements in navigation permit north-south trade.[46] The earlier suggestion that commerce went together with frugality seems to be replaced now by the notion that commerce produces wealth, wealth produces luxury, and luxury produces "the perfection of the arts."[47] If we put this account together with what Montesquieu said of England—that men are judged by "wealth and personal merit," and that "[t]here would be a solid luxury, founded not on the refinement of vanity, but on that of real needs"—Montesquieu thinks that commerce supports political liberty in the form of security.[48]

This discussion of the constituent parts of political liberty reveals a tension between the Christian religion and the preferred spirit of the laws for the nation. Montesquieu addresses this in book XXIV, when he turns to religion. Since he is "not a theologian, but one who writes about politics," Montesquieu limits himself to "things that would be wholly true only in a human way of thinking, for they have not been considered in relation to the more sublime truths."

> With regard to the true religion, the slightest fairness will show that I have never claimed to make its interests cede to political interests, but to unite them both; now, in order to unite them, they must be known.
> The Christian religion, which orders men to love one another, no doubt wants the best political laws and the best civil laws for each people, because those laws are, after it, the great good men can give and receive.[49]

But Montesquieu's method in book XII involves limiting laws in the strict sense to matters pertaining to security; as a result, religious matters are relegated to noncriminal rules or admonitions. In the subsequent discussion of religion, I think it becomes clear that Montesquieu's intention is precisely to make religion, including Christianity, cede to the political interest in liberty as security.

In chapter two of book XXIV, Montesquieu defends religion against the atheism of Pierre Bayle. To Bayle's claim that it is better to be an atheist than an idolater, because it is better never to have existed than to exist and be a bad man, Montesquieu replies that this is "sophistry," since "it is quite useful [to mankind] for one to believe that god is."[50] In chapter 3, Montesquieu approvingly describes the Christianity of the Gospels as gentle, and he credits Christianity with bringing about a certain political right and a right of nations that leaves to the vanquished "these great things: life, liberty, laws, goods, and always religion."[51] But is that so? Are these things due to Christianity? Or is it commerce that makes for gentle mores, and hence facilitates a change in laws supportive of liberty?[52] First, Montesquieu did not say that about religion when he introduced the law of nations. Second, Montesquieu provides examples where Christian rulers did not act in a spirit of gentleness. Montesquieu's point, I take it, is that the spirit of Christianity, from the Gospels, is one of gentleness. He thus notes with approval that "it is much more evident to us that a religion should soften the mores of men than it is that a religion is true."[53] That seems to describe Montesquieu's intention with respect to Christianity.

At this point, in chapter 6, Montesquieu takes up another of Bayle's paradoxes: that a state formed by true Christians could not continue to exist because the people would have a stronger attachment to the kingdom of heaven than to their earthly homeland.[54] Montesquieu, in reply, distinguishes "orders for the establishment of Christianity" from "Christianity itself," which corresponds to his distinction between precepts and counsels. As he says in his next chapter, "Human laws made to speak to the spirit should give precepts and no counsels at all; religion, made to speak to the heart, should give many counsels and few precepts." The question is, how effective will the counsels of restraint be if the laws permit the fullest activity of the peaceful passions?

The next three chapters suggest that morality can be supported without true religion, or perhaps without religion at all. First, Montesquieu says that in countries "having a religion not given by god," it is important that the religion agree with morality, "because religion, even a false one, is the best warrant men can have of the integrity of men."[55] This implies that for Montesquieu the correct understanding of morality and integrity does not require religion. Moreover, after briefly praising the Essenes for their justice, Montesquieu describes the Stoics with high praise: "If I could for a moment cease to think that I am a Christian, I would not be able to keep myself from numbering the destruction of Zeno's sect among the misfortunes of human kind."[56] Two points are noteworthy. First, Montesquieu might have regarded the Stoics as atheists; then his praise calls into question his support for Christianity.[57] Second, the Stoics' selfless dedication to the happiness of others and their scorn for pleasures and pains puts them in the category of the ancient republics, not the modern republics of political liberty. Perhaps Montesquieu's position is that it's too difficult for people to live as the Stoics did; men need to be allowed the liberty to satisfy their passions, and religion of a certain kind is necessary to support gentleness.

In book XXV, on religion in each country and their external police, Montesquieu advocates toleration, which he distinguishes from approval.[58] He also says that penal laws should be avoided in matters of religion. Montesquieu recommends appeals to hopes rather than fears:

> A more certain way to attack religion is by favor, by the comforts of life, by the hope of fortune, not by what reminds one of it, but by what makes one forget it; not by what makes one indignant, but by what leads one to indifference when other passions act on our souls and when those that religion inspires are silent. General rule: in the matter of changing religion, invitations are stronger than penalties.[59]

In book XXVI, titled, "On the laws in the relation they should have with the order of things upon which they are to enact," Montesquieu identifies the following sorts of laws: by natural right, by divine right, by ecclesiastical right, by right of nations, by the general political right, by the particular political right, by the right of conquest, by the civil right of each society, and by domestic right.[60] Divine right refers to religion in general; ecclesiastical right refers to canonical matters, which Montesquieu also refers to as the "police of religion." The sphere of the police appears to cover counsels, or regulations, rather than precepts, or laws.[61] In chapter 2, Montesquieu says that human laws aim at the good, which changes, while religion aims at the best, which is unchanging. The sphere of religion remains private, however: "The principal force of religion comes from its being believed; the force of human laws come from their being feared."[62] What does this mean for marriage, a subject of importance to religion and to civil society? Up to a point there is no conflict, since the civil laws might add requirements: "The law of religion wants certain ceremonies, and the civil laws want the consent of the fathers. In this way they ask something more, but they ask nothing that is contrary to it." But what about divorce? "It follows that it is for the laws of religion to decide whether or not the bond will be indissoluble, for if the laws of religion had established an indissoluble bond and the civil laws had ruled that it could be broken, these two things would be contradictory."[63] Montesquieu emphasizes counsels, or advice, over precepts, or laws, in religious matters.[64] This goes together with his observation that, while religious laws aim at "the goodness of the man who observes them," civil laws aim at "the general good of society."[65]

Montesquieu thus proposes to change Christianity's effect on human life by encouraging men to indulge in their peaceful passions, especially in commercial activity, and to regard religion as a matter of private concern, not a political matter requiring the attention of the laws. This revision of religion is due to his view of political liberty as the end of good government. If political liberty, understood as security, is the end of government, then freedom of speech is a logical support to such an end. While the American founders relied on Locke on religion and generally did not consider alternatives to the common law approach to free speech—no prior restraint but subsequent punishment was permitted—until 1800, Montesquieu's reflections on religion were taken up by Tocqueville, who applied them to American democracy.[66] Therefore, I think it is reasonable to say that Montesquieu's new form of republican government describes the principles of American government, as applied to the First Amendment freedoms as much as to the structure of government.

Notes

1. *The Spirit of the Laws* was published in 1748 in France, and in 1750, Thomas Nugent's English translation was published.

2. Harvey C. Mansfield, Jr. *Taming the Prince: Modern Executive Power* (New York: The Free Press, 1989) chapter 9.

3. *The Spirit of the Laws*, ed. by Anne Cohler, Basia Miller, and Harold Stone (Cambridge, Cambridge University Press, 1989) book 2, chapter 2. All subsequent citations will be to this edition.

4. See book 3, chapter 3; pp. 22–23, and book 4, chapter 4, pp. 35.

5. Id., book 4, chapter 4, p. 35.

6. Id. See book 4, chapter 6, p. 37 and book 5, chapter, 2; pp. 42–43.

7. Id., book 3, chapters 6 and 7; pp. 26, 27.

8. Id., book 5, chapter 19, p. 70.

9. Id., book 11, chapter 6.

10. Id., book 11, chapter 7.

11. Id., book 11, chapter 8, pp. 167–68.

12. Id., book 11, chapter 3, p. 155.

13. Id., book 11, chapter 4, pp. 155–66.

14. Id., book 19, chapter, 27, p. 325.

15. Id., book 20, chapter 7, p. 343.

16. See Leo Strauss, *What is Political Philosophy? And Other Studies* (Chicago: University of Chicago, 1959) p. 49.

17. *The Spirit of the Laws*, book 1, chapter 1, p. 3.

18. Id.

19. Id.

20. Id., p. 4.

21. Id., p. 5.

22. Id.

23. Id., book 1, chapter 2, p. 6 (emphasis in original).

24. Id.

25. These include the nature and principles of government, physical characteristics, such as climate, terrain, location and extent of territory, the amount of liberty

the constitution can sustain, religion, wealth, number, commerce, and the manners and mores of the people, the origin of the laws, the purpose of the legislator, and the order of things on which they are established. See book 1, chapter 3, pp. 8–9.

26. Book 4, chapter 4, p. 35.

27. Id. 12, 2.

28. Id. 12, 3.

29. Id. 12.4. p. 191.

30. Id. 12, 4; p. 190.

31. Id.

32. Id. at p. 190. In chapter 13, Montesquieu distinguishes between an "object of police" and a crime, p. 200. The editors refer the reader to book XXVI, chapter 24 for Montesquieu's explanation of the meaning of "police." Montesquieu's discussion in 26.24 conforms to what he said in 12.3 about penalties and punishments. The law must punish serious matters, those affecting security; the magistrate may punish lesser matters, those involving tranquility. This latter action is what he means by "the police;" today we would consider it limited to discretionary warnings. See book XXVI, chapter 24, pp. 517–18.

33. Id. p. 191.

34. Id. p. 191.

35. Id. p. 193.

36. See Id. p. 194.

37. Montesquieu, book XII, chapter 8, p. 195.

38. Id.

39. Id. book XII, chapter 12, p. 198.

40. Id. at pp. 198–99.

41. Id., book XII, chapter 13, p. 199.

42. Id., book IXX, chapter 27, p. 328.

43. Id., book IXX, chapter 27, p. 330.

44. Id., p. 332.

45. Id., book XX,, chapter 2, p. 338.

46. Id., book XXI, chapter 4, p. 356.

47. Id., book XXI , chapter 6, p. 357.

48. Id., book IXX, chapter 27, p. 331.

49. Id., book XXIV, chapter 1; p. 459.

50. Id., book XXIV, chapter 2, p. 460.

51. Id., pp. 461–62.

52. Id., book XXI, chapters, 1 and 2; p. 338.

53. Id., book, XXIV, chapter 4, p. 462.

54. Id., book XXIV, chapter 6, pp. 463–64.

55. Id., book XXIV, chapter 8, p. 465.

56. Id., book XXIV, chapter 10, p. 466.

57. In book XXIV, chapter 19, Montesquieu writes: "The religion of Confucius denies the immortality of the soul, and the sect of Zeno did not believe in it." p. 473.

Moreover, Montesquieu expressly calls the Stoics atheists in his *Defense de L'Esprit Des Lois*, in Montesqueiu, *Oeuvres completes*, vol. II, ed. and annotated by Roger Caillois (Edition Gallimard, 1951) p. 1136.

58. Id., book 25, chapter 9, p. 487.
59. Id., book 25, chapter 12; p. 489.
60. Id., p. 494.
61. See book 24, chapter 6.
62. Id., book 26, chapter 2, p. 495.
63. Id., book 26, chapter 13, p. 506.
64. Id., book 24, chapter 6, p. 464.
65. Id., book 26, chapter 9, p. 502.
66. Rousseau also drew on Montesquieu's account of religion. In his *Social Contract*, Rousseau coined the term "civil religion," which Spinoza, Locke and Montesquieu were introducing in different forms (see book 4, chapter 8). Rousseau's account of religion was too candidly anti-Christian for the Americans, however.

CHAPTER EIGHT

John Stuart Mill's *On Liberty*

John Stuart Mill's *On Liberty* (1859) develops the argument of his philosophic predecessors to the limit of its logic. He strictly limits government's authority, he adopts the "marketplace of ideas" argument for all opinions, and he seeks to limit social constraint on individual development as much as government coercion.

Mill describes his "anti-paternalistic" principle this way:

> The object of this essay is to assert one very simple principle, as entitled to govern absolutely the dealings of society with the individual in the way of compulsion and control, whether the means used be physical force in the form of legal penalties, or the moral coercion of public opinion. That principle is, that the sole end for which mankind are warranted, individually or collectively, in interfering with the liberty of action of any of their number, is self protection. That the only purpose for which power can be rightfully exercised over any member of a civilized community, against his will, is to prevent harm to others. His own good, either physical or moral, is not a sufficient warrant.[1]

Mill identifies three areas of individual freedom: liberty of conscience, liberty of tastes and pursuits, and a resulting liberty of association.[2] Since freedom of conscience includes the fullest freedom of expression, to allow individuals to attain the goal of self-development, Mill must show that society benefits from, or at least is not harmed by, this freedom. Here is Mill's first statement against the suppression of opinions:

If all mankind minus one, were of one opinion, and only one person were of the contrary opinion, mankind would be no more justified in silencing that one person, than he, if he had the power, would be justified in silencing mankind. Were an opinion a personal possession of no value except to the owner; if to be obstructed in the enjoyment of it were simply a private injury, it would make some difference whether the injury was inflicted only on a few persons or on many. But the peculiar evil of silencing the expression of an opinion is, that it is robbing the human race; posterity as well as the existing generation; those who dissent from the opinion, still more than those who hold it. If the opinion is right, they are deprived of the opportunity of exchanging error for truth: if wrong they lose, what is almost as great a benefit, the clearer perception and livelier impression of truth, produced by its collision with error.[3]

Mill begins his discussion under the first hypothesis—that the opinion suppressed by authority may be true—by noting that the silencing of discussion presumes infallibility, which no human can possess. Mill's first counterargument emphasizes the need for action: "Judgment is given to men that they may use it." An awareness that no one is infallible could lead to inaction, which would "leave all our interests uncared for, and all our duties unperformed."[4] He replies: "There is the greatest difference between presuming an opinion to be true, because, with every opportunity for contesting it, it has not been refuted, and assuming its truth for the purpose of not permitting its refutation."[5] Mill's argument presupposes that the relevant body of judges must be the entire citizenry, not merely the legislature. After all, whenever democratic legislatures limit freedom of expression, a debate precedes the voting, and further discussion occurs whenever legislators reconsider the policy.[6]

Assuming that "there is on the whole a preponderance among mankind of rational opinions and rational conduct," Mill speculates that it must be due "to a quality of the human mind . . . that his errors are corrigible. He is capable of rectifying his mistakes, by discussion and experience."[7] But how does this follow from Mill's earlier statement that "on any matter not self-evident there are ninety nine persons totally incapable of judging of it, for one who is capable?"[8] Mill appears to trust in a kind of long-term trial and error; political and social development advances over time, as science does. He describes the wise man, who shows "the steady habit of correcting and completing his own opinion by collating it with those of others," as the model for all. Mill's wise man resembles the disinterested scientist or scholar. His knowledge may not encompass prudent political action, and even if it did, he might not be able to persuade democratic citizens, who are skeptical of "political scientists" who might claim to have superior knowledge of politics.

For Mill, since human beings are fallible, all questions must remain open to questioning.[9] Mill considers the contention that certain beliefs are "so useful, not to say indispensable to well-being, that it is as much the duty of government to uphold those beliefs, as to protect any other of the interests of society."[10] He rejects this because "the usefulness of an opinion is itself a matter of opinion," and "the truth of an opinion is part of its utility."[11] "In the opinion . . . of the best of men, no belief which is contrary to truth can really be useful." But suppose there are moral opinions that cannot be demonstrated, or that cannot be persuasively demonstrated to all men? Mill takes this up by considering attacks on "the belief in God and in a future state, or any of the commonly received doctrines of morality." In reply to the question whether this too is an opinion about which one cannot assume infallibility, Mill replies "it is not the feeling sure of a doctrine . . . which I call an assumption of infallibility," but "the undertaking to decide that question *for others*, without allowing them to hear what can be said on the contrary side."[12] Mill thus wants each person to think for himself as fully as possible, without pressure, legal or social. Is it for the sake of individual self-development, or is it because the truth emerges under such conditions?

To illustrate his position, Mill discusses the deaths of Socrates and Jesus and the persecution of Christians by the Roman emperor Marcus Aurelius. Socrates was "put to death by his countrymen, after a judicial conviction, for impiety and immorality." Jesus was put to death as a blasphemer, even though he left "such an impression of his moral grandeur, that eighteen subsequent centuries have done homage to him as the Almighty in person." Finally, Marcus Aurelius, "a better Christian in all but the dogmatic sense of the word, than almost any of the ostensibly Christian sovereigns who have since reigned, persecuted Christianity." Failing to see "that Christianity was to be a good and not an evil to the world," Aurelius "deemed it his duty not to suffer society to fall in pieces, and saw not how if its existing ties were removed. . . . The new religion openly aimed at dissolving these ties." Aurelius could have adopted Christianity but did not, because "this strange history of a crucified God was not credible to him."[13]

Mill judiciously avoids pronouncing on the truth of either the Christian or the Roman conceptions of human excellence. The man who claims that the truth of an opinion is part of its utility does suggest that in a moderated form Christianity has been useful—that is, it has been a "renovating agency."[14] Calling the dictum "that truth always triumphs over persecution . . . one of those pleasant falsehoods which men repeat after one another till they pass into commonplaces," Mill nonetheless accepts a modified version of the proposition;

> It is a piece of idle sentimentality that truth, merely as truth, has any inherent power denied to error, of prevailing against the dungeon and the stake. Men are not more zealous for truth than they often are for error, and a sufficient application of legal or even of social penalties will generally succeed in stopping the propagation of either. The real advantage which truth has, consists in this, that when an opinion is true, it may be extinguished once, twice, or many times, but in the course of ages there will generally be found persons to rediscover it, until some one of its reappearances falls on a time when from favourable circumstances it escapes persecution until it has made such head as to withstand all subsequent attempts to suppress it.[15]

Later, Mill writes that "as mankind improve, the number of doctrines which are no longer disputed or doubted will be constantly on the increase: and the well being of mankind may almost be measured by the number and gravity of the truths which have reached the point of being uncontested."[16]

Mill notes with approval the rise of "Socratic philosophy" after Socrates was put to death, and the growth of the Christian church after persecution of Christians. These results are offered, without discussion, as evidence of the advance of truth. Mill's main point is that while "our merely social intolerance kills no one," it stifles independent thinking. Mill wants "the multitude of promising intellects" to be freed from those constraints.[17] He thinks that their freedom to act in bold ways will be fully consistent with the overall regime of tolerance.

Mill then contends that even if its received opinions are true, civil society must allow the fullest expression of counter arguments. Otherwise, the true opinion "will be held as a dead dogma, not as a living truth." To make his case, or to illustrate it, Mill describes the activity of Cicero, "the greatest orator, save one, of antiquity," who "always studied his adversary's case with as great, if not with still greater, intensity than even his own. What Cicero practiced as the means of forensic success, requires to be imitated by all who study any subject in order to arrive at the truth."[18] But are the situations similar? Cicero engaged in forensic or deliberative rhetoric; that is, he either brought a charge against or defended individuals before the law, or he advocated a certain policy before the Roman Senate. He did not constantly engage in controversies over the fundamental principles of the Roman Republic. Such debates arose from necessity, not choice. Some policy debates may touch on the meaning of the principles of the regime, but they rarely focus on questioning the soundness of those very principles.

Mill insists that England's future Ciceros, who seem to include all citizens, should hear the arguments of their adversaries not from their teachers but directly. Without indicating how this involves a political discussion, Mill says: "He must be able to hear [the arguments] from persons who actually believe them; who defend them in earnest, and do their very utmost for them."[19] One wonders how that would work for either a legislature or an academic institution. Should Marxists be hired to teach Marxism in the universities? And members of the neo-Nazi party and the Ku Klux Klan to present the views of racial hate groups?

To illustrate the problem of creeds losing their vitality, Mill describes the limited or half-hearted way in which many Christians subscribe to the maxims and precepts of the New Testament, which he contrasts to the faith of the early Christians.[20] It's not clear that Mill opposes this development of Christianity, as we shall see.

Mill uses the Platonic dialogues as an example of "a negative discussion of the great questions of philosophy and life, directed with consummate skill to the purpose of convincing any one who had merely adopted the commonplaces of received opinion, that he did not understand the subject."[21] But where Plato's Socrates describes the education of the philosophic few as a movement from opinion to knowledge, which may involve no more than a clarification of fundamental alternatives,[22] Mill believes that mankind as a whole is capable of intellectual progress and that progress involves liberation from authority and more and more reliance on one's own rational faculties. How does that work, if most individuals are not capable of independent thinking and hence rely on common opinion?

Finally, Mill considers the most common case, where each side possesses a part of the truth:

> Hence, even in revolutions of opinion, one part of the truth usually sets while another rises. Even progress, which ought to superadd, for the most part only substitutes, one partial and incomplete truth for another; improvement consisting chiefly in this, that the new fragment of truth is more wanted, more adapted to the needs of the time, than that which it displaces.[23]

This progress, which increasingly satisfies human needs, seems to take place without the help of statesmanship but simply as a result of a condition of freedom.

Mill provides two examples of partial truths that have combined with other truths to become more complete. The first is Rousseau's critique of the Enlightenment, "exploding like bombshells in the midst, dislocating the compact mass of one-sided opinion, and forcing its elements to recombine in a better form and with additional ingredients."[24]

Mill's brief treatment of Rousseau does not acknowledge, let alone criticize, Rousseau's account of the importance of vanity and compassion as related forms of self-love that affect political life. Rousseau may have introduced historical reasoning in his account of natural man and the characteristic of "perfectibility,"[25] but he did not think that political problems could be solved once and for all. For that reason, he emphasized the difference between natural freedom and civil freedom and he discussed the need for human beings to be made into citizens—that is, parts of an artificial whole. Rational calculations of self-interest would not suffice to keep citizens attached to their country; a civil religion was needed. Mill disagrees with Rousseau on these points, but he does not present his argument. Mill simply asserts that "the current opinions were . . . nearer to [the truth]," but that "there lay in Rousseau's doctrine, as has floated down the stream of opinion along with it, a considerable amount of exactly those truths which the popular opinion wanted."[26]

Mill's second example of a partial truth concerns Christianity. Addressing the objection that "the Christian morality . . . is the whole truth on that subject," Mill demurs. "The Gospel always refers to a preexisting morality, and confines its precepts to the particulars in which that morality was to be corrected, or superseded by a wider and higher [one]."[27] Rejecting the Old Testament as "in many respects barbaric," and identifying this position with St. Paul, Mill says that "what is called Christian but should rather be termed theological, morality, was not the work of Christ or the Apostles," but developed by the Catholic Church over five centuries. "Its ideal is negative rather than positive; passive rather than active; Innocence rather than Nobleness; abstinence from evil rather than energetic Pursuit of Good: in its precepts . . . 'thou shalt not' predominates unduly over 'thou shalt.'"[28] Mill criticizes the Christian teaching regarding reward and punishment as well as its emphasis on duty without any connection to interest. Mill still claims that Christian ethics can be reconciled with "the many requisites of a complete moral doctrine":

> I believe that the sayings of Christ . . . are irreconcilable with nothing which a comprehensive morality requires; that everything which is excellent in ethics may be brought within them, with no greater violence to their language than has been done to it by all who have attempted to deduce from them any practical system of conduct whatever. But it is quite consistent with this, to believe that they contain, and were meant to contain only a part of the truth; that

many essential elements of the highest morality are among the things which are not provided for, nor intended to be provided for, in the recorded deliverances of the Founder of Christianity, and which have been entirely thrown aside in the system of ethics erected on the basis of those deliverances by the Christian Church.[29]

Mill is "tactful," to say the least, in his treatment of Christianity's teachings on human excellence and happiness. At the same time, his expressed confidence in society's improvement, as more and more truths become accepted, suggests something akin to Christian faith in divine providence.[30] As freedom triumphs over the authority of custom and tradition, Mill seems to expect everyone to develop the faculty of exercising intelligent judgment.[31] At the same time, latitude is given to the manner of expression. "With regard to what is commonly meant by intemperate discussion, namely invective, sarcasm, personality, and the like, the denunciation of these weapons would deserve more sympathy if it were ever proposed to interdict them equally to both sides."[32]

In his central chapter, on individuality, Mill argues that men should be free to act on their own opinions, "so long as it is at their own risk and peril." He presents this formulation of the boundary between speech and action:

> No one pretends that actions should be as free as opinions. On the contrary, even opinions lose their immunity, when the circumstances in which they are expressed are such as to constitute their expression a positive instigation to some mischievous act. An opinion that corn dealers are starvers of the poor, or that private property is robbery, ought to be unmolested when simply circulated through the press, but may justly incur punishment when delivered orally to an excited mob assembled before the house of a corn dealer, or when handed about among the same mob in the form of a placard.[33]

Mill treats the line-drawing activity in the next chapter. In this one, he argues for the importance of the freedom of self-development. In addition to different opinions, "there should be different experiments of living"[34] for the sake of self-development. Mill's individual does not realize himself in and through activities with others. Mill encourages "individual spontaneity," which "is hardly recognized by the common modes of thinking, as having an intrinsic worth, or deserving any regard on its own."[35] This applies to the moral as well as to intellectual development:

> The human faculties of perception, judgment, discriminative feeling, mental activity, and even moral preference, are exercised only in making a choice. He

who does anything because it is the custom, makes no choice. He gains no practice either in discerning or in desiring what is best. The mental and the moral, like the muscular powers, are improved only by being used.[36]

Mill assumes that moral habits develop the same way that intellectual faculties do. But does one benefit by giving serious consideration to leading a life of crime or tyranny? And does society benefit by encouraging such experimentation? What accounts for his sanguine view concerning the results of the fullest freedom of action as well as opinion? The answer lies in Mill's two-part account of human nature. He likens human nature "not [to] a machine to be built after a model, and set to do exactly the work prescribed for it, but [to] a tree, which requires to grow and develope itself on all sides, according to the tendency and inward forces which make it a living thing."[37] Mill emphasizes desires and impulses, not understanding and restraint.[38]

Mill argues for a renewed individualism without any change in government's purpose. As an example, he praises "a Greek ideal of self-development. . . . It may be better to be a John Knox than an Alcibiades, but it is better to be a Pericles than either, nor would a Pericles . . . be without anything good which belonged to John Knox."[39] Why, in terms of his praise of energy, should Mill prefer Pericles to Alcibiades, and even prefer the Christian John Knox to Alcibiades? Instead of acknowledging the conflict between true individuals and civil society, Mill has recourse to the notion that there is a social as well as a selfish side to individual development:

> The means of development which the individual loses by being prevented from gratifying his inclinations to the injury of others, are chiefly obtained at the expense of the development of other people. And even to himself there is a full equivalent in the better development of the social part of his nature, rendered possible by the restraint put upon the selfish part.[40]

Mill expects his individualists to agree "to be held to rigid rules of justice for the sake of others," since it "developes the feelings and capacities which have the good of others for their object."[41] He argues that the development of the exceptional human beings benefits everyone. Moreover, these "persons of genius" are capable of all sorts of good. They "discover new truths," they "point out when what were once truths are true no longer," they "commence new practices," and they "set the example of more enlightened conduct, and better taste and sense in human life."[42]

Mill laments the rule of mediocrity and public opinion. Apparently, when things were less advanced socially, they were better in terms of individual activity. Mill blames custom for modern society's aversion to individuality, and its resulting mediocrity. And yet, even as he concludes his chapter, Mill reveals his awareness that the replacement of an aristocratic class hierarchy by a liberal, commercial democracy goes along with a more uniform civil society.[43] Fully aware of the drawbacks of uniformity, Mill seems to be unaware of the dangers of unrestricted individualism.

In his final two chapters, Mill explains how to draw the line between individual matters and matters of social concern, and then he gives several illustrations. He distinguishes between self-regarding virtues and vices on the one hand and social virtues and vices on the other. The self-regarding vices include folly, "lowness or deprivation of taste," "rashness, obstinacy [and] self-conceit," and "indulgences" in "animal pleasures at the expense of those of feeling and intellect." The proper response to a person manifesting these qualities is to avoid his company, to warn others against him, or to prefer others for "optional good offices." Social vices, or acts injurious to others, include "encroachment on their rights, falsehood or duplicity in dealing with them; unfair or ungenerous use of advantages over them, even selfish abstinence from defending them against injury."[44] Beyond noting that the more serious offenses are liable to "moral retribution and punishment," and less serious offenses only to "moral reprobation," Mill does not make clear where the legal line should be drawn, perhaps because his main interest is to protect individuals from either moral censure or governmental retribution for any self-regarding vice. Society may respond to the dispositions that lead to injury to others; these include

> cruelty of disposition, malice and ill-nature; . . . envy; dissimulation and insincerity; irascibility on insufficient cause, and resentment disproportioned to the provocation; the love of domineering over others; the desire to engross more than one's share of advantages . . . the pride which derives gratification from the abasement of others; the egoism which thinks self and its concerns are more important than everything else.[45]

These are all moral vices and "constitute a bad and odious moral character"; they differ in kind from the self-regarding faults "which are not properly immoralities and . . . do not constitute wickedness."[46]

If Mill is so concerned about fully developed individualism, why is he willing to leave individuals alone to waste their talents? This is his answer:

> But with regard to the merely contingent, or, as it may be called, constructive injury, which a person causes to society, by conduct which neither violates any specific duty to the public, nor occasions perceptible hurt to any assignable individual except himself; the inconvenience is one which society can afford to bear, for the sake of the greater good of human freedom.[47]

Furthermore, Mill asks why, if society did not succeed when it had power over its weaker individuals when they were minors, should anyone expect success when they are adults? And "the strongest of all the arguments against the interference of the public with purely personal conduct, is that when it does interfere, the odds are that it interferes wrongly, and in the wrong place."[48]

Mill's illustrations of the harms that result from society's interference in individual matters usually involve religion. His discussion of the Mormon doctrine of polygamy is the most interesting. After expressing his own disapproval of the institution for the way it treats women, Mill notes that the institution of marriage is voluntary and many women might prefer to share a husband with other women to having no husband at all. Mill's proposed solution is to not require other countries to recognize such marriages but to leave the Mormons, and any other practitioners of polygamy, to settle in an uninhabited part of the world.[49]

Mill concludes with his argument in favor of individual activity and against energetic government. He expresses reservations about a proposal for filling the civil service with competitive examinations. "It is not, also, to be forgotten, that the absorption of all the principal ability of the country into the governing body is fatal, sooner or later, to the mental activity and progressiveness of the body itself."[50] Mill thus advocates the dissemination of power combined with the centralization of information and "diffusion of it from the centre."[51] "The worth of a State, in the long run, is the worth of the individuals composing it."[52] Mill assumes a harmony between individuals and the state while he virtually ignores citizenship, and his emphasis on the line between the individual and the social denigrates any sense of civic obligation.

Notes

1. *On Liberty and Other Writings*, ed. by Stefan Collini (Cambridge: Cambridge University Press, 1989), at p. 13, (hereinafter cited as Mill). Mill limits the application of his principle to adults and to mature civil societies, since "liberty, as a principle, has no application to any state of things anterior to the time when mankind have become capable of being improved by free and equal discussion." When he discusses "backward states," Mill is paternalistic: "Despotism is a legitimate mode of government in dealing with barbarians, provided the end be their improvement and the means justified by actually effecting that end." pp. 13–14.

2. Id., pp. 15–16.

3. Id. at p. 20.

4. Id. at p. 22.

5. Id. at pp. 22–23.

6. Likewise, one might distinguish between outlawing a political party, such as the Communist Party, and prohibiting the publication or sale of *The Communist Manifesto*. As long as Marx, and other Communist writings may be read, a debate may take place on the best policy regarding a political party whose principle of action is violent revolution.

7. Mill, p. 23.

8. Id. p. 23.

9. Id. See p. 25.

10. Id. p. 25.

11. Id. p. 25.

12. Id. p. 26; emphasis in original.

13. Id. p. 29.

14. Id.

15. Id. p. 31.

16. Id. p. 45.

17. Id., p. 35.

18. Id. p. 38.

19. Id., p. 38.

20. See Id pp. 43–44

21. Id. at p. 45.

22. See Leo Strauss, *What is Political Philosophy And Other Studies* (Glencoe, IL, Free Press, 1959) pp. 38–41.

23. Id. at p. 47.

24. Id., p. 48.

25. See Rousseau's *Discourse on the Origin and Foundation of Inequality among Men*, ed. Roger D. Masters (New York: St. Martin's Press, 1964).

26. Mill, op. cit, p. 48.

27. Id. at pp. 49–50.

28. Id. at p. 50.

29. Id. at p. 51.

30. Hegel's "cunning of reason" consisted in the passions of men, especially suprahistorical ones, advancing the condition of rational liberty in the world "behind the backs" of the individuals' conscious intentions. (See *Introduction to the Philosophy of History*, translated by Leo Rauch (Indianapolis: Hackett Publishing Company, 1988), p. 35. Mill makes no reference to this argument, and yet his own account of truth winning out, as more truths are accepted in society, notwithstanding the limited understanding of most human beings, resembles Hegel's account. At the same time, Mill is much less willing to allow a place for tradition and custom than Hegel is; Mill's best condition is more radically individualist than Hegel's.

31. Id. p. 53.

32. Id. p. 54.

33. Id. p. 56.
34. Id., p. 57.
35. Id. p. 57.
36. Id. p. 59.
37. Id. p. 60.
38. See Id. p. 60. Mill is clearly on the side of strong desires: "To say that one person's desires and feelings are stronger and more various than those of another, is merely to say that he has more of the raw material of human nature, and is therefore capable, perhaps of more evil, but certainly of more good." p. 60.
39. Id., p. 63.
40. Id., p. 63.
41. Id., p. 63.
42. Id., p. 64.
43. Id., p. 73.
44. Id., p. 78.
45. Id., pp. 78–79
46. Id., at p. 79.
47. Id., at p. 82.
48. Id., p. 83.
49. Id., p. 92.
50. Id., p. 112.
51. Id., p. 113.
52. Id., p. 115.

PART THREE

THE SUPREME COURT'S TREATMENT OF FREEDOM OF SPEECH AND RELIGIOUS FREEDOM

I turn now to the development of First Amendment freedoms in the authoritative decisions of the United States Supreme Court. I am interested in showing how the Court has developed principles of neutrality to interpret these clauses, in order to secure the objectives of civil peace and the quest for truth.

The first topic is freedom of speech. I will begin with a discussion of the "sedition" or "subversive speech" cases, which arose out of World War I. These cases gave rise to the "clear and present danger" test, which was first stated in *Schenck v United States* in 1919, was modified in the major Communist Party cases in the 1950s, and was revised into the "incitement test" in *Brandenburg v Ohio* in 1969. I will then turn to a discussion of the Court's "categorical approach" to free speech; this refers to categories of speech that were judged to be excluded from First Amendment protection but which have gradually gained partial protection. Then I will consider speech regulations that impose conditions without prohibiting speech according to its content. These are called "time, place, and manner" cases or, because of the importance of the place, "public forum" cases.

The second topic is religious freedom, and I will begin with a consideration of the relationship between the Free Exercise Clause and the Establishment Clause. Some of the most interesting cases involve both clauses, though most involve one or the other. The Free Exercise Clause cases raise the question of what standard should be used when the government acts for legitimate purposes but the incidental effect of that action impedes religious belief or practice. The Establishment Clause controversies arise in the context of aid to parochial schools, prayer and other religious activities in public schools, and governmental use of religious symbols.

Freedom of Speech

CHAPTER NINE

Seditious Libel and Fifty Years of "Clear and Present Danger": From *Schenck* to *Brandenburg*

As cogent as Madison's argument against the adequacy of the common law rule of "no prior restraint" was, it took more than a century before the United States Supreme Court came to accept it.[1] And it took even longer before the Court agreed on a test that protected criticism of the government. Both the speech test that was developed and the rationale for it, that truth wins out in the marketplace of ideas, drew on Mill's *On Liberty*. To some extent, the judicial opinions of Justices Brandeis and Harlan in some key twentieth century decisions reflect Madison's republican government argument. In addition, I hope to show that these Justices' arguments reflect Spinoza's arguments as well.

In 1919, the Court decided four important freedom of speech cases. The first three—*Schenck*, *Frohwerk*, and *Debs*—handed down on the same day, arose under the Espionage Act of 1917. The fourth, *Abrams*, involved a 1918 amendment to that act, which is also known as a sedition act. In addition to covering espionage and disclosure of military secrets, the Espionage Act of 1917 created three new offenses:

[1] Whoever, when the United States is at war, shall willfully make or convey false reports or false statements with intent to interfere with the operation or success of the military or naval forces of the United States, or to promote the success of its enemies, and [2] whoever, when the United States is at war, shall willfully cause or attempt to cause insubordination, disloyalty, mutiny, or refusal of duty, in the military or naval forces of the United States, or [3] shall willfully obstruct the recruiting or enlistment service of the United States, to

the injury of the service or of the United States, shall be punished by a fine of not more than $10,000 or imprisonment for not more than twenty years, or both.[2]

In the first case, Schenck v United States,[3] defendants Schenck and Baer were charged with attempting to cause insubordination in the military and naval forces of the United States and with obstructing recruiting by printing and circulating to men who had been called up for service (but who were not yet enlisted) pamphlets asserting that conscription violated the Thirteenth Amendment and urging the men to "Assert Your Rights."[4] In the second case, defendant Frohwerk was indicted for attempting to cause disloyalty and mutiny by preparing and circulating newspaper articles praising Germany and criticizing the American war effort for benefiting the wealthy few on Wall Street. In the third case, Socialist Party leader Eugene V. Debs was indicted on charges of inciting insubordination, disloyalty, mutiny, etc., and obstructing and attempting to obstruct recruiting by giving a speech supporting others who were convicted of aiding and abetting avoidance of the draft. The Supreme Court unanimously upheld each conviction. Justice Holmes wrote the Court opinions. Acknowledging for the first time that the First Amendment's Freedom of Speech clause was not limited to preventing prior restraints, he introduced the famous "clear and present danger" test this way:

> The most stringent protection of free speech would not protect a man in falsely shouting fire in a theatre and causing a panic. . . . The question in every case is whether the words used are used in such circumstances and are of such a nature as to create a clear and present danger that they will bring about the substantive evils that Congress has a right to prevent. It is a question of proximity and degree. When a nation is at war many things that might be said in time of peace are such a hindrance to its effort that their utterance will not be endured so long as men fight and that no Court could regard them as protected by any constitutional right. The statute . . . punishes conspiracies to obstruct as well as actual obstruction. If the act, (speaking or circulating a paper), its tendency and the intent with which it is done are the same, we perceive no ground for saying that success alone warrants making the act a crime.[5]

Holmes added in Frohwerk that "neither Hamilton nor Madison, nor any competent person then or later, ever supposed that to make criminal the counseling of a murder within the jurisdiction of Congress would be an unconstitutional interference with free speech."[6] While Frohwerk was a poor man turning out copy for a paper of small circulation, Holmes asserted that from the record, "it is impossible to say that it might not have been found that the circulation of the paper was in quarters where a little breath would be enough to kindle a flame and that the fact was known and relied upon by those who sent the paper out."[7] And Debs, who won nearly one million votes running for president on the Socialist Party ticket, both in 1912 and again (from jail) in 1920, stated his opposition to war and identified himself with an antiwar proclamation that called this particular war "a crime against the people of the United States and against the nations of the world."[8] The Court upheld this conviction after noting that the jury was instructed that a guilty verdict required a finding that Debs's words "had as their natural tendency and reasonably probable effect to obstruct the recruiting service."[9]

The most puzzling aspect of Holmes's opinions is that after enunciating his "clear and present danger test," which resembles Mill's corn dealers example, Holmes treated clear and present danger as no more than a "bad tendency" test.[10] Second, while the Espionage Act punished acts, not speech, the Court's upholding of these convictions amounted to interpreting the statute to outlaw popular expression of opposition to the war. In effect, the type of debate that took place in Congress—when the country maintained its neutrality in World War I until the sinking of the *Lusitania* in 1917—was not allowed among the people; or, to put it in terms similar to Madison's argument against the Sedition Act of 1798, sharp criticism against the government and the war was not permitted.

Earlier, in 1917, Federal District Court Judge Learned Hand had interpreted the Espionage Act narrowly in a civil case. The Masses Publishing Company sought an injunction against the postmaster of New York for his refusal to allow *The Masses* to be delivered through the mail.[11] Distinguishing between words as "the keys of persuasion," and others as "triggers of action," Hand found that the paper's articles and cartoons critical of the war effort fell into the permissible former category. Willful obstruction of recruiting or enlistment, Hand wrote, requires more than counsel or advice:

> Political agitation, by the passions it arouses, or the convictions it engenders, may in fact stimulate men to the violation of law. Detestation of existing policies is easily transformed into forcible resistance of the authority which puts them in execution, and it would be folly to disregard the causal relation between the two. Yet to assimilate agitation, legitimate as such, with direct incitement to violent resistance, is to disregard the tolerance of all methods of political agitation which in normal times is a safeguard of free government.
>
> This distinction is not a scholastic subterfuge, but a hard-bought acquisition in the fight for freedom, and the purpose to disregard it must be evident when

the power exists. If one stops short of urging upon others that it is their duty or their interest to resist the law, it seems to me that one should not be held to have attempted to cause its violation.[12]

Hand's statement resembles Spinoza's argument for freedom of speech as well as Madison's. Madison probably would have added that much of the political agitation took the form of political speech by people opposed to the government's policies aimed at persuading others that the policy should be changed.

After a chance encounter with Justice Holmes on a train in 1918, Judge Hand, thinking he had agreed too much with Holmes on the majority's right to control dissent, expressed his views on toleration in a letter to the Justice. Hand did not want to appear "soft" on the matter of justice:

> You say that I strike at the sacred right to kill the other fellow when he disagrees. The horrible possibility silenced me when you said it. Now, I say, 'Not at all, kill him for the love of Christ and in the name of God, but always realize that he may be the saint and you the devil. . . .
>
> I sat under the Bo Tree and these truths were revealed to me. Tolerance is the twin of Incredulity, but there is no inconsistency in cutting off the heads of as many as you please; that is a natural right. Only, and here we may differ, I do say that you may not cut off heads . . . because the victims insist upon saying things which look against Provisional Hypothesis Number Twenty-Six, the verification of which to date may be found in its proper place in the card catalogue. Generally, I insist, you must allow the possibility that if the heads are spared, other cards may be added under that subtitle which will have, perhaps, an important modification.[13]

In this formulation, Hand replaced any reference to republican or representative government with an argument for tolerance based on skepticism regarding any final knowledge of important questions, presumably concerning the best society. This argument has no connection to the constitutional and political contentions of the opponents of the draft and the war.

Holmes replied by first agreeing with Hand and then adding the qualification that "free speech stands no differently from freedom from vaccination." This explains Holmes's approach to *Schenck* in 1919, although it does not explain why he introduced the "clear and present danger" test. Holmes went on to say that since caring is the condition for every act, he did not think that self-doubt would get in the way of the action. He then related a parable concerning the abolitionist William Lloyd Garrison and the conflict between law and justice, or stability and change:

If I were an official person I should say that nothing shall induce me to do honor to a man who broke the fundamental condition of social life by bidding the very structure of society perish rather than he not have his way. If I were a son of Garrison, I should reply—Fool, not to see that every great reform has seemed to threaten the structure of society,—but that society has not perished, because man is a social animal, and with every turn falls into a new pattern like the Kaleidoscope. If I were a philosopher I should say—Fools both, not to see that you are the two blades (conservative and radical) of the shears that cut out the future. But if I were the ironical man in the back of the philosopher's head I should conclude—Greatest fool of all, Thou—not to see that man's destiny is to fight. Therefore take thy place on the one side or the other, if with the added grace of knowing that the Enemy is as good a man as thou, so much the better, but kill him if thou canst. All of which seems in accord with you.[14]

After the Supreme Court decisions were handed down, Hand sent a short note to Holmes in which, referring to *Debs*, and perhaps *Frohwerk* but not *Schenck*, he wrote: "I haven't a doubt that Debs was guilty under any rule conceivably applicable."[15] It's hard to understand that statement as anything other than accepting the inevitability of the decision. After all, later in the letter Hand restated his preference for the objective "incitement" approach over the "clear and present danger" test, and, related to that, he criticized letting juries decide on the speaker's motive. Hand seemed to have accepted the identification of the "clear and present danger" test with a "bad tendency" or motive test. Holmes's brief response includes the statement, "And now I am afraid that I don't quite get your point."[16] That's because Holmes was satisfied that Debs's speeches manifested an intent to obstruct and tended to obstruct. If Hand had said that even under the clear and present danger test, more than intent and tendency is needed, Holmes would have understood. As for Hand's incitement remark, Holmes replied that he did not understand how it was different from his clear and present danger test. Holmes never did accept the incitement test, although in the *Abrams* case he finally applied clear and present danger in a manner that distinguished it from bad tendency. And while the evidence is inconclusive, it seems that Hand's correspondence, along with critical reviews of legal scholars, eventually caused Holmes to reconsider the application of the clear and present danger test.[17]

Abrams v United States,[18] decided later in 1919, involved an appeal of convictions under the 1918 amendment to the Espionage Act. The amendment, which at least one writer has called a sedition act,[19] criminalized printing and writing intended to incite resistance to the United States or to promote the cause of its enemies, and "willfully" urging any curtailment of production

necessary for the prosecution of the war. Jacob Abrams and other Russian an-
archists, after learning of America's intervention in the Russian Revolution
on the side of the Whites, printed, wrote, and distributed leaflets, some in
English and others in Yiddish, expressing support for the Russian Revolution,
criticizing America for intervening against the Revolution, and urging a general strike as a means of assisting the Revolution. For the majority of the
Court, the First Amendment issue was easily disposed of on the basis of
Schenck. The only hard question concerned the meaning of "intent." Abrams
and his comrades obviously did not intend to obstruct the war effort against
Germany, but the Court pointed out that "men must be held to have intended, and to be accountable for, the effects which their acts were likely to
produce."[20]

Justice Holmes dissented. Reaffirming his position in *Schenck* et al.,
Holmes argued that a desire to help Russia did not amount to an intent to
hinder the war effort against Germany. Acknowledging that he might be
"technically wrong" on the intent point, Holmes asserted that "the most
nominal punishment seems to me all that possible [sic] could be inflicted unless the defendants are to be made to suffer not for what the indictment al-
leges but for the creed that they avow—a creed that I believe to be the creed
of ignorance and immaturity when honestly held."[21] Of course the degree of
punishment was not before the Supreme Court, and it is hard to square
Holmes's support for Abrams's speech with his continued support for the convictions in the earlier cases. While he did not acknowledge any change of
heart, Holmes finally applied "clear and present danger" as requiring more
than the "bad tendency" test. His dissent has become one of the most famous
statements in support of freedom of speech:

> Persecution for the expression of opinions seems to me perfectly logical. If you
> have no doubt of your premises or your power and want a certain result with
> all your heart, you naturally express your wishes in law and sweep away all op-
> position. To allow opposition by speech seems to indicate that you think the
> speech impotent, as when a man says that he has squared the circle, or that you
> do not care wholeheartedly for the result, or that you doubt either your power
> or your premises. But when men have realized that time has upset many fight-
> ing faiths, they may come to believe even more than they believe the very
> foundations of their own conduct that the ultimate good desired is better
> reached by free trade in ideas—that the best test of truth is the power of the
> thought to get itself accepted in the competition of the market, and that truth
> is the only ground upon which their wishes safely can be carried out. That at
> any rate is the theory of our Constitution.[22]

The first part of this passage reflects the position Holmes took in his correspondence with Hand. But then he shifts to the position of tolerance based on skepticism, which Hand had advocated and Holmes had refused to accept a year earlier. In so doing, Holmes brings Mill's major justification for freedom of speech into American constitutional law, modestly disclaiming any originality by identifying the position with the theory of our Constitution.

Holmes also noted that most of what Abrams and his comrades printed and circulated consisted of support for the Russian Revolution, opposition to capitalism, and criticism of American government for its intervention in the Russian civil war against the Bolsheviks. The only part of their printed words that could be connected to curtailment of production concerned their call for a general strike. Such a remark, without any specific plans to cause the action to occur, resembles the kind of exuberant political expression that both Spinoza and Madison thought best to allow in the name of democratic freedom.

The next two free speech cases, *Gitlow v New York*[23] and *Whitney v California*,[24] involved free speech challenges to state sedition laws. These laws differed from the 1917 Espionage Act but resembled part of the 1918 amendment to that act in that they criminally punished a class of speech.[25] In each case, the Court upheld the law and affirmed the conviction, claiming to apply the clear and present danger test, but in effect allowing the state legislature to define an entire category of speech—the advocacy of violence against government—as constituting a clear and present danger. In *Gitlow*, the Court applied the Free Speech Clause to state government via the Due Process Clause of the Fourteenth Amendment.[26]

Justice Holmes's dissent in *Gitlow* and Justice Brandeis's concurrence[27] in *Whitney* again asserted the speech-protective position that Holmes had first stated in *Abrams*, and that Hand presented, emphasizing incitement, in his *Masses* opinion. While each Justice concurred in the other's opinion, the opinions offer different rationales for protecting the speech at issue.

Here is Justice Holmes in *Gitlow*:

> It is said that this manifesto [Gitlow's Left Wing Manifesto, stating the orthodox Marxist position] was more than a theory, that it was an incitement. Every idea is an incitement. It offers itself for belief and if believed it is acted on unless some other belief outweighs it or some failure of energy stifles the movement at its birth. The only difference between the expression of an opinion and an incitement in the narrower sense is the speaker's enthusiasm for the result. Eloquence may set fire to reason. But whatever may be thought of the redundant discourse before us it had no chance of starting a present conflagration. If

in the long run the beliefs expressed in proletarian dictatorship are destined to be accepted by the dominant forces of the community, the only meaning of free speech is that they should be given their chance and have their way.[28]

Here is Justice Brandeis in *Whitney*:

Those who won our independence believed that the final end of the state was to make men free to develop their faculties, and that in its government the deliberative forces should prevail over the arbitrary. They valued liberty both as an end and a means. They believed liberty to be the secret of happiness and courage to be the secret of liberty. They believed that freedom to think as you will and speak as you think are means indispensable to the discovery and spread of political truth; that without free speech and assembly discussion would be futile; that with them, discussion affords ordinarily adequate protection against the dissemination of noxious doctrine; that the gravest menace to freedom is an inert people; that public discussion is a political duty; and that this should be a fundamental principle of the American government.

Those who won our independence by revolution were not cowards. They did not fear political change. They did not exalt order at the cost of liberty. To courageous, self reliant men, with confidence in the power of free and fearless reasoning applied through the processes of popular government, no danger flowing from speech can be deemed clear and present, unless the incidence of the evil apprehended is so imminent that it may befall before there is opportunity for full discussion. If there be time to expose through discussion the falsehood and fallacies, to avert the evil by the processes of education, the remedy to be applied is more speech, not enforced silence. Only an emergency can justify repression. Such must be the rule if authority is to be reconciled with freedom. Such, in my opinion, is the command of the Constitution.[29]

In *Gitlow*, Holmes began by denying the significance of Hand's distinction between persuasion and incitement. Then he offered a revised version of his *Abrams* expression of confidence in the marketplace of ideas. In this sober and cynical statement, Holmes seems to say, "Frankly, my fellow citizens, I just don't give a damn," after the fashion of his philosophical utterance, "Greatest fool of all, thou, not to see that man's destiny is to fight."[30] Having decided, in *Abrams*, to protect freedom of speech, Holmes takes the position that "the only meaning of free speech" is to allow whatever results from the "marketplace of ideas," even if the result is to shut down free government altogether and, with it, all markets, in goods and in ideas, and all other freedoms.

In *Whitney* on the other hand, Brandeis discusses free speech's importance for republican, or democratic, government, a decidedly Madisonian position. That the end of government, including democracy, is to make men free to develop their faculties resembles Spinoza, and one commentator has linked it to Thucydides' account of Pericles' Funeral Oration.[31] The reference to the discovery and spread of political truth is more akin to Spinoza and Montesquieu, as well as to the Declaration of Independence, than to Mill's or either of Holmes's open-ended formulations regarding what gets accepted in a "marketplace of ideas." In other parts of his opinion, Brandeis emphasizes the importance of the terms "clear" and "present," as well as the degree of evil that is involved. He also cites Hand's *Masses* opinion when he asserts the need to be certain about the advocacy. And because "clear and present danger" was a constitutional rule, Brandeis indicates that it must be examined by the Court, that deference to a legislature, especially regarding an entire class of speech, is inappropriate.

When Brandeis referred to the importance of time for discussion to expose falsehoods through more speech, he emphasized an essential feature of liberal democratic government: reliance on consent of the governed. His perspective was that of an active citizen as judge, not as an observer whose speculative thought tells him that there is no reason in human affairs.

The major sedition cases that arose out of World War II involved the Smith Act, which was passed as a rider to the Alien Registration Act of 1940.[32] Modeled after New York's criminal anarchy statute, the Smith Act made it unlawful to: (1) advocate or teach the duty of overthrowing the government by force or violence; (2) organize or become a member of any society which taught the violent overthrow of government; or (3) conspire to commit any of the above acts.[33] The petitioners in the first case were found guilty, in 1948, of organizing the Communist Party and willfully advocating the duty of overthrowing the government of the United States by force and violence. In 1951, the Supreme Court affirmed the convictions 6–2, in *Dennis v United States*.[34] Chief Justice Vinson's opinion, which announced the judgment but only received four votes, claimed to follow Justices Holmes and Brandeis and the clear and present danger test. The version Chief Justice Vinson and three other Justices followed, however, came from Learned Hand, then chief judge on the Court of Appeals for the Second Circuit. Bound to apply the "clear and present danger" test, Hand had written: "In each case [courts] must ask whether the gravity of the 'evil,' discounted by its improbability, justifies such invasion of free speech as is necessary to avoid the danger."[35] While this was a plausible attempt to combine considerations of degree of evil with proximity and likelihood of occurrence, it effectively read proximity out of the formula and allowed the risk of violent revolution, regardless of the probability, to control the outcome. That is why Justices Frankfurter and Jackson, concurring in the *Dennis* decision, refused to join in the Chief Justice's opinion.

Justice Frankfurter took the position that "the demands of free speech in a democratic society as well as the interest in national security are better served by candid and informed weighing of the competing interests, within the confines of the judicial process, than by announcing dogmas too inflexible for the non-Euclidean problems to be solved."[36] But for Frankfurter, judicial balancing gives substantial weight to the legislative judgment, even on First Amendment matters.[37] Yet, according to Thomas Emerson, when the Smith Act rider was added to the Alien Registration Bill in 1940, little attention was paid to it, in Congress or in the press. The rider was passed, he suggested, because members of Congress did not want to vote against a bill directed at outlawing the Communist Party.[38] Frankfurter's balancing thus amounted to judicial abdication in the name of self-restraint.

Earlier in his opinion, Justice Frankfurter described the defendants as having been "convicted of conspiring to organize a party of persons who advocate the overthrow of the Government by force and violence... On any scale of values which we have hitherto recognized, speech of this sort ranks low."[39] Notwithstanding this straightforward condemnation of the prohibited speech, Frankfurter expressed reservations, similar to Hand's, about a law that criminally punishes such speech:

A public interest is not wanting in granting freedom to speak their minds even to those who advocate the overthrow of the Government by force. For, as the evidence in this case abundantly illustrates, coupled with such advocacy is criticism of defects in our society. . . . It is commonplace that there may be a grain of truth in the most uncouth doctrine, however false and repellant the balance may be. Suppressing advocates of overthrow inevitably will also silence critics who do not advocate overthrow but fear that their criticism may be so construed. No matter how clear we may be that the defendants now before us are preparing to overthrow our Government at the propitious moment, it is self-delusion to think that we can punish them for their advocacy without adding to the risks run by loyal citizens who honestly believe in some of the reforms these defendants advance. It is a sobering fact that in sustaining the convictions before us we can hardly escape restriction on the interchange of ideas.

We must not overlook the value of that interchange. Freedom of expression is the well-spring of our civilization—the civilization we seek to maintain and further by recognizing the right of Congress to put some limitation upon expression. Such are the paradoxes of life. For social development of trial and error, the fullest possible opportunity for the free play of the human mind is an indispensable prerequisite. The history of civilization is in considerable measure the displacement of error which once held sway as official truth by beliefs which in turn have yielded to other truths. Therefore, the liberty of man to search for truth ought not to be fettered, no matter what orthodoxies he may challenge. Liberty of thought soon shrivels without freedom of expression. Nor can truth be pursued in an atmosphere hostile to the endeavor or under dangers which are hazarded only by heroes.[40]

Frankfurter's first argument resembles Spinoza's and Madison's concerning the risks of suppressing opinions; his second argument, concerning the displacement of error, follows Mill.

Justice Jackson also concurred in the *Dennis* judgment, but he regarded the "clear and present danger" test as inappropriate for the threat posed by the Communist party. To Jackson, the application of conspiracy law, which does not require an overt act, was appropriate in this case because the right to engage in all acts preparatory to an actual attempt at armed overthrow would be too dangerous.[41] Jackson's position has not been followed, although it resembles Tocqueville's warning that freedom of association is more dangerous than freedom of the press.[42]

On the dissenting side, Justice Black called the law a prior restraint,[43] and he called for a jury determination of "clear and present danger."[44] Justice Douglas also dissented, asserting his confidence in the marketplace of ideas: "Full and free discussion even of ideas we hate encourages the testing of our own prejudices and preconceptions."[45] But his account oversimplified the contest. After listing the chief works containing the doctrines of Marxism, including the *Communist Manifesto*, Justice Douglas wrote: "Those books are to Soviet Communism what *Mein Kampf* is to Nazism. If they are understood, the ugliness of Communism is revealed, its deceit and cunning are exposed, the nature of its activities becomes apparent, and the chances of its success less likely."[46] Justice Douglas did not take the *Communist Manifesto* seriously. Its error lies not in deceit so much as in asserting the inevitability and desirability of dispensing with government in any form as the condition for the realization of full freedom. If what Marx claimed to be inevitable is not, and if challenging good government in the name of perfect justice risks a great deal, Marxism may be dangerous precisely because it appears to be so attractive to lovers of liberty. The seemingly attractive end—"the free development of each is the condition for the free development of all"—causes people to look with favor on the not so temporary dictatorship of the proletariat, which we know amounted to ruthless totalitarianism.

Notwithstanding Justice Douglas's misplaced confidence, the Smith Act's reach was substantial, especially if membership in the Communist Party of the United States often connoted a political preference without any commitment to violent action. The resolution of the problem posed by the Smith

Act's outlawing of the Communist Party occurred six years later when the Supreme Court used a slight variation in a trial judge's instructions to the jury to reinterpret the reach of the statute. As a result, more than mere membership in the Party was required to uphold a conviction. In his Court opinion in *Yates v United States*, Justice Harlan distinguished between "advocacy of forcible overthrow as an abstract doctrine and advocacy of action to that end."[47] The previous distinction, from *Gitlow*, had been between advocacy of violence and teaching Marxism. Now, the Marxist doctrine of violent revolution was termed "abstract advocacy," in contrast to some overt step in preparation for the revolution, such as offering courses in sabotage and street fighting. The Court did not go so far as to say that a concrete action leading to the overthrow of the Government was necessary, but it did hold that something more than mere membership was required in order to satisfy the advocacy of action requirement.[48] While some of the defendants' cases were remanded, the trial judge dismissed them and after *Yates* no new prosecutions were instituted.[49]

Then, in 1969, the Supreme Court articulated a clear speech test as it overturned convictions against the Ku Klux Klan under Ohio's criminal syndicalism act in *Brandenburg v Ohio*.[50] That act, like the one upheld in *Whitney*, punished the advocacy of the duty or propriety of violence or terrorism. Here, members of the Klan held a rally and made vulgar threats to blacks and Jews. The Court overturned the Ohio law (and hence reversed *Whitney*) after stating the following test: "[T]he constitutional guarantees of free speech and free press do not permit a State to forbid or proscribe advocacy of the use of force or of law violation except where such advocacy is directed to inciting or producing imminent lawless action and is likely to incite or produce such action."[51]

This remains our constitutional standard for sedition, or subversive speech. Gerald Gunther described the doctrine as "a coalescing of the best features of the two contending approaches," referring to Hand's objective requirement of "incitement" and Holmes's clear and present danger.[52] It also reflects the contributions of Brandeis and Harlan. While it may be too speech-protective in cases involving militia preparing for violent action, its chief virtue as applied to political groups is that it takes into account the tendency among people to "blow off steam" without necessarily meaning everything they say. This was certainly true with the Communist Party, which many people in this country joined without intending to become hardcore revolutionaries. The best justification, then, for this speech-protective test has nothing to do with a desire to see truth win out in the marketplace. Rather, it is part of democratic freedom to allow a certain amount of loose talk. To try to stop it, on the grounds that the object of even such abstract advocacy is beyond the principles of liberal democracy, is likely to have a chilling effect on freedom and to anger well-meaning people.

The test seems to work best when it protects excessive or immoderate speech or association that is not yet truly dangerous. In the *Brandenburg* case, for example, a television reporter had been telephoned and invited to a "rally," which consisted solely of the Klan participants and the newsmen. And six weeks before *Brandenburg*, the Supreme Court overturned a conviction for threatening the life of the president of the United States.[53] An eighteen-year-old who had just received his 1-A draft classification entered into a conversation at a rally at the Washington Monument. He reportedly said: "I am not going. If they ever make me carry a rifle, the first man I want to get in my sights is L. B. J."[54] Reversing the lower courts, the Supreme Court, in a per curiam opinion, decided that under the circumstances the remarks did not constitute a threat against the life of the president:

> We do not believe that the kind of political hyperbole indulged in by petitioner fits within that statutory term [i.e., threat]. . . . We agree here with petitioner that his only offense here was "a kind of very crude offensive method of stating a political opposition to the President." Taken in context, and regarding the expressly conditional nature of the statement and the reaction of the listeners, we do not see how it could be interpreted otherwise.[55]

A more difficult case, however, would involve a form of speech that falls short of direct incitement of violence and yet might well produce it. Gunther has identified this as the "Marc Antony" problem.[56] In his funeral address in Shakespeare's *Julius Caesar*, Antony, who was allowed to speak but admonished that he should not incite the crowd to violence, managed to do just that, but without using the language of direct incitement.

Notes

1. In *Patterson v Colorado*, 205 U.S. 454 (1907) the Court assumed, without deciding whether the First Amendment applied to the states via the Fourteenth Amendment, that the common law rule of "no prior restraint" applied to the free speech clause. 205 U.S. 454, 461–62.

2. Kathleen Sullivan and Gerald Gunther, *Constitutional Law*, 14th ed. (Westbury, N.Y.: Foundation Press, 2001), p. 969; see also Emerson, *The System of Freedom of Speech* (New York: Random House, 1970), p. 62, where the law is cited as Act of June 15, 1917, ch. 30, sec 3, 40 Stat 217, 219, incorporated as amended in 18 USC s2388a. Hereinafter cited as Emerson.

3. 249 U.S. 47 (1919).

4. The defendants claimed that the draft violated the thirteenth amendment's pro-hibition on slavery and involuntary servitude. The Selective Service Act of 1917 was upheld by the Supreme Court in the Selective Draft Law Cases 245 U.S. 366 (1918).

5. 249 U.S. at 52 (1919).

6. *Frohwerk v United States*, 249 U.S. 204, 206 (1919).

7. Id. at 209.

8. *Debs v United States*, 249 U.S. 211, 216 (1919).

9. Id.

10. "If the act (speaking or circulating a paper,) its tendency and the intent with which it is done are the same, we perceive no ground for saying that success alone warrants making the act a crime." Schenck, at 52.

11. Title XII of the Act declared "non–mailable" any publication violating any provision of the Act.

12. *Masses Pub. CO v Patten*, 244 Fed. 535, 540 (S.D. N Y 1917).

13. Hand to Holmes, 22 June 1918, in Gunther, Gerald, "Learned Hand and the Origins of Modern First Amendment Doctrine: Some Fragments of History," Stanford LR vol 27, no. 3, Feb 1975, 756. The reference to the chance encounter is on p. 732.

14. Holmes to Hand, 24 June 1918, in Id. at 757.

15. Hand to Holmes, late March 1919, in Id. at p. 758.

16. Holmes to Hand, April 3, 1919, in Id. at 759.

17. Richard Polenberg discusses the arguments of Ernst Freund and Zachariah Chafee in *Fighting Faiths: The Abrams Case, The Supreme Court, and Free Speech* (New York, Penguin, 1987) pp. 219–24.

18. *Abrams v United States* 240 U.S. 616 (1919).

19. Polenberg, supra note 17, p. 34

20. *Abrams v United States*, 250 U.S. 616, 621 (1919).

21. Id. at 629 (Holmes dissenting).

22. Id. at 630 (Holmes dissenting).

23. 268 U.S. 652 (1925).

24. 274 U.S. 357 (1927).

25. The New York law defined criminal anarchy as "the doctrine that organized government should be overthrown by force and violence." 268 U.S. at 654. The California law defined criminal syndicalism "as any doctrine or precept advocating . . . the commission of crime . . . or unlawful acts of force and violence or unlawful methods of terrorism as a means of accomplishing a change in industrial ownership or control, or effecting any political change," 274 U.S. at 359.

26. This began a process of gradual incorporation, or absorption, of most of the specific provisions on the first eight amendments into the fourteenth amendment's due process clause, which made the provisions applicable against state and federal government. When this process of incorporation was completed, whatever element of federalism might have allowed the states to experiment in ways that the federal

government could not was closed off. This becomes important when we consider the Court's interpretation of the Establishment Clause, in chapters 14 and 15.

27. The opinion reads as a dissent; Brandeis concurred because he found a technical defect in the appeal.

28. *Gitlow v New York*, 268 U.S. 652, 673 (1927) (Holmes dissenting).

29. *Whitney v California*, 274 U.S. 357, 375–76, 377 (1927) (Brandeis concurring).

30. Holmes to Hand, June 24, 1918, in Gunther, supra note 13, p. 757.

31. Vincent Blasi, "The First Amendment and the Ideal of Civic Courage: The Brandeis Opinion in *Whitney v California*" 29 *William and Mary Law Review* 653 (summer 1988); see pp. 686–87.

32. Emerson, p. 110.

33. This is a paraphrase of sections 2 and 3 of the Smith Act, 54 Stat 671, 18 USC s2385, which are quoted in Chief Justice Vinson's opinion in *Dennis v United States* 341 U.S. 494, (1951) at 496.

34. 341 U.S. 494 (1951).

35. 183 F. 2d at 212, quoted in *Dennis* at 510 (1951).

36. Id. at 524–25 (Frankfurter concurring).

37. "It is not for us to decide how we would adjust the clash of interests which this case presents were the primary responsibility for reconciling it ours. Congress has determined that the danger created by advocacy of overthrow justifies the ensuing restriction on freedom of speech. The determination was made after due deliberation, and the seriousness of the congressional purpose is attested by the volume of legislation passed to effectuate the same ends." Id. at 524–25.

38. Emerson, p. 110.

39. Id. at 544–45 (Frankfurter concurring).

40. Id. at 549–50 (Frankfurter concurring).

41. See *Dennis*, p.p. 570–75.

42. "The more I view the independence of the press in its principal effects, the more I convince myself that among the moderns the independence of the press is the capital and so to speak constitutive element of freedom. A people that wants to remain free, therefore, has the right to require that one respect it at all costs. But unlimited freedom of association in political matters cannot be entirely confused with the freedom to write. The former is at once less necessary and more dangerous. A nation can set bounds for it without ceasing to be master of itself; it sometimes must do that to continue to be such." See *Democracy in America*, Mansfield and Winthrop trans., (Chicago: University of Chicago Press, 2000), vol. I, part two, chapter 4, p. 182.

43. But see Emerson, supra, p. 119.

44. Id. 175–76.

45. Id. at 584 (Douglas dissenting).

46. Id. at 584 (Douglas dissenting).

47. *Yates v United States*, 354 U.S. 298, 320 (1957).

48. The Court attempted to distinguish *Dennis* from *Yates* on the ground that the earlier case involved present advocacy of forcible action in the future while Yates involved

a conspiracy to engage in seditious advocacy at some future time. But this was a smoke-screen to conceal the Court's decision to construe the Smith Act narrowly, and thus tacitly reverse *Dennis*.

49. Emerson, p. 124. Four years later, in two related cases involving membership in the Communist Party, the Court clarified its *Yates* opinion by indicating that something more than the abstract teaching of forceful overthrow of the government was necessary to convict anyone under the membership provisions of the Act. See *Scales v United States* 367 U.S. 203 (1967) and *Noto v United States* 367 U.S. 290 (1961).

50. 395 U.S. 444 (1969).

51. 395 U.S. 444, 447.

52. Gunther, Gerald, "Learned Hand and the Origins of Modern First Amendment Doctrine: Some Fragments of History," *Stanford Law Review*, Vol. 27, No. 23, February 1975, p. 722

53. *Watts v United States* 394 U.S. 705 (1969).

54. Id. at 706.

55. Id. at 708. Even this apparently straightforward case divided the court. With Justice Douglas concurring and writing a separate opinion criticizing the statute, a bare majority granted certiorari and reversed the court of appeals. The remaining Justices would have either denied certiorari, upheld the conviction, or heard the case on oral argument. Id at 708.

56. See Sullivan and Gunther, *Constitutional Law*, 14th edition (Westbury, New York: Foundation Press, 2001) p. 983 (commenting on Hand's "incitement" approach).

CHAPTER TEN

The Preferred Position Doctrine and the Categorical Approach to Freedom of Speech: Libel

The development of the speech-protective *Brandenburg* test was part of the Supreme Court's "preferred position" doctrine, which originated in 1938 in response to the rise and fall of substantive due process in the sphere of economic liberty.[1] In a footnote to his Court opinion in *United States v Carolene Products*, Justice Stone introduced what came to be known as the "preferred position" doctrine:

> There may be narrower scope for operation of the presumption of constitutionality when legislation appears on its face to be within a specific prohibition of the Constitution, such as those of the first ten Amendments, which are deemed equally specific when held to be embraced within the Fourteenth.[2]

The Court thus rationalized its continuing deference to legislative judgments in matters affecting regulation of the economy while announcing a more activist stance toward specifically enumerated rights. Subsequent case citations included some of the early free speech cases and two due process liberty cases that became important sources for religious liberty.[3] While the preferred rights were said to be "specific provisions," meaning something more than the Due Process Clause itself, the Court preferred "personal" over property rights. In one case, famous for its view of due process as comprehending those rights that are "of the very essence of a scheme of ordered liberty,"[4] Justice Cardozo contrasted the major criminal procedures of the bill of rights with freedom of thought and speech:

We reach a different plane of social and moral values when we pass to [those guarantees of the Bill of Rights brought within the Fourteenth Amendment] by a process of absorption. These in their origin were effective against the federal government alone. If the [Fourteenth Amendment] has absorbed them, the process of absorption has had its source in the belief that neither liberty nor justice would exist if they were sacrificed. This is true, for illustration, of freedom of thought and speech. Of that freedom one may say that it is the matrix, the indispensable condition, of nearly every other form of [freedom]. Fundamental too in the concept of due process, and so in that of liberty is the thought that condemnation shall be rendered only after trial.[5]

Justice Frankfurter, in an opinion criticizing the Court's "preferred position" doctrine as simplistic, defended Justice Holmes's opinions in a manner that echoed Justice Cardozo:

But since [Holmes] also realized that the progress of civilization is to a considerable extent the displacement of error which once held sway as official truth by beliefs which in turn have yielded to other beliefs, for him the right to search for truth was of a different order than some transient economic dogma. And without freedom of expression, thought becomes checked and atrophied. Therefore, in considering what interests are so fundamental as to be enshrined in the Due Process Clause, those liberties of the individual which history has attested as the indispensable conditions of an open as against a closed society come to this Court with a momentum for respect lacking when appeal is made to liberties which derive merely from shifting economic arrangements. Accordingly, [he] was more ready to find legislative invasion where free inquiry was involved than in the debatable area of economics.[6]

Surely freedom of speech and religious freedom are important, but the underlying distinction between personal rights, which are preferred, and property rights, which are not, seems unsatisfactory. How secure would we be without protection for our property? Madison himself wrote, in 1792, that we have a property in our rights as well as a right to property.[7] Rather than balance the merits of a government regulation against the harm to free speech in each case, the Court developed an approach called "definitional balancing."[8] The "balancing" takes place at the determination of which speech is important enough to merit protection and which is not. The cases that have already been discussed are identified with "incitement to violent action"; this is one of the unprotected categories.

This "categorical approach" to free speech cases arose out of *Chaplinsky v New Hampshire*,[9] decided in 1942. The case involved a street corner confrontation between Chaplinsky, who was a member of the Jehovah's Witnesses, citizens of Rochester, and the city marshal. Chaplinksy was distributing literature and "denouncing all religion as a racket." When others complained, Marshall Bowering told them that Chaplinksy was lawfully engaged, and he told Chaplinsky that the crowd was getting restless. Later when a disturbance occurred, a traffic officer started with Chaplinsky toward the police station, without telling him whether he was under arrest. On the way, they met Bowering, who was hurrying to the scene of the disturbance, now called a riot. When Bowering repeated his warning to Chaplinksy, the latter replied, according to the complaint, "You are a God damned racketeer [and] a damned Fascist and the whole government of Rochester are Fascists or agents of Fascists."[10] Chaplinsky claimed that Bowering cursed him first—when he asked the marshal to arrest the others—and that he then replied in kind. Chaplinksy was convicted for violating a New Hampshire law that prohibited any person from addressing "any offensive, derisive, or annoying word to any other person who is lawfully in any street or other public place."[11] The Court dispensed with the religious freedom claim[12] and then addressed the free speech claim. After noting that "the right of free speech is not absolute at all times and under all circumstances," Justice Murphy wrote:

> There are certain well-defined and narrowly limited classes of speech, the prevention and punishment of which have never been thought to raise any Constitutional problem. These include the lewd and obscene, the profane, the libelous, and the insulting or "fighting" words—those which by their very utterance inflict injury or tend to incite an immediate breach of the peace. It has been well observed that such utterances are no essential part of any exposition of ideas, and are of such slight social value as a step to truth that any benefit that may be derived from them is clearly outweighed by the social interest in order and morality.[13]

Justice Murphy then quoted from an earlier state court decision explaining the meaning of the statute:

> The word "offensive" is not to be defined in terms of what a particular addressee thinks. . . . The test is what men of common intelligence would understand would be words likely to cause an average addressee to fight. . . . The English language has a number of words and expressions which by general consent are "fighting words" when said without a disarming smile. . . . Such words, ordinary men know, are likely to cause a fight.[14]

The Court found the statute narrowly drawn and not in violation of freedom of speech; the epithets "damned racketeer" and "damned Fascist" came under the "fighting words" category.

The first significant revision of an excluded category of speech involved libel. Until the Supreme Court's landmark *New York Times v Sullivan* decision,[15] libel was entirely unprotected speech. The case is famous for showing how the operation of ordinary libel laws can, in certain cases, have the effect of seditious libel laws.

On March 29, 1960, the *Times* published a ten-paragraph political advertisement, "Heed Their Rising Voices," which described civil rights demonstrations by "Southern Negro students" and the hostile reactions from government authorities in several southern cities. The account for Montgomery, Alabama, was generally correct but not in every detail. This is how Justice Brennan, author of the Court opinion, described the errors:

> Although Negro students staged a demonstration, on the State Capitol steps, they sang the National Anthem and not "My Country 'Tis of Thee." Although nine students were expelled by the State Board of Education, this was not for leading the demonstration at the Capitol, but for demanding service at a lunch counter in the Montgomery County Courthouse on another day. Not the entire student body, but most of it, had protested the expulsion, not by refusing to register, but by boycotting classes on a single day; virtually all the students did register for the ensuing semester. The campus dining hall was not padlocked on any occasion, and the only students who may have been barred from eating there were the few who had neither signed a preregistration application nor requested temporary meal tickets. Although the police were deployed near the campus in large numbers on three occasions, they did not at any time "ring" the campus, and they were not called to the campus in connection with the demonstration on the State Capitol steps, as the third paragraph implied. Dr. King had not been arrested seven times, but only four; and although he claimed to have been assaulted some years earlier in connection with his arrest for loitering outside a courtroom, one of the officers who made the arrest denied that there was such an assault.[16]

Mr. L. B. Sullivan, while not named, was the City Commissioner in charge of the police. He first demanded a full retraction from the *Times*. As a public official, he was required by Alabama law to do this before he could bring a libel action. When the *Times* responded by writing to ask Sullivan in what way he thought any of the statements had reflected on him, Sullivan filed suit. Sullivan sued the *Times* and the ad sponsors for general and punitive damages, claiming that people would know he was responsible for the behavior of the police. The state law allowed the trial judge to submit the case to the jury on the instructions that the statements made were "libelous per se," which meant that legal injury could be implied from publication and falsity, and malice could be "presumed." The jury awarded Sullivan a

$500,000 judgment against the *Times*, without differentiating between compensatory and punitive damages. Punitive damages required a proof of malice, but the state supreme court held that malice could be inferred from the *Times*'s having printed information in the advertisement that it knew, from its news files, was false.

According to the writer Anthony Lewis, Herbert Wechsler, whom the *Times* brought in to represent it after having lost in the state courts, had to persuade the newspaper to make the constitutional argument. Wechsler's associate on the case, Marvin E. Frankel, suggested that the effect of ordinary libel law as Alabama used it in this case was the same as seditious libel in the eighteenth century. This argument persuaded the *Times*, whose previous policy was to fight libel cases but to accept negative judgments when an error occurred, to press the argument that the First Amendment's Freedom of Speech Clause applied to libel cases.[17]

When Madison first thought hard about the question of free speech, he did not express confidence in truth's eventual victory, nor did he think that a freedom to print the truth was a sufficient guarantee for a press that was to act as the people's watchdog over its government. The Supreme Court recognized this in its unanimous decision in *Sullivan*. Justice Brennan's majority opinion quoted from Justice Brandeis's *Whitney* opinion on the importance of free speech and added: "Thus we consider this case against the background of a profound national commitment to the principle that debate on public issues should be uninhibited, robust, and wide-open, and that it may well include vehement, caustic, and sometimes unpleasant sharp attacks on government and public officials."[18] After rejecting errors of fact or injury to official reputation, as insufficient to justify a libel judgment, Justice Brennan drew on Madison's argument against the federal sedition act:

> If neither factual error nor defamatory content suffices to remove the constitutional shield from criticism of official conduct, the combination of the two elements is no less adequate. This is the lesson to be drawn from the great controversy over the Sedition Act of 1799, . . . which first crystallized a national awareness of the central meaning of the First Amendment.[19]

Noting that a public official's ability to win high damage awards without proof of pecuniary damage would chill freedom of the press every bit as much as criminal libel laws, the Court laid down a new constitutional rule:

> The constitutional guarantees require, we think, a federal rule that prohibits a public official from recovering damages for a defamatory falsehood relating to

his official conduct unless he proves that the statement was made with "actual malice"—that is, with knowledge that it was false and with reckless disregard of whether it was false or not.[20]

Justice Brennan elaborated on this a few pages later:

We hold today that the Constitution delimits a State's power to award damages for libel in actions brought by public officials against critics of their official conduct. Since this is such an action, the rule requiring proof of actual malice is applicable. While Alabama law apparently requires proof of actual malice for an award of punitive damages, where general damages are concerned malice is "presumed." Such a presumption is inconsistent with the federal rule.[21]

Applying these new standards to the case, the Court found that "the proof presented to show actual malice lacks the convincing clarity which the constitutional standard demands, and hence . . . would not constitutionally sustain the judgment for respondent under the proper rule of law."[22] The Court also found that the evidence "was incapable of supporting the jury's finding that the allegedly libelous statements were made 'of and concerning' the respondent."[23] To decide otherwise, the Court said, would be to "transmut[e] criticism of government, however impersonal it may seem on its face, into personal criticism, and hence potential libel, of the officials of whom the government is composed."[24] The Supreme Court thus reversed the Alabama courts' decisions by extending constitutional protection to libel against a public official, and then it decided the case before it on the merits, without sending it back to the Alabama courts.

The *Sullivan* case was well received by legal scholars,[25] but it was only the beginning of judicial consideration of libel law and its relation to freedom of speech.[26] While the Court was unanimous in its decision, Justices Black, Douglas, and Goldberg would have gone further and given citizens and the press an unconditional right to criticize government and public officials.[27] Six months after deciding *Times v Sullivan*, the Supreme Court extended the *Sullivan* rule regarding "malice" to criminal libel in *Garrison v Louisiana*.[28] The case introduced an important change in the meaning of malice. Under Louisiana law, which adopted the common law of libel, malice was defined to mean "hatred, ill will or enmity or a wanton desire to injure."[29] This definition could be consistent with a truthful account, whereas the *Times* "malice" standard required a showing of reckless disregard for the truth.

Two years later in *Rosenblatt v Bahr*, the Court reaffirmed the *Times* rule and indicated that "the 'public official' designation applied at the very least to those among the hierarchy of government employees who have, or appear to the public to have, substantial responsibility for or control over the conduct of government affairs."[30]

The following year the Court decided three more cases bearing on the *Times* malice test: *Time v Hill*,[31] *Curtis Publishing Co. v Butts* and *Associated Press v Walker*.[32] The last two, decided together, applied the *Times* malice rule to "public figures."[33] The first case applied the rule to a "false light" privacy case.[34] In the next two libel cases, the Court first extended the *Times* test to all matters of general interest, in *Rosenbloom v Metromedia*,[35] and then retreated from that position to reaffirm the "public figure" line for that test, in *Gertz v Welch*.[36] Then the Court held that the First Amendment did not extend any protection to libel of a private individual concerning a private matter.[37] In its final case on this topic, *Hustler Magazine v Falwell*, the Court held that the *Times* test did apply to a public figure's suit for intentional infliction of emotional distress.[38]

In these cases the Court considered, as Kalven pointed out, "the ambit of constitutional protection" and "the *level* of protection."[39] On the more controversial second issue, the advocates of extending the *Times* test to public figures were in the middle. Justices Black and Douglas advocated, in *Sullivan*, complete immunity for the press from libel judgments, while Justices Harlan, Clark, Stewart, and Fortas (in *Butts* and *Walker*) advocated a somewhat less rigorous standard for public figures than the *Times* test: highly unreasonable conduct, or, as Kalven put it, gross negligence.[40] In addition, Justice Harlan advocated that a private individual, such as Hill, whose privacy was invaded by a report of an incident that was presented as accurate but had been changed, only had to meet the "mere negligence" standard.[41] The *Gertz* and *Hustler* cases deserve detailed attention because of their importance for the development of libel law.

Petitioner Elmer Gertz represented the family of a youth named Nelson in civil litigation against a Chicago policeman named Nuccio. Nuccio shot and killed Nelson and was subsequently convicted of second degree murder. Respondent Welch published *American Opinion*, a monthly journal expressing the views of the John Birch Society. In March 1969, Welch published an article that he had commissioned entitled "FRAME-UP: Richard Nuccio and the War on Police." The article made several false statements about Gertz: it stated that he had been an official in the "Marxist League for Industrial Democracy"; it labeled him a "Leninist" and a "Communist-fronter"; it falsely implied that Gertz had a criminal record; and it correctly stated that Gertz had been an officer in the National Lawyers Guild but then it falsely alleged that that organization had taken part in planning the demonstrations at the 1968 Democratic National Convention in Chicago.[42] Gertz sued for defamation in federal district court. Welch argued that Gertz was a public figure and since he did not know the information was false, the First Amendment protected his publication under the *Times* standard. The district court first ruled that Gertz was not a public figure and that therefore the *Times* standard did not apply. The judge ruled that some of the statements were "libel per se;"[43] the case went to the jury, which awarded Gertz $50,000. The judge then reconsidered and decided that the *Times* standard should apply since the discussion involved a public issue; he entered a judgment for Welch, notwithstanding the jury verdict. The court of appeals affirmed the district court's decision, citing the Supreme Court's *Rosenbloom* decision as precedent. In *Rosenbloom*, a plurality of the Court applied the *Times* standard in all cases concerning a public interest. The appeals court agreed with the district court that the petitioner had failed to show with "clear and convincing evidence" that respondent acted with "actual malice" as defined by *Sullivan*.[44]

The Supreme Court reversed. Justice Powell's opinion for the court, joined by Justices Stewart, Marshall, Blackmun, and Rehnquist, held that a private citizen need not prove malice to win a libel judgment, as long as he proves liability and harm, and that Gertz was not a public figure.[45] Justices Brennan and Douglas dissented, maintaining that the decision did not protect free speech enough. Justice Brennan favored the *Rosenbloom* plurality approach. Justice Douglas reiterated his position that the press should enjoy absolute immunity in all matters of public concern. On the other side, Justices Burger and White both dissented from that part of the decision that required a finding of fault, meaning negligence at least, and actual harm for any defamation suit to succeed. They also dissented from the majority's limiting general and punitive damages to cases that satisfied the *Times* standard for "malice," or reckless disregard of the truth.[46]

Justice Powell's opinion described the reason for the Court's decision this way:

> We begin with the common ground. Under the First Amendment there is no such thing as a false idea. However pernicious an opinion may seem, we depend for its correction not on the conscience of judges and juries but on the competition of other ideas [He cites Jefferson's First Inaugural here.]. But there is no constitutional value in false statements of fact. Neither the intentional lie nor the careless error materially advances society's interest in "uninhibited, robust, and wide-open" debate on public issues.[47]

Justice Powell's contention that there are no false ideas resembles Justice Jackson's statement that there is no orthodoxy, at least none that can be required.[48] The distinction between facts and opinions reflects the twofold interest in giving speech adequate "breathing room," not only in matters concerning criticism of government but in matters of public interest generally, and in protecting an individual's reputation against defamation. In order to protect the press against the "chilling effect" of a fear of large damage judgments, the Court is willing to protect "false facts" in certain cases. The majority is satisfied with the *Times* standard for public officials and public figures and the negligence standard for others. In the former two cases, the individuals have access to the media, and they have committed themselves to the public arena. Neither is the case for private individuals, and therefore the press is required to be more careful, to exercise reasonable care in its reporting when potentially defamatory material is involved. The limited and instrumental protection that is afforded "false facts" is reflected in a later Supreme Court case involving a private individual and a private matter. When a private credit report erroneously claimed that a construction contractor had filed for bankruptcy, that individual received compensatory and punitive damages. The Supreme Court upheld the judgment notwithstanding the fact that there was no showing of "actual malice." In his opinion announcing the judgment of the Court, Justice Powell wrote: "In light of the reduced constitutional value of speech involving no matters of public concern, we hold that the state interest adequately supports awards of presumed damages and punitive damages—even absent a showing of 'actual malice.'"[49]

The final case in the *New York Times* progeny involves the tort of intentional infliction of emotional distress. Moral majority leader Jerry Falwell was mercilessly parodied in an ad in Hustler Magazine. Utilizing the double entendre format of Campari ads, the Hustler parody had Falwell reporting that his "first time" "was during a drunken incestuous rendezvous with his mother in an outhouse." At the bottom of the spoof ad was the disclaimer: "ad parody—not to be taken seriously."[50] That was enough for the Supreme Court to overturn the compensatory and punitive damage awards that Falwell won at trial, which the court of appeals affirmed. Writing for a unanimous court, Justice Rehnquist combined the fact that Falwell was a public figure with "the fundamental importance of the free flow of ideas and opinions on matters of public interest and concern" to apply the *New York Times* test and reverse.[51] The parody was likened to political cartoons, whose aim is to ridicule. Granting that the Hustler ad was "at best a distant cousin of the political cartoons described above,"[52] Justice Rehnquist found no standard for distinguishing the outrageous from the rest. The Court's application of the *Times* standard and the distinctively speech-protective definition of "malice" produced this result.

Thus, in the name of "a profound national commitment to the principle that debate on public issues should be uninhibited, robust, and wide-open," the Supreme Court extended the *New York Times* standard regarding malice to public figures as well as public officials, and the standard applied to intentional inflictions of emotional distress as well as defamation suits.[53] Justice Powell's *Gertz* statement about false opinions and false facts explained why the negligence standard sufficed in cases involving private individuals.

Both Justice Powell's statement and Justice Jackson's in the flag salute case reflect what have come to be known as the doctrines of content and viewpoint neutrality. The term was used in *Police Department v Mosley*, decided in 1972. In that case, the Supreme Court invalidated a Chicago disorderly conduct ordinance that barred picketing within 150 feet of a school, but which exempted "peaceful picketing of any school involved in a labor dispute."[54] Justice Marshall wrote for a unanimous Court that the ordinance's "central problem" concerned its description of permissible picketing in terms of its "subject matter."[55] A later case, which will be discussed later, distinguishes between content and viewpoint discrimination and argues that the latter is the worrisome kind.[56] But Justice Marshall explained the Court's decision in terms that address both forms.

> Above all else, the First Amendment means that government has no power to restrict expression because of its message, its ideas, its subject matter, or its content. To permit the continued building of our politics and culture, and to assure self-fulfillment for each individual, our people are guaranteed the right to express any thought, free from government censorship.[57]

The "self-development" rationale for protecting speech goes together with skepticism about government's ability to make valid subject matter distinctions when it comes to regulations of speech. As the Supreme Court increasingly protects freedom of speech, its expressed faith in truth winning out in the marketplace of ideas competes with an increasing doubt concerning the significance of truth for liberal politics. On the one hand, freedom of speech is the ground for free government and the condition for every other form of freedom. But on the other hand, there is no orthodoxy because there is no such thing as a false idea. The reason for extending the sphere of protected speech apparently has less to do with confidence in the truth's winning out in any objective sense and more to do with a commitment to freedom, in terms of both self government and individual autonomy. In addition, the Court doubts that legislatures or executives will be able to make and enforce justifications for making subject matter, and especially viewpoint-based, classifications on a principled basis.

Notes

1. During the period that is identified with the Court's *Lochner* decision 198 U.S. 45 (1905), from 1905 to 1937, the Due Process Clauses of the Fifth and Fourteenth Amendments were interpreted to protect a very strong "liberty of contract." When the Court reversed itself and became more accepting of government regulations of the economy, it maintained a closer scrutiny over other rights.

2. Id. at 152.

3. The free speech cases included *Gitlow* and *Whitney*; the due process cases were *Pierce v Society of Sisters* 268 U.S. 510 (1925), and *Meyer v Nebraska* 262 U.S. 390 (1923). In *Meyer* the Court struck down a law which punished a teacher for teaching German and thus violated a state law prohibiting the teaching of foreign languages; and in *Pierce*, the Court struck down an Oregon law that required students to attend public school. Justice McReynolds, who wrote both Court opinions, presented a broad view of liberty in the first case.

4. *Palko v Connecticut*, 302 U.S. 319, 325 (1937).

5. Id. at 326.

6. *Kovacs v Cooper*, 336 U.S. 77, 95 (1949).

7. Essay on Property, in the *National Gazette*, March 29, 1792, in *The Mind of the Founder: Sources of the Political Thought of James Madison*, ed. by Marvin Meyers (Indianapolis, Bobbs Merrill, 1973) p. 244. ("In a word, as a man is said to have a right to his property, he may be equally said to have a property in his rights.")

8. See Nimmer, "The Right to Speak from Times to Time: First Amendment Theory Applied to Libel and Misapplied to Privacy," in 56 *Calif.L.Rev* 935 (1968). pp. 942ff.

9. 315 U.S. 569 (1942).

10. Id. at 569.

11. Id.

12. "[W]e cannot conceive that cursing a public officer is the exercise of religion in any sense of the term," at Id. 571.

13. Id. at 571–72.

14. Id. at 573. Harry Kalven called this the "judicial ratification of the well-known bon mot from Owen Wistar's *The Virginian*, 'When you call me that, smile.'" See Kalven, *A Worthy Tradition: Freedom of Speech in America*, p. 17.

15. 376 U.S. 254 (1964).

16. Id. at 258–59.

17. See Lewis, Anthony, *Make No Law: The Sullivan Case and the First Amendment*, (New York, Vintage Books, 1992), 106–67.

18. 376 U.S. at 271.
19. Id. 273.
20. Id. 279–80.
21. Id. 283–84.
22. Id. 285–86.
23. Id. 288.
24. Id. 292.
25. Harry Kalven concluded his essay on the case by reporting and joining in Alexander Meiklejohn's opinion that the decision was "an occasion for dancing in the streets," and by suggesting that the Court should go further. See "The New York Times Case: A Note on 'The Central Meaning of the First Amendment,'" in Philip Kurland, ed., *Free Speech and Association: The Supreme Court and the First Amendment* (Chicago, University of Chicago Press), 1975, 114, hereinafter Kurland, *Free Speech*.
26. No Justice discussed the case of a private individual's suing for libel, although Justice Brennan did reserve the question concerning "the boundaries of the 'official conduct' concept," 376 at 283, note 23.
27. See their concurring opinions in Id. at 293 and 298.
28. 379 U.S. 75 (1966).
29. *Garrison v Louisiana* 379 U.S. 64, 78 (1964).
30. 383 U.S. 75, 85 (1966).
31. 385 U.S. 374 (1967).
32. 388 U.S. 130 (1967).
33. The justification for the extension was that public figures had access to the news media "to expose through discussion the falsehood and fallacies of defamatory statements." *Curtis v Butts* 388 U.S. 130, 155 (internal quotation omitted).
34. "False light" refers to an inaccurate representation. In the case, *Life Magazine* published an account of a play—based on a novel—which depicted the Hill family's experience when escaped convicts held them as hostages. While in fact the family was released unharmed, without any violence having occurred, the novel included considerable violence, as did the play, and this was reported as true in the *Life* article. For a full description, see the syllabus to the case 385 U.S. 374.
35. 403 U.S. 29 (1971).
36. 418 U.S. 323 (1974).
37. *Dun and Bradstreet v Greenmoss Builders* 472 U.S. 749 (1985).
38. *Hustler Magazine v Falwell* 485 U.S. 46 (1988).
39. Kalven, Harry, Jr., "The Reasonable Man and the First Amendment: Hill, Butts, and Walker," in Kurland, supra, note 25, p. 218.
40. Id. at 238. See also *Rosenblatt* at 155.
41. *Time v Hill*, 385 at 406–9. The incident is described in note 34 above.
42. This comes from Justice Powell's Court opinion in *Gertz v Welch*, 418 U.S. 323, 326 (1974).
43. This means that no special damage needs to be shown. The law presumes that anyone so slandered has suffered damage.

44. 418 U.S. at 328–32.

45. Id. at 345–7, 351–52.

46. See especially Justice White's dissent at id. 365–77. Chief Justice Burger agreed with much of what Justice White states," at id. 355.

47. Id. at 339–40 (1974).

48. *West Virginia State Board of Education v Barnette*, 319 U.S. 624, 634 (1943).

49. *Dun and Bradstreet v Greenmoss Builders*, 472 U.S. 749, 761 (1985). Justices Rehnquist and O'Connor concurred in the opinion. Chief Justice Burger and Justice White concurred in the judgment that *Gertz* did not apply; they did not join Justice Powell's opinion because they disagreed with the *Gertz* limitations on presumed and punitive damages. Dissenting Justices Brennan, Marshall, Blackmun, and Stevens would have applied the *Gertz* limitations in this case as well.

50. *Hustler Magazine, Inc. v Falwell*, 485 U.S. 46 (1988). Chief Justice Rehnquist describes the ad in his Court opinion at 48.

51. Id. 50, 57.

52. Id. 55.

53. *Gertz* 361–62.

54. 408 U.S. 92 (1972).

55. Id. 95.

56. *R. A. V v St. Paul* 505 U.S. 377 (1992).

57. In *Mosley* 408 U.S. at 95–96.

CHAPTER ELEVEN

The Increased Protection for "Fighting Words" and Other "Offensive Speech": Obscenity, Pornography, and Commercial Speech

In this chapter, I examine the Supreme Court's expansion of free speech protection in areas that it first identified as categorically excluded: "fighting words"—including "offensive" expression (verbal and symbolic)—obscenity and pornography, and commercial speech. The Court's justifications invoke individual autonomy more than either self-government or the quest for truth. In that respect, the cases reflect the Court's inclusion of Mill's interest in individual autonomy within the ambit of the First Amendment's free speech protection.

"Fighting Words"

The Court limited the "fighting words" doctrine in *Terminiello v Chicago*, an important "hostile audience" case decided in 1949.[1] Terminiello delivered a lecture in an auditorium under the auspices of the Christian Veterans of America. With over eight hundred people in the auditorium and a thousand protesting outside, Terminiello spoke passionately and crudely against Communists and Jews.[2] He was found guilty of a breach of the peace after the trial judge instructed the jury that the statute covered speech that "stirs the public to anger, invites dispute, brings about a condition of unrest, and creates dissatisfaction with conditions as they are, or even stirs people to anger."[3] The Court reversed, 5 to 4. In his opinion for the court, Justice Douglas emphasized the importance of free discussion. "Accordingly, a function of free speech under our system of government is to invite dispute. It may indeed best serve its high purpose when it induces a condition of unrest, creates dissatisfaction with conditions as they are, or even stirs people to anger."[4] Dissenting, Justice Jackson argued that the trial court "was dealing with a riot and with a speech that provoked a hostile mob and incited a friendly one, which threatened violence between the two."[5]

The case was difficult because political speech was involved and the audience presented what Harry Kalven called the "heckler's veto" problem.[6] The notion that speech serves a high purpose by creating unrest and dissatisfaction requires civil society to tolerate every form of expression short of direct incitement to violence.

Cohen v California, decided in 1971, was an important case for the expansion of coarse, or emotive, expression, and thus a narrowing of the excepted category of "fighting words." Justice Harlan, who wrote the Court opinion, described the case as "at first blush too inconsequential to find its way into our books."[7] (It also was the first time that the "F word" was published in the United States Reports.) On April 26, 1968, Robert Paul Cohen was observed in the corridor of the Los Angeles County Courthouse wearing a jacket on which the words "Fuck the Draft" were plainly visible.[8] He was convicted in municipal court of "maliciously and willfully disturb[ing] the peace . . . by . . . offensive conduct," and was sentenced to thirty days in prison.[9] The court of appeals affirmed the conviction. It held that offensive conduct means "behavior which has a tendency to provoke others to acts of violence or to in turn disturb the peace" and that the state had proven this element against Cohen.[10] Cohen, who wore the jacket to convey the depth of his feelings against the Vietnam War, argued that the statute as applied infringed on his First Amendment rights.

Justice Harlan began by describing what was *not* involved in the case. The case involved words, not conduct, and it did not fall within "those relatively few categories" that are unprotected. The words were not obscene, because they were not erotic. Moreover, they were not "fighting words," because they were not directed to any particular person, nor was there any showing that anyone was violently aroused.[11] This treatment of "fighting words" anticipated a Supreme Court decision the following year, in *Gooding v Wilson*.[12] In that case the category was narrowed to include only words that have a "direct tendency to cause acts of violence by the person to whom, individually, the remark is addressed."[13] The other part of the *Chaplinsky* definition of "fighting words," "those [words] which by their very utterance inflict injury," was silently dropped.[14]

In the second part of his *Cohen* opinion, Justice Harlan asked whether California could "excise, as 'offensive conduct,' one particular scurrilous epithet from the public discourse," either because it is likely to cause violence or on the paternalistic grounds that states, "acting as guardians of public morality, may properly remove this offensive word from the public vocabulary."[15] He rejected the first ground, which he had implicitly ruled out already, by saying that there was no evidence of citizens standing ready to strike out at Cohen. He recognized that the second ground had some weight, but he rejected it also, citing Justice Brandeis's statement that "the constitutional right of free expression is powerful medicine in a society as diverse and populous as ours."[16]

> It is designed and intended to remove governmental restraints from the arena of public discussion, putting the decision as to what views shall be voiced largely into the hands of each of us, in the hope that use of such freedom will ultimately produce a more capable citizenry and more perfect polity and in the belief that no other approach would comport with the premise of individual dignity and choice upon which our political system rests.[17]

While this seems to be a stretch, Cohen's crude four-letter word message did express a political opinion. After remarking "that the air may at times seem filled with verbal cacophony is . . . not a sign of weakness but of strength,"[18] Justice Harlan questioned whether criminal law can treat vulgarity:

> For, while the particular four-letter word being litigated here is perhaps more distasteful than most others of its genre, it is nevertheless often true that one man's vulgarity is another's lyric. Indeed, we think it is largely because government officials cannot make principled distinctions in this area that the Constitution leaves matters of taste and style so largely to the individual.[19]

Just as Socrates identified the democratic regime with an indiscriminate love of useful and useless pleasures,[20] so Justice Harlan's democratic citizen cannot distinguish between vulgarity and lyrics. Justice Harlan comes closer to explaining the importance of the decision when he writes that

> much linguistic expression serves a dual communicative function: it conveys not only ideas capable of relatively precise, detached explication, but otherwise inexpressible emotions as well. In fact, words are often chosen as much for their emotive as their cognitive force. We cannot sanction the view that the Constitution, while solicitous of the cognitive content of individual speech, has little or no regard for that emotive function, which, practically speaking, may often be the more important element of the overall message sought to be communicated.[21]

When the Court's deference to emotive expression is combined with its recognition of "symbolic expression," constitutionally protected freedom of speech includes the right to burn the American flag. The key symbolic expression case involved draft card burning.

Two years before *Cohen*, in *United States v O'Brien*, the Supreme Court held that symbolic expression was protected under the First Amendment. On March 31, 1966, David Paul O'Brien and three companions burned their draft cards on the steps of the South Boston Courthouse. This action violated the Universal Military Training and Service Act of 1948, as amended in 1965. The original act required all registrants to keep their certificates in their personal possession "at all times." The 1965 amendment made it an offense if any person "forges, alters, knowingly destroys, knowingly mutilates, or in any manner changes any such [registration] certificate."[22] O'Brien argued that the amendment was unconstitutional because its purpose was to abridge freedom of speech. The district court rejected those arguments but the court of appeals agreed, reversing the conviction and invalidating the amendment. The Supreme Court reversed, holding the amendment constitutional as enacted and applied.[23] After asserting that the amendment did not abridge free speech "on its face," the Court then considered O'Brien's "as applied" argument:

> This Court has held that when "speech" and "non-speech" elements are combined in the same course of conduct, a sufficiently important governmental interest in regulating the non-speech element can justify incidental limitations on First Amendment freedoms. . . . We think it clear that a government regulation is sufficiently justified [1] if it is within the constitutional power of the government; [2] if it furthers an important or substantial governmental interest; [3] if the governmental interest is unrelated to the suppression of free expression; and [4] if the incidental restriction on alleged First Amendment freedoms is no greater than is essential to the furtherance of that interest.[24]

This case turned out to be more important for its recognition of symbolic expression than for its dubious application of the new test to draft card burning.[25] The key question turned out to be whether the governmental interest was or was not related to the suppression of free expression. In an important article, John Hart Ely identified the third part of the test as performing the "switching function": if the governmental interest is related to the suppression of speech, strict scrutiny is applied to the statute, which almost always means it is invalidated; if the governmental interest is not related to the suppression of speech, then some form of balancing takes place, and the statute is likely to survive constitutional review.[26]

From *O'Brien* to Flag Burning

The Supreme Court took more than twenty years before it faced up to the significance of its *O'Brien* test for flag desecration statutes. In the first three cases, convictions for flag burning or some form of misuse of a flag were overturned, without the Court's having to rule directly on the flag burning issue. In the first case, Sidney Street burned his flag and uttered, "We don't need no damn flag," after learning that James Meredith had been shot. The Court held that the statute allowed Street to be punished for "speaking defiant or contemptuous words about the American flag."[27] The second case involved flag abuse: Defendant Goguen wore a version of the flag on his trousers. The Court held that the misuse statute was too broad, especially since "display of the flag is so common and takes so many forms."[28] In the third case, college student Spence attached a peace sign to a flag that he hung from the window of his apartment, to protest the invasion of Cambodia and the killings at Kent State. The Court reversed his conviction under a state misuse statute on the grounds that the flag was private property, that there was no trespass and no breach of the peace, and that Spence engaged in a clear form of communication.[29] The *per curiam* opinion presented a clear account of when symbolic conduct comes under the protection of the First Amendment: "An intent to convey a particularized message was present, and in the surrounding circumstances, the likelihood was great that the message would be understood by those who viewed it."[30] The Court finally confronted flag burning directly in 1989.

Flag Burning I: *Texas v Johnson* (1989)

The Texas "desecration of venerated objects" statute covered public monuments, places of worship or burial, and state or national flags. It defined "desecrate" as "defac[ing], damag[ing], or otherwise physically mistreat[ing] [any of these objects] in a way that the actor knows will seriously offend one or more persons likely to observe or discover his action."[31] While the Republican National Convention was nominating President Reagan in Dallas in 1984, Gregory Lee Johnson participated in a political demonstration. It ended in front of Dallas City Hall, where Johnson unfurled an American flag, doused it with kerosene, and set it on fire. While the flag burned, the protestors chanted, "America the red, white, and blue, we spit on you."[32] No one was injured or threatened, although many reported being seriously offended by the burning of the flag.

Johnson was convicted and sentenced to one year in prison and fined $1,000. The state court of appeals affirmed the conviction, but the court of criminal appeals reversed, on First Amendment grounds. Justice Brennan handed down the Supreme Court opinion affirming that reversal,[33] which was joined by Justices Marshall, Blackmun, Kennedy, and Scalia; Justices Rehnquist, White, O'Connor, and Stevens dissented.

Justice Brennan began his *O'Brien* analysis by determining that Johnson's burning of the flag constituted expressive conduct, under *Spence*. Then he considered whether the state's regulation was related to the suppression of free expression. Addressing the state's interest in preventing breaches of the peace, Justice Brennan noted that no disturbance of the peace actually occurred; he also rejected the state's claim that since the audience had taken serious offense a disturbance was likely to occur.[34] Justice Brennan also distinguished Johnson's expressive conduct from "fighting words."[35] He then finds that the second interest—preserving the flag as a symbol of nationhood and national unity—was related to speech, on the authority of *Spence*, and concluded: "we are thus outside of *O'Brien's* test altogether."[36]

Justice Brennan next considered whether the state's interest in preserving the flag as a symbol of the nation justified the restriction: first, he determines that "strict scrutiny" applies and then, in a longer discussion, he explains why such a law does not pass the strict scrutiny test. The test requires the government to demonstrate (1) a "compelling interest" and (2) there is a lack of alternative means of addressing that interest.

On the first point, Justice Brennan concluded that "strict scrutiny" applies by demonstrating that the law was "content based," and not "content neutral." Johnson "was prosecuted for his expression of dissatisfaction with the policies of this country, expression situated at the core of our First Amendment values."[37] Justice Brennan referred to the language of the Texas law to describe Johnson's act: he was prosecuted for burning the flag "because he knew that his politically charged expression would cause 'serious offense,'" not because the flag "was dirty or torn."[38] Finally, because the question of whether Johnson's treatment of the flag violated the Texas law "depended on the likely communicative impact of his expressive conduct," Justice Brennan found that "this restriction on Johnson's expression is content based" and therefore must be subjected "'to the most exacting scrutiny.'"[39]

When he applied strict scrutiny to the Texas statute, Justice Brennan drew on Justice Jackson's *Barnette* opinion. "If there is a bedrock principle underlying the First Amendment, it is that the Government may not prohibit the expression of an idea simply because society finds the idea itself offensive or disagreeable."[40] Moreover, the combination of protection of symbolic expression plus tolerance for different forms of expression, including offensive speech, meant that it was not enough that Johnson and others may express their opposition to American government in numerous ways besides flag burning.

Justice Brennan remarked that the Government does have "a legitimate interest in making efforts to 'preserv[e] the national flag as an unalloyed symbol of our country,'" as long as it does not use coercion to do so.[41] "Precatory regulations" and recommendations are permitted; use of the criminal law is not. Then, in a burst of Millian and Brandeisian optimism, Justice Brennan urged those who disagree with the flag burners "to persuade them that they are wrong," to wave our own flag, to "salut[e] the flag that burns," and to give "its remains a respectful burial."[42] "We do not consecrate the flag by punishing its desecration, for in doing so we dilute the freedom that this cherished emblem represents."[43]

Chief Justice Rehnquist wrote a long dissenting opinion and included extensive quotations from patriotic poetry to support his contention that the flag is a special symbol of American unity and nationhood. He also used the slogan of the American Revolution ("No taxation without representation") to expound his understanding of American government:

> Those who submitted to government should have some say as to what kind of laws would be passed. Surely one of the high purposes of a democratic society is to legislate against conduct that is regarded as evil and profoundly offensive to the majority of people—whether it be murder, embezzlement, pollution, or flag burning.[44]

Flag burning seems out of place in such company, especially in light of the *Brandenburg* and *Cohen* decisions, and the decision upholding the right of the American Nazi Party to march in Skokie, Illinois, a town with a substantial Jewish population, including survivors of the Nazi concentration camps.[45]

Justice Stevens's dissent maded two points. First, he argues that the question of whether Texas or the federal government "has the power to prohibit the public desecration of the American flag . . . is unique."[46] A country's flag is a symbol of more than "nationhood and national unity," but also of "the ideas that characterize the society that has chosen that emblem as well as the special history that has animated the growth and power of those ideas."[47] Stevens disagreed with the majority's suggestion that this decision will enhance the flag's symbolic importance: "[S]anctioning the public desecration of the flag will tarnish its value—both for those who cherish the ideas for which it waves and for those who desire to don the robes of martyrdom by burning it."[48] In the relatively short time since *Johnson*, Justice Stevens's fears have not been borne out.

Justice Stevens also likened flag burning to putting graffiti on the Washington Monument, or conveying a political message by spray painting the Lincoln Memorial. But these examples can be distinguished from flag burning. Unlike flags, which are many and privately owned, the memorial and the monument are each singular publicly owned objects, and the government can therefore demonstrate a substantial interest in protecting them that is unrelated to the suppression of speech.

On this reasoning, should government not also be able to restrict the expressive activity of the Ku Klux Klan and the American Nazi Party? Those organizations disagree with the fundamental principles of American government, such as equal rights for all. The Court's decisions upholding freedom of speech in those cases go against the arguments of Justice Stevens and Chief Justice Rehnquist here; they also account for the reluctant concurrence of Justice Kennedy as well as Justice Scalia's vote with the majority.

Justice Stevens also argued that the prohibition on flag burning differed significantly from the flag salute requirement of *Barnette* and that the statute did not violate content neutrality, since "the concept of 'desecration' does not turn on the substance of the message the actor intends to convey, but rather on whether those who view the *act* will take serious offense."[49] The flag salute requirement may be different, and yet Justice Jackson's "no orthodoxy" principle, when combined with recognition of symbolic expression, leads to the majority's decision. As for Justice Stevens's "content neutrality" argument, if the object of the law is to protect the flag as a unique symbol of the country, that is not only content based, but also viewpoint based. And, as Justice Brennan pointed out, the *Boos v Barry* decision stands squarely against Justice Stevens's interpretation. In that case, the Court struck down a law that prohibited picketing near foreign embassies where the message conveyed brought any foreign government into "public odium" or "disrepute."[50]

Public opposition to the decision prompted Congressional Hearings on ways to protect the flag.[51] Aware of the difficulty they faced in fashioning a law that would pass constitutional muster, Congress nonetheless passed the Flag Protection Act of 1989. It criminalized the conduct of anyone who "knowingly mutilates, defaces, defiles, burns, maintains on the floor or ground or tramples upon" a United States flag, "except conduct related to the disposal of a 'worn or soiled' flag."[52] In the two resulting cases, the lower courts invalidated the law on the authority of *Johnson*.

The two cases were consolidated on expedited appeal to the Supreme Court, which heard oral argument on May 14, 1990, and handed down its decision just four weeks later, affirming the District Courts by the same 5 to 4 vote that had decided *Johnson* a year earlier. As they had in *Johnson*, Justice

Brennan wrote the Court opinion, and Justice Stevens wrote a dissent. There were no other opinions.

Justice Brennan first declined to reconsider the Court's conclusion in *Johnson* that flag burning enjoys full First Amendment protection. Then he considered whether the Flag Protection Act, which proscribed all "conduct (other than disposal) that damages or mistreats a flag, without regard to the actor's motive, his intended message, or the likely effects of his conduct on onlookers" was distinguishable from the Texas statute, which was directed at acts which "the actor knows will seriously offend onlookers."[53]

The government asserted "an interest in 'protecting the physical integrity of the flag under all circumstances' in order to safeguard the flag's identity 'as the unique and unalloyed symbol of the nation.'" [54] The Court reasoned that the government's objective, to preserve the flag as a symbol of the nation, was not threatened by private acts of destruction but, was "implicated 'only when a person's treatment of the flag communicates [a] message' to others that is inconsistent with those ideals."[55] That made the statute content based.

Justice Brennan concluded that the Flag Protection Act "still suffers from the same fundamental flaw" as the Texas law: "it suppresses expression out of concern for its likely communicative impact."[56] Examined under strict scrutiny, the new law failed the constitutional test just as the previous law had. "We decline the Government's invitation to reassess this conclusion in light of Congress's recent recognition of a purported 'national consensus' favoring a prohibition on flag burning."[57] Regardless of whether such a consensus exists, any suggestion that popular opposition to political expression strengthens the Government's interest in suppressing it "is foreign to the First Amendment."[58]

In his dissent, Justice Stevens restated his arguments from *Johnson*. He also offered the following test:

> Certain methods of expression may be prohibited if (a) the prohibition is supported by a legitimate societal interest that is unrelated to suppression of the ideas the speaker desires to express; (b) the prohibition does not entail any interference with the speaker's freedom to express those ideas by other means; and (c) the interest in allowing the speaker complete freedom of choice among alternative methods of expression is less important than the societal interest supporting the prohibition.[59]

On the first point, Justice Stevens began by identifying two components to the government's interest in the flag: "in times of crisis, it inspires and motivates the average citizen to make personal sacrifices . . . [and] at all times, it serves as a reminder of the paramount importance of pursuing the ideals that characterize our society."[60] For Justice Stevens, "the Government's legitimate interest in preserving the symbolic value of the flag" should trump the "specific content of the flag burner's speech."[61]

The flag burning cases illustrate the significance of content and viewpoint neutrality for freedom of speech in American constitutional law. The justification for this doctrine may appear to be faith in the truth winning out in the marketplace of ideas, if we take Justice Brennan's concluding remarks in *Johnson* at face value. In light of Justice Harlan's Court opinion in *Cohen*, however, the sounder justification is a "lesser of two evils" approach, when government authority, in the form of a criminal law, is directed at crude expression that is likely to offend people. This can be related to "autonomy," or it can be identified with a strong judicial sense (not shared by all the Justices) that because the United States is a free country, crude forms of symbolic expression, if not directed at another person face to face, should be tolerated. The category of "fighting words" still exists, but it has been reduced to something resembling incitement to imminent violence.

Hate Speech

In *R. A. V. v St. Paul*,[62] the Court extended its "viewpoint neutrality" analysis to the unprotected category of "fighting words." The city of St. Paul prosecuted "R. A. V." (the name of the juvenile was withheld for confidentiality) under a Bias Motivated Crime Ordinance for allegedly constructing a crudely made cross and burning it inside the fenced yard of an African-American family.[63] The ordinance made it a misdemeanor for anyone to place "on public or private property any symbol, object, appellation, characterization, or graffiti, including but not limited to, a burning cross or Nazi swastika, which one knows or has reasonable grounds to know arouses anger, alarm, or resentment in others on the basis of race, color, creed, religion, or gender."[64] The state district court found the ordinance in violation of the First Amendment, but the Minnesota Supreme Court reversed, upholding the ordinance by interpreting it to reach no more than unprotected expression under the "fighting words" doctrine.[65]

The United States Supreme Court unanimously reversed, holding the ordinance unconstitutional. Justice Scalia delivered the Court opinion, which Chief Justice Rehnquist, and Justices Kennedy, Souter, and Thomas joined.[66]

Accepting the state's interpretation of the ordinance as limited to "fighting words," Justice Scalia applied the "content neutrality" rule to strike it down. The doctrine had previously been applied to protected speech, which could be indirectly regulated by means of time, place, and manner regulations, or through "secondary effects,"[67] but could not be prohibited. For the first time, the Court majority applied the content neutrality requirement to categories of proscribable speech. Justice Scalia reinterpreted the Court's earlier account of its categorical approach to mean "that these areas of speech can, consistently with the First Amendment, be regulated because of their constitutionally proscribable content (obscenity, defamation, etc.)—not that they are categories of speech entirely invisible to the Constitution, so that they may be made the vehicles for content discrimination unrelated to their distinctively proscribable content."[68] Thus, under *R. A. V.*, it is now impermissible to pick out certain "fighting words" on the basis of content (or especially "viewpoint") for punishment.

The other four justices concurred in the decision because they thought the statute prohibited much protected—as well as unprotected—speech and was therefore fatally "overbroad." Justice White criticized the Court's position, however, by saying that it introduced a prohibition on "under-inclusiveness," that the Court was insisting on an "all or nothing" approach to proscribable speech.[69] And Justice Stevens argued that the Court has not always followed content neutrality and that it should not in this case.[70]

Justice Scalia responded first by arguing that a content neutrality requirement was narrower than under-inclusiveness. Then he argued that content discrimination was permissible when "the basis for [it] consists entirely of the very reason the entire class of speech at issue is proscribable."[71] His first illustration was a state's choosing to prohibit only the most patently offensive of obscenity, when it could prohibit all; that was permissible, but a state's choosing to prohibit "only that obscenity which includes offensive political messages" would not be permitted.[72] Justice Scalia's second example drew on *Watts v United States*, where the Court upheld a federal act criminalizing threats of violence directed against the president.[73] Justice Scalia found this legitimate "under inclusiveness," where criminalizing only those threats "that mention his policy on aid to inner cities" would be invalid.[74] Justice Scalia then argued that content-based classifications are possible where they are associated with "particular 'secondary effects' of the speech which produce harms that can be prohibited." Justice Scalia maintained that content discrimination may be allowed as long as "there is no realistic possibility that official suppression of ideas is afoot."[75] The worst form of content discrimination, in other words, is viewpoint discrimination, and that cannot be allowed at anytime.

According to Justice Stevens, the ordinance, assuming that it was not fatally overbroad, "regulates speech not on the basis of its subject matter or the viewpoint expressed, but rather on the basis of the harm the speech causes."[76] The ordinance regulates "only a subcategory of expression that causes *injuries* based on 'race, color, creed, religion, or gender,' not a subcategory that involves *discussions* that concern those characteristics."[77] But according to Justice Scalia, the effect is a viewpoint-based ordinance: there were many content and viewpoint neutral alternatives available to St. Paul—the laws on the books were available for use—but "the only interest distinctively served by the content limitation is that of displaying the city council's special hostility towards the particular biases thus singled out. That is precisely what the First Amendment forbids."[78] Justice Scalia seems to be right that the ordinance, as it had been interpreted by the Minnesota Supreme Court in an effort to keep it within constitutional bounds, singles out for special prohibition those fighting words that convey hostility and are likely to incite to violence on the basis of certain categories only.

R. A. V. v St. Paul involved a constitutional challenge to a legislative attempt to "denounce" certain forms of speech that, as Justice Stevens has written, rank very low.[79] In two cases, Justice Stevens wrote plurality opinions affirming his position that not all speech deserves full protection. But in each case, other Justices voting with Stevens on the result offered a different rationale for the decision. In *Young v Mini-Theatres*, the Court upheld Detroit's "Anti-Skid Row Ordinance," which required the dispersal of "adult" theatres and bookstores. After quoting Voltaire on the importance of free speech ("I disapprove of what you say, but I will defend with my life your right to say it"), Stevens offered this justification for granting less than full protection to erotic (but not obscene) speech:

> Whether political oratory or philosophical discussion moves us to applaud or to despise what is said, every schoolchild can understand why our duty to defend the right to speak remains the same. But few of us would march our sons and daughters off to war to preserve the citizen's right to see 'Specified Sexual Activities' exhibited in the theatres of our choice.[80]

But Justice Powell, who voted with the majority in the 5 to 4 decision, saw the case "as presenting an example of an innovative land use regulation, implicating First Amendment concerns only incidentally and to a limited extent."[81]

The same 5 to 4 majority, with the same division within the majority, prevailed in a case that involved an FCC warning to a radio station concerning the broadcasting of offensive words at a time when children were likely to hear the program.[82] In voting to uphold the FCC warning, both Justices Stevens and Powell emphasized the special character of the broadcast medium as a justification for allowing the regulation of "offensive, indecent material," which "confronts the citizen…in the privacy of the home."[83] During the day, listeners are likely to include children, and as they tune in at any time, effective warnings are not possible. So the Court affirmed the FCC's warning to the radio station that it should "channel" certain programs to times of day when children are not exposed. But Justice Powell explicitly disavowed that part of Justice Stevens's opinion that would have upheld the FCC regulation even though it was content based.[84]

Justice Stevens wanted to expand on the Court's categorical approach to free speech by introducing a category between no protection and full protection: low value speech would receive some protection. More generally, he favored a case-by-case examination of free speech claims, where political speech is accorded the highest protection. This "sliding scale" approach would require more judicial discriminations than the categorical approach, which requires but one judgment at the outset: is the speech protected or not? Justice Powell preferred the "content-neutral" character of the categorical approach: all protected speech is treated in the same manner.

In 2003, the Court revisited the expressive character of cross burning. In *Virginia v Black*,[85] it reaffirmed its *R. A. V.* decision and also provided some support for a state's authority to punish this form of threatening conduct. The Virginia statute banned cross burning with "the intent of intimidating any person or group of persons," and it declared "any such burning of a cross shall be prima facie evidence of an intent to intimidate a person or group of persons."[86] The case involved two different incidents. In one, Barry Black led a Ku Klux Klan rally on private property with permission of the owner. In the other, Richard Elliott and Jonathan O'Mara planted a cross and set it on fire in the yard of their neighbor, an African American, after he complained about Elliot's using his backyard as a firing range. The defendants were convicted at trial,[87] and the court of appeals affirmed, but a divided Virginia Supreme Court reversed. The majority found the statute similar to the St. Paul ordinance and unconstitutional, since "it selectively chooses only cross burning because of its distinctive message."[88] The dissenting justices thought the statute passed constitutional muster because it addressed "conduct that constitutes a true threat," and unlike the St. Paul ordinance, it did not refer to any specific motive or viewpoint.[89]

The United States Supreme Court reversed, with six justices voting to uphold the main part of the statute and seven justices voting to strike down the evidentiary provision. In her opinion stating the judgment, which was also a Court opinion on the main issue, Justice O'Connor was joined by Chief Justice Rehnquist and Justices Stevens, Scalia, and Breyer. After providing a history to show that cross burning is often used to intimidate, and after acknowledging that cross burning is "symbolic expression," Justice O'Connor concluded that

> Virginia's statute does not run afoul of the First Amendment insofar as it bans cross burning with intent to intimidate. Unlike the statute at issue in R. A. V., the Virginia statute does not single out for opprobrium only that speech directed toward "one of the specified disfavored topics. [citation omitted]" It does not matter whether an individual burns a cross with intent to intimidate because of the victim's race, gender, or religion, or because of the victim's political affiliation, union membership, or homosexuality.[90]

Therefore, the statute was an example of a permissible form of content regulation; cross burning was prohibited because it is a "particularly vehement form of intimidation," not in order to stifle a viewpoint.[91] Because a burning cross may signify an ideological position as well as constitute a threat, Justices O'Connor, Rehnquist, Stevens, and Breyer found that the jury instructions under the statute's evidentiary provision ran the risk of causing juries to take the act of cross burning as sufficient evidence of intimidation, especially when a defendant chose not to testify.[92] They therefore invalidated the provision, albeit inviting the state supreme court, on remand, to "interpret the provision . . . in order to avoid the constitutional objections we have described."[93] Justices Scalia and Thomas would have upheld this part of the law also, since the provision did not amount to an irrebuttable presumption of intimidation, although Justice Scalia did provide a fifth vote for remanding to the Virginia Supreme Court to get an authoritative interpretation of the prima facie evidence provision.[94]

Justice Souter, joined by Justices Kennedy and Ginsburg, thought the statute's focus on cross burning as the sole form of expressive intimidation, and especially the evidentiary provision, made the statute impermissibly viewpoint-based, and therefore would have invalidated the entire law on the basis of R. A. V.[95]

Obscenity and Pornography

When the Court first held that obscenity was not within the scope of constitutionally protected speech in Roth v United States (1957), it described obscenity as "utterly without redeeming social importance."[96] Obscene material was defined as that "which deals with sex in a manner appealing to the pruri-ent interest."[97] The judicial test required the average person's application of community standards, looking at the work as a whole. The *Roth* test was re-vised nine years later, in the *Memoirs* case, to require a three-part test for ob-scene material: (1) the dominant theme of the material, taken as a whole, had to appeal to the prurient interest in sex; (2) it had to do so in a manner patently offensive to the community; and (3) the work had to be "utterly without redeeming social value."[98] This test was then revised slightly in *Miller v California*[99] in 1973: The patently offensive sexual conduct had to be specif-ically defined by an applicable state statute, and the third part of the test asked "whether the work, taken as a whole, lacks serious literary, artistic, political or scientific value."[100]

The Supreme Court divided 5 to 4 in *Miller* and its companion case.[101] Jus-tice Brennan, who wrote the *Roth* opinion in 1957, had concluded that ob-scenity could not be adequately defined for a criminal statute, although he was willing to allow states to prevent minors from receiving obscene materi-als. Subsequent cases have revealed, however, that the legal definition of ob-scenity covers "hardcore" pornography and nothing more; anything else will be protected under the *Miller* test. Whereas in *Roth* the entire category was said to be without social value, in *Memoirs*, and now in *Miller*, the "serious value" test must be applied for each work, and the Court has not been strict in its application of that test.[102]

Two recent Internet cases illustrate the significance of the narrowing of obscenity as an unprotected category of speech. The first is *Reno v ACLU*,[103] which addressed a provision of the Communications Decency Act of 1996 that prohibited the knowing transmission of obscene or indecent messages to anyone under eighteen years of age. The lower court enjoined the gov-ernment from enforcing the indecency provisions but preserved the govern-ment's right to prosecute obscenity or child pornography activities prohib-ited by the law. The Supreme Court affirmed. The CDA was described as a content-based blanket restriction on speech.[104] The lower court noted that the Internet was not like the radio, in that one did not encounter its con-tent by accident. In addition, the Supreme Court noted that there was no effective way for noncommercial chat rooms to separate adults from minors. Consequently, the Court was unwilling to sanction a substantial restriction on minors' exposure to sexually explicit material if it would also restrict adult access.

In 1998, Congress passed the Child Online Protection Act to address the infirmities in the Communications Decency Act. In *Ashcroft v ACLU*,[105] the Court remanded the case back to the third circuit. As Justice Thomas pointed out in his opinion stating the judgment of the Court, this law prohibited anyone from knowingly making available on the World Wide Web any communication for commercial purposes that is harmful to minors. The law defined material that was harmful to minors on analogy to the three-part *Miller* test for obscenity.[106] The good faith defenses against prosecution included restricting access by minors to the website by means of a credit card, debit account, or adult access code or adult personal ID number, or some other verification of age. The challengers claimed that the material on their Web sites was valuable to adults and that their fear of prosecution "created an effective ban on constitutionally protected speech by and to adults." The district court agreed and granted a preliminary injunction. The court of appeals affirmed, but on a different ground: it held that the community standard requirement, as applied to the Internet in this case, would allow the most restrictive community standard to apply to the Internet at large, thus making the statute "substantially overbroad."

The Supreme Court remanded the case to the court of appeals, saying that the statute was not substantially overbroad on its face. Justices Thomas, Rehnquist, and Scalia thought that the different community standards as applied to material harmful to minors might not be significant enough to invalidate the statute. Justices O'Connor and Breyer thought that Congress intended a national community standard for the Internet, but they also voted for the remand. Justice Kennedy filed an opinion concurring in the judgment, in which Justices Souter and Ginsburg joined. Only Justice Stevens dissented, arguing that the court of appeals was correct and that too much protected speech was restricted.[107]

Justice Thomas described the nature of the restriction in the following sentence: "Respondents argue that COPA is 'unconstitutionally overbroad' because it will require Web publishers to shield some material behind age verification screens that could be displayed openly in many communities across the Nation if Web speakers were able to limit access to their sites on a geographic basis."[108] The First Amendment issue is not whether adult access to sexually explicit material can be prohibited— although most of it is probably legally obscene—but whether access may be subject to a gatekeeper procedure that would screen out minors while admitting adults. The First Amendment requirement of the least restrictive means places the burden on parents to put blocking devices on their computers if they do not want their minor children to have access to pornography. To support this position, the Court defends adult access to pornography in the name of autonomy.

Commercial Speech

The Court's treatment of commercial speech illustrates the limits to the application of "truth wins out in the marketplace of ideas." Perhaps it is more accurate to say that the Court treats the marketplace differently from the "marketplace of ideas," which tells us something about our polity's alleged reliance on truth winning out.

The Court first regarded this form of speech as another unprotected category in 1942.[109] In the 1970s, however, the Court reconsidered in *Virginia Pharmacy*:

> [Our] question is whether speech which does "no more than propose a commercial transaction" is so removed from any "exposition of ideas" and from "truth, science and morality and arts in general, in its diffusion of liberal sentiments on the administration of Government" that it lacks all protection. Our answer is that it is not.[110]

The Court noted that consumers might be more interested in the free flow of commercial information concerning drug prices than they are in politics. In his opinion for the Court in *Virginia Pharmacy*, Justice Blackmun, citing the *Gertz* distinction between facts and opinions, noted that much commercial speech "is not provably false, or even wholly false, but only deceptive or misleading. We foresee no obstacle to a State's dealing effectively with this problem."[111] In a footnote elaborating this point, Justice Blackmun gave two reasons for commercial speech's receiving less protection than other speech. First, "the truth of commercial speech . . . may be more easily verifiable by its disseminator than...news reporting or political commentary."[112] Second, commercial speech "may be more durable than other kinds [of speech]," since advertising is essential for profits.[113] This reveals something interesting about the conviction that truth wins out in the marketplace of ideas. In the name of democratic freedom, people should be left to decide for themselves in matters where the truth is in dispute. But more regulation of commercial speech is permissible because the Court has confidence in government's ability to distinguish truth from falsehood where the question concerns the presentation of the price of goods offered for sale.

In *Central Hudson Gas v Public Service Corp* (1980), the Supreme Court articulated its test for First Amendment protection of commercial speech. Central Hudson challenged the New York Public Service Commission's ban on promotional advertising for electrical utilities. Delivering the Court opinion, Justice Powell presented a four-part test:

At the outset, we must determine whether the expression is protected by the First Amendment. For commercial speech to come within that provision, it at least must concern lawful activity and not be misleading. Next, we ask whether the asserted governmental interest is substantial. If both inquiries yield positive answers, we must determine whether the regulation directly advances the governmental interest asserted, and whether it is not more extensive than is necessary to serve that interest.[114]

Applying the test, the Court concluded that the Commission's order was more extensive than necessary, since it prohibited promotional advertising that might have reduced energy use. Subsequent cases have led to different interpretations of the closeness of the "fit" between the regulation and the governmental interest. The decision in *Board of Trustees, SUNY v Fox* stated that the "least restrictive means" was not required.[115] This was consistent with the "intermediate scrutiny" approach that seemed to reflect less than full protection. But the Court later indicated that commercial speech would not be treated differently from noncommercial speech for aesthetic or safety purposes.[116] And after suggesting that regulations of commercial speech that aimed at discouraging gambling would be upheld under a "vice" exception, the Court reversed itself. In *Rubin v Coors Brewing Co.*, it invalidated a law that prohibited advertising the alcohol content of beer on labels.[117] Justice Thomas wrote the Court opinion; he emphasized the irrationality of the government's policy, since there was no prohibition on the disclosure of alcohol content in advertising.

When Rhode Island justified its total ban on advertising liquor prices as a means of serving the state's goal of temperance, the Court unanimously reversed.[118] Justices Stevens, Kennedy, and Ginsburg thought that truthful, nonmisleading commercial speech deserved full First Amendment protection. Justice Thomas would have held that a ban on truthful price information was per se illegitimate. And Justices O'Connor, Rehnquist, Souter, and Breyer thought that the regulation failed the *Hudson* test. As Justice O'Connor put it, the "fit" between bans on price advertising, high prices, and lower consumption of alcohol was not close enough. A sales tax, she suggested, would have been a more direct way to effect the state's policy. The Court's position may be inconsistent if one tries to determine whether commercial speech is subjected to "strict" or to "intermediate" scrutiny. The Court seems to be saying that paternalistic justifications for restricting commercial speech will not be upheld when that speech pertains to a lawful activity and is truthful. Where the truth or falsity of the speech can readily be determined, regulations requiring the truth will be upheld; regulations attempting to keep information from people allegedly for their own good will be invalidated.

Notes

1. 337 U.S. 1.
2. Justice Jackson, in his dissenting opinion, quotes substantially from the speech. See Id. at 14–22.
3. Id. at 3 (1949).
4. Id. at 4 (1949).
5. Id. at 13 (Justice Jackson dissenting).
6. See Harry Kalven Jr. A *Worthy Tradition: Freedom of Speech in America* (Harper and Row Publishers: New York, 1998), pp. 89, 97–98.
7. *Cohen v California*, 403 U.S. 15, 16 (1971).
8. Id. at 16.
9. Id. at 17.
10. Id. at 17.
11. See Id. at 18–21.
12. 405 U.S. 518 (1972).
13. Id. at 523 (1972).
14. The appellants, whose breach of the peace convictions were overturned, were black; in a scuffle with a police officer, they said: "White son of a bitch, I'll kill you," etc., at 520.
15. *Cohen*, 403 U.S., at 22–23.
16. Id. at 24. The Brandeis citation came from *Whitney v New York*.
17. Id.
18. Id. at 26.
19. Id. at 25.
20. See *Republic* VIII, 558c–561b.
21. 403 U.S. at 26. Four Justices dissented from this decision. Justice Blackmun, joined by Chief Justice Burger and Justice Black, thought that the case came within the *Chaplinsky* definition of "fighting words."
22. *United States v O'Brien*, 391 U.S. 367, 370 (1968) (emphasis in original).
23. See Id. at 372.
24. Id. at 376–77.
25. Chief Justice Warren maintained that the Court "will not strike down an otherwise constitutional statute on the basis of an alleged illicit legislative motive." Id. at 383. But, in light of the substantial overlap between the earlier law, which required possession of one's draft card, and the 1965 amendment, which criminalized its willful destruction, one can understand how the court of appeals concluded that the law's purpose was the suppression of expression. *O'Brien* resembles *Schenck*: in each case, the Court articulates a speech test and then applies it in a dubious manner.

26. See John Hart Ely, "Flag Desecration: A Case Study in the Roles of Categorization and Balancing in First Amendment Analysis," 88 *Harvard Law Review* 1482, 1484 (1975). In Ely's formulation, the "switching function" the second part, since he omits the first, that the power be constitutional, as given.

27. *Street v New York*, 394 U.S. 576, 577–78 (1969).

28. *Smith, Sheriff v Goguen*, 415 U.S. 566, 581 (1974).

29. *Spence v Washington*, 418 U.S. 405 (1974).

30. Id. at 410–11.

31. *Texas v Johnson*, 491 U.S. 397, 400 (1989).

32. Id. at 399.

33. Id. at 401.

34. Id. at 408–9

35. Id at 409

36. Id. at 410.

37. Id. at 411.

38. Id. In this context, he cites Justice Blackmun's dissent in *Goguen*, which we will consider later.

39. Id. at 412. The intended quotation is from *Spence*, 418 U.S. at 412.

40. *Johnson*, supra, at 414.

41. Id. at 418.

42. Id. at 419.

43. Id. In his brief concurrence, Justice Kennedy indicated that his conception of the judicial power and his understanding of "the law and the Constitution" compelled him to decide the case as he did, notwithstanding his "distaste for the result." Id. p. 421. Since Johnson's "acts were speech, in both the technical and the fundamental meaning of the Constitution," "he must go free." Id.

44. Id. at 435 (Chief Justice Rehnquist dissenting).

45. See *National Socialist Party v Skokie* 432 U.S. 43 (1977).

46. Id. at 436 (Justice Stevens dissenting).

47. Id.

48. Id. at 437 (Justice Stevens dissenting).

49. Id. 438 (Justice Stevens dissenting; emphasis in original).

50. *Boos v Barry* 485 U.S. 312 (1988).

51. For a discussion of the Congressional Hearings and debate, see Dry, "Flag Burning and the Constitution," in *The Supreme Court Review 1990*, pp. 85–91.

52. From syllabus to *US v Eichman*, 496 U.S. 310, 311 (1990).

53. Id. at 315. The passage was quoted in the opinion; it came from the government's brief.

54. Id. at 315; the internal quotes are from the government's brief.

55. Id.

56. Id. at 317.

57. Id. at 318.

58. Id.

59. Id. at 319 (Justice Stevens dissenting). This test resembles the one the government offered in its brief in these cases; see *United States v Henchman* Nos. 89–1433 and 89–1434, pp. 32–33.

60. Id. at 319–20 (Justice Stevens dissenting).

61. Id., 321.

62. 505 U.S. 377 (1992).

63. The authorities apparently chose to prosecute under the ordinance, rather than more specific felony statutes to highlight the city's condemnation of "hate crimes." Justice Scalia identifies the following statutes that covered RAV's criminal conduct: one providing for up to five years imprisonment for terrorist threats; one providing for up to five years for arson; and one providing for up to one year and a $3,000 fine for damage to property. See *R. A. V., Petitioner v City of St. Paul, Minnesota,* 505 U.S. 377 (1992) 380.

64. Id.

65. *In the Matter of the Welfare of R. A. V.* 464 N.W.2d 507 (Minn 1991).

66. Justice White, with whom Justices Blackmun, O'Connor, and Stevens agreed, wanted to hold that the state supreme court had not narrowed the ordinance sufficiently, because it still criminalized "expressive conduct that causes only hurt feelings, offense, or resentment," 505 U.S. at 414, which is protected by the First Amendment.

67. See *Renton v Playtime Theatres, Inc.* 475 U.S. 41 (1986).

68. 505 U.S. at 383–84. Justice Scalia cited *New York v Ferber,* 458 U.S. 747 (1982) in which the Court upheld the state's prohibition on child pornography, since there was no question of censoring a particular literary theme, which is to say no content discrimination was involved. *R. A. V.* at 386. But that case involved protected speech—that is, nonobscene pornography—where an otherwise impermissible prohibition was upheld because of the special harm associated with the use of minors in making such protected pornography. Justice Scalia remarked that no content discrimination was involved.

69. Id. at 401. "Underinclusiveness" means that a law covers only some of the instances of a given mischief that it intended to prohibit or regulate.

70. Justice Stevens drew on his plurality opinions in *Young v American Mini Theatres Inc.* and *FCC v Pacifica,* in which he introduced the concept of levels of protected speech to justify restrictions on "adult entertainment" and crude words on the radio, as well as his concurring opinion in the child pornography case, in which the prohibition of otherwise protected expression was upheld because of the demonstrated harm to children used as participants. He also drew on certain commercial speech cases, Id. at 422, 426–29.

71. Id. at 388.

72. Id. at 388.

73. See below, text at chapter 9, footnote 53.

74. Id. at 388.

75. Id. at 390.

76. Id. at 433.

77. Id. at 433.

78. Id. at 396

79. In addition to his *R. A. V.* opinion, see Justice Stevens' recent essay, "The Freedom of Speech," in 102 *Yale LR* 1293 no. 6 April 1993.

80. *Young v American Mini-Theatres*, 427 U.S. 50, 70 (1976).

81. Id. at 73 (Justice Powell concurring).

82. *FCC v Pacifica* 438 U.S. 726 (1978).

83. Id. at 748; Justice Powell emphasizes the privacy of the home at 759.

84. Id. at 761. Gerald Gunther expressed concern about Justice Stevens's approach in this case; see "The Highest Court, The Toughest Issues," *Stanford Magazine*, Fall–Winter 1978, p. 34.

85. 123 S. Ct. 1536.

86. 18.2–423, as quoted in Justice O'Connor's opinion announcing the judgment of the court, at 1541–42.

87. Black objected to the jury instruction, which allowed an inference of intent to intimidate from the act of cross burning. At Elliot's trial, the court instructed the jury that it had to find an intent to intimidate. O'Maura pleaded guilty, reserving his right to contest the constitutionality of the statute. See 1542–43.

88. Id., 1543, quoting from 262 Va. 764, at 777.

89. Id., 1543.

90. Id., 1549; the internal quote is from *R. A. V.* at 391.

91. Id., 1549–50.

92. Id., 1549–50.

93. Id., 1552.

94. Id., 1552. The Court therefore agreed with the Virginia Supreme Court that Black conviction could not stand; it vacated the judgments in the cases of Elliot and O'Maura, remanding the case for further proceedings.

95. See 1561 for the discussion of the evidentiary provision.

96. *Roth v United States* 354 US 476, 485 (1957).

97. Id. at 486.

98. *A Book Named "John Cleland's Memoirs of a Woman of Pleasure" v Attorney General of Massachusetts*, 383 U.S. 413, 418 (1966).

99. 413 U.S. 15 (1973).

100. Id. at 25.

101. *Paris Adult Theatre I v Slaton* 413 U.S. 49 (1973).

102. For example, in *Jenkins v Georgia* 418 U.S. 153 (1974), the Court unanimously reversed a state conviction for showing "Carnal Knowledge," on the grounds that, while the movie was about sex and depicted scenes in which sexual conduct was understood to be taking place, the presence of prominent actors (including Jack Nicholson) made it "mainstream" and allowed it to pass the *Miller* test.

103. 521 U.S. 844 (1997).

104. Id. at 902.

105. 535 U.S. 564 (2002).

106. Id. at 570.

107. Id. at 612. This seems to represent a shift from Justice Stevens' position in the "offensive speech" cases in the 1970s.

108. Id. at 584.

109. *Valentine v Christensen*, 316 U.S. 52 (1942).

110. *Virginia Pharmacy Board v Virginia Citizens Consumer Council*, 425 U.S. 748, 762 (1976), citations omitted.

111. Id. at 771.

112. Id. at 772 (note 24).

113. Id.

114. *Central Hudson Gas v Public Service Corporation*, 447 U.S. 557, 566 (1980).

115. 492 U.S. 469 (1989).

116. *City of Cincinnati v Discovery Network*, 507 U.S. 410 (1993).

117. *Rubin v Coors Brewing Co.*, 514 U.S. 476 (1995). For the "vice" exception, see *Posadas de Puerto Rico Associates v Tomism Co. of Puerto Rico*, 478 U.S. 328 (1986).

118. *44 Liquormart v Rhode Island* 517 U.S. 484 (1996).

CHAPTER TWELVE

Money and Speech and the Public Forum (or Time, Place, and Manner) Doctrine

Money and Speech in Political Campaigns

While most of the Supreme Court's freedom of speech decisions support democratic freedom, either in the name of self-government or individual expression, the Court has upheld one form of symbolic expression that reflects liberal democracy's commitment to property rights: the use of money to publicize opinions in political campaigns. The campaign finance cases—especially *Buckley v Valeo* (1976),[1] the principal decision—are perhaps the most striking illustrations of how judicial protection of freedom of speech in the name of democratic politics can intrude into the very core of democratic politics. Congressional determination that fair elections required overall limitations on expenditures and contributions, by candidates, political parties, other associations, and individuals, was held unconstitutional in some key respects and constitutional in others. That decision and others that followed severely limited what lawmakers could do to restrict the influence of money in political campaigns.

Congress passed a Federal Election Campaign Act in 1971. It limited personal contributions by candidates for the major federal offices and their immediate families. It also limited media spending, and it required reporting of most contributions and expenditures. This law was never tested in the courts, however; in reaction to the Watergate scandal and the record campaign spending levels in the 1972 elections, Congress passed the Federal Election Campaign Act Amendments of 1974. This comprehensive law contained four general provisions. First, it set individual contribution and expenditure limits of $1,000 "relative to a clearly identified federal candidate" for each national election and an overall annual limit of $25,000 for any contributor. Campaign contributions by candidates for various federal offices were also subject to prescribed limits. Second, contributions and expenditures above a certain threshold ($100 for individuals) had to be publicly disclosed. Third, a system of public funding for presidential campaigns was established. Fourth, a Federal Election Commission (FEC) was established to administer the act.[2] All of these provisions were subject to constitutional challenge in *Buckley v Valeo*, decided in 1976. Appellants included a United States Senator who was running for reelection (James Buckley) and a Presidential candidate (Eugene McCarthy). The district court, on instructions from the court of appeals, provided fact-finding and certified the constitutional questions. The court of appeals then found that Congress had demonstrated "a clear and compelling interest" in preserving the integrity of the electoral process and sustained the Act, with one minor exception.[3]

The Supreme Court, in a per curiam opinion that only Justices Brennan, Stewart, and Powell joined in its entirety, upheld the reporting requirements, the system of public funding of the Presidential campaign, and the contribution limits, but invalidated the expenditure limits.

In its discussion of general principles, the per curiam opinion began by affirming that the act's contribution and expenditure limitations implicated the First Amendment."[4] The act's defenders, citing *O'Brien*, contended that the regulations affected conduct and that the effect on speech was incidental. The court of appeals had found that the money that finances campaign speech was conduct unrelated to the suppression of speech. The Supreme Court disagreed: "This Court has never suggested that the dependence of a communication on the expenditure of money operates itself to introduce a nonspeech element or to reduce the exacting scrutiny required by the First Amendment."[5] Even if the expenditure of money were considered conduct, the Act failed the *O'Brien* test because "the interests served by [it] include restricting the voices of people and interest groups who have money to spend and reducing the overall scope of federal campaigns."[6]

A more interesting argument in support of these limits on contributions and expenditures likened them to the "time, place, and manner" regulation of a maximum decibel level for sound trucks.[7] Was Congress not simply regulating the volume of dollars that could be expended in a political campaign? The per curiam opinion said no: "The critical difference . . . is that the present Act's contribution and expenditure limitations impose direct quantity restrictions on political communication and association by persons, groups, candidates and political parties, in addition to any reasonable time, place, and manner regulations otherwise imposed."[8]

Finding the Act directly related to the suppression of expression, the Court applied "strict scrutiny." The test consists of a two-part examination of the challenged law or regulation; the purpose must be compelling and the means chosen to effect that purpose must be the least restrictive on the affected right, here free speech. Before addressing the intended purposes and their relation to the means chosen, however, the per curiam opinion distinguished the two different regulations in terms of their effects on freedom of speech. Expenditure limits can directly limit the speech of a given individual. Contribution limits do not necessarily have that effect.[9] This distinction became the basis for the "compromise" decision, which upheld the contribution limits and invalidated the expenditure limits.[10]

The Court upheld the contribution limits by recognizing the importance of the primary interest served: "the prevention of corruption and the appearance of corruption spawned by the real or imagined coercive influence of large financial contributions on candidates' positions and on their actions if elected to office."[11] To the contention that bribery laws and narrowly drawn disclosure laws constituted a less restrictive means of addressing corruption, the Court replied that bribery laws deal with only the most blatant attempts to influence government action and that Congress could have concluded that "disclosure was only a partial measure, and that contribution ceilings were a necessary legislative concomitant to deal with the reality or appearance of corruption inherent in a system permitting unlimited financial contributions."[12] The Court concluded that the restriction focused on the problem of corruption, or its appearance, and did not seriously undermine the right of political association.[13] Consequently: "We find that under the rigorous standard of review established by our prior decisions, the weighty interests served by restricting the size of financial contributions to political candidates are sufficient to justify the limited effect upon First Amendment freedoms caused by the $1,000 contribution ceiling."[14]

In its consideration of expenditure limits, the Court began by interpreting expenditures "relative to a clearly identified candidate" as "limited to communications that include explicit words of advocacy of election or defeat of a candidate."[15] Turning to the basic First Amendment question, the Court first disagreed with the court of appeals's finding that the expenditure limit was a valid "loophole-closing" measure for the contribution limit. "The markedly greater burden on basic freedoms caused by [the expenditure limitation provision] thus cannot be sustained simply by invoking the interest in maximizing the effectiveness of the less intrusive contribution limitations."[16] The Court then found the governmental interest in preventing corruption and the appearance of corruption inadequate to justify this limit. Assuming that expenditures could pose such a problem, the means would not be adequate, since large expenditures not advocating the election or defeat of a candidate could not be covered.[17] But such expenditures would be furthest removed from corruption. The better argument was that even independent advocacy generated by large expenditures "does not presently appear to pose dangers of real or apparent corruption comparable to those identified with large campaign contributions."[18]

The Court's response to the government's interest "in equalizing the relative ability of individuals and groups to influence the outcome of elections,"[19] was decisive: "The concept that government may restrict the speech of some elements of our society in order to enhance the relative voice of others is wholly foreign to the First Amendment."[20] The Court emphasized the widest possible dissemination of ideas and the unfettered exchange of ideas.[21] Thus, just as the Court refused to draw lines with respect to content or viewpoint, it also refused to draw a line at what constituted excessive and hence "unfair" speech.

Chief Justice Burger and Justice Blackmun would have struck down the contribution limits along with the expenditure limits; Justice White would have upheld both. He thought that once the Court accepts Congress's judgment about "the evils of unlimited contributions," it should accept its claim that "other steps must be taken to counter the corrosive effects of money in federal election campaigns."[22] Justice Marshall thought that the governmental interest "in promoting the reality and appearance of equal access to the political arena justified limits on candidate expenditures."[23] Chief Justice Burger and Justice Rehnquist dissented from the public financing provisions for presidential campaigns.[24]

The Supreme Court's post-*Buckley* decisions on campaign financing have followed the distinction between permissible contribution limits and impermissible expenditure limits.[25] In *Colorado Republican Federal Campaign Committee v FEC*, the Court held that political parties also have a right to make unlimited independent expenditures. Justice Breyer wrote the plurality opinion, which Justices O'Connor and Souter joined. Justices Kennedy, Rehnquist, and Scalia would have held that party expenditure limits were invalid whether applied to coordinated or uncoordinated expenditures: party spending on campaigns was, they felt, the equivalent of spending one's own money. Justice Thomas would have gone further and repudiated the contribution-expenditure distinction. Justices Stevens and Ginsburg dissented; they would have upheld the party expenditure limits as to both independent and coordinated expenses. Their justifications were (1) avoiding corruption and (2) "leveling the electoral playing field by constraining the cost of federal campaigns."[26]

When considering restrictions on corporations, the Supreme Court has invalidated some and upheld some. In *First National Bank of Boston v Bellotti*, the Court overturned a prohibition on corporate spending to influence a referendum. Writing for the Court, Justice Powell said: "In the realm of protected speech, the legislature is constitutionally disqualified from dictating the subjects about which persons may speak and speakers who may address a public issue."[27] But limitations on how a corporation could contribute to an election campaign were upheld as applied to for-profits and associations that worked closely with for-profits. In *FEC v National Right to Work Committee*,[28] the Court upheld the requirement that unions and corporations must establish "separate segregated funds," raised by solicitations of their employees or membership, in order to support candidates.[29] Since the state had given the corporate form certain advantages, it could restrain corporations, and unions, from using their economic power to unfair advantage in electoral campaigns. The Court made an exception in *FEC v Massachusetts Citizens for Life, Inc*,[30] holding that this non-profit corporation was more like a voluntary political association and that therefore corruption—which the Court had identified as an important factor in *Buckley*—was not an issue. But it reaffirmed the limitation on for-profit corporations and associations that work closely with them in *Austin v Michigan Chamber of Commerce*.[31]

In *Nixon v Shrink*,[32] the Court upheld state contribution limits 6 to 3, even though there was no showing that corruption or appearance of corruption was a problem. The Justices took three distinct positions, with minor variations:

1. Justices Souter, who wrote the Court opinion, O'Connor, and Rehnquist accepted, without reservations, that *Buckley* controlled.
2. Dissenting Justices Scalia and Thomas would have rejected *Buckley* in the name of free speech. Justice Kennedy would have overruled *Buckley*, on the grounds that the differing treatment of independent expenditures and contributions, combined with limitless "soft money," was constitutionally indefensible; he remained open, however, to the possibility that Congress could regulate both expenditures and contributions in a constitutional manner.

3. Justices Breyer and Ginsburg, concurring, wanted to reopen the discussion of whether limits on expenditures might be constitutional. Justice
   Stevens, also concurring, concluded that the issue involved property,
   not speech, and hence all regulations were constitutional.

Buckley and its progeny thus stand for the following propositions: Money
spent in political campaigns is political speech and subject to extensive
protection. Corruption and its appearance justify contribution limits. Neither that rationale nor the desire to equalize the influence of wealth or
even the desire to limit the amount of money in political campaigns, justifies limits on independent expenditures. Corporate spending can be con-
fined, due to the unique benefits of that organizational form (which applies
to unions as well).

In 2002, Congress passed The Bipartisan Campaign Reform Act
(BCRA)[33] for the purpose of closing "soft," or "non-federal," money loopholes in FECA. "Soft money" refers to any money that is not subject to the
disclosure requirements and source and amounts limitations of the FECA.
This includes contributions to political parties (and other organizations) that
are spent on state and local campaigns or are spent on federal campaigns but
not for the express advocacy or defeat of a candidate.[34] Passage of BCRA cul-
minated a seven-year effort by Senators McCain and Feingold to achieve
campaign finance reform. According to Congressional Quarterly, the Enron
scandal and the revelation that the company had spent $3.6 million in soft
money donations to the two major parties, "put the legislation over the top,"
but momentum for the reform came from the increasing amounts of unregulated soft money that went into political campaigns. In the 2000 elections,
the Republicans raised $250 million and the Democrats $245 million in soft
money.[35] The two main features of BCRA ban national political parties from
accepting or spending soft money and forbid corporations and labor unions
from directly funding issue ads, or "electioneering communications," during
the final sixty days of a general election and final thirty days of a primary.[36]
In addition to closing these two spending loopholes in the current law, the
new law, which went into effect on November 6, 2002 (after the national
elections), raised the hard money contribution limits.[37]

On May 1, 2003, a three-judge district court handed down four opinions
(a per curiam stating the results and a separate memorandum opinion from
each judge) totaling more than sixteen hundred pages in the first suit to challenge the act, McConnell v FEC. By 2 to 1, the court upheld the major provisions of the act, with these modifications: The ban on party use of soft
money was limited to "campaign communications (particularly candidate-

advocacy 'issue' advertisements), which are designed to, and which do, directly affect federal elections"; the restriction on corporate and union spending was limited to "electioneering communications which promote, oppose, attack, or support specific candidates for the office which they seek," but this ban was extended without limit of time.[38]

On December 10, the Supreme Court, by a 5 to 4 vote, upheld the main features of the law as passed by Congress; these were contained in Titles I and II.[39] Justices O'Connor and Stevens wrote the Court opinion upholding these titles, and Justices Souter, Ginsburg, and Breyer concurred. The five-justice majority applied heightened scrutiny to these provisions and agreed with Congress that they were necessary to close loopholes that had developed as a result of the narrow definition of "hard money" and the subsequent large amounts of unregulated money that flowed into campaigns. Regarding Title I, Justices O'Connor and Stevens wrote:

> The question for present purposes is whether large *soft-money* contributions to national party committees have a corrupting influence or give rise to the appearance of corruption. Both common sense and the ample record in these cases confirm Congress' belief that they do. . . . The FEC's allocation regime [allowing a percentage of money given to national and state parties for election drives to count as nonregulated soft money] has invited widespread circumvention of FECA's limits on contributions to parties for the purpose of influencing federal elections. Under this system, corporate, union, and wealthy individual donors have been free to contribute substantial sums of soft money to the national parties, which the parties can spend for the specific purpose of influencing a particular candidate's federal election.[40]

As for Title II, the Court noted that *Buckley v Valeo* "drew a constitutionally mandated line between express advocacy and so-called issue advocacy," prohibiting the former and allowing the latter in order to make the 1974 law clear.[41] But that was

> the product of statutory interpretation rather than a constitutional command. . . . In short, the concept of express advocacy and the concomitant class of magic words were born of an effort to avoid constitutional infirmities. . . . Indeed, the unmistakable lesson from the record in this litigation, as all three judges on the District Court agreed, is that *Buckley's* magic-words requirement [express advocacy for the election or defeat of a candidate] is functionally meaningless.[42]

Two of the four dissenting justices—Scalia and Thomas—reiterated their views that *Buckley* itself was mistaken and should be overruled. Chief Justice

Rehnquist and Justice Kennedy rejected the majority's "loophole closing" rationale on the grounds that too much core political speech, not related to corruption, was prohibited.[43] Where the majority accepted Congress's contention that large soft money contributions buy access—and that access produces results, especially blocking legislation[44]—Justice Kennedy, speaking for the minority, did not:

> Access in itself, however, shows only that in a general sense an officeholder favors someone or that someone has influence on the officeholder. There is no basis, in law or in fact, to say favoritism or influence in general is the same as corrupt favoritism or influence in particular. By equating vague and generic claims of favoritism or influence with actual or apparent corruption, the Court adopts a definition of corruption that dismantles basic First Amendment rules, permits Congress to suppress speech in the absence of a quid pro quo threat, and moves beyond the rationale that is *Buckley's* very foundation.[45]

Notwithstanding the final part of Justice Kennedy's remark, in upholding the major provisions of BCRA, the Court has reaffirmed the *Buckley* approach to campaign finance regulation. The approach—a compromise—recognizes the government's demonstrated interest in preventing the appearance of corruption by regulating the use of money in political campaigns, on the one hand, and recognizes the individual's or association's First Amendment right to use money to influence elections and policy, on the other hand. The dissent insists on a narrower definition of corruption—limited to actual quid pro quo transactions. This is consistent with their support—contra *Buckley*—of a free speech right to unlimited contributions as well as expenditures.

Time, Place, and Manner, or the Public Forum Doctrine

Apart from deciding cases involving categories of previously unprotected speech, the Supreme Court has decided a number of free speech cases that concern "time, place, and manner" regulations. Most of these cases involve regulations concerning a particular place, and they have given rise to a set of rules regarding "public forums." As early as 1939, the Court has emphasized the importance of the public forum:

> Wherever the title of streets and parks may rest they have immemorially been held in trust for purposes of assembly, communicating thoughts between citizens, and discussing public questions. Such use of the streets and public places has, from ancient times, been a part of the privileges, immunities, rights and liberties of citizens.[46]

These cases also reflect the Court's emphasis on "content neutrality," which we noted in *Police Department v Mosley* and the *R. A. V.* case. The weight given to the content neutrality principle in time, place, and manner cases has caused some scholars to question whether too little attention is paid to guaranteed access to certain modes or places of expression.[47] The cases suggest that the decisions vary with the specific regulation. For example, required permits for parades were upheld, but a total ban on leaflets was overturned. Sound trucks emitting "raucous sounds" could be banned, but a ban on signs posted on private property, with exceptions for on-site advertising, etc., was overturned, on the grounds that too much speech was prohibited. And while a license fee to meet the expense incident to the administration of a content-neutral act was upheld, a user fee calculated according to the anticipated hostility of the audience was invalidated.[48]

In *Cox v Louisiana*, the Supreme Court invalidated breach of the peace and obstruction of public passageway convictions against Cox and other civil rights demonstrators at the same time that it upheld the ordinance against picketing near a courthouse. (The Court held the demonstrators had not violated the ordinance.)[49] In a famous article about this case, Harry Kalven called for "a set of Robert's Rules of Order for the new uses of the public forum, albeit the designing of such rules poses a problem of formidable practical difficulty."[50] Kalven's sympathies were clearly on the side of free speech. "When the citizen goes to the street, he is exercising an immemorial right of a free man, a kind of First Amendment easement."[51] Since the primary activity in public places is ordinarily not speech making, and the two activities— peaceful recreation and a public address, with or without a demonstration— might conflict with one another, the question often is, what kind of accommodation does the First Amendment require? An advocate of free speech may want more than a guarantee of content neutrality, or equal access where access is given; that advocate will want guaranteed access. Since speech is significantly protected against content-based regulations, the concern becomes the proper weight to be placed on guaranteed access.

The best the Court has done in terms of a general approach to this question concerns regulations affecting "place" rather than manner: Is the place a traditional public forum? If not, has the government acted in such a way to make it a public forum? Or, is it a "non-public forum"? The Court attempted to "codify" its approach to the public forum in *Perry Education Association v Perry Local Educators' Association*, decided in 1983. This case involved access to teacher mailboxes in a public school. A collective bargaining contract gave access to the school mail system and teacher mailboxes to the incumbent union only; a rival union sued for access, claiming that its denial violated content neutrality. The Court upheld the regulation, interpreting the restriction as based on "status," not content or viewpoint. The four dissenting Justices saw the distinction as impermissible viewpoint discrimination. In his Court opinion, Justice White presented the following schema for a right of access to public property:

> In places which by long tradition or by government fiat have been devoted to assembly and debate, the rights of the state to limit expressive activity are sharply circumscribed. At one end of the spectrum are [streets and parks *Hague v CIO*]. In these quintessential public forums, the government may not prohibit all communicative activity. For the state to enforce a content-based exclusion it must show that its regulation is necessary to serve a compelling state interest and that it is narrowly drawn to achieve that end. The state may also enforce regulations of the time, place, and manner or expression which are content-neutral, are narrowly drawn to serve a significant government interest, and leave open ample alternative channels of communication.
>
> A second category consists of public property which the state has opened for use by the public as a place for expressive activity. The Constitution forbids a state to enforce certain exclusions from a forum generally open to the public even if it was not required to create the forum in the first place. . . . Although a state is not required to indefinitely retain the open character of the facility, as long as it does so it is bound by the same standards as apply to the traditional public forum.
>
> Public property which is not by tradition or designation a forum for public communication is governed by different standards. . . . In addition to time, place and manner regulations, the state may reserve the forum for its intended purposes, communicative or otherwise, as long as the regulation on speech is reasonable and not an effort to suppress expression merely because public officials oppose the speaker's view.[52]

This three-part formulation reveals the importance of the public forum designation as well as the content neutrality principle. The formulation includes three distinct levels of scrutiny: "strict scrutiny" is applied to all content-based regulations in traditional or designated public forums (it may also be applied to the nonpublic forum setting); "heightened scrutiny" is applied to content neutral regulations in traditional and designated public forums; and "rational basis" scrutiny is applied to regulations in nonpublic forums.

A balancing approach to time, place, and manner regulations of speech might look at the importance of the expression, the extent to which the regulation restricts the expression, and the availability of alternative modes of expression as well as alternative regulations. With the *Perry* formulation, the Court has attempted to provide rules that can be applied across the board.

The question lingers whether a typology that focuses on place can do justice to the relevant constitutional concerns.

A case involving members of the Hari Krishna Movement and airport regulations reveals the difficulties of this approach.[53] The Port Authority of New York and New Jersey promulgated bans on the solicitation of money and the distribution of literature in public airport terminals. (The activities could take place on the sidewalks outside the airports.) The International Society for Krishna Consciousness (ISKON) challenged the rules. The Court decided, in a 5 to 4 vote, that the airport terminals were "nonpublic forums." The close vote on this issue reflected a disagreement over how much weight should be given to "tradition" in considering whether an airport terminal was a public forum. For the dissenting justices, airports were like streets and parks. Since the majority's position meant application of the "rational basis" test, one might have expected a similar 5 to 4 vote to uphold the two content-neutral regulations. The solicitation ban was upheld, but by a 6 to 3 vote. Chief Justice Rehnquist wrote the Court opinion and applied the "rational basis" test. Justice Kennedy, who argued that airport terminals were like streets and parks, and hence public forums, also voted to uphold the ban. He applied "heightened scrutiny" and distinguished between a total ban on solicitation and this one: "In-person solicitation of funds, when combined with immediate receipt of that money, creates a risk of fraud and duress which is well recognized, and which is different in kind from other forms of expression or conduct."[54] The ban on distribution and sale of literature was overturned 5 to 4. Here, the four justices who thought that airport terminals were public forums found this regulation failed "heightened scrutiny." They emphasized that the distribution of flyers "lies at the heart" of the First Amendment. Justice O'Connor, who voted that the terminals were not public forums, provided the fifth vote on this issue. She thought the prohibition failed even the lenient "reasonableness" test. "While the difficulties posed by solicitation in a nonpublic forum are sufficiently obvious that its regulation may 'ring of common sense,' the same is not necessarily true of leafleting. [The] distribution of literature does not require that the recipient stop in order to receive the message the speaker wishes to convey; instead, the recipient is free to read the message at a later time."[55] The decisive point in this case was not the public forum designation but that leafleting, even with selling attached, was accorded more protection than solicitation. And why did those justices accord as much weight to leafleting with selling as to leafleting alone? It probably had something to do with the Krishna practice of *Sankirtan*, which enjoins the members of that religion to distribute and sell religious literature in public places.

In an earlier case involving this practice, the Court upheld a Minnesota State Fair regulation that prohibited the sale and distribution of any merchandise within the fair grounds, except at booths that could be rented first-come first-served on a nondiscriminatory basis. The Krishnas raised a free exercise claim, but Justice White, writing the Court opinion, treated the case in terms of free speech and upheld the content neutral regulation on grounds of crowd control.[56] The Krishnas' activity points to the occasional overlap between free speech and religious free exercise cases.

Several other public forum cases have involved religious speech on public property. In these cases, a public authority has prohibited religious activity in the name of the requirements of the Establishment Clause. The Supreme Court has then struck down the prohibition in the name of freedom of speech (content neutrality). In *Widmar v Vincent* (1981), the University of Missouri at Kansas City prohibited the use of its facilities "for purposes of religious activity or worship."[57] In *Lamb's Chapel v Center Moriches Union Free School District* (1993), the school district made its public school facilities available to the community after school hours, but provided that "the school premises shall not be used by any group for religious purposes."[58] In each case, the Court struck down the prohibitions as unconstitutional forms of content-based regulations. Justice Powell addressed the Establishment Clause justification this way in *Widmar*: "An open forum in a public university does not confer any imprimatur of State approval on religious sects or practices."[59] Justice White was the lone dissenter in *Widmar*. His position was that the case "involves religious worship only; the fact that that worship is accomplished through speech does not add anything to [the challengers'] argument."[60] The *Lamb's Chapel* case was different for Justice White, who wrote the Court opinion there; he thought that the local evangelical group's desire to show a film series on Christian family values did not amount to religious worship. For every other Justice, religious activity that is expressive is treated as no different from any other form of expression under the content neutrality rule.

The different levels of judicial scrutiny reflected in the Court's *Perry* schema for time, place, and manner regulation of speech resemble the Court's *O'Brien* test for symbolic expression. The Court acknowledged this in *Clark v Community for Creative Non-Violence*,[61] a time, place, and manner case decided in 1984, one year after *Perry*. The National Park Service regulations for parks in the District of Columbia prohibited camping, which included sleeping in Lafayette Park and on the Mall. The Park Service had issued a permit to CCNV to conduct a demonstration in the park; the permit even allowed the erection of two symbolic tent cities, to demonstrate the plight of the homeless. But it refused CCNV's request that the demonstrators be permitted to sleep in the symbolic tents. The district court granted summary judgment for the Park Service, but the court of appeals reversed, 6 to 5, noting the importance of sleep as part of the symbolic message and suggesting other ways in which the Park Service could regulate so as to preserve the parks. Thus, the case involved symbolic expression as well as a time, place, and manner regulation. The Supreme Court, 7 to 2, reversed the Court of Appeals and upheld the regulation. Writing for the court, Justice White stated: "We have often noted that restrictions of this kind are valid provided that they are justified without reference to the content of the regulated speech, that they are narrowly tailored to serve a significant government interest, and that they leave open ample alternative channels for communication of the information."[62] Acknowledging that symbolic expression was involved, Justice White also wrote: "Symbolic expression of this kind may be forbidden or regulated if the conduct itself may be constitutionally regulated, if the regulation is narrowly drawn to further a substantial governmental interest, and if the interest is unrelated to the suppression of free speech."[63]

Justice White went on to say that the *O'Brien* standard for expressive conduct, which he used, "is little if any different from the standard applied to time, place, and manner restrictions."[64] In this case, the regulation—a prohibition on sleeping in the parks—could be viewed as a time, place, and manner regulation on a demonstration and an indirect restriction on symbolic expression. In a footnote, Justice White elaborated: "Reasonable time place and manner restrictions are valid even though they directly limit oral or written expression. It would be odd to insist on a higher standard for limitations aimed at regulable conduct and having only an incidental impact on speech."[65]

In dissent, Justices Brennan and Marshall gave greater weight to the importance of the symbolic expression that the actual sleeping in the tents would have represented. Their constitutional objection was not to the equating of the *O'Brien* and the time, place, and manner tests. Their position can be described in one of two ways: Narrowly viewed, they did not think that heightened scrutiny was fairly applied in this case. More generally viewed, they were sufficiently committed to guaranteed access that they would have applied the same "strict scrutiny" to content neutral regulations that reduce access to public places for expressive activity as the majority applied to content based regulations. In other words, where the majority, following *O'Brien*, only applies strict scrutiny if the government *purpose* is judged to be the suppression of expression, the dissent would apply strict scrutiny wherever the *effect* is the suppression of expression.

While the categorical approach suggests a final "in or out" determination, the Court's approach to many of these cases has been more nuanced. Under both the O'Brien test and the time, place, and manner, or public forum, test, the Court exercises a certain level of scrutiny: strict if the regulation is either content based or has as its object the suppression of expression; "heightened" if the regulation is content neutral and concerns a public forum or incidentally affects speech. This means that, apart from regulations affecting speech in what are called "nonpublic forums," speech receives more protection than conduct even when the government's action has an independent and legitimate purpose. In addition, public forum doctrine has allowed religious organizations to gain access to public facilities for their expressive activities, notwithstanding Establishment Clause concerns.

In 1990, the Court held that a school's refusal to allow high school students to form a Christian Club and meet after school on school premises, when other student groups were given permission, violated the Equal Access Act, since a "limited public forum" had been created.[66] The school contended that allowing the club to use school facilities violated the Establishment Clause. Justice O'Connor's opinion announcing the judgment of the court stated, "there is a crucial difference between government speech endorsing religion, which the Establishment Clause forbids, and private speech endorsing religion, which the Free Speech and Free Exercise Clauses protect."[67] Justice O'Connor went on to quote from a Senate report accompanying the Equal Access Act: "Students below the college level are capable of distinguishing between State-initiated school sponsored, or teacher-led speech on the one hand and student initiated, student-led religious speech on the other."[68]

Rosenberger v Rector and Visitors of University of Virginia, decided in 1995, involved the request of a recognized student organization for reimbursement from the Student Activities Fund for the costs of printing its newspaper, called *Wide Awake*. The paper's viewpoint was Christian. Each page of the publication was marked by a cross, and its mission was "to challenge Christians to live, in word and deed, according to the faith they proclaim and to encourage students to consider what a personal relationship with Jesus Christ means."[69] The university cited the Establishment Clause in defending its rule prohibiting such organizations from receiving funding from student activities fees. The court of appeals held that the viewpoint discrimination would have violated the Free Speech Clause, had it not been required by the Establishment Clause.

Justice Kennedy wrote the 5 to 4 Court opinion extending the principle of neutrality regarding speech in public fora from access to places (*Mergens* and *Widmar*) to access to funding. He noted "disbursements from the fund go to private contractors for the cost of printing that which is protected under the Speech Clause of the First Amendment."[70] Because the university had clearly separated itself from the expression of the student activities, and because it had intended to establish a limited public forum for educational purposes, its exclusion of religious viewpoints from reimbursement for costs amounted to "viewpoint discrimination." In dissent, Justice Souter argued that the Establishment Clause prohibited such financial support for religion,[71] that money differed from space for the purpose of "public forum analysis,"[72] and that the discrimination was content based, not viewpoint based, and did not violate the Free Speech Clause.[73]

Finally, in *Good News Club v Milford Central School* (2001),[74] the Court held, 6 to 3, that once a school district opened its facilities to the general public for "social, civic and recreational meetings and entertainment events,"[75] it could not exclude a club on the basis of its religious nature. In his Court opinion, Justice Thomas described the Good News Club as an organization that "chooses to teach moral lessons from a Christian perspective through live storytelling and prayer, whereas Lamb's Chapel taught lessons through films."[76] He also likened Good News Club's religious activities to *Wide Awake* publications in *Rosenberger*.[77]

Justices Stevens, Souter, and Ginsburg dissented. In their separate dissenting opinions both Justice Stevens and Justice Souter argued that religious worship can and should be distinguished from religious speech.[78] The Court's refusal to make that distinction indicates that free exercise claims now receive strong support from the Free Speech Clause.

Notes

1. 424 U.S. 1 (1976).
2. The provisions of the law are described in the *Buckley* Court's per curiam opinion.
3. Id. at 10.
4. Id. at 14.
5. Id. at 16.
6. Id. at 17.
7. *Kovacs v Cooper* 336 U.S. 77 (1949).
8. *Buckley*, 424 U.S. at 18. In a footnote, the per curiam made this distinction: "The decibel restriction upheld in *Kovacs* limited the manner of operating a sound truck, but not the extent of its proper use. By contrast, the Act's dollar ceilings restrict the extent of the reasonable use of virtually every means of communicating information." Id. note 17. Of course, the decibel level limit had the effect of limiting

the reach of the message, but the interest in allowing people to enjoy public streets and parks without loud noise is not directly related to the suppression of expression.

9. Id. at 20–21.

10. Gerald Gunther and Kathleen Sullivan have suggested that the Court applied a lower degree of scrutiny to the contribution limits than it did to the expenditure limits. Kathleen Sullivan and Gerald Gunther, *Constitutional Law*, 14th Edition, (Westport, New York: Foundations Press, 2001), p. 1378. I think a more accurate, if more complicated, explanation is that the Court applied both "strict scrutiny" and a form of "balancing." Subsequent Supreme Court decisions have confirmed the Sullivan and Gunther analysis, however. See also Daniel Ortiz, in *Campaign Finance Reform: A Source Book*, ed by Corrado, Mann, Ortiz, Potter and Sourauf (Washington: Brookings, 1997), p. 63.

11. 424 U.S. at 25.

12. Id. at 28.

13. Id. at 28–29.

14. Id. at 29.

15. Id. at 43. This interpretation produced developments that eventually led to a new federal law to close the "loopholes" in FECA, described later.

16. Id. at 44.

17. Id. at 45.

18. Id. at 46.

19. Id. at 48.

20. Id. at 48–49.

21. Id., citing *Times v Sullivan* and other cases.

22. Id. at 260.

23. Id. at 287.

24. The Court also struck down the original mode of selecting the FEC as in violation of the president's appointment power. Congress revised that provision to conform to the constitutional requirement that the president nominate and, with the advice and consent of the Senate, appoint executive branch officials.

25. *California Medical Assn v FEC*, 453 U.S. 182 (1981); *FEC v National Conservative PAC*, 470 U.S. 480 (1985); and *Colorado Republican Federal Campaign Committee v FEC*, 518 U.S. 604 (1996).

26. *Colorado Republican Federal Campaign Committee*, supra, note 25, at 649 (Justice Stevens dissenting).

27. *First National Bank of Boston v Bellotti*, 435 U.S. 765,785 (1978).

28. *FEC v National Right to Work Committee* [NRWC], 459 U.S. 197 (1982).

29. Federal Election Campaign Act of 1971, 2 U. S. C. § 441b(a), as quoted in the syllabus in NRWC, supra, note 28.

30. 479 U.S. 238 (1986).

31. 494 U.S. 652 (1990).

32. 120 S. Ct. 897 (2000).

33. PL 107–55.

34. See *Congressional Quarterly Weekly*, May 18, 2003, pp. 1347–48 for a discussion of the provisions of the law. The Court opinion of Justices Stevens's and O'Connor, in *McConnell v FEC*, discussed below, also describes "soft money." See 540 U.S. at 11–17 (slip opinion).

35. *Congressional Quarterly Weekly*, March 23, 2003, pp. 799, 802.

36. "Electioneering communications" are "broadcast, cable, or satellite communications that name candidates for federal office or show their likeness within 60 days of a general election and 30 days of a primary, and that are targeted to candidates' states or districts." See *Congressional Quarterly Weekly*, March 23, 2002, p. 1348.

37. Contribution limits to candidates were raised from $1,000 to $2,000 per election, indexed for inflation. The aggregate contribution limits for individuals for a two-year election cycle was set at $95,000: $37,500 to candidates and $57,500 for parties and political action committees. Independent expenditures of $1,000 or more calling for the election or defeat of a candidate, made on behalf of a candidate within twenty days of an election must be reported. *Congressional Quarterly Weekly*, May 18, 2003, p. 1347. The law also imposed reporting requirements on independent expenditures of $1,000 or more if given within twenty days of an election, $10,000 or more otherwise.

38. The quoted passages come from Judge Leon's memorandum opinion in *McConnell v FEC*, p. 5. As the separate opinions, and the chart at the beginning of the per curiam opinion make clear, Judge Leon's was the "swing vote" on most of the provisions in the law; Judge Kollar-Kotelly would have upheld the law as written, and Judge Henderson would have struck down most of the limiting provisions as incompatible with the First Amendment.

39. *McConnell v FEC*, 540 U.S. (2003) (slip opinion). "In the main, we uphold BCRA's two principal, complementary features: the control of soft money and the regulation of electioneering communications. Accordingly, we affirm in part and reverse in part the District Court's judgment with respect to Titles I and II." Id. at 118–19 (slip opinion). There are five titles to the Bipartisan Campaign Reform Act of 2002. I limit myself to a general discussion of the major titles.

40. Id. at 35–36.

41. Id. at 83, 84.

42. Id. at 84–86.

43. Chief Justice Rehnquist's opinion, 540 U.S. at 2 to 3 (slip opinion); Justice Kennedy's opinion at 540 U.S. at 5 to 15 (slip opinion).

44. "The evidence connects soft money to manipulations of the legislative calendar, leading to Congress' failure to enact, among other things, generic drug legislation, tort reform, and tobacco legislation (citations omitted)." From the Stevens-O'Connor Court opinion, in *McConnell* 540 U.S. at 40 (slip opinion).

45. Justice Kennedy's opinion, 540 U.S. at 13 (slip opinion).

46. *Hague v CIO*, 307 U.S. 496, 515 (1939).

47. See Redish, "The Content Distinction in First Amendment Analysis," 34 *Stanford L Rev* 113 (1981).

48. *Cox v New Hampshire*, 312 U.S. 569 (1941) (parade permit); *Schneider v State*, 308 U.S. 147 (1939) (leaflets); *Kovacs v Cooper*, 336 U.S. 77 (1949) (sound trucks); *City of Ladue v Gilleo*, 512 U.S. 43 (1994)(sign on private property); *Forsyth Co. v Nationalist Movement*, 505 U.S. 123 (1992)(sliding scale permit fee). The fifth example in the text refers to *Cox*, in which the Court assumed a content neutral license fee would be constitutional, although no fee was actually assessed (see *Cox*, 312 U.S. at 577).

49. 379 U.S. 536 (1965).

50. Harry Kalven, "The Concept of the Public Forum," in Kurland, Free Speech p. 127.

51. Id.

52. *Perry Education Association v Perry Local Educators' Association*, 460 U.S. 37, 45–46 (1983).

53. *International Society for Krishna Consciousness v Lee* 505 U.S. 672 (1992).

54. 505 US at 705 (1992).

55. Id. at 690.

56. *Heffron v ISKCON*, 452 U.S. 640 (1981).

57. 454 U.S. 263, 264 (1981).

58. 508 U.S. 384, 387 (1993).

59. 454 U.S. at 274.

60. Id. at 283 (Justice White dissenting).

61. 468 U.S. 288 (1984).

62. *Clark v Community for Creative Non-Violence*, 468 U.S. 288, 293 (1984).

63. Id. at 294.

64. Id. at 298.

65. Id. at 299, note 8.

66. *Board of Education v Mergens* 489 U.S. 226 (1990).

67. Id. at 250.

68. Id. at 250–51 (internal citation omitted).

69. *Rosenberger v Rector and Visitors of University of Virginia*, 515 U.S. 819, 826 (1995).

70. Id. at 841.

71. Id. at 878.

72. Id. at 887–89.

73. Id. at 895.

74. 2001 U.S. Lexis 4312.

75. Id., p. 9.

76. Id., p. 21.

77. Id., p. 22.

78. Justice Stevens at p. 56; Justice Souter at pp. 68–70.

Religious Freedom
and the Constitution

The last free speech cases discussed in chapter 12 provide a transition to our examination of the Supreme Court's treatment of religious freedom. In many cases, the question arises whether the two religion clauses are mutually consistent, because a strict separation approach to Establishment Clause cases appears to conflict with an accommodation approach to Free Exercise Clause cases. In some cases, as we have seen, the strict separation approach also conflicts with the Court's content neutrality approach to freedom of speech. And the limited discussion in the First Congress did not clarify the relation between the two clauses.[1] Phillip Kurland's proposed interpretation reflects Locke's teaching in his *Letter on Toleration*:

> The principle tendered is a simple one. The freedom and separation clauses should be read as stating a single precept: that government cannot utilize religion as a standard for action or inaction because these clauses, read together as they should be, prohibit classification in terms of religion either to confer a benefit or to impose a burden.[2]

The Supreme Court's interpretation of the religion clauses approaches Kurland's principle but also reflects Tocqueville's observation: "Religion, which, among Americans, never mixes directly in the government of society, should therefore be considered as the first of their political institutions; for if it does not give them the taste for freedom, it singularly facilitates their use of it."[3] In Free Exercise Clause cases, the conflict is between an approach that looks exclusively to the purpose of the legislation and one that provides special accommodation when legislation not aimed at religion nonetheless affects religious adherents. In Establishment Clause cases, the conflict is between neutrality and different forms of accommodation, including the doctrine of "non-preferentialism." The most recent Supreme Court decisions reflect a resolve to follow the neutrality rule. The Court has tempered its Establishment Clause decisions with accommodations toward religion, and it has allowed legislative accommodation in certain free exercise matters. In both situations, the prevailing neutrality doctrine minimizes the occasions when the Court has to define religion.

Notes

1. See chapter 3 for a discussion of the work of the First Congress.

2. Phillip Kurland, *Religion and the Law: Of Church and State and the Supreme Court* (Chicago: Aldine Pub. Co., 1961 and 1962), p. 112.

3. *Democracy in America*, vol. 2, part 2, chapter 9, p. 280.

CHAPTER THIRTEEN

The Free Exercise Clause

The first "Free Exercise" case concerned a challenge to the Mormon Church practice of polygamy. In *Reynolds v United States*, decided in 1878, the Supreme Court affirmed a criminal conviction for violating the law against polygamy.[1] Appellant claimed that his Mormon religion required him to practice polygamy and that the Free Exercise Clause protected such practice. In an opinion by Chief Justice Waite, the Court drew on the common law to support the proposition that "polygamy has always been odious among the northern and western nations of Europe."[2] Chief Justice Waite went on to say "it is impossible to believe that the constitutional guaranty of religious free-dom was intended to prohibit legislation in respect to this most important feature of social life."[3] Since the law prohibiting polygamy was a valid exer-cise of Congressional power over the territory, the remaining question was whether those who practiced polygamy as a part of their religion were ex-empt from the law. The answer was a clear "no." "Laws are made for the gov-ernment of actions, and while they cannot interfere with mere religious be-liefs and opinions, they may with practices."[4]

The Supreme Court did not consider other free exercise cases until 1940. In *Cantwell v Connecticut*,[5] the Supreme Court confronted two issues that arose out of Jesse Cantwell's proselytizing for the Jehovah's Witnesses. Cantwell an-gered some of his listeners when he played phonograph records with messages attacking Catholics. Cantwell was charged with a breach of the peace and with soliciting without prior approval, as required by state law. The state supreme court upheld the convictions, emphasizing Cantwell's solicitation.

The Supreme Court reversed. While the Court treated the statute as a time, place, and manner regulation of speech, it also discussed the meaning of free exercise and held, for the first time, that the Fourteenth Amendment's Due Process Clause made the Free Exercise Clause applicable to the states.[6] Justice Roberts's Court opinion acknowledged that "the Amendment embraces two concepts—freedom to believe and freedom to act. The first is absolute but, in the nature of things, the second cannot be."[7] He then proceeded to find that the administrative discretion to identify a religious cause was "a censorship of religion" and "a denial of liberty protected by the First Amendment and included in the liberty which is within the protection of the Fourteenth."[8]

Two weeks after deciding *Cantwell,* the Court applied the "freedom to believe—freedom to act" distinction and rejected a clear "free exercise" claim in *Minersville v Gobitis,* its first flag salute decision.[9] The Gobitis family, members of the Jehovah's Witnesses, objected to the requirement on the grounds that it forced them to violate their religious beliefs, bowing down to, or recognizing, a graven image, in violation of the Ten Commandments.[10] Justice Frankfurter wrote the Court opinion upholding the local requirement that all public school teachers and pupils participate in the pledge of allegiance and flag salute. "The religious liberty which the Constitution protects has never excluded legislation of general scope not directed against doctrinal loyalties of particular sects."[11] Justice Frankfurter rejected the freedom of speech claim this way: "National unity is the basis of national security."[12]

Justice Stone was the lone dissenter; for him the requirement violated both freedom of speech and the free exercise of religion. "For by this law the state seeks to coerce these children to express a sentiment which, as they interpret it, they do not entertain, and which violates their deepest religious convictions."[13] For Justice Stone, the constitutional line should be drawn between eliciting expressions of loyalty, which is permissible, and compelling them, which is not.[14] Justice Stone did not say whether the argument from conscience applied to nonreligious beliefs.

The difference between the free speech claim and the Free Exercise claim came to the forefront in the *Barnette* case, the second flag salute decision, thanks to Justice Jackson. The case came to the Court on appeal from a three-judge district court that had decided the case in favor of Barnette on free exercise grounds. District court Judge Parker, who wrote the opinion, noted that Justices Black, Douglas, and Murphy had since disassociated themselves from *Gobitis,* which they had originally supported. Along with Justice Stone, that meant that four of the seven justices on the 1942 Court who were part of the *Gobitis* Court now opposed that decision.[15] District

Judge Parker "anticipated" the Supreme Court's reversal of *Jones v Opelika*,[16] a reversal made possible by Justice Rutledge's vote. In light of that change, one would have expected *Gobitis* to have been overruled by a similar 5 to 4 vote and on free exercise grounds, or with reference to a right of conscience, without distinguishing freedom of speech from the free exercise of religion.

Justice Jackson, however, viewed the flag salute issue in terms of freedom of speech (coerced expression), rather than a free exercise claim of exemption from an otherwise valid exercise of the state's police power. "To sustain the compulsory flag salute we are required to say that a Bill of Rights which guards the individual's right to speak his own mind, left it open to public authorities to compel him to utter what is not in his mind."[17] Now the issue between the majority and the minority turned on the level of scrutiny that was to be applied to a requirement that implicated freedom of speech directly. The flag salute requirement did not suppress speech, but it did coerce all public schoolchildren to express a belief.[18] And, as Justice Jackson maintained, "It would seem that involuntary affirmation could be commanded only on even more immediate and urgent grounds than silence."[19]

Justice Jackson's reply to Justice Frankfurter's "national unity" argument was similar to Justice Stone's: "National unity as an end which officials may foster by persuasion and example is not in question. The problem is whether under our constitution compulsion as here employed is a permissible means for its achievement."[20] For Justice Jackson, "the test of [freedom's] substance is the right to differ as to things that touch the heart of the existing order."[21] This is followed by the now famous "fixed star" statement proscribing orthodoxy.[22]

The brief concurring opinions of Justices Black and Douglas and Justice Murphy emphasized the religious freedom aspect of the case, but Jackson's Court opinion made it clear that any person could now refuse to participate in the pledge of allegiance and salute to the flag without suffering expulsion from public school.

In his dissent, Justice Frankfurter restated his argument concerning the proper understanding of the Free Exercise Clause. "The constitutional protection of religious freedom terminated disabilities, it did not create new privileges. It gave religious equality, not civil immunity."[23] As for the free speech issue—the only issue upon which he and Justice Jackson disagreed— Justice Frankfurter defended the use of symbols in civic education.[24] The disagreement concerned the coercive use of symbols to inculcate belief. Justice Frankfurter disapproved, but he did not find it unconstitutional.[25]

The Supreme Court had occasion to revisit the meaning of the Free Exercise Clause in the 1960s. The cases involved Sunday closing laws, a Seventh

Day Adventist who was denied unemployment compensation, and conscientious objectors.

The Supreme Court decided two Sunday closing laws cases in 1961: McGowan v Maryland[26] and Braunfeld v Brown.[27] In McGowan, the Court, by a vote of 8 to 1, upheld the denial of appellants' claim that the Sunday closing law violated the Establishment Clause as well as the Due Process and Equal Protection Clauses. The Court found that the practice of a day of rest, while religious in origin, satisfied the secular purpose of providing a restful break from ordinary activities. In the Braunfeld case, Orthodox Jews argued that their religion commanded them to rest on their Sabbath, which was Saturday, and the Pennsylvania law, which provided for criminal sanctions, forced them to choose between practicing their religion, and—as a result of being limited to a five-day workweek—being driven out of business. By a vote of 6 to 3, the Court affirmed the lower court's rejection of appellant's claim: "[the statute] simply regulates a secular activity and, as applied to appellants, operates so as to make the practice of their religious beliefs more expensive."[28] Their choice was not criminal prosecution or abandonment of their religious practice, but rather retaining their present occupations "and incurring economic disadvantage," or engaging in "some other commercial activity which does not call for either Saturday or Sunday labor."[29] Justice Brennan dissented on the free exercise claim in Braunfeld, and Justice Stewart joined him.[30] Justice Brennan maintained that the Free Exercise Clause required an accommodation where possible; that meant granting an exemption to the appellants, and presumably any other Saturday Sabbatarians who were similarly affected by the Sunday Closing law. Twenty-one of the thirty-four states with Sunday closing laws made such an exemption.

The Court changed its position on its approach to free exercise claims in Sherbert v Verner, decided in 1963.[31] Miss Sherbert, a Seventh Day Adventist, had been denied unemployment compensation on the grounds that she was not "available for work," since she refused to work on Saturday, her Sabbath. The Court reversed the lower court and upheld Sherbert's claim, 7 to 2; Justice Brennan wrote the Court opinion.[32]

Drawing on a recently decided freedom of association case,[33] Justice Brennan proclaimed the "compelling interest" test now applicable to "any incidental burden on the free exercise of appellant's religion."[34] In his application of the "compelling state interest," Justice Brennan considered and rejected the state's concern about fraudulent claims or the need to judicially examine the truth or falsity of religious beliefs. The first concern was merely a possibility and the second not likely; in any case, the state would have to demonstrate the absence of any alternative means to deal with such a problem.[35]

Justice Brennan distinguished *Sherbert* from *Braunfeld* by saying there was "a strong state interest in providing one uniform day of rest for all workers," and that granting exemptions for Sabbatarians in that case might have given the exempted class a competitive advantage.[36] Still, Justice Brennan applied the same test in *Sherbert* that he advocated in his *Braunfeld* dissent. Both Justice Stewart, who concurred in the Court opinion, and dissenting Justices Harlan and White were unimpressed with the attempt to distinguish the two cases.

In his dissenting opinion, Justice Harlan described the purpose of the legislation in social and economic terms: "to tide people over, and to avoid social and economic chaos, during periods when *work was unavailable*."[37] Since all mills in the area were on a six-day workweek, appellant was "unavailable for work" for a personal reason just like any other personal reason. However, Justice Harlan thought "it would be a permissible accommodation of religion for the State, if it chose to do so, to create an exception to its eligibility requirements for persons like the appellant."[38] He did not say whether accommodating some reasons of conscience, but not all, would also pass an equal protection analysis. And he barely mentioned, in a final footnote, the equal protection argument that Sherbert made on the basis of the state emergency Sunday work provisions.[39]

Justice Brennan pointed out that the statute authorized work on Sundays during emergencies but protected employees who conscientiously opposed working on Sunday.[40] Instead of deciding the case on an Equal Protection Clause basis, Justice Brennan chose to introduce the broader "compelling interest" test whenever statutes that are neutral in purpose nevertheless indirectly restrict religious practice.[41]

In the conscientious objector cases, however, the Court did employ equal protection analysis. The framers of the Bill of Rights considered and then rejected an amendment that would have guaranteed—after "the right of the people to keep and bear arms"—that "no person religiously scrupulous, shall be compelled to bear arms."[42] The controlling sentiment, as expressed by Egbert Benson, a Federalist from New York, was that "No man can claim this indulgence of right. It may be a religious persuasion, but it is no natural right, and therefore ought to be left to the discretion of the government."[43] Both state governments and Congress have exercised this discretion to provide for exemptions for conscientious objectors. Congress passed conscription laws with exemptions in 1863 through 1864, 1917, 1940, and again in 1948.[44] The Supreme Court had three occasions to determine the scope of the conscientious objector exemption. The Universal Military Training and Service Act of 1940, as amended in 1948, contains the following statement (section 6j) on conscientious objector exemptions:

> Nothing contained in this title shall be construed to require any person to be subject to combatant training and service in the armed forces of the United States who, by reason of religious training and belief, is conscientiously opposed to participation in war in any form. Religious training and belief in this connection means an individual's belief in a relation to a Supreme Being involving duties superior to those arising from any human relation, but does not include essentially political, sociological, or philosophical views, or a merely personal moral code.[45]

In the first case, in 1965, three individuals, including Daniel Andrew Seeger, claimed conscientious objector status but did not sign the Selective Service System form without changing it. Seeger, for example, put quotation marks around "religious belief" and "left his belief in a Supreme Being open." Instead, he referred to his "belief in and devotion to goodness and virtue for their own sakes, and a religious faith in a purely ethical creed."[46] On the basis of such a creed, Seeger opposed war in any form. The court of appeals reversed his conviction on constitutional grounds; it held that the "Supreme Being" requirement was an "impermissible classification" under the Due Process Clause of the Fifth Amendment.[47] In his unanimous Supreme Court opinion, Justice Clark noted that there were over 250 sects in the United States, with some believing "in a purely personal God" and others emphasizing the goals of peace and understanding.[48] After also noting that Congress deliberately chose the term "Supreme Being" rather than "God," Justice Clark offered the following test: "A sincere and meaningful belief which occupies in the life of its possessor a place parallel to that filled by the God of those admittedly qualifying for the exemption comes within the statutory definition."[49] Applying such a test the Court held that Seeger and the two other individuals qualified for the 6 (j) exemption.

The next case arose when Eliot Ashton Welsh struck out the words "my religious training and," before signing the required form. The Supreme Court, voting 5 to 3, reversed Welsh's conviction. Justice Black announced the judgment of the Court in an opinion that only Justices Douglas, Brennan, and Marshal joined. After quoting the Court's test from *Seeger*, Justice Black wrote:

> If an individual deeply and sincerely holds beliefs that are purely ethical or moral in source and content but that nevertheless impose upon him a duty of

conscience to refrain from participating in any war at any time, those beliefs certainly occupy in the life of that individual "a place parallel to that filled by . . . God" in traditionally religious persons. Because his beliefs function as a religion in his life, such an individual is as much entitled to a "religious" conscientious objector exemption under S6 (j) as is someone who derives his conscientious opposition to war from traditional religious convictions."[50]

As for Welsh's explicit denial that his position was based on religious beliefs, Justice Black remarked that "very few registrants are fully aware of the broad scope of the word 'religious' as used in 6 (j), and accordingly a registrant's statement that his beliefs are nonreligious is a highly unreliable guide for those charged with administering the exemption."[51]

For Justice Harlan, however, who supplied the fifth vote, intellectual candor required a different judicial route to the same result. "The natural reading of S6 (j), which quite evidently draws a distinction between theistic and nontheistic religions, is the only one that is consistent with the legislative history."[52] He charged the Court opinion with having "performed a lobotomy and completely transformed the statute by reading out of it any distinction between religiously acquired beliefs and those deriving from 'essentially political, sociological, or philosophical views or a merely personal moral code.'"[53] In *Seeger*, Justice Clark cited several authorities, including Paul Tillich, in support of what could be called "non-theistic religion," and Justice Douglas, in his concurring opinion, argued that Buddhism might also be viewed that way.[54] The inclusion of *Seeger* and *Welsh* within the language of 6 (j) expands the exemption category, and yet, as Justice Black pointed out, Congress responded to the Court's *Seeger* decision by deleting the reference to a "Supreme Being" in section 6(j).[55]

The Supreme Court thus applied the exemption statute to any conscientious opposition to war in any form. That result was confirmed in *Gillette v United States*,[56] where the Court rejected, 8 to 1, Gillette's claim that his opposition to the war in Vietnam as unjust came within the statutory exemption. Criticism of a particular war was central to the political deliberations, and hence a part of the political process.

The most interesting part of Justice Harlan's opinion in *Welsh* concerned the reasons why he voted for Welsh's exemption, after having argued that the expanded interpretation of the statute did not respect Congressional intent:[57]

The constitutional question that must be faced in this case is whether a statute that defers to the individual's conscience only when his views emanate from adherence to theistic religious belief is within the power of Congress. Congress, of course, could, entirely consistently with the requirements of the Constitution, eliminate all exemptions for conscientious objectors.[58]

Justice Harlan found the statute "under-inclusive" in its treatment of "conscientiousness" as a ground for gaining exemption from required enlistment. He went beyond the distinction between theistic and nontheistic religions to embrace "conscience" as the ground that must be treated in an "all or nothing" manner:

> [The statute] not only accords a preference to the "religious," but also disadvantages adherents of religions that do not worship a Supreme Being. The constitutional infirmity cannot be cured, moreover, even by an impermissible construction that eliminates the theistic requirement and simply draws the line between religious and nonreligious. This in my view offends the Establishment Clause and is that kind of classification. . . . If the exemption is to be given application, it must encompass the class of individuals it purports to exclude, those whose beliefs emanate from a purely moral, ethical, or philosophical source. The common denominator must be the intensity of moral conviction with which a belief is held.[59]

On the basis of the "severability clause"[60] and the government's longstanding policy of "exempting religious conscientious objectors," Justice Harlan concluded that the right choice was to expand the statute.[61] He was "prepared to accept the prevailing opinion's conscientious objector test, not as a reflection of congressional statutory intent but as a patchwork of judicial making that cures the defect of under-inclusion in S 6(j) and can be administered by local boards in the usual course of business."[62]

Justice White wrote a dissenting opinion, which Chief Justice Burger and Justice Stewart joined. These Justices agreed with Justice Harlan that the plurality had misconstrued the statute but disagreed with his contention that, rightly interpreted, the statute violated the Establishment Clause. "I would not frustrate congressional will by construing the Establishment Clause to condition the exemption for religionists upon extending the exemption also to those who object to war on nonreligious grounds."[63] Justice White's best reply to Justice Harlan's Establishment Clause argument was that the Free Exercise Clause extended beyond belief to conduct as well.[64] Justice White reminded Justice Harlan that in *Sherbert* he recommended a legislative accommodation for Sabbatarians regarding unemployment benefits. Justice Harlan responded that the accommodation had to "be sufficiently broad to be religiously neutral."[65]

The Supreme Court's *Wisconsin v Yoder*[66] decision reaffirmed the *Sherbert* approach but also revealed the difficulties involved in carving out special exemptions for religious groups. The case involved a challenge to Wisconsin's policy of requiring that all children attend school until the age of sixteen. Yoder and other members of the Old Order Amish religion and the Conservative Amish Menonite Church in Wisconsin contended that requiring their children to attend high school, public or private, was contrary to their "religion and way of life." When they declined to send their children, ages fourteen and fifteen, to school, respondents were charged with violating the state's compulsory education requirement and fined five dollars each.[67] The Wisconsin Supreme Court reversed on free exercise grounds, citing *Sherbert*. The United States Supreme Court affirmed. Much of Chief Justice Burger's Court opinion drew on expert testimony concerning the Amish way of life: "[It was] in harmony with nature and the soil, as exemplified by the simple life of the early Christian era that continued in America during much of our early national life."[68] The environment at high school stressed "competition in class work and sports and . . . pressure to conform to the styles, manners, and ways of the peer group." And being in high school took the Amish away from their own community "physically and emotionally, during the crucial and formative adolescent period of life."[69]

Chief Justice Burger cited *Pierce v Society of Sisters*,[70] which recognized the liberty interest that parents have in educating their children, for the proposition that "there must be a state interest of sufficient magnitude to override the interest claiming protection under the Free Exercise Clause."[71] But *Pierce* held that the state, which may require the education of the young and set general standards, may not require all children to attend public schools. So *Pierce* stands for an option the Amish did not choose: the right to send one's children to a private school.[72] After holding that the First and Fourteenth Amendments prevented Wisconsin from compelling respondents to send their children to attend high school until they are sixteen, Chief Justice Burger concluded his opinion by suggesting some form of accommodation regarding vocational education.

Chief Justice Burger relied on *Walz v Tax Commission*,[73] to demonstrate the Court's longstanding position of flexibility and accommodation of the relationship between free exercise and establishment.[74] But the *Walz* Court upheld the property tax exemption for religious organizations because they were a subset of charitable organizations to whom the law granted the exemption.[75] The *Yoder* case followed the *Sherbert* approach in subjecting a neutral law to strict scrutiny as applied to the Amish.

A way of life, however virtuous and admirable, may not be interposed as a barrier to reasonable state regulation of education if it is based on purely secular considerations; to have the protection of the Religion Clauses, the claims must be rooted in religious belief. Although a determination of what is a 'religious' belief or practice entitled to constitutional protection may present a most delicate question, the very concept of ordered liberty precludes allowing every person to make his own standards on matters of conduct in which society has important interests. Thus, if the Amish asserted their claims because of their subjective evaluation and rejection of the contemporary secular values accepted by the majority, much as Thoreau rejected the social values of his time and isolated himself at Walden Pond, their claims would not rest on a religious basis. Thoreau's choice was philosophical and personal rather than religious, and such belief does not rise to the demands of the Religion Clauses.[76]

The Chief Justice concluded his opinion by suggesting that few religious peoples would satisfy the test as the Amish did.[77] This contrasts sharply with the Court's approach to religion in the *Seeger* and *Welsh* cases.

Chief Justice Burger added something to the *Sherbert* test when he rejected the state's contention that a neutral regulation should not be subject to special scrutiny when it is challenged in the name of religion: "A regulation neutral on its face may, in its application, nonetheless offend the constitutional requirement for government neutrality if it unduly burdens the free exercise of religion."[78] Hence, an "undue" or "substantial" burden is necessary to trigger the "compelling interest" test.

After *Yoder*, the Court decided nine cases involving free exercise claims to exemptions from otherwise legitimate laws: in three of them, where the facts were similar to *Sherbert*, the claimants won.[79] The disposition of the other six cases indicated disagreement about the soundness of the *Sherbert* approach to free exercise. The editors of one prominent casebook described the Court's opinions in these cases as follows:

In the preceding cases the Court used three techniques to distinguish Sherbert and Yoder. In some cases, it found an overriding government interest in uniformity, for example in the administration of the tax laws [*United States v Lee*, 455 U.S. 252 (1982)]. In others it found that free exercise interests were attenuated and government interests paramount in specialized environments such as prisons and the military [*Olone v Estate of Shabaz*, 482 U.S. 342 (1987); *Goldman v Weinberger*, 475 U.S. 503 (1986)]. And in others, it applied a narrow definition of what constitutes a burden on religious practice, rejecting free exercise claims seeking to alter 'internal' government operations such as the use of social security numbers and the development of federal property [*Bowen v Roy* 476 U.S. 693 (1986); *Lyng v Northwest Indian Cemetery Protective Association*, 485 U.S. 439 (1988)].[80]

Two years later, in *Employment Division v Smith* (1980), the Supreme Court repudiated the *Sherbert* compelling interest test for free exercise cases. Justice Scalia wrote the Court opinion, which Chief Justice Rehnquist and Justices White, Stevens, and Kennedy joined. Justice O'Connor wrote a partial concurrence and partial dissent, holding to the *Sherbert* test, and Justice Brennan wrote a dissent, which Justices Marshall and Blackmun joined.

Respondents Alfred Smith and Galen Black were fired from their jobs with a private drug-rehabilitation clinic for ingesting the drug peyote for sacramental purposes at a ceremony of their Native American Church. They applied for unemployment compensation, but the Employment Division in Oregon determined that they were ineligible for benefits because "they had been discharged for work related 'misconduct.'"[81] The Oregon Court of Appeals reversed, holding that the denial violated their free exercise rights. The Oregon Supreme Court agreed, reasoning that the "misconduct" provision under which respondents were disqualified was intended to preserve "the financial integrity of the compensation fund," not to enforce the state's criminal law, and that such a rationale was not sufficient to justify the burden placed on respondents' religious practice.[82] The United States Supreme Court remanded the case to the Oregon Supreme Court to determine whether respondents' sacramental use of peyote was in fact a violation of the criminal law. The Oregon Court answered that it was because the statute made no exception for the religiously inspired use of peyote, but it reaffirmed its earlier ruling in favor of the respondents.

Justice Scalia's Court opinion laid down the neutrality approach to the Free Exercise Clause, in opposition to the *Sherbert* accommodation approach. "It is a permissible reading of the text . . . to say that if prohibiting the exercise of religion . . . is not the object . . . but merely the incidental effect of a generally applicable and otherwise valid provision, the First Amendment has not been offended."[83]

We would expect an account of why the *Sherbert/Yoder* approach was mistaken. Instead, the usually candid Justice Scalia did his best to distinguish these two cases. He distinguished *Yoder* as a hybrid case, resting on both the Free Exercise Clause and the right of parents, presumably under the Due Process Clause, to direct the education of their children.[84] He distinguished *Sherbert*, as well as two other unemployment compensation cases, as not involving exemption from "a generally applicable criminal law."[85]

While the Court's attempt to limit *Sherbert* and *Yoder* is not persuasive, its argument against the use of the "compelling interest" test in the free exercise context is. The *Sherbert* "free exercise" test was triggered by the effect of the law, not its purpose. Unlike "purpose" tests or other kinds of "effects" tests, the application of this test could result in a decision that exempted some from an otherwise legitimate law.[86] There seem to be two related difficulties with such an approach. First, as Justice Scalia points out, there is no way for the courts to determine what is a substantial burden on religion without assessing the relative importance of a given belief.[87] Second, it is not clear that courts either can or should grant special consideration to religious objections to otherwise valid laws. And to the extent to which making such distinctions is possible and desirable, it seems best to leave that business to the legislature. Justice Scalia closed his opinion by suggesting that the Oregon legislature consider exempting the ingesting of peyote from the criminal law that prohibited the use of controlled substances.[88]

Justice O'Connor wrote an opinion concurring in the result but dissenting from the majority's treatment of the *Sherbert* test. She argued that the compelling interest test "effectuates the First Amendment's command that religious liberty is an independent liberty, that it occupies a preferred position, and that the Court will not permit encroachments upon this liberty, whether direct or indirect, unless required by clear and compelling government interests 'of the highest order.'"[89] On the matter of precedent, Justice O'Connor quoted a lengthy passage from *Yoder*, which concluded: "A regulation neutral on its face, may, in its application, nonetheless offend the constitutional requirement for government neutrality if it unduly burdens the free exercise of religion."[90]

Justice O'Connor joined the majority because the underlying behavior that led to the firing was against a criminal law.[91] Consequently, she thought the state's decision to regard respondents as not qualified to receive unemployment compensation, as a result of being fired for ingesting peyote at a religious ceremony, passed the compelling interest test, "although the question is close."[92]

In his dissenting opinion, which Justices Brennan and Marshall joined, Justice Blackmun pointed out that Oregon had never sought to prosecute respondents, and offered no evidence to demonstrate that religious use of peyote constituted a health risk.[93]

The Supreme Court continued to debate the *Smith* decision in a case involving the Church of Lakumi Babalu Aye.[94] The church practiced the Santeria religion, which features ritualized animal sacrifice. When it announced plans to open a house of worship in Hialeah, Florida, the city council passed a series of ordinances related to the State's laws subjecting to criminal punishment anyone who "unnecessarily or cruelly . . . kills any animal."[95] Justice Kennedy's description of one ordinance in particular highlighted the constitutional difficulties surrounding these regulations:

It [87–71] prohibits the sacrifice of animals, but defines sacrifice as 'to unnecessarily kill . . . an animal in a public or private ritual or ceremony not for the primary purpose of food consumption.' The definition excludes almost all killings of animals except for religious sacrifice, and the primary purpose requirement narrows the proscribed category even further, in particular by exempting kosher slaughter.[96]

The Court unanimously concluded: "the suppression of the central element of the Santeria worship service was the object of the ordinance."[97] From the perspective of any legitimate interest in health and safety, say concerning proper disposal or inspection, the regulations were "under-inclusive," to the point of discriminating against a particular religious practice no less. After showing that the law did not pass the *Smith* tests of neutrality and general applicability,[98] Justice Kennedy went on to apply the compelling interest test to "a law burdening religious practice," on the analogy to the *O'Brien* test for legislation that aims at the suppression of expression.[99]

Justice Souter, in his concurring opinion, restated the case against the *Smith* rule.[100] He emphasized different kinds of neutrality:

A secular law, applicable to all, that prohibited consumption of alcohol, for example, would affect members of religions that require the use of wine differently from members of other religions and nonbelievers disproportionately burdening the practice of, say Catholicism or Judaism. Without an exemption for sacramental wine, Prohibition may fail the test of religion neutrality.[101]

Justice Souter distinguished between formal and substantive neutrality. The former looks at the purpose of the law; the latter looks at the effect and would require governmental accommodation "by exempting religious practices from formally neutral laws."[102] The *Smith* case announced the rule of formal neutrality while the dissenters' position advocated substantive neutrality. The "non-persecution principle," as Justice Souter also described the *Smith* rule, did not, in his view, satisfy the requirements of the Free Exercise Clause. But, the Sherbert/Yoder approach required the Court to determine which religious claims were legitimate and then give such claims a privileged treatment. The *Seeger* and *Welsh* cases stand for the proposition that the Court will not allow the line to be drawn between religious belief and categorical moral belief in the matter of exemption from combat.[103] Finally, Justice Kennedy described the relationship between the two religion clauses this way:

These [Establishment Clause] cases, however, for the most part have addressed governmental efforts to benefit religion or particular religions, and so have dealt with a question different, at least, in its formulation and emphasis, from the issue here. Petitioners allege an attempt to disfavor their religion because of the religious ceremonies it commands, and the Free Exercise Clause is dispositive in our analysis.[104]

The suggestion here is that the two clauses complement one another in the service of a certain form of neutrality.

Congress responded to the *Smith* decision by passing the Religious Freedom Restoration Act (RFRA) in 1993.[105] Congress wrote a detailed finding to the effect that the Court's neutral approach toward religion, as manifested in the *Smith* case, "may burden [the] religious exercise" that the First Amendment protected and that the "compelling interest" test struck "sensible balances between religious liberty and competing prior governmental interests."[106] Then in section 3, entitled Free Exercise of Religion Protected, Congress enacted the following:

a. In General: Government shall not substantially burden a person's exercise of religion even if the burden results from a rule of general applicability, except as provided in subsection b.
b. Exception: Government may substantially burden a person's exercise of religion only if it demonstrates that application of the burden to the person
   1. is in furtherance of a compelling governmental interest; and
   2. is the least restrictive means of furthering that compelling governmental interest.
c. Judicial Relief: A person whose religious exercise has been burdened in violation of this section may assert that violation as a claim or defense in a judicial proceeding and obtain appropriate relief against a government. Standing to assert a claim or defense under this section shall be governed by the general rules of standing under article III of the Constitution.[107]

In *City of Boerne v Flores*,[108] the St. Peter Catholic Church sought a building permit to enlarge its church but city authorities, relying on a recently passed ordinance aimed a preserving historic landmarks or buildings in a historic district, declined to give its permission. The church sued, relying on RFRA. The district court found the law unconstitutional but the court of appeals reversed, upholding the law. The Supreme Court reversed the court of appeals, holding the law unconstitutional.

Justice Kennedy delivered the Court opinion, which Chief Justice Rehnquist and Justices Stevens, Scalia, Thomas, and Ginsburg joined. Justices O'Connor, Souter, and Breyer dissented. Justice Kennedy's opinion accepted the *Smith* precedent and addressed the case in terms of the Fourteenth Amendment: could Congress through its Fourteenth Amendment enforcement power expand the scope of the First Amendment's protection of free exercise of religion? His answer for the Court, not surprisingly, was "no." He quoted from *Katzenbach v Morgan*[109] to support the contention that congressional action under the Fourteenth Amendment must address constitutional violations, either actual or anticipated ones. In light of some of the Court's precedents in the voting rights cases, defenders of the RFRA argued that rather than wait for, or limit the law to, cases that target religious beliefs, which might be difficult to prove, "Congress can simply invalidate any law which imposes a substantial burden on a religious practice unless it is justified by a compelling interest and is the least restrictive means of accomplishing that interest."[110] Justice Kennedy's response to that argument was: "While preventive rules are sometimes appropriate remedial measures, there must be a congruence between the means used and the ends to be achieved. The appropriateness of remedial measures must be considered in light of the evil presented."[111] Using such a test, Justice Kennedy distinguished RFRA from the Voting Rights Act of 1965: that law suspended voting tests in states and parts of states where the combination of the tests and low registration among black voters suggested the presence of discrimination, but the record in support of RFRA cited no laws passed due to religious bigotry.[112] As a result, Justice Kennedy concluded for the court that RFRA "cannot be considered remedial, preventive legislation, if those terms are to have any meaning."[113] Toward the end of his opinion, Justice Kennedy offered a general defense of the neutrality rule:

> It is a reality of the modern regulatory state that numerous state laws, such as the zoning regulations at issue here, impose a substantial burden on a large class of individuals. When the exercise of religion has been burdened in an incidental way by a law of general application, it does not follow that the persons affected have been burdened because of their religious beliefs.[114]

Justices Scalia, in his concurring opinion, and O'Connor, in her dissent, continued the debate on the merits of "compelling interest" versus neutrality. Justice O'Connor argued that "the [Free Exercise] Clause is best understood as an affirmative guarantee of the right to participate in religious practices and conduct without impermissible governmental interference, even when such conduct conflicts with a neutral, generally applicable, law."[115] She cited colonial charters and the state constitutions, quoting from four eighteenth century state constitutional provisions on free exercise. Here is New York's:

> The free exercise and enjoyment of religious profession and worship, without discrimination or preference shall forever hereafter be allowed, within this

State, to all mankind: Provided, That the liberty of conscience, hereby granted, shall not be so construed as to excuse acts of licentiousness, or justify practices inconsistent with the peace or safety of this State.[116]

Justice Scalia's rejoinder was twofold: First, the protection was against discriminatory action by government; second, if the "free exercise" provisos go further, they mean that the religious practice "shall be permitted *so long as it does not violate general laws governing conduct*."[117] Justice O'Connor argued that the constitutional provisos "make sense only if the right to free exercise was viewed as generally superior to ordinary legislation, to be overridden only when necessary to secure important governmental purposes."[118]

Justice O'Connor also cited Madison's proposed language, for the Virginia Bill of Rights, protecting the right of conscience.[119] To Justice Scalia, this argument and Madison's *Memorial and Remonstrance*, also against a legislative assessment for religious instruction, did not address free exercise so much as "establishment."[120]

Finally, Justice O'Connor referred to the actions of various states and the Continental Congress to exempt anyone who "from religious principles cannot bear arms in any case."[121] Justice Scalia replied that these were examples of legislative exemption, which he supported. Justice O'Connor acknowledged that fact but noted that this action had been taken before the practice of judicial review was initiated, and that "the drafters and ratifiers of the First Amendment—many of whom served in state legislatures—assumed courts would apply the Free Exercise Clause similarly, so that religious liberty was safeguarded."[122] But there were examples of state courts ruling on the constitutionality of state laws during the Confederation period.[123] More significantly, the framers of the Bill of Rights debated the very question of exemptions for conscientious objectors to war and decided to omit it from what became the Second Amendment and leave it to legislative discretion.[124] The Court majority's position leaves it to the legislative branch to decide whether and how to accommodate conscientious objections to laws.

Notes

1. The federal law, cited as Revised Statutes sect. 5352 in *Reynolds*, applied to "a Territory, or any other place over which the United States have exclusive jurisdiction." 98 U.S. 145.
2. Id.
3. Id. at 165.
4. Id. at 166.
5. 310 U.S. 296 (1940).

6. Id. at 303.

7. Id. at 303–4.

8. Id. at 305. The breach of the peace conviction was thrown out on free speech grounds, at 309.

9. The flag salute cases were also discussed in the introduction, pp. 4–6.

10. *Minersville v Gobitis*, 310 U.S. 586, 601–2 (1940).

11. Id. at 594.

12. Id. at 595. Earlier, Frankfurter had distinguished *Cantwell*: that case protected individuals against penalties resulting from their religious activities' offending the religious views of others. See 593.

13. Id. at 601 (Justice Stone dissenting).

14. Id. at 605 (Justice Stone dissenting).

15. 47 F. Supp. 251, 253 (1942).

16. 316 U.S. 584 (1942); overturned by *Murdock v Pennsylvania* 319 U.S. 105, 117 (1943).

17. *West Virginia State Board of Education v Barnette*, 319 U.S. 624, 633–634 (1943).

18. The private school option was available, as Justice Frankfurter had pointed out, but that cost additional money.

19. Id. at 633.

20. Id. at 640.

21. Id. at 642.

22. Id. See my discussion of this in the introduction.

23. Id. at 653 (Justice Frankfurter dissenting). And: "The essence of the religious freedom guaranteed by our Constitution is therefore this: no religion shall either receive the state's support or incur its hostility. Religion is outside the sphere of political government." Id. at p. 654. Justice Frankfurter expressed sympathy for legislative accommodation to religious scruples in such cases; he does not say whether the accommodation can be limited to religious beliefs.

24. Id. 662.

25. See 646–47 and 667–71 for classic statements of Justice Frankfurter's doctrine of "judicial self-restraint."

26. 366 U.S. 420 (1961).

27. 366 U.S. 599 (1961).

28. Id. at 605 (1961). Justice Frankfurter concurred in a separate long opinion that Justice Harlan joined.

29. Id. at 606 (1961).

30. Justice Douglas dissented in both cases, on both Free Exercise and Establishment Clause grounds.

31. 374 U.S. 398.(1960).

32. Since the Sunday closing laws cases, Justices Frankfurter and Whitaker had retired from the Court, replaced by Justices Goldberg and White. Justice Goldberg joined the majority while Justice White dissented with Justice Harlan. Justices Black,

Clark, and Warren voted with Justice Brennan in this case where they had voted in the majority and against him in *Braunfeld*.

33. *NAACP v Button* 371 U.S. 415 (1963).

34. *Sherbert*, at 403.

35. Id., at 407.

36. Id. at 408–9.

37. Id. at 419 (Justice Harlan dissenting, italics in original).

38. Id. at 422 (Justice Harlan dissenting).

39. Id. at 423 at note 4.

40. Id. at 406.

41. Id. at 410.

42. Helen E.Veit et al., *Creating the Bill of Rights*, (Baltimore: Johns Hopkins University Press, 1991), p. 182. See chapter 3.

43. Id., p. 184.

44. *U.S. v Seeger* 380 U.S. 163 (1965) 171–73.

45. 62 Stat 612, as quoted in Justice Black's Court opinion in *Welsh v United States* 398 U.S. 333 (1970). Justice Black noted that after the *Seeger* decision Congress deleted the reference to a "Supreme Being," but retained the rest of that sentence. Note 2, p. 336.

46. *Seeger*, 380 U.S. at 166

47. Id. at 167 (from Justice Clark's opinion).

48. Id. at 174.

49. Id. at 176.

50. *Welsh v United States*, 398 U.S. 333, 340 (1970). The internal quote is from *Seeger* at 176.

51. Id. at 341.

52. Id. at 348 (Justice Harlan concurring).

53. Id. at 351 (Justice Harlan concurring).

54. *Seeger*, 380 U.S. at 180, 191.

55. *Welsh*, 398 U.S. at 336, footnote 2.

56. 401 U.S. 437 (1971).

57. If Justice Harlan had joined Justices White, Burger, and Stewart, the Court would have divided 4 to 4, thus leaving the conviction standing, since Justice Blackmun did not participate in the decision.

58. *Welsh*, 398 U.S. at 356 (Justice Harlan concurring).

59. Id. at 357–58.

60. This provision states that whatever part of a statute that is found unconstitutional should be "severed" from the rest of the statute, which is to remain in force.

61. Id. at 364.

62. Id. at 366–67.

63. Id. at 372 (Justice White dissenting). Also: "We should thus not labor to find a violation of the Establishment Clause when free exercise values prompt Congress to relieve religious believers from the burdens of the law at least in those instances

where the law is not merely prohibitory but commands the performance of military duties that are forbidden by a man's religion." Id. at 373.

64. See Id. at 372.

65. Id. at 358 (note 9).

66. 406 U.S. 205 (1972).

67. Id. at 208 (1972).

68. Id. at 210.

69. Id. at 211. The Amish did not object to sending their children to elementary school, apparently because the atmosphere was not yet so alien to their way of life.

70. 268 U.S. 510 (1925).

71. Id. at 214.

72. The Amish did propose to satisfy the compulsory education requirement with vocational school for three hours a week, during which time they would be taught standard academic subjects by an Amish teacher; for the rest of the week they would perform farm and household duties under parental supervision. The Superintendent reportedly rejected the proposal as not providing "substantially equivalent education" to what other schools in the area provided. Id. at 208, note 3.

73. 397 U.S. 664 (1970).

74. 406 U.S. at 221.

75. 397 U.S. at 672–74.

76. Yoder, 406 U.S. at 215–16.

77. Id. at 236.

78. Id. at 220.

79. Thomas v Review Board, 450 U.S. 707 (1981), Hobbie v Unemployment Appeals Comm'n, 480 U.S. 136 (1987), and Frazee v Illinois Employment Security Department, 489 U.S. 829 (1989).

80. Kathleen Sullivan and Gerald Gunther, Constitutional Law, 14th Edition, (New York: Foundation Press, 2001) p. 1461.

81. Employment Division v Smith, 494 U.S. 872, 874 (1990).

82. Id. at 875. The state supreme court cited Sherbert and Thomas to support its position.

83. Id. at 878.

84. Id. at 881–82.

85. Id. at 884.

86. See Justice Scalia's opinion at Id. 886.

87. Id.

88. Oregon did pass a law allowing individuals "to present their religious beliefs as an 'affirmative defense' if convicted under the state law proscribing peyote." Carolyn Long, Religious Freedom and Indian Rights: The Case of Oregon v Smith (Lawrence, Kansas: University Press of Kansas, 2000), p. 225. Long does not indicate what effect this law might have on the issue of unemployment compensation benefits.

89. Id. at 895 (Justice O'Connor concurring); the internal quote at the end from Yoder, 406 U.S. at 215.

90. Id. at 896, is from *Yoder*, 406 U.S. at 220.

91. She noted that the Oregon law followed federal law in identifying peyote as a "Schedule 1 controlled substance, which means that Congress has found that it has a high potential for abuse, that there is no currently accepted medical use, and that there is a lack of accepted safety for use of the drug under medical supervision." Id. at 904.

92. Id. at 905 (Justice O'Connor concurring).

93. Id. at 911–12 (Justice O'Connor concurring).

94. *Church of Lakumi Babalu Aye v City of Hialeah* 508 U.S. 520 (1993).

95. Id. at 526 (1990). This ordinance—87–40—incorporated Florida's animal cruelty laws, "except as to penalty." Id.

96. Id. at 535.

97. Id. at 534. As Justice Kennedy described the effects of the various regulations, they amounted to what Justice Harlan, whom he quoted, referred to as a "religious gerrymander"; the council members wanted to prohibit this one religious practice and no other form of killing of animals, such as fishing and hunting, or even orthodox Jews' form of kosher butchering.

98. Justice Kennedy wrote that "neutrality and general applicability are interrelated." Id. at 531. In his concurring opinion, Justice Scalia was more emphatic: "the terms are not only 'interrelated,' *ante* at 531, but substantially overlap." Id. 557.

99. Id. at 546.

100. Justice Souter was appointed to replace retiring Justice Brennan in 1990, after the Court decided the *Smith* case.

101. Id. at 561. Justice Souter observed in a footnote that the National Prohibition Act did provide for such an exemption, which is precisely the position that Justice Scalia took in *Smith* and that Justice Harlan did before him. Justice Souter's point, following Justice Brennan, is that the legislative process might not be as responsive to comparable accommodation requests from other less accepted religions and religious practices. He drew on the work of two scholars, Michael McConnell and Douglas Laycock, who favored the Court's *Sherbert* approach.

102. Id. 562. Souter cites Laycock's article, "Formal, Substantive, and Disaggregated Neutrality Toward Religion," 39 *DePaul L. Rev* 993 (1990).

103. On the other hand, to the extent to which the Court allows legislatures to make accommodations for free exercise claimants, the differential treatment between action based on religious beliefs and action based on sincere moral beliefs remains. Justice Harlan suggested that legislative accommodations had to be religiously neutral.

104. Id. at 532.

105. PL 103–41

106. 42 U.S.C. S 2000bb(a) in *City of Boerne v Flores*, 521 U.S. 507, 515 (1997). The detailed finding is in (2) and the conclusion is in (5).

107. Id.

108. 521 U.S. 507 (1997).

109. 384 U.S. 641 (1966). Justice Kennedy quoted from *Morgan*, 384 U.S. at 651, in his *Flores* opinion, U.S. 521 U.S. at 517–18. The Supreme Court upheld section 4e of the Voting Rights Act of 1965, which mandated that nonnative English speakers who completed the sixth grade in an accredited school in Puerto Rico could not be denied the right to vote in any election. The Court's opinion raised but did not settle the question, how extensive is Congress's power to legislate under the enforcement clause of the Fourteenth Amendment?

110. Id. at 520.

111. Id. at 530.

112. Id.

113. Id. at 532.

114. Id. at 535. In his brief concurrence, Justice Stevens argued that the RFRA violated the Establishment Clause. That argument would not allow local governments to accommodate religious free exercise; the ground of accommodation would have to be broader.

115. Id. at 546 (Justice O'Connor dissenting).

116. Id. at 553 (Justice O'Connor dissenting), quoting the New York Constitution, Article XXXVIII; Massachusetts had a similar provision which was quoted above in part one.

117. Id. at 539 (Justice Scalia concurring). Emphasis in original.

118. Id. at 555 (Justice O'Connor dissenting).

119. That no one "on account of conscience, should be invested with peculiar emoluments or privileges, nor subjected to any penalties or disabilities, unless under color of religion the preservation of equal liberty, and the existence of the State be manifestly endangered." Id. at 556 (Justice O'Connor dissenting).

120. "[T]he pamphlet argues that the assessment wrongly placed civil society ahead of personal religious belief and, thus, should not be approved by the legislators." Id. at 542 (Justice Scalia concurring).

121. Id. at 558 (Justice O'Connor dissenting), quoting from *2 Journals of Continental Congress*, 1774–1789, pp. 187, 189.

122. Id at 559, 560.

123. Crosskey, William W., *Politics and the Constitution in the History of the United States* (Chicago: University of Chicago Press: 1953), vol. 2, Ch. XXVII.

124. See discussion in part 1, chapter 3.

CHAPTER FOURTEEN

The Establishment Clause: I

In light of Tocqueville's observation that religion "never mixes directly in the government of society" in America, but is "the first of their political institutions,"[1] the Establishment Clause questions concern when and why a governmental accommodation of religion is or is not constitutional. The early cases involved aid to parochial schools, "released time" programs to accommodate religious education during the school day, authorized prayer in public schools, and tax-exempt status for religious institutions. In working through these cases, the Court developed its three-part *Lemon* test for Establishment Clause cases: "First, the statute must have a secular legislative purpose; second, its principal or primary effect must be one that neither advances nor inhibits religion; finally the statute must not foster 'an excessive legislative entanglement.'"[2] The opinions in these cases reveal a disagreement in the Court concerning permissible accommodation, as well as the strictness of the *Lemon* test. The cases decided after *Lemon* reflect an increasing willingness to accommodate religion in some respects—such as aid to parochial schools—but not in others, such as prayer or any other religious activity in public schools. This chapter will start with the early cases and then turn to the reconsideration of parochial school cases. The next chapter will treat the more recent prayer cases and other cases involving government "endorsement" of religion.

The Early Cases: From *Everson* to *Lemon*

The Supreme Court first considered the meaning of the Establishment Clause in *Everson v Board of Education*.[3] In that case, the Court, 5 to 4, interpreted the clause to require separation of religion from politics and upheld transportation reimbursement for travel to private parochial as well as public schools. It also, unanimously, "incorporated" the Establishment Clause into the Due Process Clause of the Fourteenth Amendment. This meant that the same rule regarding separation of religion from politics would be applied to the several states as applied to Congress.

The township of Ewing, New Jersey, authorized reimbursement to parents of schoolchildren for transportation on public buses. Money was paid to parents of public school and Catholic school children only. (There were no other not-for-profit schools in the township.) A taxpayer's lawsuit charged that the aid violated the Establishment Clause, as applied to the states through the Fourteenth Amendment. Justice Black's Court opinion provided a broad account of the requirements of the clause.

> The "establishment of religion" clause of the First Amendment means at least this: Neither a state nor the Federal Government can set up a church. Neither can pass laws which aid one religion, aid all religions, or prefer one religion over another. Neither can force nor influence a person to go to or to remain away from church against his will or force him to profess a belief or disbelief in any religion. . . . No tax in any amount, large or small, can be levied to support any religious activities or institutions, whatever they may be called, or whatever form they may adopt to teach or practice religion.[4]

While the state could not "contribute tax-raised funds to the support of an institution which teaches the tenets and faith of any church,"[5] Justice Black explained that the money was going to the parents, not the school, and the legislation was a kind of "public welfare legislation."[6] He likened it to providing police protection to students going to school, including parochial school, although he acknowledged that the legislature was not constitutionally obligated to extend its reimbursement program to parents of private school children.[7]

In dissent, Justice Jackson, joined by Justice Frankfurter, preferred a stricter separation.

> Our public school, if not a product of Protestantism, at least is more consistent with it than with the Catholic culture and scheme of values. It is a relatively recent development dating from about 1840. It is organized on the premise that secular education can be isolated from all religious teaching so that the school can inculcate needed temporal knowledge and also maintain a strict and lofty neutrality as to religion. The assumption is that after the individual has been instructed in worldly wisdom he will be better fitted to choose his religion.[8]

Catholics—and perhaps Baptists—might well reply that the prominence of a Protestant-based public school education, funded by taxes, is precisely what made it so important for them to institute their own schools. And, unlike in *Yoder*, the parochial school satisfied the state's education requirement while it also provided religious instruction. No Justice took issue with the incorporation argument or with the strong neutrality statement.

The next two cases concerned "released time" programs. They used public school time to facilitate religious instruction. In *McCollum v Board of Education*[9], the Court, 8 to 1, invalidated an Illinois program that brought religious teachers into the public schools to give weekly thirty- to forty-five-minute religious instruction to those pupils in grades four through nine whose parents requested it. The other students were required to stay in school but regular classes were suspended.[10] Four years later, in *Zorach v Clausen*,[11] the Court, 6 to 3, upheld New York City's released time program, which allowed students, with their parents' permission, to leave school during school hours for religious instruction or devotional exercises. Justice Black wrote the Court opinion invalidating the Illinois program:

> The operation of the State's compulsory education system thus assists and is integrated with the program of religious instruction carried on by separate religious sects. Pupils compelled by law to go to school for secular education are released in part from their legal duty upon the condition that they attend the religious classes.[12]

But four years later, Justice Douglas's Court opinion in *Zorach* emphasized the absence of religious instruction in public schools and the absence of the expenditure of public funds.[13] After finding that the school authorities were neutral and there was no showing of "coercion,"[14] Justice Douglas gave this rationale for accommodation.

> We are a religious people whose institutions presuppose a Supreme Being. We guarantee the freedom to worship as one chooses. We make room for as wide a variety of beliefs and creeds as the spiritual needs of man deem necessary. We sponsor an attitude on the part of government that shows no partiality to any one group and that lets each flourish according to the zeal of its adherents and the appeal of its dogma. When the state encourages religious instruction or cooperates with religious authorities by adjusting the schedule of public events to sectarian needs, it follows the best of our traditions.[15]

To the dissenters, Justices Black, Frankfurter, and Jackson, the program unconstitutionally used the compulsory public school machinery to encourage religious activity, and this divided public school pupils along lines of religious observance.[16] While *Zorach* has never been explicitly overturned, the prayer cases suggest that it is no longer valid.

The Court decided its first two prayer cases a decade later; in each case it held that voluntary prayer in the public schools violated the Establishment Clause. In *Engel v Vitale*,[17] the Board of Education of Union Free School District No. 9, acting on the recommendation of the Board of Regents of New York State, directed its principal to have the following prayer said in class at the start of every school day: "Almighty God, we acknowledge our dependence upon Thee, and we beg Thy blessings upon us, our parents, our teachers and our Country."[18] In *Abington v Schempp*,[19] ten verses of the Bible were read without comment and the Lord's Prayer was recited in Abington High School at the opening of each public school day.[20] In the companion case, the Board of School Commissioners of Baltimore City provided for a "reading, without comment, of a chapter in the Holy Bible and/or the use of the Lord's prayer."[21] In each case, a child could be excused from the exercise with a letter from his parent or guardian. In *Engel*, Justice Black delivered the 6 to 1 Court opinion: "We think that the constitutional prohibition against laws respecting an establishment of religion must at least mean that in this country it is no part of the business of government to compose official prayers for any group of the American people to recite as a part of a religious program carried on by government."[22]

Justice Black's elaboration noted: "The Establishment Clause, unlike the Free Exercise Clause, does not depend upon any showing of direct governmental compulsion and is violated by the enactment of laws which establish an official religion whether those laws operate directly to coerce nonobserving individuals or not."[23] But he also wrote that the "indirect coercive pressure on religious minorities to conform . . . is plain."[24]

In dissent, Justice Stewart emphasized the voluntary character of the exercise and the common practice for government officials to invoke divine support. He also suggested that there is little difference between this prayer and the reference to God in the Pledge of Allegiance, in the motto on our coins, and in the Star-Spangled Banner.[25]

In the *Schempp* case, Justice Clark's Court opinion referred to the constitutional goal of "wholesome neutrality" and then offered this test: "What are the purpose and primary effect of the enactment? If either is the advancement or inhibition of religion then the enactment exceeds the scope of legislative power as circumscribed by the Constitution."[26] He then applied the test to Bible reading and struck it down.[27] In his lengthy concurring opinion, Justice Brennan attempted to reconcile Justice Douglas's statement that

Americans are "a religious people whose institutions presuppose a Supreme Being,"[28] with the Establishment Clause: "While our institutions reflect a firm conviction that we are a religious people, those institutions by solemn constitutional injunction may not officially involve religion in such a way as to discriminate against, or oppress, a particular sect or religion."[29]

Justice Brennan thought that the views of the founders on religious freedom did not yield a clear answer to the question concerning prayer in public schools, since such schools did not yet exist and the framers were concerned about "far more flagrant intrusions of government into the realm of religion."[30] He did suggest that with the increased importance of public schools, government supported prayers "sufficiently threaten . . . those substantive evils the fear of which called forth the Establishment Clause."[31]

In dissent, Justice Stewart argued that to keep prayer and religion generally out of the public schools amounted to a violation of the Free Exercise Clause.[32] Justice Stewart acknowledged the problem of peer pressure in schools but thought it could be addressed.[33]

In its next religion case, *Allen v Board of Education*,[34] the Supreme Court returned to the issue of aid to parochial schools. In a 5 to 3 decision, Justice White wrote the Court opinion upholding New York State's program of purchasing and lending textbooks "to all children residing in such district who are enrolled in grades seven to twelve of a public or private school which complies with the compulsory education law."[35] After quoting the purpose-and-effect test from *Schempp*, Justice White noted that the case was no different from *Everson*, since "each book loaned must be approved by the public school authorities; only secular books may receive approval."[36] His argument relied on both the constitutionality of private schools and the legislative judgment that the schools must be doing "an acceptable job of providing secular education to their children."[37]

Justices Black, Douglas, and Fortas, in separate opinions, rejected the majority's contention that the aid supported the secular purpose of the private parochial schools. They each feared that the books would "tend to propagate the religious views of the favored sect."[38]

The next case, *Walz v Tax Commissioner, New York*,[39] involved the tax-exempt status of religious organizations. The Court upheld the exemption 8 to 1, with only Justice Douglas dissenting. Chief Justice Burger offered this approach to the Establishment Clause in his Court opinion:

> We will not tolerate either governmentally established religion or governmental interference with religion. Short of those expressly proscribed governmental acts there is room for play in the joints productive of a benevolent neutral-

ity which will permit religious exercise to exist without sponsorship and without interference.[40]

No perfect or absolute separation is really possible; the very existence of the Religion Clauses is an involvement of sorts, one that seeks to mark boundaries to avoid excessive entanglement.[41]

The Chief Justice pointed out that the legislature had granted exemption to all houses of religious worship within a broad class of property owned by non-profit, quasi-public corporations, which include hospitals, libraries, and playgrounds, and scientific, professional, historical, and patriotic groups.[42] Having introduced "entanglement," the Chief Justice argued that granting tax exemptions entailed less involvement than having to value church property for taxes.[43] Thus "entanglement" became a separate part of the Establishment Clause test.

Justices Brennan and Harlan both wrote concurring opinions. The former emphasized the difference between a subsidy and an exemption[44]; the latter noted that the statute "satisfies the requirement of neutrality."[45]

Justice Douglas dissented. Tax exemptions were like subsidies, he argued, because dollars were indirectly being given to religious organizations.[46] He thought the exemption category had to be limited to nonsectarian social welfare operations.[47]

In 1971, the Supreme Court, by a vote of 8 to 1, struck down two related statutes providing for aid to parochial schools and formulated its *Lemon* test. *Lemon v Kurtzman*[48] involved a Pennsylvania law that provided aid to non-public schools for teachers' salaries, textbooks, and instructional materials. *Earley v DiCenso*,[49] involved a Rhode Island law that provided for salary supplements for teachers of secular subjects in nonpublic schools, to equal the salary levels of public school teachers.[50] In each case, provisions were made to assure that the teachers taught only subjects also taught in the public schools and that they used teaching materials also used in public schools—or that were approved by the Superintendent of Public Instruction (in the Pennsylvania case). The three-judge district court in Rhode Island held that state's statute unconstitutional. The three-judge district court in Pennsylvania upheld that state's statute. Chief Justice Burger began his Court opinion by calling the language of the Religion Clauses "at best opaque;" he then drew on the criteria mentioned in *Allen* and *Walz* to present the "*Lemon* test":

Every analysis in this area must begin with consideration of the cumulative criteria developed by the Court over many years. Three such tests may be gleaned from our cases. First, the statute must have a secular legislative purpose; second, its principal or primary effect must be one that neither advances nor inhibits religion; finally, the statute must not foster "an excessive government entanglement with religion."[51]

After noting that the state statutes passed the purpose test, Chief Justice Burger skipped over any consideration of the "effect test," because he found that the "cumulative impact" of the statutory provisions that restrict the aid in order to guarantee a separation between secular and religious educational functions "involves excessive entanglement between government and religion."[52]

Chief Justice Burger's opinion considered the entanglement question in terms of the character of Roman Catholic elementary and secondary schools, since most of the parochial schools were Catholic, and the need to oversee the teachers as well as the schools' finances. "With the best of intentions such a teacher would find it hard to make a total separation between secular teaching and religious doctrine."[53]

Justice Douglas's concurring opinion reflected hostility to parochial schools.[54] Justice Brennan's concurring opinion emphasized the distinction he drew in *Walz* between a subsidy and an exemption; the former involves a transfer of funds; the latter does not.[55] He manifested a clear preference for public schools.[56]

Justice White was the sole dissenter in these cases. He emphasized the educational purpose that the private schools provided and that in these cases two states and the federal government had elected to provide educational aid for all students, including those who attend church-related schools.[57] He also pointed out how the Court's opinion set two elements of the *Lemon* test against one another:

> The State cannot finance secular instruction if it permits religion to be taught in the same classroom; but if it exacts a promise that religion not be so taught—a promise the school and its teachers are quite willing and on this record able to give—and enforces it, it is then entangled in the 'no entanglement' aspect of the Court's Establishment Clause jurisprudence.[58]

At this time, the Court had yet to apply the "principal effect" part of the *Lemon* test.[59] In subsequent Establishment Clause cases, the Court revised its treatment of aid to parochial schools while remaining consistent in its treatment of public school prayer. I think that is so because there is a more persuasive case for accommodation consistent with neutrality in the parochial school cases than in the prayer cases.

Public Aid to Private Schools: From *Nyquist* to *Zelman*

After *Lemon*, the Court continued to invalidate most legislative attempts to provide aid to parochial schools, although it upheld a tax-deduction law in *Mueller v Allen*[60] (1983). With the appointment of Justices O'Connor (1981) and Kennedy (1988), the Court shifted to a more accommodating position, which eventually upheld vouchers for private schools.

In *Committee for Public Education & Religious Liberty v Nyquist* (1973), the Court, by a vote of 6 to 3, invalidated three amendments to New York's Education and Tax Laws. One part of the law provided grants for health and safety for "qualifying" nonpublic schools; qualifying schools received a certain amount of money per pupil per year if they served "a high concentration of pupils from low income families."[61] The other part of the program involved either a tuition reimbursement or a tax deduction for low-income parents.

In his Court opinion, Justice Powell acknowledged "the State's interests in promoting pluralism and diversity among its public and nonpublic schools," and the financial reasons why the state wanted to support nonpublic schools.[62] Applying the effect and entanglement criteria, however, he threw out the grants since there were no restrictions on how the money could be used. Consequently, this program failed the "effect" test.[63] The Court rejected tuition reimbursement even though the money went to the parents: "the effect of the aid is unmistakably to provide desired financial support for nonpublic, sectarian institutions."[64] The tax deduction, or tax forgiveness, provisions also failed the "effect" test.[65]

Chief Justice Burger and Justice Rehnquist dissented on the tuition grants and the tax provisions. Justice White, following his *Lemon* opinion, dissented from the entire opinion. He concentrated on the admittedly secular purpose of such laws.[66]

After deciding two other cases similarly,[67] the Supreme Court upheld a Minnesota tax deduction plan, 5 to 4, in *Mueller v Allen* (1983).[68] The Minnesota law allowed a deduction for tuition, texts, and transportation; parents of public as well as nonpublic schoolchildren could benefit from it.[69] Justice Powell concluded that the broader coverage distinguished this law from the New York law. The other six Justices who decided this case and *Nyquist* saw no difference. But Justice Powell's vote plus the appointment of Justice O'Connor, who supported the Minnesota law, turned a 6 to 3 decision against tax deductions into a 5 to 4 majority in favor of it here.[70]

Two years later a bare majority of the Court reaffirmed its strict approach to aid to parochial schools. In *Grand Rapids v Ball* and *Aguilar v Felton*, decided together in 1985, the Court reviewed state and federal programs that provided supplementary instruction and instructional materials in nonpublic schools. In the first case, Michigan's Shared Time and Community Education programs sent public school teachers into nonpublic school classrooms to teach "core curriculum" courses.[71] The lower courts held the program invalid on both "effect" and "entanglement" grounds, and the Supreme Court affirmed.

Justice Brennan's Court opinion pointed out that forty of the forty-one participating schools were sectarian, and twenty-eight of them were Roman Catholic.[72] Citing the *Meek* case,[73] Justice Brennan held that the programs failed the "effect" test for three reasons: public school teachers, while teaching in sectarian schools, "may subtly or overtly indoctrinate the students in particular religious tenets at public expense"; "state provided instruction in the religious school buildings threatens to convey a message of state support for religion to students and to the general public"; and "the programs in effect subsidize the religious functions of the parochial schools by taking over a substantial portion of their responsibility for teaching secular subjects."[74]

In the companion case, *Aguilar v Felton*,[75] New York City used federal funds under Title I of the Elementary and Secondary Education Act of 1965 to pay the salaries of public school employees who taught in local educational institutions serving children from low-income families. Of the students eligible for funds, 13 percent were enrolled in private schools; 84 percent of those schools were Catholic and 8 percent were Hebrew day schools. The programs included reading, mathematics, English as a second language, and guidance services. The teachers were supervised and told to have minimum contact with private school personnel, and supervisors made periodic unannounced visits to the classrooms.[76] Justice Brennan's Court opinion found that

> the supervisory system established by the City of New York inevitably results in the excessive entanglement of church and state. . . . Even where state aid to parochial schools does not have the primary effect of advancing religion, the provision of such aid may nonetheless violate the Establishment Clause owing to the nature of the interaction of church and state in the administration of that aid.[77]

In his dissent, Justice Rehnquist restated Justice White's earlier position: "The Court takes advantage of the 'Catch 22' paradox of its own creation, whereby aid must be supervised to ensure no entanglement but the supervision itself is held to cause an entanglement."[78] Justice O'Connor, also dissenting, questioned "the utility of 'entanglement' as a separate Establishment Clause standard in most cases."[79] She also thought that teachers were professionals who could be counted on to abstain from indoctrination when they taught secular subjects in parochial schools.[80]

Twelve years later, Justice O'Connor wrote the Court opinion overturning these decisions in *Agostini v Felton* (1997).[81] The Court reconsidered the *Aguilar* case (and its companion) because the Title I program was still in effect for public schoolchildren and petitioners argued that five Justices had "called for the overruling of *Aguilar*" in the Court's decision in *Board of Education of Kiryas Joel Village School District v Grumet*.[82]

The *Kiryas Joel* case arose as a direct result of *Aguilar*. It concerned members of the Satmar Hasidic sect, Orthodox Jews who spoke Yiddish and eschewed the dress and behavior of modern American society. The controversy originated with the Satmars' purchase of an undeveloped subdivision in the town of Monroe in Orange County, New York. A zoning dispute led the Satmars to request that a new village be formed within the town. As Justice Souter noted in his Court opinion, this was "a right which New York's village law gives almost any group of residents who satisfy certain procedural niceties."[83] When neighbors objected to the plan to secede from the town of Monroe, boundaries were drawn so that the new Village of Kiryas Joel included only the land owned and inhabited by the Satmars.[84] The Satmar children attended private, sex-segregated religious schools. As of 1984, children who qualified for special educational services under federal and state law[85] received these services at an annex to the girls' private school. The Court's 1985 decisions invalidated this arrangement. The children who needed special services then were forced to attend public school outside the village. The families were not satisfied with this experience, for the same reason the Amish refused to send their fifteen-year-olds to public school; the lower court record referred to "the panic, fear and trauma [the children] suffered in leaving their own community and being with people whose ways were so different."[86] By 1989, with all but one of the handicapped children from Kiryas Joel receiving only privately funded services or going without any assistance, the state legislature made the Village of Kiryas Joel a separate school district, "with all the powers of a union free school district."[87] The newly created school district proceeded to run the special education programs for handicapped children. Two-thirds of the fulltime students came from outside the village, and the school had many more part-time students who attended parochial schools than fulltime students.[88]

As sympathetic as it was to the plight of the Satmar families, the Court struck down the law creating a separate school district for the Village of Kiryas Joel. Justice Souter, author of the Court opinion, said the law "effectively identifies these recipients of governmental authority by reference to doctrinal adherence, even though it does not do so expressly."[89] Justice Souter wondered whether the legislature would extend the same opportunity to other groups seeking similar accommodation.[90] The other options were to provide the special educational services at the nearby public school or "at a neutral site near one of the village's parochial schools."[91] The first option was unsatisfactory to the Satmar families; the second was more costly.[92]

In his brief concurrence, which Justices Blackmun and Ginsburg joined, Justice Stevens suggested "the State could have taken steps to alleviate the children's fear by teaching their schoolmates to be tolerant and respectful of Satmar customs."[93] Justice Kennedy concurred in the Court's judgment, since the school district was "drawn along religious lines,"[94] but he also wrote that the *Grand Rapids* and *Aguilar* decisions "may have been erroneous."[95] Justice Scalia's dissent, in which Chief Justice Rehnquist and Justice Thomas concurred, "heartily" agreed with Justice Kennedy on this point.[96] The fifth vote for a reconsideration of *Grand Rapids* and *Ball* came from Justice O'Connor, whose sympathies were clearly with the Satmars. She suggested that the New York legislature could "allow all villages to operate their own school districts."[97] She then offered her view of the religion clauses and urged reconsideration of *Aguilar*.

> The Religion Clauses prohibit the government from favoring religion, but they provide no warrant for discriminating *against* religion. All handicapped children are entitled by law to government-funded special education. [citation omitted] If the government provides this education on-site at public schools and at nonsectarian private schools, it is only fair that it provide it onsite at sectarian schools as well.
>
> I thought this to be true in Aguilar [citation omitted] and I still believe it today. . . . The court should, in a proper case, be prepared to reconsider Aguilar, in order to bring our Establishment Clause jurisprudence back to what I think is the proper track—government impartiality, not animosity, towards religion.[98]

Two other Court decisions supported reconsideration of *Aguilar* and *Grand Rapids*. In *Witters v Washington Department of Services for the Blind* (1986),[99] the Court unanimously held that the Establishment Clause did not forbid the state from extending assistance under a state rehabilitation program to a blind student who desired to pursue a degree at a private Christian college, in order to become a pastor, missionary, or youth director. Justice Marshall's Court opinion emphasized that the aid was available to the individual student and could be used at all schools.[100] In *Zobrest v Catalina Foothills School District* (1993),[101] the Court, 5 to 4, held that the Establishment Clause did not forbid the school district from providing a sign language interpreter for the petitioner, who was going to attend a Catholic high school.[102] Chief Justice Rehnquist's Court opinion noted that the parent chose where to send the individual student, and the aid did not relieve sectarian schools of any educational expense.[103]

After the *Kiryas Joel* decision, petitioners in *Agostini v Felton* (1997), who were bound by the *Aguilar* decision, sought relief from the injunction on the grounds that "it is no longer equitable that the judgment should have prospective application."[104] Justice O'Connor's Court opinion, joined by Chief Justice Rehnquist and Justices Scalia, Kennedy, and Thomas, overturned the two 1985 decisions. Title I funds could now be made available for public school teachers to instruct students who were at risk of failing the state's student performance standards in private, including parochial, schools. The schools had to be located within the attendance boundaries of a public school located in a low-income area and the services provided had to be "secular, neutral, and nonideological."[105] Justice O'Connor restated the *Lemon* test by reducing "entanglement" to an element of the "effect" prong. Justice Souter wrote a dissenting opinion, which Justices Stevens, Ginsburg, and Breyer joined.[106]

Justice O'Connor used the *Zobrest* and *Witters* cases to argue that the Court no longer assumed that putting public school teachers into religious schools to teach secular subjects had the impermissible effect of advancing religion. There was no evidence that teachers, who are professionals, would attempt to indoctrinate students, or that having public school teachers instruct students in remedial math or English constituted an inappropriate "symbolic union between government and religion."[107] Nor did the provision of Title I aid by public employees on parochial campuses "impermissibly finance religious indoctrination."[108] Justice O'Connor maintained that "a financial incentive to undertake religious indoctrination . . . is not present where the aid is allocated on the basis of neutral, secular criteria that neither favor nor disfavor religion, and is made available to both religious and secular beneficiaries on a nondiscriminatory basis."[109] Finally, the concern about an excessive "entanglement" between church and state is best treated "as an aspect of the inquiry into a statute's effect."[110] That is because the Court no longer considered "administrative cooperation" between a school board and parochial schools or the dangers of "political divisiveness" as sufficient grounds for a finding of excessive "entanglement."[111] Justice O'Connor's summary restated the "effect" test:

> New York City's Title I program does not run afoul of any of the three primary criteria we currently use to evaluate whether government aid has the effect of

advancing religion: it does not result in governmental indoctrination; define its recipients by reference to religion; or create an excessive entanglement. We therefore hold that a federally funded program providing supplemental, remedial instruction to disadvantaged children on a neutral basis is not invalid under the Establishment Clause when such instruction is given on the premises of sectarian schools by government employees pursuant to a program containing safeguards such as those present here.[112]

Justice Souter's dissent argued that, at most, the *Witters* and *Zobrest* decisions only went part of the way toward justifying this decision. "What was so remarkable [about the programs in *Aguilar* and *Ball*] was that the schemes in issue assumed a teaching responsibility indistinguishable from the responsibility of the schools themselves."[113] For Justice Souter and the three other dissenting justices, this aid was substantial and direct, whereas the programs in *Witters* and *Zobrest* were insubstantial and indirect. Furthermore, "if a State may constitutionally enter the schools to teach in the manner in question, it must in constitutional principle be free to assume, or assume payment for, the entire cost of instruction provided in any ostensibly secular subject in any religious school."[114]

The problem raised by *Kiryas Joel* provided the best argument for the majority's decision. Special education programs for handicapped students or low-income students who were failing (and who were in poor schools) were too expensive for state and local governments alone to support. Most private schools, especially parochial schools, could not afford them either, and if those schools failed, the financial burden on state and local government would be even greater. Creating special facilities for parochial school students to receive these important federally funded programs was unnecessarily costly, since there had been no showing of an attempt to indoctrinate students receiving this instruction from public teachers in parochial schools.

The Court decided another case very similar to *Agostini* in 2000. In *Mitchell v Helms*,[115] it upheld 6 to 3 a federal program that distributed funds to state and local government agencies that loaned educational materials and equipment to elementary and secondary schools.[116] Justice Thomas wrote the opinion stating the judgment of the Court, which Chief Justice Rehnquist and Justices Scalia and Kennedy joined. Justice O'Connor wrote a separate concurrence that Justice Breyer joined. Justice Souter dissented, joined by Justices Stevens and Ginsburg.

The only arguable difference between this case and *Agostini* was that the educational materials could be "diverted" to inappropriate uses, whereas the Court determined that public school teachers could be trusted to follow the guidelines regarding nonreligious instruction. Justice Thomas's plurality opinion maintained that the issue was not divertibility but "impermissible content."[117] He described a focus on divertibility as "boundless—enveloping all aid, no matter how trivial," and hence reasonably related to preventing an establishment of religion.[118] Returning to the two *Agostini* criteria, Justice Thomas found that Chapter 2 aid followed the child and was therefore neutral. The plurality dismissed evidence that some equipment was diverted for religious use and that the safeguards against diversion were allegedly weak as "not relevant to the constitutional inquiry, whatever relevance they may have under the statute and regulations."[119]

Justices O'Connor and Breyer refused to join the plurality because of that statement. Justice O'Connor thought there was a difference between per capita aid programs and "true private choice programs considered in *Witters* and *Zobrest*." In the earlier cases, what the individual chose to do with the funds did not implicate the government; in the current case, it did, and therefore a check was needed to make sure that funds were not diverted to improperly advance religion.[120] Rejecting the dissent's contention that the possibility of divertibility invalidated the program, Justices O'Connor and Breyer concurred because they found that adequate checks were in place and the violations were minimal.[121]

Justice Souter's lengthy dissent surveyed the Court's treatment of aid to parochial schools from *Everson* on, in order to argue that the majority had erred in allowing the divertibility of funds for religious objectives and that the plurality's treatment of neutrality would oversimplify and depart from the original understanding of the principle.

Justice Souter described three founding concerns regarding religion: "compelling an individual to support religion violates the fundamental principle of freedom of conscience"; "government aid corrupts religion"; and "government establishment of religion is inextricably linked with conflict."[122] With these principles, Justice Souter consistently opposes aid to parochial schools. He interpreted *Everson* narrowly: the school transportation aid was likened to fire and police protection. His position does not allow for a distinction between government support for the education of all students, including those who attend private schools, and the religious missions of parochial schools. Support for one is support for the other and impermissible.

The most recent aid case came in 2002, when the Supreme Court, 5 to 4, upheld Ohio's Pilot Project Scholarship Program, which included Cleveland's voucher program for private, including parochial, schools. *Zelman v Simmons-Harris*[123] confirmed the new majority position, which supports neutral aid to schools for the purpose of enhancing education, even if a substantial portion of private school aid goes to parochial schools.

After a federal court and the state auditor found the Cleveland city school district in a "crisis," Ohio enacted a law providing two kinds of assistance to parents of children in that district. Tuition aid was given for students in kindergarten through third grade (expanding each year through eighth grade) to attend a participating public or private school of the parents' choosing. Tutorial aid was provided for parents who chose to have their children remain enrolled in their neighborhood public school.[124] The tuition could be used at any private school within the district, as long as it met statewide educational standards and agreed not to discriminate on the basis of race, religion, or ethnic background. A tuition grant of up to $2,250 would be made to any school, including any public school in an adjacent district.[125] During the 1999–2000 school year, fifty-six private schools participated in the program; forty-six had a religious affiliation, and none of the public schools in adjacent districts participated. More than 3,700 students participated in the scholarship program, and 96 percent of them enrolled in religiously affiliated schools. The program also allowed Cleveland's students to elect to attend community and magnet schools in the district.[126] The lower courts invalidated the law on the grounds that its "primary effect" was the advancement of religion. The Supreme Court reversed.[127]

Chief Justice Rehnquist wrote the Court opinion, in which Justices O'Connor, Kennedy, Scalia, and Thomas joined; Justices O'Connor and Thomas wrote concurring opinions. Justice Souter wrote another lengthy dissent, in which Justices Stevens, Ginsburg, and Breyer joined.

Characterizing this case as involving "true private choice," Chief Justice Rehnquist cited *Mueller, Witters,* and *Zobrest* for the following proposition:

> Where a government aid program is neutral with respect to religion, and provides assistance directly to a broad class of citizens who, in turn, direct government aid to religious schools wholly as a result of their own genuine and independent private choice, the program is not readily subject to challenge under the Establishment Clause. . . . The incidental advancement of a religious mission, or the perceived endorsement of a religious message, is reasonably attributable to the individual recipient, not to the government, whose role ends with the disbursement of benefits.[128]

The Cleveland program fit this description because it provided a range of "educational opportunities to the children of a failed school district."[129] Given this context, the Court rejected the challengers' contention that the program created a public perception of government endorsement of religion.[130] To the contention that 96 percent of the choices for religious schools indicated government support for religion, the Chief Justice referred to the more than 1,900 children enrolled in alternative community schools, the more than 13,000 children enrolled in alternative magnet schools, and the more than 1,400 children receiving tutorial assistance in regular public schools. Counting these children brought the percentage enrolled in religious schools down to under 20 percent.[131]

Justice O'Connor wrote separately to emphasize that the decision did not mark a break with past decisions and that the students in religious schools "have exercised 'true private choice.'"[132] Conceding that the voucher program allowed significant funds to reach religious schools "without restrictions" on their use, Justice O'Connor referred to the range of school choices and cited the value of tax exemptions for religious institutions and charitable giving to put the dollar amount in perspective.[133] She then justified the revision of the *Lemon* test and its application here. The key points were that the aid was provided in a neutral fashion and the beneficiaries of the indirect aid (the religious schools) received it as a result of the free choices of parents, not the government.[134]

Justice Thomas's concurring opinion began with a quote from Frederick Douglass that "education . . . means emancipation," and a refreshing reminder that the legislative focus was to ameliorate a disgraceful failure of public education. He observed, in conclusion, that ten states had tried "some form of publicly funded private school choice as one means of raising the quality of education provided to underprivileged urban children. These programs address the root of the problem with failing urban public schools that disproportionately affect minority students."[135]

Justice Souter's dissent acknowledged the seriousness of Cleveland's failing schools but insisted that "constitutional limitations are placed on government to preserve constitutional values in hard cases, like these."[136]

His opinion moved from (1) a general discussion of the shift in constitutional doctrine from *Everson* to the present, to (2) a detailed examination of the choice options here, which he regarded as skewed toward parochial schools, to (3) a most general discussion of the dangers to both government and religion that such programs of support risk.

Justice Souter first drew on *Everson:* "no tax . . . can be levied to support any religious activities of institutions" and a voucher scheme that provides amounts covering almost all the tuition costs does just that.[137] The majority's test erroneously made neutrality in offering aid and private choice suffice.[138] Then he contended that the limited number of nonreligious private schools and the amount of tuition rebate both supported parental choices for the religious schools. He did not count public schools as part of the parents' choice, since that was not part of the voucher plan (it may be for adjacent districts) although he conceded that two of the community schools used to be private schools. Moreover, the tuition support levels covered all of the religious schools' tuition but perhaps only half the amount for other private schools. As a result, some parents chose parochial schools even though the school's religious affiliation was not their own.[139] Justice Souter's final point emphasized the substantial nature of the aid that flowed to religious institutions; he claimed that such programs would corrupt religion and cause more strife.[140]

Justice Breyer's brief dissent developed the argument that publicly financed voucher programs would produce "religiously based social conflict."[141] Justice Breyer cited different authorities for the contention, similar to the one I have been making, that the purpose of the religion clauses taken together, and before that the purpose of religious freedom, was to eliminate religious strife. Both sides agreed on that. The question is how to assess aid to parochial schools in general and voucher programs, including this one in particular.[142] Justice Breyer, who concurred in *Helms*, explained that school vouchers "direct financing to a core function of the church: the teaching of religious truths to young children."[143] And voucher programs "permit a considerable shift of taxpayer dollars from public secular schools to private religious schools."[144] Granting this, I note that leaving the decision in the hands of the legislatures, who have responded in the name of educational opportunity, has not yet led to religious strife.

As a postscript to this discussion, the Court has not interpreted the Free Exercise Clause to prevent state courts from interpreting their own religion clauses to forbid aid to religious education that the federal Establishment Clause allows.[145]

Notes

1. *Democracy in America*, vol. 1, part 2, chapter 9, p. 280.
2. *Lemon v Kurtzman*, 403 U.S. 602, 613–14 (1971). Internal case citations omitted.
3. 330 U.S. 1 (1947).
4. Id. at 15–16.
5. Id. at 16.
6. Id.
7. Id.
8. Id. at 23–24 (Justice Jackson dissenting). Justice Rutledge's dissent also contained a strong statement against the aid. "[D]aily religious education commingled with secular is 'religion' within the guaranty's comprehensive scope. So are religious training and teaching in whatever form. . . . The [Amendment's] prohibition broadly

forbids state support, financial or other, of religion in any guise, form or degree. It outlaws all use of public funds for religious purposes." Id. at 33.

9. 333 U.S. 203 (1948).

10. Id. at 207–8.

11. 343 U.S. 306 (1952).

12. 333 U.S. at 209–10.

13. 343 U.S. at 308–9.

14. Id. at 311.

15. Id. at 313–14.

16. See Id. at 317 (Justice Black, dissenting). Justices Frankfurter and Jackson made the same point about the improper use of the school attendance to get children to receive religious instruction. Id. at 321, 323–24.

17. 370 U.S. 421 (1962).

18. Id. at 422.

19. 374 U.S. 203 (1963).

20. This was a statewide requirement; see Id. at 205.

21. Id. at 211. These were two cases decided together: one from Pennsylvania and one from Maryland.

22. 370 U.S. at 425. Justices Frankfurter and White did not participate in the case. Since the former justice retired in 1962, and the latter was appointed in his place, Justice White probably was sworn in after oral argument in the case.

23. Id. at 430. Justice Douglas' concurrence emphasized the use of tax funds, which seems minimal here (Id. at 442). Moreover, he recanted his vote in *Everson*, the school bus case, without saying a thing about his *Zorach* Court opinion (Id. at 443).

24. Id. at 431. The Court later relies on an expanded conception of "coercion" when it continues to disallow government-supported prayer in public schools but allows prayer in legislative assemblies.

25. Id. at 449. For a discussion of the pledge language, see below.

26. 374 at 222.

27. Id. at 223.

28. Id. at 230 (Justice Brennan concurring), quoting from 333 U.S. at 313.

29. Id. at 231 (Justice Brennan concurring). Justice Brennan distinguished *Zorach* by emphasizing that public school buildings were not used in that released-time case. Id. at 223. The logic of the argument against prayer in the public schools was clearly against using required school attendance to facilitate religious activities, but the Court was unwilling to overturn *Zorach* explicitly. In his concurring opinion in *Abington*, Justice Douglas made no reference to his Court opinion in *Zorach*.

30. Id. at 237 (Justice Brennan concurring).

31. Id. at 241 (Justice Brennan concurring). Justice Goldberg's brief concurrence, agreed with Justices Clark and Brennan: "The fullest realization of true religious liberty requires that government neither engage in nor compel religious practices, that it effect no favoritism among sects or between religion and nonreligion, and that it work deterrence of no religious belief." Id. at 304. Justice Goldberg noted that providing military

chaplains and having schools teach "about religion," in contrast to "the teaching of re-ligion," would pass constitutional muster. Id at 306.

32. Id. at 317 (Justice Stewart dissenting).

33. He would remand the cases for the trial courts to determine if there was any inappropriate pressure on children.

34. 392 U.S. 236 (1965).

35. Id. at 239.

36. Id. at 244–45.

37. Id. at 248.

38. Id. at 252; see also Justice Douglas at 258–59 and Justice Fortas at 271.

39. 397 U.S. 663 (1970).

40. Id. at 669.

41. Id. at 670.

42. Id. at 673. The Chief Justice pointed out that all fifty states provide for tax ex-emption for places of worship and that federal law exempts religious and other eleemosynary groups from the income tax. Id at 676, note 4.

43. Id. at 674.

44. Id. at 690 (Justice Brennan concurring).

45. Id. at 696 (Justice Harlan concurring). This reminds us of Justice Harlan's concurring opinion in the second conscientious objector case (*Welsh v United States*). See chapter 13.

46. Id. at 707 (Justice Douglas dissenting).

47. Id. at 708 (Justice Douglas dissenting).

48. 403 U.S. 602 (1971).

49. This case was decided with *Lemon*, the lead case. In Rhode Island, 25 percent of the State's pupils were in nonpublic schools, and 95 percent of them were enrolled in Catholic schools. In Pennsylvania, 20 percent of that State's pupils were in non-public schools, and more than 96 percent were enrolled in church-related schools, most of which were Catholic.

50. On the same day it decided these cases, the Court handed down a decision up-holding federal construction grants to colleges and universities. See following foot-note 59.

51. *Lemon*, supra, 612–13 (internal citations omitted).

52. Id. at 614.

53. Id. at 618.

54. "[T]he raison d'etre of parochial schools is the propagation of a religious faith. They also teach secular subjects; but they came into existence in this country because Protestant groups were perverting the public schools by using them to propagate their faith. The Catholics naturally rebelled. If schools were to be used to propagate a par-ticular creed or religion, then Catholic ideals should also be served. Hence the ad-vent of parochial schools." Id. at 628.

55. Id. at 652–53 (Justice Brennan concurring).

56. "This Nation long ago committed itself to primary reliance upon publicly supported public education to serve its important goals in secular education. Our religious diversity gave strong impetus to that commitment." Id. at 658.

57. Id. at 661–62 (Justice White dissenting).

58. Id. at 668 (Justice White dissenting).

59. In addition, on the same day that it handed down its *Lemon* decision, the Court upheld federal construction grants to colleges and universities, including parochial schools, as long as the facilities were never used for religious purposes. Chief Justice Burger's plurality opinion in *Tilton v Richardson* stated: "There are generally significant differences between the religious aspects of church-related institutions of higher learning and parochial elementary and secondary schools. . . . There is substance to the contention that college students are less impressionable and less susceptible to religious indoctrination." *Tilton v Richardson* 403 U.S. 672, 685 (1971).

60. 463 U.S. 388.

61. *Committee For Public Education & Religious Liberty v Nyquist*, 413 U.S. 756, 762–763 (1973).

62. Id. at 773.

63. Id. at 779–80. This was the first time the Court employed the "effect test."

64. Id. at 783. In a footnote, Justice Powell refused to consider the distinction between a primary and a secondary effect. "Our cases simply do not support the notion that a law found to have a 'primary effect' to promote some legitimate end under the State's police power is immune from further examination to ascertain whether it also has the direct and immediate effect of advancing religion." Id. at 783–4, note 39.

65. Justice Powell distinguished this tax deduction from the tax exemption in *Walz*; the tax exemption had the support of tradition, and it was extended to more than religious organizations. Id. at 794.

66. See Id. at 823–24.

67. In *Meek v Pittance*, 421 U.S. 349 (1975), the Court struck down all parts of a Pennsylvania law providing auxiliary services and instructional materials to nonpublic schools meeting the State's compulsory attendance requirements except the textbook loan provisions. Some of the Justices in the majority wanted to invalidate the textbook provisions as well, and overturn *Allen* in the process. Chief Justice Burger and Justices White and Rehnquist dissented from those parts that invalidated most of the law. Then in *Wolman v Walter*, decided in 1977, the Court considered a similar law from Ohio. Here is Justice Blackmun's summary: "We hold constitutional those portions of the Ohio statute authorizing the State to provide nonpublic school pupils with books, standardized testing and scoring, diagnostic services, and therapeutic and remedial services. We hold unconstitutional those portions relating to instructional materials and equipment and field trip services" (433 U.S. 229, 235, 1977). Justice Marshall wanted to overturn *Allen* and strike the textbook aid. Justice Powell would have upheld the support for field trips, which Justice Blackmun's summary must have included under therapeutic aid. And Justices Rehnquist and White would have upheld the entire statute.

68. 463 U.S. 388.

69. Of course, everyone knew that the main expense was tuition and that public schools do not charge tuition, as the money comes from taxes.

70. Chief Justice Burger and Justices Rehnquist and White joined the majority here, while they dissented in Nyquist. Likewise, Justices Brennan, Marshall, and Blackmun dissented here, where they joined the majority in Nyquist. In addition, retiring Justices Douglas and Stewart, who were in the Nyquist majority, were replaced by Justice O'Connor, who voted with the majority in Mueller, and Justice Stevens, who dissented. This indicates the importance of Justice O'Connor's appointment for the Court's changing approach to Establishment Clause cases.

71. The Community Education program involved elective activities and took place after school; nonpublic schoolteachers volunteered their time for the program. In addition, the public school system "leased" classroom space for the Shared Time teachers and the classrooms had to be free of all religious symbols.

72. School District of the City of Grand Rapids v Ball, 473 U.S. 373, 379 (1985).

73. See note 66 above.

74. Id. at 397. Chief Justice Burger and Justice O'Connor concurred in the decision on the Community Education, since parochial school teachers were employed, but they dissented on the Shared Time program. Justices White and Rehnquist also dissented.

75. 473 U.S. 402 (1985).

76. Aguilar v Felton, 473 U.S. 402, 405–407 (1985).

77. Id. at 409. Justice Powell, who provided the fifth vote in these cases, agreed on "entanglement," at 415–16.

78. Id. at 420–21 (Justice Rehnquist dissenting). Justice White made this point above in his Lemon dissent. See above, text at note 77.

79. Id. at 422 (Justice O'Connor dissenting).

80. Id. at 424–25 (Justice O'Connor dissenting).

81. 521 U.S. 203.

82. Justice Anthony Kennedy replaced retiring Justice Powell in 1987. His opinion in Kiryas Joel expressed doubt about the soundness of the Aguliar and Ball decisions.

83. Board of Education of Kiryas Joel Village School District v Grumet, 512 U.S. 687, 691 (1994).

84. Id.

85. Justice Souter cited the Federal Individuals with Disabilities Act and Act 89 of New York Education law at 692.

86. Id. at 692.

87. Id. at 693.

88. Id. at 694.

89. Id. at 699. The majority relied on Larkin v Grendal's Den, 459 U.S. 116 (1982). In that case the Court invalidated a law that granted religious bodies a veto over applications for liquor licenses.

90. Id. at 703.

91. Id. at 707.

92. In *Agostini v Felton*, 521 U.S. 203 (1997), Justice O'Connor reports that the New York City Board of Education spent an additional $15 million a year leasing sites and transporting students etc. from 1986 to 1994; see 213. The case is discussed below.

93. 512 U.S. at 711 (Justice Stevens dissenting).

94. Id. at 729 (Justice Kennedy concurring).

95. "In light of the case before us, and in the interest of sound elaboration of constitutional doctrine, it may be necessary for us to reconsider them at a later date. A neutral aid scheme, available to religious and nonreligious alike, is the preferable way to address problems such as the Satmar handicapped children have suffered. But for *Grand Rapids* and *Aguilar*, the Satmars would have had no need to seek special accommodations or their own school district. Our decisions led them to choose that unfortunate course, with the deficiencies I have described." Id. at 731 internal citation omitted.

96. Id. at 750 (Justice Scalia dissenting). In his dissent, Justice Scalia argued that this case differed from *Larkin*, since civil authority was given to a community who happened to be of the same religion, not to the religious authority per se. He also thought that the Court should not second guess the legislature's motive, even though the school district was created by a special act rather than according to the State's general laws regarding school districts. See 735, 738–39.

97. Id at 717.

98. Id. at 717–18 (Justice O'Connor concurring).

99. 474 U.S. 481 (1986).

100. Id. at 487–88.

101. 509 U.S. 1 (1993).

102. Id. at 3–4.

103. Id. at 10, 12. As for the state-supported interpreter working in a parochial school, the Chief Justice wrote: "Nothing in this record suggests that a sign-language interpreter would do more than accurately interpret whatever material is presented to the class as a whole." Justices Blackmun and Souter dissented on this point. Justices Stevens and O'Connor thought the case should have been remanded for consideration of statutory questions.

104. 521 U.S. 203, 215, quoting from Rule 60(b) (5).

105. Id. at 209–10.

106. Justice Breyer joined the part on the merits only. Justice Ginsburg also wrote a separate dissent objecting to the use of a procedural rule 60(b)(5) to reconsider a decided case, rather than waiting for another one to raise the same issue. 521 U.S. 203, 259.

107. Id. at 223.

108. Id. at 228.

109. Id. at 231.

110. Id. at 233.

111. Id. at 233.

112. Id. at 234–5. This reverses *Aguilar* and that part of *Ball* that invalidated Grand Rapids' Shared time program. The Court did not consider whether nonpublic school teachers could provide the instruction.

113. Id. at 245.

114. Id. at 246.

115. 530 U.S. 793 (2000).

116. The chapter 2 program channeled federal funds through local educational agencies (LEAs, usually public school districts) via state educational agencies (SEAs) to implement programs to assist children in primary and secondary schools. The law offered assistance to public and (nonprofit) private schools on an equal basis. The funds could only "supplement" the funding that is made available from non-Federal sources and the materials offered to private schools must be "secular, neutral, and non-ideological." Id. 801–2 (Justice Thomas's Court opinion).

117. Id. at 822.

118. Id. at 824.

119. Id. at 834. There was also evidence of improperly loaned textbooks. That violation was discovered and the books were returned.

120. "Because the religious indoctrination is supported by government assistance, the reasonable observer would naturally perceive the aid program as *government* support for the advancement of religion." 843 (emphasis in the original).

121. "To establish a First Amendment violation, plaintiffs must prove that the aid in question actually is, or has been, used for religious purposes." Id. at 857.

122. Id. at 870–72.

123. *Zelman v Simmons-Harris* 536 U.S. 639.

124. Id. at 645. I assume that referred to the neighborhood school.

125. For the lowest income families, the copayment could not be more than $250; the copay limit did not apply for other families, who received a grant of up to $1,875. The tutorial assistance amounts to 90 percent of the amount charged, up to $360, for the low income students, and $300 for the rest. See Id. at 646–47.

126. The funding for these schools, from state and local sources, was considerably more than the tuition scholarship. See Id. at 647–48. There were ten start-up community schools and twenty-three magnet schools.

127. Id. at 648.

128. Id. at 652.

129. Id. at 653.

130. Id. at 655.

131. Id. at 659.

132. Id. at 663.

133. Id. at 664.

134. The three-part test was reduced to two parts: purpose and effect. The "effect" part of the test considers whether the program administers aid in a neutral fashion

and "whether beneficiaries of indirect aid have a genuine choice among religious and nonreligious organizations when determining the organizations to which they will direct that aid." Id. at 669.

135. Id. at 683.

136. Id. at 686.

137. Id. at 687, 688. The *Everson* quote is in U.S. 330 at 16.

138. That is how I understand Justice Souter's statement that since *Mueller* (1983) the *Lemon* test has been transformed so that "[n]ow...the substantial character of government aid is held to have no constitutional significance, and the espoused criteria of neutrality in offering aid, and private choice in directing it, are shown to be nothing but examples of verbal formalism." Id. at 688–89.

139. See Id. at 703 and note 12 at 704. Justice Souter does acknowledge that he would not support a higher aid level, which would cover tuition at all private schools, since the increased financial support for "religious teaching" would make it "more egregiously unconstitutional than the current scheme." See Id. at 706, note 16.

140. Id. at 715–16. Justice Souter notes increases in dollar spending and that in another state's voucher program, many parochial schools received more than their tuition. Justice Souter refers to Milwaukee's program at 174.

141. Id. at 717.

142. Justice Souter pointed out that two out of three parents sent children to a religious school not of their own religion (704). Did this suggest that the program would produce religious strife or that it was giving poor families an educational alternative to the failed public schools?

143. Id. at 726.

144. Id. at 727.

145. Witters, who won in the U.S. Supreme Court, lost in the Washington state supreme court, on the grounds that the state Constitution prohibited state funding of religious education [*Witters v State Commission for the Blind* 112 Wash. 2d 363 (1989)]. The U.S. Supreme Court refused to hear the case on certiorari, 493 U.S. 850 (1989). Then, in 2004, in *Locke v Davey*, the Supreme Court upheld Washington state's "Promise Scholarships," which were awarded to qualified students attending state colleges or universities but excluded students majoring in devotional theology. The Court held that the exclusion, required by the state constitution's stricter "establishment clause" did not violate the federal Free Exercise Clause. See 72 U.S.L.W. 4206 (2004).

CHAPTER FIFTEEN

The Establishment Clause: II

Government Endorsement of Religious Activity

We turn now to the cases involving some form of government authorization or endorsement of religious activity in public schools and other public places. The Court has followed the neutrality principle, although a minority of justices currently sitting has questioned it, and the Court has accommodated religion to different degrees in different contexts.

Marsh v Chambers (1983),[1] the legislative prayer case, is an excellent example of accommodation. The Nebraska legislature began each session with a prayer offered by a chaplain who was chosen by an executive board of the legislature and paid out of public funds. Ernest Chambers, as a member of the legislature and a taxpayer, brought suit to stop the practice. The district court held that the practice was valid but the payment from public funds violated the Establishment Clause. The court of appeals, applying the *Lemon* test, held that both the prayer and the payment violated all three parts of the test.[2]

Chief Justice Burger's Court opinion, which Justices White, Blackmun, Powell, Rehnquist, and O'Connor joined, made no attempt to reconcile legislative prayer with the *Lemon* test. The opinion noted that the lower courts that heard the case "opened with an announcement that concluded 'God save the United States and this Honorable Court,'" described the colonial practice of having prayer open legislative sessions, and referred to the First Congress's appointment of paid chaplains.[3] Based on this "unique history," the Court "conclude[d] that legislative prayer presents no more potential for establishment than provision of school transportation, beneficial grants for higher education, or tax exemptions for religious organizations [citations omitted]."[4] Chief Justice Burger distinguished this prayer case from the earlier ones: "Here, the individual claiming injury by the practice is an adult, presumably not readily susceptible to 'religious indoctrination,' or peer pressure [citing *Abington*]."[5]

Justice Brennan, in a dissent that Justice Marshall joined, had an easy time demonstrating how legislative prayer and payment of a chaplain's salary violated the *Lemon* test. Justice Brennan thought it was a good sign that the majority did not use a test, since "it simply confirms that the Court is carving out an exception to the Establishment Clause rather than reshaping doctrine to accommodate legislative prayer."[6]

Both opinions referred to Madison's disapproval of legislative prayer. Justice Brennan quoted from Madison's "Detached Memoranda," written some time between 1817 and 1832:[7]

Is the appointment of Chaplains to the two Houses of Congress consistent with the Constitution, and with the pure principle of religious freedom?

In strictness, the answer on both points must be in the negative. The Constitution of the U.S. forbids everything like an establishment of a national religion. The law appointing Chaplains establishes a religious worship for the national representatives to be performed by Ministries of religion, elected by a majority of them; and these are to be paid out of the national taxes. Does not this involve the principle of a national establishment, applicable to a provision for a religious worship for the Constituent as well as of the representative Body, approved by the majority, and conducted by Ministers of religion paid by the entire nation?[8]

Neither Justice quoted or made reference to Madison's final statement about this form of prayer: "Rather than let this step beyond the landmarks of power have the effect of a legitimate precedent, it will be better to apply to it the legal aphorism *de minimis non curat lex*: or to class it *cum 'maculis quas aut incuria fudit, aut humana parum cavit natura.*'"[9] The first Latin phrase means "the law does not care about little things." The second means this is to be classed with "little blemishes that have come about through inattention, or because human nature didn't guard against them strictly enough." Madison's remarks explain the *Marsh* decision more fully than Chief Justice Burger's opinion does.[10]

A year later, the Court decided *Lynch v Donnelly*.[11] Pawtucket, Rhode Island's annual Christmas display included a banner reading "Season's Greetings!" and a crèche, or Nativity scene. The city owned the Christmas display, which it erected in a park owned by a nonprofit organization and located "in the heart of the shopping district."[12] The entire display also included "among other things, a Santa Claus house, reindeer pulling Santa's sleigh, candy-striped poles, a Christmas tree, carolers," etc. The district court ruled that the inclusion of the crèche violated the Establishment Clause by endorsing and promulgating religious beliefs. A divided court of appeals agreed; the Supreme Court reversed. In his Court opinion, Chief Justice Burger emphasized accommodation[13] and described the display this way:

> When viewed in the proper context of the Christmas Holiday season . . . there is insufficient evidence to establish that the inclusion of the crèche is a purposeful or surreptitious effort to express some kind of subtle governmental advocacy of a particular religious message. . . . The city . . . has principally taken note of a significant historical religious event long celebrated in the Western world. The crèche in the display depicts the historical origins of this traditional event long recognized as a National Holiday.[14]

In applying the *Lemon* test, the Chief Justice said that the purpose was a secular celebration of the holiday[15] and the primary effect of including the crèche was not to advance religion, because the display "is no more an advancement or endorsement of religion than the Congressional and Executive recognition of the Holiday itself as 'Christ's Mass,' or the exhibition of literally hundreds of religious paintings in governmentally supported museums."[16]

Justice O'Connor, who joined the majority opinion, wrote a more persuasive account in her concurring opinion. "The central issue in this case is whether Pawtucket has endorsed Christianity by its display of the crèche. To answer that question, we must examine both what Pawtucket intended to communicate in displaying the crèche and what message the city's display actually conveyed."[17] Justice O'Connor concluded that "the evident purpose of including the crèche in the larger display was not promotion of the religious content of the crèche but celebration of the public holiday through its traditional symbols. Celebration of public holidays, which have cultural significance even if they also have religious aspects, is a legitimate secular purpose."[18]

The setting in which the crèche was displayed "changes what viewers may fairly understand to be the purpose of the display." Such a celebration of a holiday that is both secular and religious was likened to Thanksgiving and the motto on our coins ("In God we Trust"); they serve "the legitimate secular purposes of solemnizing public occasions, expressing confidence in the future, and encouraging the recognition of what is worthy of appreciation in society."[19] Justice O'Connor's "no endorsement" principle can be viewed as a variant of the *Lemon* test's inquiry into the primary effect. Is it persuasive? Can Justice O'Connor rely on the secular setting within which the crèche was displayed to claim "non-endorsement" of religion and also describe the crèche's use in such a display as solemnizing a public occasion? Is it not more accurate, if impolitic, to say that the mixed setting sufficiently commercialized the crèche to allow its inclusion to pass constitutional muster?[20]

Justice Brennan, in a dissent joined by Justices Marshall, Blackmun, and Stevens, noted the narrow basis of the Court's ruling and expressed appreciation that the opinion returned to a consideration of the *Lemon* test. He still disagreed with the majority. "The 'primary effect,' of including a nativity scene in the city's display is, as the District Court found, to place the government's imprimatur of approval on the particular religious beliefs exemplified by the crèche."[21]

Five years later, the Court divided again over a city-sponsored display that included a crèche. In *Allegheny v American Civil Liberties Union* (1989),[22] a crèche was prominently displayed on the grand staircase of the Allegheny County Courthouse in Pittsburgh and a large Christmas tree and a large menorah were displayed outside an office building owned jointly by Pittsburgh and Allegheny Counties. Justices Blackmun and O'Connor, whose votes decided the case, were the only ones to agree that the crèche display, standing prominently by itself, violated the Establishment Clause, while the Christmas tree and the menorah represented the secular aspects of the holiday season and religious pluralism and were constitutional.[23] Justice Blackmun wrote the opinion stating the judgment of the Court. Despite his dissent in *Lynch*, he agreed with Justice O'Connor's approach.[24]

The most combative opinion came from newly appointed Justice Kennedy, who charged the majority with "an unjustified hostility toward religion" in holding the crèche display in violation of the Establishment Clause.[25] Justice Kennedy favored a "non-coercion," "non-proselytizing" approach to the Establishment Clause.[26] He thought that as long as there was a secular component to a given holiday, every manner of celebration should be permitted. [27]

The remaining cases in this analysis involve prayer or some other religiously inspired activity in public schools. In this context, the Court majority has refused to accommodate religion.

In *Wallace v Jaffree* (1985),[28] Alabama passed a law authorizing public schools to set aside one minute "for meditation or voluntary prayer." The Court's 6 to 3 decision made it clear that legislative prayer was unique. Justice Stevens's Court opinion, which Justices Brennan, Marshall, Blackmun, and Powell joined (Justice O'Connor concurred in the judgment), identified three Alabama statutes that were involved in the early stages of litigation: one authorized a moment of silence "for meditation"; the one at issue in this case authorized a period of silence "for meditation or prayer";[29] and another authorized teachers to lead "willing students" in a prayer to "Almighty God . . . the Creator and Supreme Judge of the world."[30] The district court judge had upheld the first statute and found the other two invalid for encouraging a religious activity; then, the same judge reconsidered and held the latter two statutes constitutional on the grounds that the Establishment Clause did not apply to the states, contrary to *Everson*. The court of appeals reversed the district judge on that point and the appellees did not challenge the holding that the first statute was constitutional.

Justice Stevens referred to the testimony of two state senators to show that "the legislation was an 'effort to return voluntary prayer to the public schools.'"[31] Noting the changes in the law along with the subsequent testimony, he distinguished between a legislative intent to return prayer to the public schools and a student's right to engage in voluntary prayer during a moment of silence. He then concluded "that the Alabama Legislature intended to change existing law . . . for the sole purpose of expressing the State's endorsement of prayer activities for one minute at the beginning of each school day."[32]

Chief Justice Burger's dissent referred to legislative and judicial invocations of divine assistance.[33] He also rejected the distinction between the statute that only mentioned meditation and the one at issue here, which mentioned meditation or prayer. The mention of prayer as a possible activity during the moment of silence was the same, for Chief Justice Burger, as the words "under God," which were added to the Pledge of Allegiance in 1954.[34]

Justice White's brief dissent saw no difference between the first and second statutes: "if a student asked whether he could pray during that moment, it is difficult to believe that the teacher could not answer in the affirmative."[35]

Justice Rehnquist took the occasion of this case to challenge the Court's view, from *Everson*, that the Establishment Clause required neutrality as between religion and irreligion as well as among different religions. He reviewed constitutional discussions in the First Congress and argued that Madison's expression of concern that no "national religion" should be established manifested a limited purpose, in contrast to his strict separation position in Virginia. Justice Rehnquist thus attributed to Madison and others a willingness to grant Congress the power to assist religion, as long as the assistance was "non-preferential." Justice Rehnquist's review notwithstanding, the clearest conclusion from the limited discussion in the First Congress is that Congress was not to have any authority over religion.[36] In addition, considering the variety of religious sects in America in the late twentieth century, it is difficult to envision how government support for prayer could be "non-preferential."[37]

What happens when a religiously inspired interest in how science is taught in public schools leads to legislation that reflects an educational interest in the origins of life?[38] This is what the Court confronted in the case of *Edwards v Aguilard* (1987).[39] In his Court opinion, Justice Brennan described Louisiana's Creation Act, also known as the Balanced Treatment for Creation-Science and Evolution-Science in Public School Instruction Act,[40] this way:

> The Creationism Act forbids the teaching of the theory of evolution in public schools unless accompanied by instruction in "creation science." No school is required to teach evolution or creation science. If either is taught, however, the other must also be taught. The theories of evolution and creation science are statutorily defined as "scientific evidences for [creation or evolution] and inferences from those scientific evidences."[41]

The appellants, arguing on behalf of Louisiana, claimed that the secular purpose of the act was to protect academic freedom, but Justice Brennan: "appellants have identified no clear secular purpose for the Louisiana Act."[42] First, Justice Brennan said the term did not apply to what teachers may teach, since they "are not free, absent permission, to teach courses different from what is required."[43] But even if the term applied, the act "actually serves to diminish academic freedom by removing the flexibility to teach evolution without also teaching creation science, even if teachers determine that such curriculum results in less effective and comprehensive science instruction."[44] Justice Brennan quoted the statute's legislative sponsor, Senator Bill Keith: "My preference would be that neither [creationism nor evolution] be taught."[45] Senator Keith drew on the expert testimony of Dr. Edward Boudreaux to define "creation science" as "the religious belief that a supernatural creator was responsible for the creation of humankind."[46] Drawing on Senator Keith's testimony, Justice Brennan concluded: "the purpose of the Creationism Act was to restructure the science curriculum to conform with a particular religious viewpoint."[47]

In his concurrence,[48] Justice Powell focused on the kinship between the creation science and the Biblical accounts of creation and the fact that Dr. Boudreaux and the other "recognized creation scientists" in the United States were affiliated with one of two religiously based research organizations.[49] This was enough for him—and Justice O'Connor, concurring—to conclude that "religious belief" is the "Balanced Treatment Act's reason for existence."[50]

Justice White, who usually supported religious accommodation, wrote a separate opinion concurring in the judgment. He thought the language of the act and the lower courts' interpretation of "creation science" indicated that hostility to science rather than academic freedom was the decisive factor in the legislation.

Still, as Justice Scalia pointed out in dissent, this was not a clear case of an impermissible religious purpose prompting a law, and normally the Court deferred to legislatures on matters of educational policy. As Justice Scalia summarized the testimony, there were two possible explanations for the beginning of life and the legislation assured that if one was taught, the other would be also. He also quoted Senator Keith denying that his intent "was to advance a particular religious doctrine."[51]

The most recent public school prayer cases involved a graduation ceremony and a college football game. In *Lee v Weisman*,[52] Deborah Weisman, with her father, sued to prohibit school officials from including a planned invocation and benediction in the graduation ceremony at Nathan Bishop Middle School in Providence, Rhode Island, just four days before graduation day. The federal district court denied the motion for lack of time and the ceremony took place as planned. The school principal, Robert E. Lee, had invited a rabbi to deliver the prayers, supplying him with a pamphlet prepared by the National Conference of Christians and Jews, entitled, "Guidelines for Civil Occasions." The rabbi's fifteen-line invocation began, "God of the Free, Hope of the Brave"; and his equally brief benediction began and ended with expressions of gratitude to "God" and "to You, Lord." The students and the rest of the assembly stood for the Pledge of Allegiance and remained standing for at least one of the rabbi's prayers. After allowing the Weismans to amend their lawsuit, since Deborah would be confronted with the same kind of ceremony in high school, the judge held such "non-denominational" prayers to be in violation of the Establishment Clause, citing the *Lemon* test. The court of appeals, 2 to 1, agreed with the district court, and the Supreme Court affirmed that decision, 5 to 4, in a Court opinion by Justice Kennedy, joined by Justices Souter, Blackmun, O'Connor, and Stevens.

Justice Kennedy presented the question this way: "whether including clerical members who offer prayers as part of the official graduation ceremony is consistent with the Religion Clauses of the First Amendment."[53] He emphasized the school context[54] and detailed the state's role in the religious exercise: the school principal decided to have an invocation and benediction, chose the clergyman, and provided him with guidelines, to ensure that the prayer was nonsectarian.[55]

Justice Kennedy noted that student opinion was divided on prayer; if such a difference of opinion were viewed in terms of speech, living in a pluralistic society would require exposure to different ideas. But religion was different:

> In religious debate or expression the government is not a prime participant, for the Framers deemed religious establishment antithetical to the freedom of all. The Free Exercise Clause embraces a freedom of conscience and worship that has close parallels in the speech provisions of the First Amendment, but the Establishment Clause is a specific prohibition on forms of state intervention in religious affairs with no precise counterpart in the speech provisions.[56]

Justice Kennedy, who was willing to accommodate religious symbols on government property during national holidays,[57] and who supported accommodation for the private speech and association rights of students who wish to engage in religious activities,[58] opposed accommodation for public school prayer:

> The sole question presented is whether a religious exercise may be conducted at a graduation ceremony in circumstances where . . . young graduates who object are induced to conform. No holding by this Court suggests that a school can persuade or compel a student to participate in a religious exercise. That is being done here, and it is forbidden by the Establishment Clause of the First Amendment.[59]

Justice Blackmun's concurring opinion noted that *Marsh* was the only case that did not follow the *Lemon* test and the prohibition on government participation in religious activity or pressure, however subtle, to participate in religious activity:

> When the government arrogates to itself a role in religious affairs, it abandons its obligation as guarantor of democracy. Democracy requires the nourishment of dialog and dissent, while religious faith puts its trust in an ultimate divine authority above all human deliberation. When the government appropriates religious truth, it "transforms rational debate into theological decree." Those who disagree no longer are questioning the policy judgment of the elected but the rules of a higher authority who is beyond reproach.[60]

This strong statement might not be reconcilable with the Court's legislative prayer and religious symbolism cases. But if one associates the school environment, including the graduation ceremony, with education, then the distinction drawn accounts for the strict application of separation in the public school setting.

In his concurrence, Justice Souter reviewed the framers' deliberations on religion in the First Congress and concluded that the case for "non-preferential" promotion of religion was "not so convincing as to require reconsideration of our settled law."[61] He made two interesting points. First, if the framers had intended to allow "non-preferential" promotion of religion, they could have expressed that intention more clearly by placing the indefinite article before religion, not establishment ("Congress shall make no law respecting an establishment of religion.") Second, the concept of "non-preferential" promotion presupposed a clear distinction between sectarian and nonsectarian religious practices, which is not easily made. For example, the rabbi drew on the King James Version of Micah for his exhortation to "do justly, love mercy, and walk humbly."[62]

Justice Scalia's dissent made the argument from history, akin to the kind of argument that supported legislative prayer. He played down "coerciveness" of the peer pressure to stand for the prayer; he likened the student's option to sit silently through the prayer, while others stood and recited it, to the option to sit silently through the flag salute exercise.[63] He also offered a justification similar to Justice O'Connor's argument from *Lynch* concerning solemnizing public occasions: "The narrow context of the present case involves a community's celebration of one of the milestones in its young citizens' lives, and it is a bold step for this Court to seek to banish from that occasion, and from thousands of similar celebrations, throughout the land, the expression of gratitude to God that a majority of the community wishes to make."[64] Justice Scalia thought that graduation prayer was permissible as long as the audience was informed—by an announcement or a written assertion in the program—"that while all are asked to rise for the invocation and benediction, none is compelled to join in them, nor will be assumed, by rising, to have done so."[65]

Then, in *Santa Fe School District v Doe*,[66] the Court, 6 to 3, applied its *Lee* reasoning to the football setting. Justice Stevens wrote the Court opinion; Chief Justice Rehnquist dissented, joined by Justices Scalia and Thomas.

Litigation regarding prayer at Santa Fe High School in Texas began in 1995, and originally involved prayer at graduation as well as prayer at football games. The original plaintiffs, now respondents,[67] alleged that the school district had engaged in several proselytizing practices "such as promoting attendance at a Baptist revival meeting, encouraging membership in religious clubs," etc., as well as allowing students to read Christian prayers at graduation ceremonies and over the public address system at football games.[68] The district court entered an interim order prohibiting the proselytizing practices and ordering that "a nondenominational prayer" consisting of "an invocation and/or benediction" could be presented by a student selected by the graduating class.[69] The district adopted policies for graduation (in May and June) and football games (in August and October) in line with this order. In the May policy, the board chose

> to permit the graduating senior class, with the advice and counsel of the senior class principal or designee, to elect by secret ballot to choose whether an invocation and benediction shall be part of the graduation exercise. If so chosen the class shall elect by secret ballot, from a list of student volunteers, students to deliver nonsectarian, nonproselytizing invocations and benedictions for the purpose of solemnizing their graduation ceremonies.[70]

The students chose to have such a prayer and it was given at the graduation in 1995. Then in July, the district enacted another policy eliminating the requirement that the prayers be nonsectarian and nonproselytizing, provided that if the district court disallowed it, the previous policy would take effect. The August policy, entitled "Prayer at Football Games," incorporated the same features—the choice whether or not to have a prayer, followed by the election of the person or persons to give it—as the graduation prayer policy. In addition, it contained two versions, identical in every respect except that the one limiting the prayers to nonsectarian invocations would only go into effect if a court order enjoined the district from sponsoring a sectarian prayer. The final October policy omitted prayer from the title (it was now called "Student Activities: Pre-Game Ceremonies at Football Games") and referred to "a brief invocation and/or message."[71] Justice Stevens observed that the students chose to have a student say a prayer under the August policy, and there was no additional election under the final October policy.

The district court interpreted *Lee v Weisman* to allow nonsectarian prayers led by students at graduation and at football games; both parties appealed, and the court of appeals reversed. The Supreme Court affirmed that reversal.[72]

The Court announced that it was following *Lee*, which meant "government may not coerce anyone to support or participate in religion or its exercise."[73] The school district defended its policy in two ways. First, it claimed that the student election to determine whether or not there would be prayer or some other "message" or "statement" and the student selection of the individual who would speak created a "public forum" in which what was said amounted to "private student speech, not public speech."[74] Justice Stevens replied by distinguishing the "public forum" cases: the pregame ceremony was not open to "indiscriminate use . . . by the student body generally." In addition, only the majority-approved message was conveyed.[75] Nor did the two-step election process establish "private speech," since the entire policy was the board's. In addition, the reference to "solemnizing the event" "invites and encourages religious messages,"[76] and the school's endorsement of the ceremony was clear, in light of the context.[77]

The school district also claimed that the football policy was distinguishable from the graduation prayer in *Lee* because there was no coercion: the messages were chosen by students and attendance was not required at the games.[78] Justice Stevens addressed each of these two points. The election mechanism did not remove the prayer from government sponsorship; it only "encourages divisiveness along religious lines in a public school setting."[79] And many people, such as cheerleaders, members of the band, and the team members, were required to attend. Beyond that, "the constitutional command will not permit the District 'to exact religious conformity from a student as the price' of joining her classmates at a varsity football game."[80]

Chief Justice Rehnquist, dissenting, thought the decision was premature, since it was not clear that a prayer would be said.[81] He also argued that the election provisions produced "private speech," not "government speech."

Conclusion

The Supreme Court has used or considered three different types of test in its examination of Establishment Clause cases: the *Lemon* Test, the Endorsement Test, and the No Coercion test. The first has been questioned and criticized but not rejected. To some extent it has evolved into the Endorsement Test, with the major difference that "entanglement" has ceased to be an independent criterion. That came about in connection with the aid to parochial-school cases, where the accommodation position has won out. Advocates of that position have urged the adoption of a No Coercion test in prayer cases, but they remain a minority. The majority position on the Court with regard to prayer and religious activity is that accommodation may be appropriate for legislative prayer and for some displays of religious symbols, but it is not appropriate when government acts as educator. Perhaps the Endorsement Test and the No Coercion Test intersect, if one views coercion as including government and peer pressure in the primary or secondary school context.

The public forum analysis for free speech cases has become another source of accommodation for religious activity in public places. The Court started by holding that religious organizations could not for that reason be excluded from a designated public forum (*Lamb's Chapel*); then it applied the public forum concept to a public university's funding of student organizations' educational activities and held that religious speech had an equal right to funding (*Rosenberger*); then it held that clubs holding meetings resembling religious services could not be excluded from the designated forum created when a public school opened its facilities to the public for educational activities (*Good News Club*). These activities did not violate the Establishment Clause largely because in each case the speaker was a private individual or group, not the school, and hence not the government. In yet another case, the Court held that the city of Columbus, Ohio, could not forbid the Ku Klux Klan from erecting a large Latin cross on a public square adjacent to the statehouse; since the speaker was not the government, the Establishment Clause was not violated.[82]

The separation, or neutrality, principle is the starting point, but in accommodation is more feasible in some contexts than in others. The Court is least likely to accommodate public school support for religion in the form of authorization to pray, or a religion-based restriction on the academic program. This result is due especially to the views of Justices O'Connor and Kennedy, and, occasionally, Justice Breyer. The other Justices have been firmly divided between strict separation and accommodation, regardless of the context.

Notes

1. 463 U.S. 783 (1983).
2. Id. at 785–86 (1983).
3. Id. at 789–90.
4. Id. at 791.
5. *Marsh*, supra, at 792.
6. Id. at 796 (Justice Brennan dissenting).
7. See Elizabeth Fleet, ed., "Madison's Detached Memoranda," William and Mary Quarterly, 3rd Series, vol. III, no. 4, October 1946, pp. 534–68
8. Detached Memoranda, 558, quoted by Justice Brennan, in Marsh, supra, at 807.
9. Detached Memoranda 559.
10. In fairness to the Chief Justice, perhaps a judicial opinion cannot be so candid when it comes to the need for some pragmatic tempering of a constitutional principle, such as neutrality or separation. I am indebted to Eve Adler for the Latin translation.
11. 465 U.S. 668 (1984).
12. *Lynch v Donnelly*, 465 U.S. 668 (1984). If the same organization that owned the park had owned the crèche, the city would have been able to enjoy the Christmas display with no constitutional controversy. Id. at 671.

13. Id. at 674–77.He referred to *Marsh*, and the Presidential proclamation delivered every Thanksgiving, and to religious paintings in the National Gallery and a representation of Moses and the Ten Commandments in the Supreme Court.

14. Id. at 681. The Chief Justice used the "no more than" approach in *Marsh* as well. See text at note 4.

15. Id., 681.

16. Id., 683. The entanglement issue was not as difficult, since there was no administrative oversight. 684.

17. Id. at 689 (Justice O'Connor concurring).

18. Id. at 691 (Justice O'Connor concurring).

19. Id. at 693 (Justice O'Connor concurring).

20. For a trenchant critique of the Supreme Court's opinions in this case, see Winnifred Fallers Sullivan, *Paying the Words Extra: Religious Discourse in the Supreme Court of the United States* (Cambridge, MA: Harvard University Center for the Study of World Religions, 1994).

21. Id. at 701. The inclusion of secular symbols of Christmas did not persuade Justice Brennan, because for non-Christians "the symbolic reenactment of the birth of a divine being who has been miraculously incarnated as a man stands as a dramatic reminder of their differences with Christian faith." 708.

22. 492 U.S. 573 (1989).

23. Justices Brennan, Marshall, and Stevens would have invalidated both displays, and Justices Kennedy, Rehnquist, White, and Scalia would have allowed both displays.

24. "Thus, despite divergence at the bottom line, the five Justices in concurrence and dissent in *Lynch* agreed upon the relevant constitutional principles; the government's use of religious symbolism is unconstitutional if it has the effect of endorsing religious beliefs, and the effect of the government's use of religious symbolism depends upon the context." Id. at 597. The reference is to Justice O'Connor and the four dissenters in *Lynch*.

25. Id. at 655 Justice Kennedy devotes a substantial part of his opinion to criticizing Justice O'Connor's "endorsement" approach to the "primary effect" test ("A test for implementing the protections of the Establishment Clause that, if applied with consistency, would invalidate longstanding traditions cannot be a proper reading of the Clause.") 670.

26. Id. at 660, 664–65 (Justice Kennedy concurring in part and dissenting in part).

27. "If government is to participate in its citizens' celebration of a holiday that contains both a secular and a religious component, enforced recognition of only the secular aspect would signify the callous indifference toward religious faith that our cases and traditions do not require; for by commemorating the holiday only as it is celebrated by nonadherents, the government would be refusing to acknowledge the plain fact, and the historical reality, that many of its citizens celebrate its religious aspects as well." 663–64.

28. *Wallace v Jaffree* 472 U.S. 38 (1985).

29. The Court had already affirmed the court of appeals' invalidation of teacher-led prayer; see *Wallace v Jaffree* 466 U.S. 924 (1984) cited at 472 U.S. 38, note 8.

30. Id. at 40.

31. Id. at 57. The internal quote is from a statement submitted into the legislative record; see note 43.

32. Id. at 59–60. Justice O'Connor's concurrence reiterated her "no endorsement" interpretation of the *Lemon* test. Id. at 69–70. She also noted that a "rigid application of the *Lemon* test would invalidate legislation exempting religious observers from generally applicable government obligations." 82.

33. Id. at 84–85 (Chief Justice Berger dissenting). This comparison fails to note the significance of the distinction the Chief Justice made in his own *Marsh v Chambers* opinion, between an assembly of adults and one of children in school, susceptible to "peer pressure." See *Marsh*, supra 187.

34. Justice O'Connor replied to this by referring to her *Lynch* opinion: the words "serve as an acknowledgement of religion with 'the legitimate secular purposes of solemnizing public occasions [and] expressing confidence in the future.'" See Id. at 78, quoting from *Lynch* at 693. For a discussion of the recent "under God" case, see the conclusion.

35. Id. at 91.

36. See discussion in part one.

37. Justice Stevens, in his Court opinion, cited Cantwell and Barnette in support of the incorporation position. See pp. 50–51. He could have cited Justice Brennan's Schempp opinion also; 374 U.S. 203, (1963) 256 (the Establishment Clause is a "coguarantor," with the Free Exercise Clause, of religious liberty).

38. The Court tends to avoid questions of religious truth. See *United States v Ballard* 322 U.S. 78 (1944). The federal government brought an indictment against the Ballards for defrauding people by making knowingly false statements about their abilities. The Ballards claimed that they were exercising their religious freedom and that government could not put their beliefs to a test of truth. The district court judge charged the jury with considering the defendants' good faith only; this led to convictions that the Supreme Court upheld.

39. *Edwards v Aguilard* 482 U.S. 578 (1987). For an earlier judicial confrontation between Darwinian evolution and the Bible's story of creation, see *Epperson v Arkansas*, 397 U.S. 97 (1968).

40. Id. at 581.

41. Id. at 581. Justices Marshall, Blackmun, Powell, and Stevens joined the Court opinion.

42. Id. at 585.

43. Id. at 586.

44. Id. at 586.

45. Id. at 587.

46. *Edwards v Aguilard* at 591, text and note 12.

47. Id. at 593.

48. Justice Powell's concurring opinion clarified the issue by providing dictionary definitions of the key terms. "The 'doctrine or theory of creation' is commonly defined as 'holding that matter, the various forms of life, and the world were created by a transcendent God out of nothing (citation omitted). 'Evolution' is defined as 'the theory that the various types of animals and plants have their origin in other preexisting types, the distinguishable differences being due to modifications in successive generations.' Id. at 598–99.

49. Id. at 601–2. The Creation Research Society had a four-part statement of belief that spelled out the Biblical, and especially Christian, foundations of their position.

50. Id. at 603. See also 604 ("Whatever the academic merit of particular subjects or theories, the Establishment Clause limits the discretion of state officials to pick and choose among them for the purpose of promoting a particular religious belief. The language of the statute and its legislative history convince me that the Louisiana Legislature exercised its discretion for this purpose in this case.")

51. Id. at 625 (Justice Scalia dissenting).

52. 505 U.S. 577 (1992).

53. Id. at 580.

54. Id. at 586.

55. Id. at 588.

56. Id. at 591.

57. See his opinion in *County of Alleghaney v ACLU* 492 U.S. 573, 664–65 (1989). (Discussed above in text at note 26.)

58. Id. at 599, citing *Board of Education v Mergens*, 496 U.S. 226 (1990).

59. Id. at 599.

60. Id.at 607 (Justice Blackmun concurring).

61. Id. at 612.

62. Id. at 617. Justice Souter cited Justice Blackmun, who identified the prayer as "Judeo-Christian" since it came from Micah. Neither Justice noted the rabbi's omission of the phrase, "with thy God," which occurs immediately after "walk humbly." There is more than one reason to object to such a prayer in a public school graduation.

63. Id. at 638–39 (Justice Scalia dissenting).

64. Id. at 645 (Justice Scalia dissenting).

65. Id.

66. 530 U.S. 290 (2000).

67. They were called "Doe" to protect their privacy.

68. *Santa Fe v Doe* 530 U.S. 290, 295 (2000).

69. Id. 296.

70. Id. at 296–97 (quoted from the Court of Appeals decision).

71. Id. at 298, note 6.

72. Id. at 299, 301.

73. Id. at 302, quoting from Lee at 587.

74. Id. at 302.

75. Id. at 303–4.
76. Id. at 306.
77. Id. at 307–8.
78. Id. at 310.
79. Id. at 311.
80. Id. at 311, 312 (internal quote from *Lee v Weisman*).
81. Id. at 318.
82. *Capitol Square Review and Advisory Board v Pinette* 515 U.S. 753 (1995).

Conclusion

I have argued that the prominence of our First Amendment freedoms pre-supposes and devolves from the establishment of limited government. Be-cause the First Amendment freedoms all require limited government, we should study them together and study them in the light of modern political philosophy, which justified the creation of limited government. Beginning in the seventeenth century, the aim of Enlightenment philosophers was to se-cure civil peace and, at the same time, preserve the right to engage in phi-losophy or science, that is, the quest for the truth. Their dual goal required that they "tame" religion by "privatizing" all questions concerning how a cit-izen should live. This act of privatizing separates the individual's efforts to de-fine and pursue his ends from the tasks and ends of government. The philoso-phers wanted to limit government to the job of securing the means for individual pursuits.

The philosophical advocates of limited government—Spinoza, Locke, Montesquieu, and Mill—all prescribe tolerance of differing opinions on the highest questions. We have seen how Milton first used the notion that truth would win out against falsehood to argue for no prior restraints—in the form of licensing requirements—on publishing. Taking up this argu-ment, Locke extended it to all speculative doctrines in religion. He in-tended to deny to religion any legitimate governmental authority. Govern-ment would regulate matters affecting the preservation of life, liberty, and estate. This regulation included the affirmation, on the part of govern-ment, of a belief in God. While Locke argues for toleration of religious opinions and practices, he includes freedom of speech as well. On behalf of religious tolerance and freedom, Spinoza reduced the scope of true Christian principles to piety and justice, which he claimed were further reducible simply to obedience to the sovereign. He then offered distinctive and explicit arguments for democracy and for freedom of speech, basing his position on the limited objectives of security and a healthy life.

By referring to the development of the mind in the context of democratic government, Spinoza supported two different and related justifications for freedom of speech: the quest for truth and the requirements of democratic government. He distinguished the rational activity of philosophic thought from the subrational pursuits connected to security; he argued for a wide range of freedom of speech, taking note of the spiritedness of well-intentioned but misguided advocates of freedom. Spinoza thus offers a two-track argument for freedom of speech: One track corresponds to the activity of the philosophic few and the other to the efforts of the nonphilosophic many. While he does not argue that the philosophers should rule (only that they may safely be given their freedom), he does say that the democratic and nonphilosophic many should rule. His approach to freedom of speech reflects what that low but solid government must look like.

In his *Second Treatise*, Locke emphasizes freedom of political speech when he discusses the relationship between the people and their representatives in government. This argument differs from what he says about speculative opinions—that the truth can shift for itself—in his *Letter Concerning Toleration*. In that context, Locke writes that there is no need for government to concern itself with such opinions.

Montesquieu defined political liberty as security and, consequently, argued for limiting criminal law. First, this meant emphasizing counsels and admonitions in matters concerning religion. Second, Montesquieu's approach to freedom of speech and the press, like Spinoza's, followed the speech-conduct distinction. "Speech becomes criminal only when it prepares, when it accompanies, or when it follows a criminal act. Everything is turned upside down if speech is made a capital crime instead of being regarded as the sign of a capital crime."[1]

In *On Liberty*, Mill extended the argument that truth wins out in the marketplace of ideas to use as the basis for full freedom of speech and opinion. He also wrote that individual autonomy, or individuality, was good and energetic government was bad. In addition to the arguments for free speech as the necessary precondition for the quest for truth and as a requirement of democratic self-government, Mill introduced autonomy as the third argument in support of freedom of speech.

The American founders took up Locke's view on toleration when they fashioned bills for establishing religious liberty. Jefferson even included the Lockean suggestion that the truth will win out in a contest among religious opinions. Madison added that the friends of Christianity should have no fear that religion might not prosper without the support of government.

In the matter of freedom of speech, the founders at first followed English common law. Relying on Blackstone, they considered the notion of "no prior restraint" a sufficient protection for freedom of speech. Milton had taken this position, earlier. While the federal sedition law allowed the claim of truth as a defense and permitted the jury to decide the libel question, Madison, in 1799 and 1800, concluded that republican government in America needed a more speech-protective approach if the people, as sovereign, were going to be able to present and to hear criticism of their government officials. Madison's argument against the criminal law of seditious libel resembled Spinoza's argument regarding the requirements of democratic—he used the term "republican"—government more than any notion of truth winning out.

The modern Supreme Court's interpretation of these freedoms represents an understandable and defensible development of the founding principles of American government. There are, of course, differences between the founders' understanding and our current constitutional law doctrines. But the differences come from the democratization of American government, which the founders anticipated, combined with the Court's need to convert general principles into workable legal tests. The prominence of neutrality, as applied to freedom of speech and religion, has largely succeeded in securing the objectives of limited government for a democratic and diverse people.

The Court's neutrality doctrines as applied to freedom of speech have become widely accepted. Some scholars who disagree with these doctrines defend seditious libel laws, as long as truth and good motive are allowed as a defense and juries decide questions of law and fact.[2] Others, rejecting seditious libel, argue that the freedom of speech should be limited to political speech.[3] On the first point, I think Madison rightly rejected as inadequate any form of seditious, or criminal, libel law; he thought that political opinions, especially those expressed against the government—its men or its measures—cannot be held to a strict truth requirement, as judgments regarding the soundness of policy are not like facts whose veracity can be clearly determined. On the second point, not only would it be difficult to draw the line between the political and the nonpolitical in many cases, but also, if freedom of speech accompanies democracy, it surely extends to private speech as well as political speech. An important part of democratic freedom is to "live as one wants," as Aristotle said; or, as Americans say, "It's a free country, I can say what I want."

Starting with Justice Holmes, the Supreme Court adopted the "marketplace of ideas" rationale in support of freedom of speech. In more recent cases, the Court has interpreted that doctrine to proscribe any government restriction on expression. Recall Justice Powell's statement in the *Gertz* libel case: "We begin with the common ground. Under the First Amendment, there is no such thing as a false idea."[4] Justice Powell was drawing on Justice Jackson's famous flag salute opinion: "If there is any fixed star in our constitutional constellation, it is that no official, high or petty, can prescribe what shall be orthodox in politics, nationalism, religion, or other matters of opinion or force citizens to confess by word or act their faith therein."[5]

I think we can and should defend this libertarian position on freedom of speech on conservative pragmatic grounds, rather than place our faith on the uncertain claim that truth arises or even prevails in the marketplace of ideas. After all, the philosophers who invented the marketplace metaphor used it rhetorically to gain support for toleration. Whether or not Holmes believed in it, the Supreme Court's approach to drawing the legal line between permissible and impermissible speech can be defended on the basis of arguments from both Spinoza and Montesquieu. The Court has taken the position that government should not be in the business of forcing people to espouse orthodoxies. That is not inconsistent with government speech that affirms orthodoxies, such as the inalienable rights of life, liberty, and pursuit of happiness. Rather, the heterogeneity and robustness of American democracy requires that we not ask governmental authority to expend the resources of the criminal law on matters that do not threaten security, especially when doing so runs the risk of losing the attachment of its citizenry.

This is the way to understand the modern Supreme Court's expansive free speech decisions. The constitutionally conservative Justice Harlan signaled the development of this approach to free speech law in his opinions in *Yates v United States* and *Cohen v California*. In *Yates*, he reinterpreted the Smith Act to allow prosecution for overt acts only, but not for mere membership in the Communist Party. And in *Cohen*, he recognized the expressive value of emotive feelings, when he struck down Cohen's conviction for disturbing the peace. The *Yates* decision led to the *Brandenburg* "incitement" test, and the *Cohen* decision led to the protection of the expressive conduct of flag burning. We benefit from the removal of such behavior from the criminal law, because as Spinoza pointed out, insisting on attachment to tolerance and civility puts spirited but decent citizens at odds with their government. We should acknowledge, however, that we pay the price of legitimating irresponsible and emotive expression.[6]

Controversy over religious freedom is more extensive, since a minority of the Court advocates "non-preferentialism," rather than the *Everson* Court's neutrality as between religion and irreligion.[7] Still, the Court has accommodated religion, sometimes in the way it interprets the Establishment Clause—concerning aid to parochial schools but not prayer in the public schools—and sometimes in its use of the public forum doctrine, borrowed from free speech law. Justice O'Connor has been the most forceful advocate of religious freedom on the Court, although she failed to persuade a majority of the Court to retain the "strict scrutiny" test for free exercise challenges to generally applicable laws whose effects hinder the free exercise of religion. I think the majority was correct for two reasons. First, Justice Harlan's "equal protection" approach in Free Exercise cases makes good sense, given that there are many religions in America and we have difficulty in agreeing on a definition of religion. Second, the Court's effort to apply the "compelling interest" test to Free Exercise claims, in cases where the purpose of the law was valid but the effect still seriously hindered a religious practice, yielded close divisions among the justices over the significance of particular facts.

Justice O'Connor did succeed in persuading a majority of the Court, thanks to the support of Justice Kennedy, to support accommodation of strict neutrality with her "no endorsement" approach to Establishment Clause questions. As a result, the Court has allowed certain forms of religious symbolism in public places, and it has allowed aid, including vouchers, for private, including parochial, schools. I think the Court was right to follow Justice O'Connor's lead in these cases.

An important difference between free speech and religious freedom becomes clear when we compare the Court's treatment of the flag salute ceremony with its treatment of school prayer. Government may express its own view of sound political and constitutional principles, as long as it does not compel an individual to express a given view. It may for example, require a civics course as part of the educational curriculum, and it can encourage voluntary participation in the flag salute (*Barnette*). However, as both Justices Kennedy and Blackmun pointed out in the opinions in *Lee v Weisman*,[8] government must stay clear of theological statements or other forms of religious activity.

Of course there are exceptions to the neutrality principle: legislative prayer, Thanksgiving Proclamations, mottoes on coins, certain religious symbols, and "under God" as a part of our pledge of allegiance, for example. The Court has allowed these forms of "accommodation" of religion or indicated that it would allow them.[9]

In the area of free speech we have surely witnessed the effects of the democratization of republican government.[10] What has that meant for the twin objectives of civil peace and the quest for the truth? Does the freedom of speech that we enjoy allow us to enjoy civil peace as we carry out our civic duties and to pursue inquiries, no matter how controversial, as we engage in our individual search for truth? By and large, to this two-pronged question I respond "yes," although we must acknowledge that our democratic protection of both the "emotive" function as well as the cognitive content of speech, which protection includes flag burning or cross burning, does not encourage rational discourse. Mill argued for the fullest freedom of speech for the sake of self-development as well as to benefit others. He wanted individuals to be free from social constraint as well as the coercion of law. Of course he could not, consistent with his support for individual freedom, prevent "the many" from impressing their opinions and tastes on others. We have seen that a regime of full legal freedom of expression cannot guarantee that all thoughtful opinions will receive a hearing. Why not? People might not listen, or those who can provide a forum for diverse opinions might not do so.

Our inability to guarantee that all thoughtful opinions will receive a hearing should remind us of the difference between the ancient philosophers' views on speech and religion and ours. Plato, Aristotle, and Thucydides knew that democratic speech was not the same as philosophic inquiry; democratic freedom does not necessarily produce a prudent, practical, wise politics. The teachings of the Enlightenment philosophers I have examined have liberated us from the constraints of revealed religion, and in so doing have paved the way for the celebration of liberal democracy as the best practical form of government. The constitutional and legal doctrines that followed from that teaching have produced substantial freedom and security. We have all the conditions we need for the quest for truth. However, to pursue the rational life in our practical affairs and our other inquiries as well, we will need recourse to one more condition, Socratic moderation. For this we can turn to the ancients for thoughtful guidance. While modern liberal democracy consigns the search for wisdom, which requires control over the emotive function, largely to each individual as a private citizen, in our public affairs we need a corresponding appreciation of the value of moderation as the political virtue.

Notes

1. *The Spirit of the Laws*, book 12, chapter 12, 199.

2. See Walter Berns, *The First Amendment and the Future of American Democracy*, chapter 3; David Lowenthal, *Present Dangers: Rediscovering the First Amendment*, chapter 2.

3. See Robert Bork, "Neutral Principles and Some First Amendment Problems," *47 Indiana Law Journal* 1–35, pp. 22–23.

4. 418 U.S. 323, 329 (1974).

5. *West Virginia State Board of Education v Barnette* 319 U.S. 624, 642 (1943).

6. While most judges and scholars accept the Court's overall approach to free speech, the Justices as well as scholars disagree over whether hate speech should be protected, as well as over the status of money in political campaigns.

7. Philip Hamburger's recently published book, *Separation of Church and State* (Cambridge: Harvard University Press, 2002), argues against the separation thesis. In his view, advocates of freedom from religious establishment "did not demand a separation of church and state." p. 89. "The religious dissenters [who opposed establishments] made demands for a religious liberty that limited civil government, especially civil legislation, rather than for a religious liberty conceived as a separation of church and state." p. 107. He also contends that Madison's position on the First Amendment differed from his earlier position in Virginia. He also thinks that Madison might have "slightly modified his views," p. 106, but the Detached Memoranda portray a separationist Madison.

8. See above, chapter 15.

9. While the court chose not to decide whether the words "under god" transformed the Pledge of Allegiance into an unconstitutional exercise (see introduction note 24), I believe that it should (and will) eventually decide, following Madison's position on chaplains in Congress, that the two words can be accommodated, because they do not convert the Pledge of Allegiance into a prayer.

10. As Harvey Mansfield has pointed out, the founders' distinction between republican government and democracy has been lost to sight. See *Taming the Prince: The Ambivalence of Modern Executive Power*, p. 279.

Bibliography

All United States Supreme Court decisions and other judicial decisions can be found in the index.

Alexander, James. *A Brief Narrative of the Case and Trial of John Peter Zenger.* Cambridge, Mass.: Belknap Press of Harvard University, 1963.

Anastaplo, George. *The Constitutionalist.* Dallas: Southern Methodist University Press, 1971.

Aristotle, *Nicomachean Ethics.* Trans. Martin Ostwald. New York: Macmillan Publishing Company, 1962.

———. *The Politics.* Trans. Carnes Lord. Chicago: University of Chicago Press, 1984.

Ballagh, James Curtis, ed. *The Letters of Richard Henry Lee.* New York: Da Capo, 1970 [c.1911].

Berns, Walter. *The First Amendment and the Future of American Democracy.* New York: Basic Books, 1976.

———. "Freedom of the Press and the Alien and Sedition Acts: A Reappraisal." *The Supreme Court Review, 1970.* Chicago: University of Chicago, 1970.

Beveridge, Albert J. *The Life of John Marshall,* vol. 2. Boston and New York: Houghton Mifflin Company 1919.

Blackstone, William. *Commentaries on the Laws of England.* Chicago and London: University of Chicago Press, 1979.

Blasi, Vincent. "The Checking Value in First Amendment Theory." *American Bar Association Research Journal* 3 (1977).

———. "The First Amendment and the Ideal of Civic Courage: The Brandeis Opinion in *Whitney v California*." *William and Mary Law Review* vol. 29, 653 (Summer 1988).

——. "Free Speech and the Widening Gyre of Fund-Raising: Why Campaign Spending Limits May Not Violate the First Amendment After All." *Columbia Law Review* vol. 95, 1281 (1994).

Bork, Robert. "Our Judicial Oligarchy." First published in *First Things*. 67 (Nov. 1996), 23. Reprinted in *The End of Democracy? Judicial Usurpation of Politics*. Ed. Mitchell S. Muncy. Dallas: Spence Publishing Company, 1997.

——. "Neutral Principles and Some First Amendment Problems," *Indiana Law Journal* 47, 1–35.

——. *Slouching Toward Gomorrah: Modern Liberalism and American Decline*. New York: Regan Books, 1996.

——. *The Tempting of America: The Political Seduction of the Law*. New York: Free Press, 1990.

Boyd, Julian P., ed. *Papers of Thomas Jefferson*, vol. 1. Princeton: Princeton University Press, 1950.

Brann, Eva. "Madison's Memorial and Remonstrance." *The Past-Present: Selected Writings of Eva Brann*. Annapolis, Md.: St. John's College Press, 1997.

Buckley, Thomas E. *Church and State in Revolutionary Virginia 1776–1787*. University Press of Virginia 1977.

Canavan, Francis. *Freedom of Expression*. Durham, N.C.: Carolina Academic Press, 1984.

Chafee, Zechariah, Jr. *Free Speech in the United States*. New York: Atheneum, 1969.

Choper, Jesse H. *Securing Religious Liberty*. Chicago: University of Chicago Press, 1995.

Cropsey, Joseph. *Plato's World: Man's Place in the Cosmos*. Chicago: University of Chicago Press, 1995.

——. "The United States as a Regime." In *Political Philosophy and the Issues of Politics*. Ed. Joseph Cropsey. Chicago: University of Chicago Press, 1977.

Crosskey, William W. *Politics and the Constitution in the History of the United States*, vol. 2. Chicago: University of Chicago Press: 1953.

Curry, Thomas. *The First Freedoms: Church and State in America to the Passage of the First Amendment*. New York: Oxford University Press, 1986.

Davis, James Calvin. "A Return to Civility: Roger Williams and Public Discourse in America." *Journal of Church and State* vol. 43, 4 (Autumn 2001), 689–706.

Dowling, Paul M. *Polite Wisdom: Heathen Rhetoric in Milton's Areopagitica*. Lanham, Md.: Rowman and Littlefield, 1995.

Dry, Murray. "The Debate Over Ratification of the Constitution." In *Encyclopedia of the American Revolution*. Ed. Jack P. Greene and J. R. Pole. Cambridge, Mass: Blackwell, 1991.

Dunn, John. *The Political Thought of John Locke: An Historical Account of the 'Two Treatises of Government.'* Cambridge: Cambridge University Press, 1969.

——. "What is Living and What Is Dead in John Locke." In *Interpreting Political Responsibility: Essays 1981–1989*. Princeton: Princeton University Press, 1990.

Ely, John Hart. "Flag Desecration: A Case Study in the Roles of Categorization and Balancing in First Amendment Analysis." *Harvard Law Review* vol. 88, 1482 (1975).

Emerson, Thomas I. *The System of Freedom of Expression*. New York: Random House, 1970.

———. *Toward a General Theory of the First Amendment*. New York: Random House, 1964.

Farber, Daniel A. *The First Amendment*. New York: Foundation Press, 1998.

Farrand, Max ed. *Records of the Federal Convention of 1787*. Vol. 2. New Haven: Yale University Press, 1937, 364.

Fiss, Owen M. *The Irony of Free Speech*. Cambridge, Mass.: Harvard University Press, 1996.

Fleet, Elizabeth, ed. "Madison's Detached Memoranda." *William and Mary Quarterly*, 3rd series, vol. 3, 4 (October 1946).

Greenawalt, Kent. *Fighting Words: Individuals, Communities, and Liberties of Speech*. Princeton, N.J.: Princeton University Press, 1995.

———. *Speech, Crime, & The Uses of Language*. New York: Oxford University Press, 1989.

Gunther, Gerald. "The Highest Court, The Toughest Issues," *Stanford Magazine*. (Fall–Winter) 1978.

———. "Learned Hand and the Origins of Modern First Amendment Doctrine: Some Fragments of History." *Stanford Law Review* vol. 27, 23 (Feb 1975).

Hamburger, Philip. *Separation of Church and State*. Cambridge: Harvard University Press, 2002.

Hegel, Georg Wilhelm Friedrich. *Introduction to the Philosophy of History*. Translated by Leo Rauch. Indianapolis: Hackett Publishing Company, 1988.

Howe, Mark DeWolfe. *The Garden and the Wilderness: Religion and Government in American Constitutional History*. Chicago: University of Chicago Press, 1965.

Hunt, Gaillard. "James Madison and Religious Liberty." *Annual Report of the American Historical Association* vol.1 (1901).

Hunt, Gaillard. ed. *The Writings of James Madison*. 9 vols. New York: Putnam, 1900–1910.

Kalven, Harry. *A Worthy Tradition: Freedom of Speech in America*. New York: Harper & Row, 1988.

Kurland, Phillip, and Ralph Lerner, eds. *The Founders' Constitution*. Vol. 5. Chicago: University of Chicago Press, 1987.

Kurland, Philip, ed. *Free Speech and Association: The Supreme Court and the First Amendment*. Chicago, University of Chicago Press, 1975.

———. *Religion and the Law: Of Church and State and the Supreme Court*. Chicago: Aldine Publishing Company, 1961, 1962.

Laycock, Douglas. "Formal, Substantive, and Disaggregated Neutrality toward Religion." *DePaul Law Review* vol. 39, 993 (1990).

Levy, Leonard. *Emergence of a Free Press*. New York: Oxford University Press, 1985.

———. *The Establishment Clause: Religion and the First Amendment*. New York: MacMillan, 1986.

———. *Freedom of Speech and Press in Early American History: Legacy of Suppression*. New York: Harper and Row, 1960.

Lewis, Anthony. *Make No Law: The Sullivan Case and the First Amendment*. New York: Vintage Books, 1992.

Locke, John. *Epistola de Tolerantia: A Letter on Toleration*. Bilingual edition. Ed. Raymond Klibansky. Trans. J. W. Gough. Oxford: Clarendon P., 1968.

——. *A Letter Concerning Toleration*. Ed. James H. Hully. Indianapolis: Hackett Publishing Company; 1983.

——. *The Reasonableness of Christianity, with a Discourse of Miracles and part of a Third Letter Concerning Toleration*. Ed. I. T. Ramsey. Stanford: Stanford University Press, 1958.

——. *Two Treatises of Government*. Ed. Peter Laslett. Cambridge: Cambridge University Press, 1960.

Long, Carolyn. *Religious Freedom and Indian Rights: The Case of Oregon v Smith*. Lawrence: University Press of Kansas, 2000.

Lowenthal, David. *No Liberty For License: The Forgotten Logic of the First Amendment*. Dallas: Spence Publishing Company, 1997.

——. *Present Dangers: Rediscovering the First Amendment*. Dallas: Spence Publishing Company, 2002.

Lutz, Donald S., ed. *Colonial Origins of the American Constitution*. Indianapolis: Liberty Fund, 1997.

Madison, James. *The Papers of James Madison*. Ed. William T. Hutchinson, William M. E. Rachal, and Robert A. Rutland. Vols. 1–10. Chicago: University of Chicago Press. Vols. 11– . Charlottesville:University Press of Virginia, 1962–.

Maimonides. *The Guide of the Perplexed*. 2 vols. Trans. Sholomo Pines. Chicago: University of Chicago Press, 1963.

Malbin, Michael. *Religion and Politics: The Intention of the Authors of the First Amendment*. Washington D.C.: American Enterprise Institute, 1978.

Mansfield, Harvey C., Jr., and Delba Winthrop, trans. *Democracy in America*. By Alexis de Tocqueville. Chicago: University of Chicago Press, 2000.

Mansfield, Harvey, Jr. "The Religious Issue and the Origin of Modern Constitutionalism." In *America's Constitutional Soul*. Ed. Harvey Mansfield Jr. Baltimore and London: John's Hopkins University Press, 1991.

——. "Party Government and the Settlement of 1688." *American Political Science Review* vol. LVIII, 4 (December 1964).

——. *Machiavelli's Virtue*. Chicago: University of Chicago Press, 1996.

——. *Taming the Prince: The Ambivalence of Executive Power*. New York: Free Press, 1989.

Mansfield, Harvey, Jr., ed. *Thomas Jefferson: Selected Writings*. Arlington Heights, Ill.: AHM Publishing Corp. 1979.

Mattern, David B., ed. *Papers of James Madison*. Vol. XVII Charlottesville: University of Virginia Press.

Meiklejohn, Alexander. *Political Freedom: The Constitutional Powers of the People*. Oxford: New York, 1965.

Meyers, Marvin, ed. *The Mind of the Founder: Sources of the Political Thought of James Madison*. Indianapolis: Bobbs Merrill, 1973.

Mill, John Stuart. *On Liberty and Other Writings.* Ed. Stefan Collini. Cambridge: Cambridge University Press, 1989.

Miller, Perry. *Roger Williams: His Contribution to the American Tradition.* New York: Atheneum, 1962.

Milton, John. "Areopagitica." In *Areopagitica and Education.* Ed. George H. Sabine. Arlington Heights, Ill.: Harlan Davidson, Inc., 1951.

Montesquieu. *Oeuvres completes.* Ed. and annotated Roger Caillois. Paris: Gallimard, 1951.

———. *The Spirit of the Laws.* Ed. Anne Cohler, Basia Miller, and Harold Stone. Cambridge: Cambridge University Press, 1989.

Ortiz, Daniel, Anthony Corrado, Thomas E. Mann, Trevor Potter, and Frank J. Sourauf, eds. *Campaign Finance Reform: A Source Book.* Washington, D.C.: Brookings, 1997.

Nimmer, Melville B. "The Right to Speak from Times to Time: First Amendment Theory Applied to Libel and Misapplied to Privacy." In *California Law Review* vol. 56, 935 (1968).

Peterson, Merrill D., ed. *The Portable Thomas Jefferson.* New York: Penguin Books, 1975.

Plato. *The Republic of Plato.* Trans. Allan Bloom. New York: Basic Books, 1968.

———. *Phaedrus.* Trans. Alexaader Nehamas and Paul Woodruff. Indianapolis: Hackett Publishing Company Inc., 1994.

Polenberg, Richard. *Fighting Faiths: The Abrams Case, The Supreme Court, and Free Speech.* New York: Penguin, 1987.

Rabban, David M. *Free Speech in Its Forgotten Years.* Cambridge: Cambridge University Press, 1997.

Redish, Martin H. "The Content Distinction in First Amendment Analysis." *Stanford Law Review* vol. 34 ,113 (1981).

Reid, John Phillip. *The Concept of Liberty in the Age of the American Revolution.* Chicago: University of Chicago Press, 1988.

Rousseau. *Discourse on the Origin and Foundation of Inequality Among Men.* Trans. Roger D. Masters and Judith R. Masters. New York: St. Martin's Press, 1964.

Rutland, Robert. *The Birth of the Bill of Rights: 1776–1791.* Boston: Northeastern University Press, 1991.

Schauer, Frederick. *Free Speech: A Philosophical Enquiry.* New York: Cambridge University Press, 1982.

Schwartz, Bernard. *The Roots of the Bill of Rights: An Illustrated Source Book of American Freedom.* New York: Chelsea House Publishers, 1980.

Shattuck, Roger. *Forbidden Knowledge: From Prometheus to Pornography.* New York: St. Martin's Press, 1996.

Spinoza, Benedict. *Theological-Political Treatise.*Trans. Samuel Shirley. Indianapolis: Hackett Publishing Company, 1998.

Stoner, James R., Jr. *Common Law and Liberal Theory: Coke, Hobbes, & The Origins of American Constitutionalism.* Lawrence: University of Kansas, 1992.

———. *Common Law Liberty: Rethinking American Constitutionalism.* Lawrence: University Kansas, 2003.

Storing, Herbert. *The Complete Anti-Federalist.* Chicago: University of Chicago Press, 1981.

———. *What the Anti-Federalists Were For!* Chicago: University of Chicago Press, 1981.

———. "The Constitution and the Bill of Rights." In *Writings of Herbert J. Storing: Toward a More Perfect Union.* Ed. Joseph M. Bessette. Washington, D.C.: AEI, 1995.

Strassler, Robert B., ed. *The Landmark Thucydides: A Comprehensive Guide to the Peloponnesian War.* Trans. Richard Crawley. New York: Free Press, 1996.

Strauss, Leo. *The City and Man.* Chicago: Rand McNally, 1964.

———. "Liberal Education and Responsibility." In *Liberalism: Ancient and Modern.* Ed. Leo Strauss. New York: Basic Books, 1968.

———. *Natural Right and History.* Chicago: University of Chicago, 1953.

———. "How to Study Spinoza's Theological-Political Treatise." In *Persecution and the Art of Writing.* Ed. Leo Strauss. Glencoe, Ill.: Free Press, 1952.

———. "Plato's Apology of Socrates and Crito." In *Studies in Platonic Political Philosophy.* Ed. Leo Strauss. Chicago: University of Chicago, 1983.

———. *What is Political Philosophy? And Other Studies.* Chicago: University of Chicago Press, 1959.

Sullivan, Kathleen. "Against Campaign Finance Reform." *Utah Law Review* (1998), 311.

Sullivan, Kathleen and Gerald Gunther. *Constitutional Law.* 14th ed. Westbury, N.Y.: Foundation Press, 2001.

Sullivan, Winnifred Fallers. *Paying the Words Extra: Religious Discourse in the Supreme Court of the United States.* Cambridge, Mass.: Harvard University Center for the Study of World Religions, 1994.

Sunstein, Cass. *Democracy and the Problem of Free Speech.* New York: Free Press, 1993.

———. "A New Deal for Speech." In *The Partial Constitution.* Ed. Cass Sunstein. Cambridge: Harvard University Press, 1993.

Surluck, Ernest, ed. *The Complete Prose Works of John Milton.* Vol. 2. Yale, 1959.

Thorpe, Francis Newton, ed. *The Federal and State Constitutions, Colonial Charters, and Other Organic Laws of the States Territories and Colonies Now or Heretofore Forming the United States of America.* Vol. 3 [1841]. Washington, D.C.: GPO, 1909.

Tuck, Richard, ed. *Leviathan.* By Thomas Hobbes. Cambridge: Cambridge University Press, 1991.

Veit, Helen E., Kenneth R Bowling, and Charlene Bangs Bickford, eds. *Creating the Bill of Rights: The Documentary Record From the First Federal Congress.* Baltimore: Johns Hopkins University Press, 1991.

Waldron, Jeremy. *God, Locke, and Equality: Christian Foundations of John Locke's Political Thought.* Cambridge: Cambridge University Press, 2002.

Warhoft, Sidney, ed. "A Letter to Mr. Matthew, Upon Sending to Him Part of 'Instauratio Magna.'" In *Francis Bacon: A Selection of His Works.* Odyssey Press, 1981.

West, Thomas G., and Grace Starry West, trans. *Plato and Aristophanes: Four Texts on Socrates.* Ithaca, N.Y.: Cornell University Press, 1984.

Winthrop, John, "A Model of Christian Charity." In Allen Heimert and Andrew Delbanco, eds. *The Puritans in America: A Narrative Anthology*. Cambridge: Harvard University Press, 1985.

Zuckert, Michael P. "Locke and the Problem of Civil Religion: Locke on Christianity." In *Launching Liberalism: On Lockean Political Philosophy*. By Michael P. Zuckert. Lawrence: University Press of Kansas, 2002.

———. *Natural Rights and the New Republicanism*. Princeton: Princeton University Press, 1994.

Index

Montesquieu on, 128–29; Williams on, 29
treason, Montesquieu on, 125
truth: Aristotle on, 83; Declaration of Independence on, 6; Milton on, 99, 101–2; Plato on, 84, 87
truth, quest for, 6–7, 9–10, 43–44; Milton on, 99
truth, victory of: Alexander on, 47; Holmes on, 8–9, 154; Jefferson on, 40; Locke on, 106, 108; Mill on, 135–36; Milton on, 8, 98; Supreme Court on, 194

under God clause, 12n25, 270, 287, 289n9
underinclusiveness, 188, 198n69
United States v Carolene Products, 165
United States v Lee, 230
United States v O'Brien, 181
Universal Military Training and Service Act, 181, 226

Van Dam, Rip, 46
Vermont, constitution of, 32, 33, 48n3
Vietnam War, 181
viewpoint neutrality, 174, 187–89
Virginia: Bill of Rights, 20; constitution of, 33, 34–44
Virginia Pharmacy, 194
Virginia Report, 15, 65, 69–72
Virginia Resolutions, 65, 67–68
Virginia v Black, 190–91
virtue: classical philosophers on, 81; Montesquieu on, 120–21
Voltaire, 189
vouchers, 9, 255–58

Waite, Morrison R., on Reynolds, 221
Wallace v Jaffree, 269–71
wall metaphor, Williams on, 27
Walz v Tax Commissioner, New York, 229, 246–47
Washington, George, 3, 73
Watts v United States, 188
Wechsler, Herbert, 169
Weisman, Deborah, 272
Welsh, Eliot Ashton, 226–27
West Virginia State Board of Education v Barnette, 5, 222–23
White, Byron R.: on Clark, 213; on Lemon, 248; on Perry, 210
Whitney v California, 155–57, 175n3
Widmar v Vincent, 212
Williams, Roger, 27–29, 42–43
Winthrop, John, 30n5; "A Model of Christian Charity," 19–31
Wisconsin v Yoder, 228–32
Witters v Washington Department of Services for the Blind, 252, 265n145
Wolman v Walter, 261n67
World War I, 149–50
World War II, 157
Wortman, Tunis, 69

Yates v United States, 160, 286
Young v Mini-Theatres, 189

Zelman v Simmons-Harris, 255–56
Zenger, John Peter, 46–48
Zobrest v Catalina Foothills School District, 252–53
Zorach v Clausen, 244–45

About the Author

Murray Dry is Charles A. Dana Professor of Political Science at Middlebury College.